# Fuzzing

# Fuzzing

## BRUTE FORCE VULNERABILITY DISCOVERY

Michael Sutton
Adam Greene
Pedram Amini

✦✦ Addison-Wesley

Upper Saddle River, NJ · Boston · Indianapolis · San Francisco
New York · Toronto · Montreal · London · Munich · Paris · Madrid
Cape Town · Sydney · Tokyo · Singapore · Mexico City

Many of the designations used by manufacturers and sellers to distinguish their products are claimed as trademarks. Where those designations appear in this book, and the publisher was aware of a trademark claim, the designations have been printed with initial capital letters or in all capitals.

The author and publisher have taken care in the preparation of this book but make no expressed or implied warranty of any kind and assume no responsibility for errors or omissions. No liability is assumed for incidental or consequential damages in connection with or arising out of the use of the information or programs contained herein.

The publisher offers excellent discounts on this book when ordered in quantity for bulk purchases or special sales, which may include electronic versions and/or custom covers and content particular to your business, training goals, marketing focus, and branding interests. For more information, please contact:

U.S. Corporate and Government Sales
800-382-3419
corpsales@pearsontechgroup.com

For sales outside the United States, please contact:

International Sales
international@pearsoned.com

 **This Book Is Safari Enabled**

The Safari® Enabled icon on the cover of your favorite technology book means the book is available through Safari Bookshelf. When you buy this book, you get free access to the online edition for 45 days.

Safari Bookshelf is an electronic reference library that lets you easily search thousands of technical books, find code samples, download chapters, and access technical information whenever and wherever you need it.

To gain 45-day Safari Enabled access to this book:

- Go to http://www.awprofessional.com/safarienabled
- Complete the brief registration form
- Enter the coupon code JZCU-T1UD-VDQ7-SRD7-WZ1E

If you have difficulty registering on Safari Bookshelf or accessing the online edition, please e-mail customer-service@safaribooksonline.com.

Visit us on the Web: www.awprofessional.com

*Library of Congress Cataloging-in-Publication Data:*

Sutton, Michael, 1973–
  Fuzzing : brute force vulnerability discovery / Michael Sutton, Adam Greene, Pedram Amini. --
1st ed.
      p. cm.
  Includes index.
  ISBN 0-321-44611-9 (pbk. : alk. paper)  1. Computer security.  2. Computer networks--Security measures.  3. Computer software--Development.  I. Greene, Adam, 1983–  II. Amini, Pedram.  III. Title.
  QA76.9.A25S89   2007
  005.8--dc22

                              2007011463

ISBN 0-32-144611-9
Text printed in the United States on recycled paper at R. R. Donnelley, Crawfordsville, Indiana
First printing, June 2007

*This book is dedicated to the two most important women in my life. Mom, without your many sacrifices, nothing would have been possible. This book is only one small example. Amanda, your unwavering love and support inspire me to achieve each and every day. I am truly a fortunate man to be married to such an amazing woman.*

—Michael Sutton

*This work is dedicated to my family and friends. Thank you all for your support and patience.*

—Adam Greene

*I dedicate this book to George W. Bush, my Commander-in-Chief, whose impressive career advancement despite remedial language skills inspired me to believe that I was capable of authoring a book.*

—Pedram Amini

# Contents

# Foreword

Vulnerabilities are the life-blood of security research. Whether you are performing a penetration test, evaluating a new product, or auditing the source code of a critical component—vulnerabilities drive your decisions, provide justification for your time, and influence your choices for years to come.

Source code auditing is a white box testing technique that has long been a popular approach for uncovering vulnerabilities in software products. This method requires the auditor to know every programming concept and function used in the product, and to have a deep understanding of the product's operating environment. Source code auditing also has one obvious pitfall—the source code for the product must be available.

Thankfully, there are black box alternatives that do not require access to source code. One such alternative is a technique known as fuzzing, which has proven successful at discovering critical vulnerabilities in products that would not be feasible to audit any other way. Fuzzing is the process of sending intentionally invalid data to a product in the hopes of triggering an error condition or fault. These error conditions can lead to exploitable vulnerabilities.

There are no real rules for fuzzing. It is a technique where success is measured solely by the results of the test. For any given product, there may be an infinite number of inputs you can provide. Fuzzing is the process of predicting what types of programming errors may exist in the product and the inputs that will trigger those errors. For this reason, fuzzing is much more of an art than a science.

Fuzzing can be as simple as randomly hitting keys on a keyboard. The 3-year-old son of a friend once discovered a vulnerability in the Mac OS X operating system's screen lock using this technique. My friend locked his screen and walked to the kitchen to get a drink. By the time he got back, his son had managed to disable the screen lock, and open a web browser, just by banging on the keyboard.

Over the last few years, I have used fuzzing tools and techniques to discover hundreds of vulnerabilities in an extensive range of software. In December 2003, I wrote a simple tool that sent a stream of random UDP packets to a remote service. This tool was used to discover two new vulnerabilities in the Microsoft WINS server. The same tool later aided in identifying serious flaws in a handful of other products. It turned out that a random stream of UDP packets was all that was needed to identify vulnerabilites in multiple Computer Associates products, the Norton Ghost management service, and a common service exposed on the Mac OS X operating system.

Fuzzers are useful for much more than network protocols. In the first quarter of 2006, I collaborated on three different browser fuzzing tools, leading to the discovery of dozens of flaws across a wide range of web browsers. In the second quarter of 2006, I wrote an ActiveX fuzzer (AxMan) that discovered over 100 unique flaws across Microsoft products alone. Many of these flaws were profiled during the Month of Browser Bugs project and led to the development of exploit modules for the Metasploit Framework. I am still finding new vulnerabilities with AxMan, nearly a year after it was originally developed. Fuzzers truly are the gift that keeps on giving.

This book is the first resource to do justice to fuzzing as a technique. The knowledge provided in this book is everything you need to start fuzzing new products and to build effective fuzzing tools of your own. The key to effective fuzzing is knowing what data to use for which products, and the tools needed to manipulate, monitor, and manage the fuzzing process. The authors of this book are pioneers in the area of fuzzing techniques and do an excellent job of covering the intricacies of the fuzzing process.

Happy bug hunting!

—HD

# Preface

*"I know the human being and fish can coexist peacefully."*

  - George W. Bush, Saginaw, Mich., Sept. 29, 2000

## INTRODUCTION

The concept of fuzzing has been around for almost two decades but has only recently captured widespread attention. A plague of vulnerabilities affecting popular client-side applications, including Microsoft Internet Explorer, Microsoft Word, and Microsoft Excel, were seen in the year 2006 and a large portion of these vulnerabilities were discovered through fuzzing. This effective application of fuzzing technologies gave rise to new tools and increased exposure. The sheer fact that this is the first published book dedicated to the subject matter is an additional indicator that there is an increasing interest in fuzzing.

Having been involved in the vulnerability research community for years, we have used a variety of fuzzing technologies in our day to day work, ranging from immature hobby projects to high end commercial products. Each of the authors has been involved in the development of both privately held and publicly released fuzzers. We leveraged our combined experience and ongoing research projects to compose this bleeding edge book, which we hope you will find beneficial.

## INTENDED AUDIENCE

Security books and articles are frequently written by security researchers for the benefit of other security researchers. We strongly believe that the quantity and severity of vulnerabilities will continue to grow so long as security is deemed to be the sole responsibility of a security team. As such, we have taken strong efforts to write for a large audience including both readers who are new to fuzzing and those who have already had significant exposure.

It is unrealistic to believe that secure applications can emerge from the development process if we simply hand completed applications to a security team for a quick audit prior to production launch. Gone are the days when a developer or a member of the QA Team can say, "security's not my problem – we have a security team that worries about that". Security must now be everyone's problem. Security must be baked into the software development lifecycle (SDLC), not brushed on at the end.

Asking the development and QA teams to focus on security can be a tall order, especially for those that have not been asked to do so in the past. We believe that fuzzing presents a unique vulnerability discovery methodology that is accessible to a wide audience due to the fact that it can be highly automated. While we are hopeful that seasoned security researchers will gain valuable insights from this book, we are equally hopeful that it will be accessible to developers and QA teams. Fuzzing can and should be an integral part of any SDLC, not just at the testing phase, but also during development. The earlier a defect can be identified, the less costly it will be to remediate.

## PREREQUISITES

Fuzzing is a vast subject. While we cover many non-fuzzing specific basics throughout the book, a number of assumptions regarding prior knowledge have been made. Readers should have at least a basic understanding of programming and computer networking prior to taking on this book. Fuzzing is all about automating security testing so naturally much of the book is dedicated to building tools. We have purposely selected multiple programming languages for these tasks. Languages were selected according to the task at hand, but this also demonstrates that fuzzing can be approached in numerous ways. It is certainly not necessary to have a background in all of the languages used, but having a language or two under your belt will go a long way in helping you to get the most from these chapters.

We detail numerous vulnerabilities throughout the book and discuss how they might have been identified through fuzzing. However, it is not our goal to define or dissect the nature of the vulnerabilities themselves. Many excellent books have been written which are dedicated to this topic. If you are looking for a primer on software vulnerabilities,

*Exploiting Software* by Greg Hoglund and Gary McGraw, books from the Hacking Exposed series and *The Shellcoder's Handbook* by Jack Koziol, David Litchfield, et al. are great references.

## APPROACH

How to best leverage this book depends upon your background and intentions. If you are new to fuzzing, we would recommend digesting the book in a sequential manner as it has been intentionally laid out to provide necessary background information prior to moving onto more advanced topics. If however, you've already spent time using various fuzzing tools, don't be afraid to dive directly into topics of interest as the various logical sections and chapter groupings are largely independent of one another.

Part I is designed to set the stage for the specific types of fuzzing that are discussed in the remainder of the book. If you're new to the world of fuzzing, consider this to be required reading. Fuzzing can be used as a vulnerability discovery methodology for just about any target, but all approaches follow the same basic principles. In Part I, we seek to define fuzzing as a vulnerability discovery methodology and detail the knowledge that will be required regardless of the type of fuzzing which is conducted.

Part II focuses on fuzzing specific classes of targets. Each target is divided across two or three chapters. The first chapter provides background information specific to the target class and the subsequent chapters focus on automation, detailing the construction of fuzzers for that particular target. Two automation chapters are provided when separate tools are deemed necessary for the Windows and UNIX platforms. For example, consider the chapter triplet on "File Format Fuzzing" starting with Chapter 11 which details background information related to fuzzing file parsers. Chapter 12, "File Format Fuzzing: Automation on UNIX" details the actual programming of a UNIX-based file fuzzer and Chapter 13, "File Format Fuzzing: Automation on Windows" details the construction of a file format fuzzer designed to run in the Windows environment.

Part III tackles advanced topics in fuzzing. For readers who already have a strong knowledge of fuzzing it may be appropriate to jump directly into Part III, while most readers will likely want to spend time in Parts I and II before moving onto these topics. In Part III, we focus on emerging technologies that are just beginning to be implemented but will become critical for advanced vulnerability discovery tools that leverage fuzzing in the future.

Finally, in Part IV, we reflect on what we've learned throughout the book and then peer into the crystal ball to see where we're headed in the future. While fuzzing is not a new concept, it still has plenty of room to grow, and we hope that this book will inspire further research in this space.

## A Touch of Humor

Writing a book is serious work, especially a book on a complex subject like fuzzing. That said, we like to have fun as much as the next person (actually probably significantly more than the average person) and have made our best effort to keep the writing entertaining. In that spirit, we decided to open each chapter with a brief quotation from the 43rd President of the United States, George W. Bush (a.k.a. Dubya). No matter what your political affiliation or beliefs may be, no one can argue that Mr. Bush has cooked up many entertaining quotes over the years, enough to fill entire calendars[1] even! We've compiled some of our favorites to share with you and hope you find them as funny as we do. As you'll see throughout the book, fuzzing can be applied against a variety of targets, evidently even the English language.

## About the Cover

At times, vulnerabilities have at times been referred to as "fish." (For example, see the thread on "The L Word & Fish"[2] from the DailyDave security mailing list.) This is a useful analogy that can be applied across the board when discussing security and vulnerabilities. A researcher can be called a fisherman. Reverse engineering the assembly code of an application, line by line, in search of a vulnerability may be referred to as "deep sea fishing." In comparison to many other auditing tactics, fuzzing for the most part only scratches the surface and is highly effective at capturing the "easy" fish. In addition, the grizzly bear is a notable "fuzzy," yet powerful animal. Combined, these are the main motivations behind our choice of cover art where the bear, representing a fuzzer, is shown capturing a fish, representing a vulnerability.

## Companion Website: www.fuzzing.org

The fuzzing.org website is an absolutely integral part of this book as opposed to a supplemental resource. In addition to housing errata that is sure to emerge post publication, the website will serve as the central repository for all source code and tools covered throughout the book. Over time, we intend to evolve fuzzing.org beyond a book-centric companion website into a valuable community resource with tools and information related to all fuzzing disciplines. We welcome your feedback in order to help make the site a valuable and open knowledgebase.

---

[1]   http://tinyurl.com/33l54g

[2]   http://archives.neohapsis.com/archives/dailydave/2004-q1/0023.html

# Acknowledgments

## GROUP ACKNOWLEDGEMENTS

While only three names appear on the cover of the book, there was a significant supporting cast behind the scenes that was responsible for making this book a reality. First and foremost are friends and family that put up with many late nights and lost weekends. We collectively owe several beers, movies, and quiet evenings at home that were missed out on during this project but to those affected, fear not, those debts will be repaid in full. While we'll miss our regular Thursday night book meetings, we recognize that others aren't likely to miss them at all.

Peter DeVries once commented, "I love being a writer. What I can't stand is the paperwork." We couldn't agree more. Coming up with the thoughts and ideas is only half the battle. Once the draft was laid out, a small army of reviewers joined the battle in an effort to convince the world that we could write a book. We would like to personally thank our technical editors who did their level best to point out our mistakes and challenge our assumptions. Most notably Charlie Miller, who went through great lengths to help make the book "cutting edge." We also sincerely appreciate the effort that H.D. Moore put in reviewing the book and writing the foreword. We would also like to thank the team from Addison-Wesley that helped guide us through the process, including Sheri Cain, Kristin Weinberger, Romny French, Jana Jones, and Lori Lyons. Last but not least, a special thanks to our acquisitions editor, Jessica Goldstein, who was willing to take a chance on three guys with a crazy idea and the naive belief that writing a book couldn't possibly be all that hard.

## MICHAEL'S ACKNOWLEDGEMENTS

I would like to take this opportunity to thank my wife Amanda for her patience and understanding throughout the writing of this book. We were planning a wedding throughout much of the writing process and there were far too many evenings and weekends spent poring over a computer screen which should have been spent enjoying a bottle of wine on the porch. I also sincerely appreciate the support given to me by all members of my family who encouraged me to pursue this project and actually believed that we could do it. Thanks also the iDefense Labs team and my coworkers at SPI Dynamics who supported and inspired me throughout the process. Finally, I want thank my co-authors for joining me on this journey, putting up with my sporadic GOYA speeches, motivating me to GOMOA and collectively producing a far stronger piece of work than I ever could have produced on my own.

## ADAM'S ACKNOWLEDGEMENTS

I would like to thank my family (especially my sister and parents), teachers and counselors at JTHS, Mark Chegwidden, Louis Collucci, Chris Burkhart, sgo, Nadwodny, Dave Aitel, Jamie Breiten, the Davis family, the Brothers Leondi, Reynolds, Kloub and AE, Lusardi, Lapilla and last and definitely least, Richard.

## PEDRAM'S ACKNOWLEDGEMENTS

I would like to thank my co-authors for the opportunity to write this book and for keeping me motivated over the long course to completion. I extend my gratitude to Cody Pierce, Cameron Hotchkies and Aaron Portnoy, my team at TippingPoint, for their ingenuity and technical reviews. Thanks to Peter Silberman, Jamie Butler, Greg Hoglund, Halvar Flake and Ero Carrera for inspiration and providing non-stop entertainment. Special thanks to David Endler, Ralph Schindler, Sunil James and Nicholas Augello, my "brothers from other mothers," for always being available to lean on. Finally, a heartfelt thanks to my family for being patient during my absence to complete this book.

# About the Authors

## MICHAEL SUTTON

Michael Sutton is the Security Evangelist for SPI Dynamics. As Security Evangelist, Michael is responsible for identifying, researching, and presenting on emerging issues in the web application security industry. He is a frequent speaker at major information security conferences, has authored numerous articles, and is regularly quoted in the media on various information security topics. Michael is also a member of the Web Application Security Consortium (WASC), where he is project lead for the Web Application Security Statistics project.

Prior to joining SPI Dynamics, Michael was a Director for iDefense/VeriSign, where he headed iDefense Labs, a team of world class researchers tasked with discovering and researching security vulnerabilities. Michael also established the Information Systems Assurance and Advisory Services (ISAAS) practice for Ernst & Young in Bermuda. He holds degrees from the University of Alberta and The George Washington University.

Michael is a proud Canadian who understands that hockey is a religion and not a sport. Outside of the office, he is a Sergeant with the Fairfax Volunteer Fire Department.

## ADAM GREENE

Adam Greene is an engineer for a large financial news company based in New York City. Previously, he served as an engineer for iDefense, an intelligence company located in Reston, VA. His interests in computer security lie mainly in reliable exploitation methods, fuzzing, and UNIX-based system auditing and exploit development.

# PEDRAM AMINI

Pedram Amini currently leads the security research and product security assessment team at TippingPoint. Previously, he was the assistant director and one of the founding members of iDefense Labs. Despite the fancy titles, he spends much of his time in the shoes of a reverse engineer—developing automation tools, plug-ins, and scripts. His most recent projects (a.k.a. "babies") include the PaiMei reverse engineering framework and the Sulley fuzzing framework.

In conjunction with his passion, Pedram launched OpenRCE.org, a community website dedicated to the art and science of reverse engineering. He has presented at RECon, BlackHat, DefCon, ShmooCon, and ToorCon and taught numerous sold out reverse engineering courses. Pedram holds a computer science degree from Tulane University.

# PART I

# BACKGROUND

# Vulnerability Discovery Methodologies

*"Will the highways of the Internet become more few?"*

—George W. Bush, Concord, N.H., January 29, 2000

Ask any accomplished security researcher how he discovers vulnerabilities and you're likely to get a multitude of answers. Why? There are a variety of approaches, each with its own advantages and disadvantages. No one approach is correct and no single method can uncover all possible vulnerabilities for a given target. At a high level, there are three primary approaches to discovering security vulnerabilities: *white box, black box,* and *gray box* testing. The differences among these approaches can be determined by the resources to which you, as the tester, have access. At one extreme, the white box approach requires complete access to all resources. This includes access to source code, design specifications, and perhaps even the programmers themselves. On the other extreme, the black box approach requires little to no knowledge of internals and is limited to blind testing for the most part. Pen testing a remote Web application with no access to source code is a good example of black box testing. Sitting in the middle is gray box testing, the definition of which varies depending on who you ask. For our purposes, gray box testing requires, for example, that you have access to compiled binaries and perhaps some basic documentation.

In this chapter we explore various high- and low-level approaches for vulnerability discovery, starting with white box testing, which you might have otherwise heard referred to as clear, glass, or translucent box testing. We then define black box and gray box testing, which would include fuzzing. We look at the pros and cons of each, as this will provide the necessary background when focusing exclusively on fuzzing throughout the remainder of the book. Fuzzing is only one approach to vulnerability discovery and it is important to recognize where alternate approaches might be more practical.

# WHITE BOX TESTING

Fuzzing as a testing methodology falls mostly in the realm of black and gray box testing. However, we start by examining a common alternate approach to vulnerability discovery used by software developers known as white box testing.

## SOURCE CODE REVIEW

A source code review can be accomplished either manually or with the assistance of automation tools. Given that computer programs are commonly comprised of tens to hundreds of thousands of lines of code, a pure manual review is generally impractical. Automated tools are an invaluable resource that will reduce the tedious task of poring over individual lines of code but can only identify *potentially* vulnerable or suspicious code segments. Human analysis is required to determine if detected issues are indeed valid.

There are a multitude of hurdles that source code analysis tools must overcome to produce useful results. Dissecting these various complex issues is beyond the scope of this book, but consider the following C language code sample, which simply copies the word *test* into a 10-byte character array:

```c
#include <string.h>

int main (int argc, char **argv)
{
    char buffer[10];
    strcpy(buffer, "test");
}
```

Next, consider the same code sample, which has been modified to allow user input to be copied into the character array.

```c
#include <string.h>
int main (int argc, char **argv)
{
    char buffer[10];
    strcpy(buffer, argv[1]);
}
```

Both code segments use the `strcpy()` routine to copy data into a stack-based buffer. The usage of `strcpy()` is generally discouraged in C/C++ programming due to its lack of bounds checking on the buffer to which data is being copied. As a result, if the programmer is not careful to add his or her own checks, an overflow can occur, placing data outside of the bounds of the intended container. The first example will not cause a buffer overflow because the size of the string "test" (including the terminating null byte) is and always will be 5, and is therefore smaller than the 10-byte buffer into which it is being copied. The second scenario might or might not cause a buffer overflow, depending on the size of the user-supplied argument on the command line. The key here is whether or not the user has control over the input provided to the vulnerable function. A rudimentary code review would flag the `strcpy()` line in both code samples as being potentially vulnerable. However, tracing of input values is required to understand if an exploitable condition truly exists. This is not to say that source code reviews cannot be valuable tools for security researchers. Source code reviews should be performed whenever the code is available. However, depending on your role and perspective, it is common not to have access to this level of detail.

People often incorrectly assume that white box testing is more effective than black box testing. What view of software can be better or more complete than access to the source code? Keep in mind, however, that what you see is not necessarily what you execute when it comes to source code. The software build process can make drastic changes during the conversion of source code to assembly code. This, among other reasons, is why it isn't possible to state that one testing approach is necessarily better than another. They are simply different approaches that will generally uncover different types of vulnerabilities. For complete coverage, it is necessary to combine multiple approaches.

## MICROSOFT SOURCE CODE LEAK

To defend the claim that a source code review is not superior to black box testing, consider an event that occurred in February 2004. Without warning, archives of code began to circulate on the Internet that were rumored to contain large excerpts of source for the Microsoft Windows NT 4.0 and Windows 2000 operating systems. Microsoft later confirmed that the archives were indeed genuine. Many corporations were extremely nervous that this leak would quickly lead to a flood of vulnerabilities in the two popular operating systems. That didn't happen. In fact, to this day we can attribute only a handful of vulnerabilities to the leaked source code. Among that short list of vulnerabilities is CVE-2004-0566, which details an integer overflow that could be triggered when rendering bitmap files.[1] Interestingly, Microsoft disputed the discovery, claiming that the software company had already uncovered the issue during an internal audit.[2] Why didn't we see a flood of vulnerabilities? Shouldn't access to source code reveal all? The truth is that a source code review, although a very important component of an application or operating system security audit, can also be difficult to perform due to the size and complexity of the code. Furthermore, disassembly analysis techniques can cover much of the same ground. For example, take a look at the TinyKRNL[3] and ReactOS[4] projects, both of which aim to provide Microsoft Windows kernel and operating system compatibility. The developers of these projects didn't have access to the Microsoft kernel source code and yet were able to create projects that at least to some extent, provide a compatible Windows environment. When auditing the Windows operating system, you won't likely have access to the Windows source code either, but the source code for these projects can be used as a guide when interpreting the Windows disassembly.

## TOOLS AND AUTOMATION

Source code analysis tools generally fall into one of three categories—compile time checkers, source code browsers, or automated source code auditing tools. Compile time checkers look for vulnerabilities as source code is compiled. The tools are generally integrated with compilers but attempt to identify security-specific issues as opposed to problems with application functionality. The /analyze compiler option in Microsoft Visual C++ is an example of a compile time checker.[5] Microsoft also provides PREfast for Drivers,[6] which can detect various classes of vulnerabilities specific to driver development that might not be detected by the compiler.

---

[1]  http://archives.neohapsis.com/archives/fulldisclosure/2004-02/0806.html

[2]  http://news.zdnet.com/2100-1009_22-5160566.html

[3]  http://www.tinykrnl.org/

[4]  http://www.reactos.org/

[5]  http://msdn2.microsoft.com/en-us/library/k3a3hzw7.aspx

[6]  http://www.microsoft.com/whdc/devtools/tools/PREfast.mspx

Source code browsers are tools designed to assist in the manual exploration and review of source code. This class of tools allows the reviewer to apply advanced searches across the code as well as enumerate and navigate cross-references between locations. For example, a reviewer might use such a tool to locate all uses of the strcpy() call in an effort to identify potential buffer overflow vulnerabilities. Cscope[7] and Linux Cross-Reference[8] are popular source code browsers.

Automated source code auditing tools are designed to scan source code and automatically identify potential areas of concern. As with most security tools, automated source code auditing tools are available as both commercial and freeware solutions. Moreover, the tools tend to focus on specific programming languages so multiple tools might be required if your target is built using different programming languages. On the commercial front, products exist from vendors such as Fortify,[9] Coverity,[10] KlocWork,[11] GrammaTech,[12] and others. Table 1.1 provides a list of some popular freeware tools, the languages they audit, and the platforms they support.

**Table 1.1**  Freeware Source Code Auditing Tools

| Name | Language(s) | Platform(s) | Download |
|---|---|---|---|
| RATS (Rough Auditing Tool for Security) | C, C++, Perl, PHP, Python | UNIX, Win32 | http://www.fortifysoftware.com/security-resources/rats.jsp |
| ITS4 | C, C++. | UNIX, Win32 | http://www.cigital.com/its4/ |
| Splint | C | UNIX, Win32 | http://lclint.cs.virginia.edu/ |
| Flawfinder | C, C++ | UNIX | http://www.dwheeler.com/flawfinder/ |
| Jlint | Java. | UNIX, Win32 | http://jlint.sourceforge.net/ |
| CodeSpy | Java | Java | http://www.owasp.org/software/labs/codespy.html |

---

[7]  http://cscope.sourceforge.net/

[8]  http://lxr.linux.no/

[9]  http://www.fortifysoftware.com/

[10] http://www.coverity.com/

[11] http://www.klocwork.com/

[12] http://www.grammatech.com/

It is important to keep in mind that no automation tool can ever replace the skills of an experienced security researcher. They are simply tools that streamline the overwhelming task of digesting thousands of lines of source code and assist in saving time and frustration. The reports generated by such tools must still be reviewed by an experienced analyst to identify false positives, and by developers to actually implement a fix. Consider, for example, the following sample output generated by the Rough Auditing Tool for Security (RATS) across the contrived vulnerable example code shown earlier in the chapter. RATS points out two potential security issues. It highlights the fact that a fixed buffer was used and that strcpy() is potentially unsafe. It does not, however, definitively state that a vulnerability exists. It only draws the attention of the user to potentially unsafe code regions and relies on him or her to determine if the code is indeed unsafe.

```
Entries in perl database: 33
Entries in python database: 62
Entries in c database: 334
Entries in php database: 55
Analyzing userinput.c
userinput.c:4: High: fixed size local buffer
Extra care should be taken to ensure that character arrays that are allocated on the
stack are used safely. They are prime targets for buffer overflow attacks.

userinput.c:5: High: strcpy
Check to be sure that argument 2 passed to this function call will not copy more data
than can be handled, resulting in a buffer overflow.

Total lines analyzed: 7
Total time 0.000131 seconds
53435 lines per second
Entries in perl database: 33
Entries in python database: 62
Entries in c database: 334
Entries in php database: 55
Analyzing userinput.c
userinput.c:4: High: fixed size local buffer
Extra care should be taken to ensure that character arrays that are allocated
on the stack are used safely.  They are prime targets for buffer overflow
attacks.

userinput.c:5: High: strcpy
Check to be sure that argument 2 passed to this function call will not copy
more data than can be handled, resulting in a buffer overflow.

Total lines analyzed: 7
Total time 0.000794 seconds
8816 lines per second
```

## PROS AND CONS

As mentioned previously, there is no single correct approach to discovering security vulnerabilities. So how does one choose an appropriate methodology? Well sometimes the decision is made for us. White box testing, for example, is not possible if we do not have access to the source code of the target. This is the case for most security researchers and end users, especially those who are dealing with commercial software in the Microsoft Windows environment. What are the advantages of white box testing?

- *Coverage.* Due to the fact that all source code is available, a code review allows for complete coverage. All possible code paths can be audited for potential vulnerabilities. This can, of course, lead to false positives as code paths might not be reachable during code execution.

Code reviews are not always possible. Even when they can be conducted, they should be combined with other vulnerability discovery methodologies. Source code analysis has the following shortcomings.

- *Complexity.* Source code analysis tools are imperfect and produce false positives. Therefore, the error reports produced by such tools are not an end game. They must still be reviewed by experienced programmers to identify issues that represent legitimate security vulnerabilities. Because significant software projects typically contain hundreds of thousands of lines of code, the reports can be lengthy and require significant time to wade through.

- *Availability.* Source code is not always available. Although many UNIX projects are open source and allow for source code to be reviewed, this situation is relatively rare in a Win32 environment and generally nonexistent when dealing with commercial software. Without access to source code, this form of white box testing is not even an option.

## BLACK BOX TESTING

Black box testing implies that you only have knowledge of what you can observe. You as the end user control the input that goes into the black box and you can observe the output that emerges from the other end, but you do not have knowledge of the inner workings of your target. This situation is most commonly found when remotely accessing Web applications and Web services. You can craft inputs in the form of Hypertext Markup Language (HTML) or Extensible Markup Language (XML) requests and observe the generated Web page or return value, respectively, but have no idea what is going on under the hood.

As another example consider that whenever you purchase an application such as Microsoft Office, you generally receive a precompiled binary application, not the source code that was used to build it. Your perspective in this situation will determine the shade of box color for the testing approach. If you do not intend to apply reverse engineering techniques, you will be effectively testing the software in a black box. Otherwise, you will be applying a gray box approach, discussed in the next section.

## MANUAL TESTING

Sticking with Web applications as an example, manual testing could involve using a standard Web browser to explore a Web site hierarchy while tediously inserting potentially dangerous inputs throughout observed areas of interest. During the most nascent stages of auditing, this technique might be applied sporadically, for example, by adding single quotes to various parameters in hopes of uncovering a SQL injection vulnerability.

Manually testing applications for vulnerabilities without the aid of automated tools is not generally a practical approach (unless your firm hires a giant horde of interns). One scenario in which it can be very beneficial is when it is used for *sweeping* multiple applications for a similar vulnerability. Sweeping takes advantage of occurrences where numerous programmers make the same mistakes in different projects. For example, perhaps a buffer overflow is found in a particular Lightweight Directory Access Protocol (LDAP) server and testing that same exploit vector against other LDAP servers reveals that they are also vulnerable. Given that programs often share code or the same programmers work on multiple projects, this is not an uncommon occurrence.

### SWEEPING

CreateProcess() is a function exposed through the Microsoft Windows application programming interface (API). As the name implies, CreateProcess() will start a new process and its primary thread.[13] The prototype of the function is shown here:

```
BOOL CreateProcess(
    LPCTSTR lpApplicationName,
    LPTSTR lpCommandLine,
    LPSECURITY_ATTRIBUTES lpProcessAttributes,
    LPSECURITY_ATTRIBUTES lpThreadAttributes,
```

---

[13] http://msdn2.microsoft.com/en-us/library/ms682425.aspx

```
        BOOL bInheritHandles,
        DWORD dwCreationFlags,
        LPVOID lpEnvironment,
        LPCTSTR lpCurrentDirectory,
        LPSTARTUPINFO lpStartupInfo,
        LPPROCESS_INFORMATION lpProcessInformation
    );
```

It is known and documented behavior that if the lpApplicationName parameter is specified as a NULL value, then the process that will be launched is the first white space delimited value in the lpCommandLine parameter. Consider, for example, this call to CreateProcess():

```
    CreateProcess(
        NULL,
        "c:\program files\sub dir\program.exe",
        ...
    );
```

In this situation, CreateProcess() will iteratively try to launch each of the following space-delimited values.

```
    c:\program.exe
    c:\program files\sub.exe
    c:\program files\sub dir\program.exe
```

This will continue until an executable is found or all possibilities have been exhausted. Therefore, if a program.exe executable were placed in the c:\ directory, applications with insecure calls to CreateProcess() with the aforementioned structure would execute program.exe. This provides attackers with a handy trick for trying to get a file executed when execute permissions are out of reach.

In November 2005, a security advisory[14] was issued identifying several popular applications that utilized insecure calls to CreateProcess(). The discoveries resulted from a successful and very simple sweeping exercise. If you'd like to sweep for the same vulnerabilities, copy and rename a simple application such as notepad.exe and place it in the c:\ directory. Now use the machine as you normally would. If the copied application suddenly launches unexpectedly, you've likely uncovered an insecure call to CreateProcess().

---

[14] http://labs.idefense.com/intelligence/vulnerabilities/display.php?id=340

## AUTOMATED TESTING OR FUZZING

Fuzzing, for the most part, is a brute force technique and what it lacks in elegance, it makes up for in simplicity and effectiveness. In Chapter 2, "What Is Fuzzing?" we define and dissect the term in full detail. In a nutshell, fuzzing consists of throwing everything but the kitchen sink at a target and monitoring the results. Most software is designed to work with specific inputs but should be robust enough to gracefully recover from situations where abnormal inputs are received. Consider the simple Web form depicted in Figure 1.1.

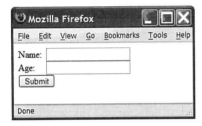

**Figure 1.1**    Simple Web form

It is fair to assume that the Name field should receive a string value and that the Age field should receive an integer. What will happen if the user accidentally reverses the input values and plugs a string into the age field? Will the string value be automatically converted to an integer based on the ASCII values of the characters? Will an error message be displayed? Will the application crash? Fuzzing seeks to answer these questions through an automated process. The researcher requires no knowledge about the internal workings of the application and is therefore conducting a black box test. You are standing back, throwing rocks at the target, and waiting to hear a window break. In this sense, fuzzing falls into the black box category. However, throughout the book we'll demonstrate how brute force fuzzing can be made more surgical to ensure that the rock flies straight and true every time; therefore fuzzing also applies in the gray box category.

## DOES MICROSOFT FUZZ?

The answer is yes. The Trustworthy Computing Security Development Lifecycle document[15] (SDL) published by Microsoft in March 2005 makes it clear that fuzzing is considered by Microsoft to be a key tool for identifying security vulnerabilities before software is released. The SDL was an initiative to embed security within the software development lifecycle, making security the responsibility of everyone participating in the development process. Fuzzing is mentioned in the SDL as a class of security testing tools that should be leveraged during the implementation phase. The document actually states that "heavy emphasis on fuzz testing is a relatively recent addition to the SDL, but results to date are very encouraging."

## PROS AND CONS

Black box testing, although not always the best approach, is always an option. Advantages of black box testing include the following:

- *Availability.* Black box testing is always applicable and even in situations when source code is available, black box testing can still be beneficial.

- *Reproducibility.* Because black box testing makes no assumptions about the target, a black box test against one File Transfer Protocol (FTP) server, for example, can be easily repurposed to test any other FTP server.

- *Simplicity.* Although approaches such as reverse code engineering (RCE) require specialized skills, pure black box testing at its most basic level can be conducted without a strong knowledge of the application internals. However, in reality, whereas basic denial of service vulnerabilities can be found simply through the use of automated testing tools, a deeper knowledge is generally required to determine if a simple application crash can be expanded into something more interesting such as code execution.

---

[15] http://msdn.microsoft.com/library/default.asp?url=/library/en-us/dnsecure/html/sdl.asp

Despite the accessibility of black box testing, it does have some shortcomings. The disadvantages of black box testing include the following:

- *Coverage.* One of the biggest challenges with black box testing is determining when to stop testing and how effective the testing has been. We address this issue in greater detail in Chapter 23, "Fuzzer Tracking."
- *Intelligence.* Black box testing is best suited to scenarios in which a vulnerability is caused by an individual input vector. Complex attacks might, however, require multiple attack vectors, some of which place the target application into a vulnerable state and others that trigger exploitation. Attacks such as these require a strong understanding of the underlying application logic and will typically only be uncovered with manual source code audits and RCE.

## GRAY BOX TESTING

Floating in between white and black box analysis, we define gray box testing to include black box auditing plus the additional insights offered through reverse engineering (RE), also known as reverse code engineering (RCE). Source code is an invaluable resource that is reasonably easy to read and provides a strong understanding of how specific functionality operates. Additionally, it communicates the inputs that specific functionality expects and the output that the same functionality can be expected to generate. Not all is lost in the absence of this great resource. Analysis of the compiled assembly instructions can help unfold a similar story, albeit with increased efforts. Security evaluation at the assembly as opposed to source code level is typically referred to as binary auditing.

### BINARY AUDITING

RCE is often used synonymously with the phrase binary auditing, but for our purposes we treat RCE as a subcategory to distinguish it from fully automated methods. The ultimate goal of RCE is to determine the underlying functionality of a compiled binary application. Although it is not possible to convert a binary file back into its original source code representation, it is possible to reverse engineer sequences of assembly instructions into a format that lies between the original source code and the machine code that makes up the binary file(s). Generally, this middle ground is a combination of assembly language and graphical representations of the flow of code within the application.

Once the binary file has been converted to a human-readable form, the code can then be reviewed for locations that could potentially contain vulnerabilities in much the same way as a source code review. As with a source code review, locating potentially vulnerable code segments is not the end game. It is also necessary to determine if an end user can influence the vulnerable code segment. Following this logic, binary auditing can be referred to as an inside-out technique: The researcher first identifies an interesting line deep within the disassembly and then traces it backward to determine if the vulnerability is exploitable.

Reverse engineering is a surgical technique that employs tools such as disassemblers, decompilers, and debuggers. Disassemblers parse illegible machine code into some flavor of assembly language suitable for digestion by a human. Various freeware disassemblers are available but for serious RCE work you will likely want to invest in a copy of DataRescue's Interactive Disassembler (IDA) Pro,[16] shown in Figure 1.2. IDA is a commercial disassembler that runs on Windows, UNIX, and MacOS platforms and is capable of dissecting binaries from a wide range of architectures.

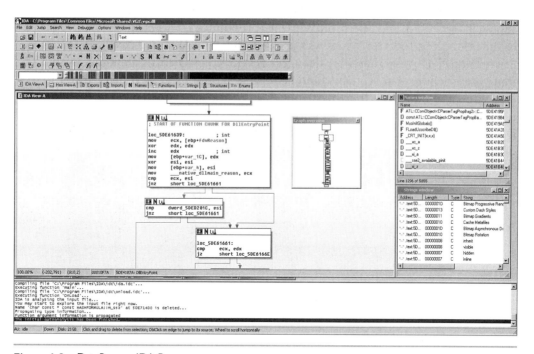

**Figure 1.2**   DataRescue IDA Pro

---

[16] http://www.datarescue.com/

Similar to a disassembler, a decompiler statically analyzes and converts binary code into a human-readable format. Instead of directly translating to assembly instructions, a decompiler attempts to produce higher level language constructs such as conditionals and loops. Decompilers are not capable of recovering the original source code because information that was contained in the source code such as comments, variable names, function names, and even basic structure is not retained when source code is compiled. Decompilers for languages that compile to machine code (e.g., C and C++) tend to have significant limitations and are mostly experimental in nature. Boomerang[17] is an example of a decompiler for machine code. Decompilers are more common for languages that compile to some intermediate form of byte code such as C#, as more detail is retained in the compiled code and decompilation is therefore generally more successful.

Unlike disassemblers and decompilers, debuggers apply dynamic analysis by opening or attaching to a target program and monitoring its execution. A debugger can display the contents of CPU registers and the state of memory while the application is running. Popular debuggers for the Win32 platform include OllyDbg,[18] a screen shot of which is shown in Figure 1.3, and Microsoft WinDbg (pronounced "wind bag").[19] WinDbg is part of the Debugging Tools for Windows[20] package and is available as a free download from Microsoft. OllyDbg is a shareware debugger developed by Oleh Yuschuk that is a bit more user friendly than WinDbg. Both debuggers allow for the creation of custom extensions and numerous third-party plug-ins are available to extend OllyDbg's functionality.[21] Various debuggers exist for the UNIX environment, with the GNU Project Debugger[22] (GDB) being the most popular and portable. GDB is a command-line debugger that is included with many UNIX/Linux distributions.

---

[17] http://boomerang.sourceforge.net/

[18] http://www.ollydbg.de/

[19] http://www.openrce.org/forums/posts/4

[20] http://www.microsoft.com/whdc/devtools/debugging/default.mspx

[21] http://www.openrce.org/downloads/browse/OllyDbg_Plugins

[22] http://www.gnu.org/software/gdb/gdb.html

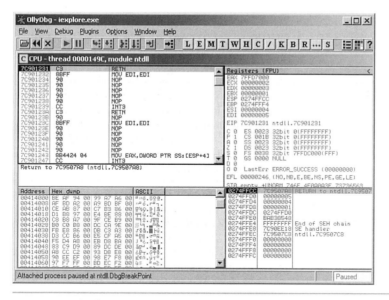

**Figure 1.3**   OllyDbg

## AUTOMATED BINARY AUDITING

There are a handful of tools emerging that attempt to automate the process of RCE in an effort to identify potential security vulnerabilities in binary applications. The primary applications include both commercial and freeware varieties and are either IDA Pro plug-ins or freestanding applications. Table 1.2 lists a handful of these.

**Table 1.2**   Automated Binary Auditing Tools

| Name | Vendor | License | Notes |
|------|--------|---------|-------|
| LogiScan | LogicLibrary | Commercial | LogicLibrary acquired BugScan in September 2004 and has since rebranded the binary auditing tool and integrated it in to the Logidex SDA management solution. |
| BugScam | Halvar Flake | Freeware | BugScam is a collection of IDC scripts for IDA Pro that enumerate the function calls within a binary to identify the potentially insecure use of various library calls. The application was mainly written as a pun or spoof on BugScan. |

*(continues)*

**Table 1.2**   continued

| | | | |
|---|---|---|---|
| Inspector | HB Gary | Commercial | Inspector is an RCE management system unifying output from various RCE tools such as IDA Pro and OllyDbg. |
| SecurityReview | Veracode | Commercial | VeraCode's product integrates a binary analysis suite directly into the development environment similar to how source code analysis suites such as Coverity operate. Analyzing at the binary level allows VeraCode to dodge some problems associated with "what you see is not what you execute." |
| BinAudit | SABRE Security | Commercial | BinAudit had not yet been released at the time of publication. However, according to the SABRE Security Web site, it is a plug-in for IDA Pro designed to identify security vulnerabilities such as out of bounds array access, double-free memory corruption, memory leaks, and so on. |

## PROS AND CONS

As mentioned, gray box testing is somewhat of a hybrid solution that incorporates traditional black box testing with insights gained from RCE efforts. As with other approaches, gray box testing has advantages and disadvantages. Advantages of gray box testing include the following:

- *Availability.* With the exception of remote Web services and applications, binary versions of software are always available.
- *Coverage.* Information gleaned through gray box analysis can be utilized to assist and improve otherwise pure black box fuzzing techniques.

The disadvantages of black box testing include the following:

- *Complexity.* RCE is a specialized skill set and therefore resources might not be available to apply this approach.

## SUMMARY

At the highest level, vulnerability discovery methodologies can be divided into white, black, and gray box testing. The resources made available to the tester determine the distinction among the three. White box testing makes all possible resources including source code available, whereas black box testing provides access only to the inputs and observed outputs. Sitting between the two, gray box testing provides additional information over black box analysis through RCE of available binaries.

White box testing involves various approaches to source code analysis. This can be accomplished manually or by leveraging automated tools such as compile time checkers, source code browsers, or automated source code auditing tools.

When conducting black box testing, source code is not available. Fuzzing via black box testing is considered blind. Inputs are generated and responses are monitored but no details regarding the internal state of the target are available for analysis. Fuzzing via gray box testing is similar to the black box approach with the addition of augmented data from RCE efforts. Fuzzing attempts to repeatedly provide an application with unexpected input and simultaneously monitor for exceptions that might result. The remainder of this book focuses on fuzzing as an approach to discovering security vulnerabilities.

# What Is Fuzzing?

*"They misunderestimated me."*

—George W. Bush, Bentonville, Ark., November 6, 2000

The term fuzzing does not exist in mainstream vocabulary, has many aliases, and might be entirely new to some readers. Fuzzing is a broad field and an exciting approach toward software security analysis. Throughout this book we dive into the specifics of various fuzzing aspects and targets. Before doing so, we begin in this chapter with a definition for the term, explore the history of fuzzing, examine the individual phases of a complete fuzzing audit, and conclude with the limitations of fuzz testing.

## DEFINITION OF FUZZING

Look up *fuzzing* in your dictionary and you're not likely to find anything that will help you to define the term as it is used by security researchers. The first public mention of fuzzing came from a University of Wisconsin-Madison research project, and the term has since been adopted to describe an entire methodology for software testing. In the academic world, fuzzing can be most closely related to boundary value analysis (BVA),[1] where you look at the range of known good values for a particular input and create test values that straddle the boundary cases of known good and bad values. The results of the

---

[1] http://en.wikipedia.org/wiki/Boundary_value_analysis

BVA can help to ensure that exception handling appropriately filters out unwanted values while allowing the full range of acceptable inputs. Fuzzing is similar to BVA, but when fuzzing, we are not solely focused on boundary values, but additionally any inputs that can trigger undefined or insecure behavior.

For the purposes of this book we define fuzzing as a method for discovering faults in software by providing unexpected input and monitoring for exceptions. It is typically an automated or semiautomated process that involves repeatedly manipulating and supplying data to target software for processing. This is, of course, a very generic definition, but it captures the basic concept of fuzzing. All fuzzers fall into one of two categories: *mutation-based* fuzzers, which apply mutations on existing data samples to create test cases, and *generation-based* fuzzers, which create test cases from scratch by modeling the target protocol or file format. Both methods carry pros and cons. In Chapter 3, "Fuzzing Methods and Fuzzer Types," we further categorize fuzzing methodologies and discuss benefits and pitfalls.

If you are new to fuzzing, consider the analogy of breaking into a house. Assume that you failed in your current career and have turned to a life of crime. If you were taking a pure white box approach to breaking into a home, you would have full access to all information about the home prior to breaking in. This might include blueprints, a list of lock manufacturers used, details of the construction materials used in building the home, and more. Although this approach provides some distinct advantages, it is not foolproof or without disadvantages. With this method you are statically analyzing the design of the home as opposed to examining it at runtime, during the actual break-in. Say, for example, you decide during your research that the side living room window represents a weak point that could be smashed to gain entry. You might not, however, anticipate the presence of the angry owner cradling a shotgun and waiting for you on the inside. On the other hand, if you were applying a pure black box testing method to breaking in, you might approach the home under the cover of darkness and quietly test all of the doors and windows, peering into the house to determine what the best point of entry is. Finally, if you chose to use fuzzing to break into the home, you might dispense with researching the blueprints or manually testing the locks. You could simply automate the process by picking up a gun and blowing your way into the home—brute force vulnerability discovery!

## HISTORY OF FUZZING

The earliest reference to fuzzing of which we are aware dates back to 1989. Professor Barton Miller (considered by many to be the "father" of fuzzing) and his Advanced Operating Systems class developed and used a primitive fuzzer to test the robustness of UNIX applications.[2] The focus of the testing was not necessarily to assess the security of the system, but rather the overall code quality and reliability. Although security considerations were mentioned in passing throughout the study, no particular emphasis was placed on setuid applications during testing. In 1995, this testing was repeated with an expanded set of UNIX utilities and operating systems being tested. The 1995 study found an overall improvement in application reliability, but still noted "significant rates of failure."

The fuzz testing method employed by Miller's team was very crude. If the application crashed or hung, it had failed the test. If it did not, it had succeeded. It accomplished this by simply throwing random strings of characters at target applications, a pure black box approach. Although this might seem overly simplistic, keep in mind that the concept of fuzzing was relatively unheard of at the time.

Around 1999, work began at the University of Oulu on their PROTOS test suite. Various PROTOS test suites were developed by first analyzing protocol specifications and then producing packets that either violated the specification or were deemed likely not to be handled properly by specific protocol implementation. Producing such test suites took considerable effort up front, but once produced, the test suites could be run against multiple vendor products. This is an example of a mixed white and black box approach and marked an important milestone in the evolution of fuzzing due to the large number of faults that were uncovered using this process.

In 2002 Microsoft provided funding to the PROTOS initiative[3] and in 2003 members of the PROTOS team launched Codenomicon, a company dedicated to the design and production of commercial fuzz testing suites. The product today is still based on the original Oulu test suite but includes a graphical user interface, user support, and fault detection through a health-checking feature, among other things.[4] More information on Codenomicon and other commercial fuzzing solutions is presented in Chapter 26, "Looking Forward."

As PROTOS matured in 2002, Dave Aitel released an open sourced fuzzer named SPIKE[5] under the GNU General Public (GPL) license. Aitel's fuzzer implements a block-based approach[6] intended for testing network-enabled applications. SPIKE takes a more

---

[2]  http://www.cs.wisc.edu/~bart/fuzz/

[3]  http://www.ee.oulu.fi/research/ouspg/protos/index.html

[4]  http://www.codenomicon.com/products/features.shtml

[5]  http://immunityinc.com/resources-freesoftware.shtml

[6]  http://www.immunityinc.com/downloads/advantages_of_block_based_analysis.html

advanced approach than Miller's fuzzer, most notably including the ability to describe variable-length data blocks. Additionally, SPIKE can not only generate random data, but also bundles a library of values that are likely to produce faults in poorly written applications. SPIKE also includes predefined functions capable of producing common protocols and data formats. Among them are Sun RPC and Microsoft RPC, two communication technologies that have been at the heart of many past vulnerabilities. As the first publicly available framework allowing users to effortlessly create their own fuzzers, the release of SPIKE marked a significant milestone. This framework is mentioned a number of times throughout the book including in Chapter 21, "Fuzzing Frameworks."

Around the same time as the initial release of SPIKE, Aitel also released a local UNIX fuzzer named sharefuzz. In contrast to Miller's fuzzer, sharefuzz targets environment variables as opposed to command-line arguments. Sharefuzz also employs a useful technique to facilitate the fuzzing process. It uses shared libraries to hook function calls that return environment variable values to return long strings as opposed to the actual values in an effort to reveal buffer overflow vulnerabilities.

The majority of fuzzing innovations following the release of SPIKE came in the form of tools for different specific classes of fuzzing. Michal Zalewski[7] (a.k.a. lcamtuf) drew attention to Web browser fuzzing in 2004 with the release of mangleme,[8] a Common Gateway Interface (CGI) script designed to continually produce malformed HTML files that are repeatedly refreshed within a targeted Web browser. Other fuzzers designed to target Web browsers soon followed. H.D. Moore and Aviv Raff produced Hamachi[9] to fuzz Dynamic HTML (DHTML) implementation flaws and the two later teamed up with Matt Murphy and Thierry Zoller to produce CSSDIE,[10] a fuzzer that targets cascading style sheet parsing.

File fuzzing came into vogue in 2004. That year Microsoft released security bulletin MS04-028 detailing a buffer overrun in the engine responsible for processing JPEG files.[11] Although this was not the first discovered file format vulnerability, it attracted attention due to the number of popular Microsoft applications that shared the vulnerable code. File format vulnerabilities also presented a unique challenge for those tasked with protecting networks. Although a surprising number of similar vulnerabilities would emerge in the following years, it was not realistic to simply block potentially vulnerable

---

[7]   http://lcamtuf.coredump.cx/

[8]   http://lcamtuf.coredump.cx/mangleme/mangle.cgi

[9]   http://metasploit.com/users/hdm/tools/hamachi/hamachi.html

[10]   http://metasploit.com/users/hdm/tools/see-ess-ess-die/cssdie.html

[11]   http://www.microsoft.com/technet/security/bulletin/MS04-028.mspx

file types from entering a corporate network. Images and media files comprise a significant portion of Internet traffic. How exciting could the Web be without images? Moreover, the majority of the vulnerabilities that would soon plague Microsoft related to Microsoft Office document files—file types critical to virtually all businesses. File format vulnerabilities turned out to be a prime candidate for mutation-based fuzzing as samples are readily available and can be mutated in rapid succession while monitoring the target application for faults. We presented at the Black Hat USA Briefings in 2005[12] and released a series of both mutation- and generation-based tools designed to fuzz file formats including FileFuzz, SPIKEfile, and notSPIKEfile.[13]

In 2005, a company named Mu Security began development of a hardware fuzzing appliance designed to mutate protocol data as it traverses a network.[14] The emergence of this commercial vendor coincides with a present trend indicating heightened interest in fuzz testing. We are beginning to see increasing availability of commercial fuzzing solutions alongside the evolution of freely available fuzzing technologies. Additionally, a large community of developers and security researchers interested in fuzzing now exists, as evident with the creation of the Fuzzing mailing list,[15] maintained by Gadi Evron. Only time will tell what exciting innovations await us.

ActiveX fuzzing became a popular target in 2006 when David Zimmer released COMRaider and H.D. Moore published AxMan.[16] Both tools focused on ActiveX controls that could be instantiated by Web applications when accessed with the Microsoft Internet Explorer Web browser. Remotely exploitable vulnerabilities in such applications represent a high risk due to the large user base. ActiveX controls, as it turns out, are an excellent fuzzing target due to the fact that they include descriptions of the interfaces, function prototypes, and member variables within the actual control, allowing for intelligent automated testing. ActiveX and browser fuzzing on a whole are studied in further detail in Chapter 17, "Web Browser Fuzzing," and Chapter 18, "Web Browser Fuzzing: Automation."

There are many other milestones and markers in the history of fuzzing, but what has been provided thus so far suffices in painting the overall picture. A graphical representation of the brief history of fuzzing is given in Figure 2.1.

---

[12] http://www.blackhat.com/presentations/bh-usa-05/bh-us-05-sutton.pdf

[13] http://labs.idefense.com/software/fuzzing.php

[14] http://www.musecurity.com/products/overview.html

[15] http://www.whitestar.linuxbox.org/mailman/listinfo/fuzzing

[16] http://metasploit.com/users/hdm/tools/axman/

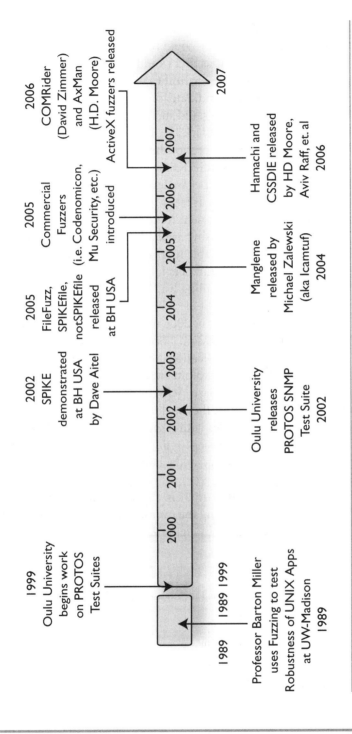

**Figure 2.1**   Fuzzing history

Despite the advances made thus far, fuzzing remains a technology in its infancy. The majority of tools to date are relatively small projects maintained by small groups of individuals or even a single programmer. It has only been in the past couple of years that early-stage startups have entered the commercial space. Although this lends credibility to fuzzing as a field on its own, it is also an indication that fuzzing will see many further innovations and reach new milestones in the coming years as increased funding is made available for research.

In the next section, we cover the various phases involved in conducting a complete fuzzing audit.

## FUZZING PHASES

Depending on various factors, the fuzzing approach chosen can vary greatly. There is no correct approach to fuzzing. It is entirely dependent on the target application, the skills of the researcher, and the format of the data being fuzzed. However, no matter what you are fuzzing or what approach you decide on, the same basic phases always apply.

1. *Identify target.* It isn't possible to select a fuzzing tool or technique until we have a target in mind. If you are fuzzing an internally developed application during a security audit, target selection will be taken care of for you. If, however, you are conducting vulnerability research to uncover vulnerabilities in third-party applications, you'll have some flexibility. When identifying a target, look at a vendor's past history with regard to previously discovered vulnerabilities. Check vulnerability aggregation sites such as SecurityFocus[17] or Secunia.[18] A vendor with a poor track record for past vulnerabilities is more than likely to have poor coding practices that will ultimately lead to the discovery of further vulnerabilities. Beyond selecting an application, it might also be necessary to target a specific file or library within the application. If that's the case, you might want to look for binaries that are shared across multiple applications, as vulnerabilities in such targets will be of higher risk due to the expanded user base.

2. *Identify inputs.* Virtually all exploitable vulnerabilities are caused by applications accepting user input and processing that data without first sanitizing it or applying validation routines. Enumerating input vectors is pivotal to the success of fuzzing.

---

[17] http://www.securityfocus.com/

[18] http://secunia.com/

Failing to locate potential sources of input or the expected input values can severely limit testing. Apply lateral thinking when looking for input vectors. Whereas some input vectors are obvious, others are subtler. In the end, anything sent from the client to the target should be considered an input vector. That includes headers, file-names, environment variables, registry keys, and so on. All should be considered input vectors and are therefore potential fuzz variables.

3. *Generate fuzzed data.* Once input vectors have been identified, fuzz data must be generated. The decision to use predetermined values, mutate existing data, or gener-ate data dynamically will depend on the target and data format. Regardless of the approach selected, automation should be applied to this process.

4. *Execute fuzzed data.* This step goes hand in hand with the previous one and is where fuzzing becomes a verb. Execution could involve the act of sending a data packet to the target, opening a file, or launching a target process. Again, automation is crucial. Without it, we're not really fuzzing.

5. *Monitor for exceptions.* A vital but often overlooked step during fuzzing is the excep-tion or fault monitoring process. Transmitting 10,000 fuzz packets to a target Web server, for example, and ultimately causing that server to crash is a useless endeavor if we are unable to pinpoint the packet responsible for the crash. Monitoring can take many forms and will be dependent on the target application and type of fuzzing being used.

6. *Determine exploitability.* Once a fault is identified, depending on the goals of the audit, it might also be necessary to determine if the uncovered bug can be further exploited. This is typically a manual process that requires specialized security knowl-edge. It might therefore be a step performed by someone other than the person con-ducting the initial fuzzing.

A graphical representation of the fuzzing phases is shown in Figure 2.2.

**Figure 2.2** Fuzzing phases

All of the phases should be addressed regardless of the type of fuzzing that is being conducted, with the possible exception of determining exploitability. The order of the phases and emphasis placed on each can be altered depending on the goals of the researcher. Although powerful, fuzzing is by no means going to uncover 100 percent of the bugs in any given software target. In the next section we outline some bug classes that are likely to fly under the radar.

## FUZZING LIMITATIONS AND EXPECTATIONS

Fuzzing by its nature lends itself to locating certain types of weaknesses in a target. It also has particular limitations in the types of vulnerabilities it will find. In this section we present several classes of vulnerabilities that typically go undiscovered by a fuzzer.

### ACCESS CONTROL FLAWS

Some applications require privilege layers to support multiple accounts or user levels. Consider, for example, an online calendaring system that might be accessed via a Web front end. The application might specify an administrator that controls who is allowed to log on to the system. There might be a special group of users capable of creating calendars. All other users might only have read privileges. The most basic form of access control will ensure that a regular user cannot perform administrative tasks.

A fuzzer might be able to discover a fault in the calendaring software that allows an attacker to take complete control of the system. At a low level, software faults are generic across different targets so the same logic can be applied to detect them across the board. During the testing process the fuzzer might also successfully access admin-only functionality with only the credentials of a regular user. However, it is very unlikely that this access control bypass will be detected. Why? Well, consider the fact that the fuzzer does not have an understanding of the logic of the program. There is no way for the fuzzer to know that the admin area should not be accessible to a regular user. Implementing logic-aware functionality into the fuzzer is plausible but can be extremely complex and most likely cannot be reapplied when testing other targets without significant modification.

## Poor Design Logic

Fuzzers are also not the best tools to use for identifying poor design logic. Consider, for example, the vulnerability discovered in Veritas Backup Exec that allows attackers to remotely access the Windows server registry to create, modify, or delete registry keys.[19] Such access can almost trivially lead to a complete system compromise. The exposure exists thanks to a listening service that implements a remote procedure call (RPC) interface on a Transmission Control Protocol (TCP) endpoint that requires no authentication and yet accepts commands for manipulating the registry. This was not an authentication issue, as by design there was no authentication required. Rather, it was an inappropriate design decision that likely stemmed from a failure to assume that attackers would be willing to invest the time to decipher the Microsoft Interface Description Language (IDL) used to describe the target routine and subsequently build a custom utility to communicate with the server.

Although a fuzzer might uncover poor parsing of data supplied over the RPC connection that results in some form of low-level fault, it is incapable of determining that the exposed functionality is insecure. This concept plays an important role later when we take a look at ActiveX fuzzing in Chapter 18, "Web Browser Fuzzing: Automation," as many controls simply expose methods allowing an attacker, for example, to create and execute files. Special consideration is given to detecting these design bugs.

## Backdoors

For a fuzzer, with limited or no information about the structure of a target application, a backdoor is seen no differently than any other target logic, such as a login screen. Both are simply input vectors receiving authentication credentials. Furthermore, unless the

---

[19] http://labs.idefense.com/intelligence/vulnerabilities/display.php?id=269

fuzzer has been given enough information to recognize successful logins, it will have no way to identify a successful login attempt using a hard-coded password even if it does randomly uncover one. For example, during the fuzzing of the password field a malformed input that resulted in a crash is typically discovered by a fuzzer but a randomly guessed hard-coded password is not.

## MEMORY CORRUPTION

Memory corruption issues often lead to a crash of the target process. This type of issue can then be recognized by the same symptoms as in a denial of service. However, some memory corruption issues are gracefully handled by the target application and will never be recognized by a simple fuzzer. Consider, for example, a format string vulnerability that could go undetected without attaching with a debugger to the target process. A format string vulnerability often boils down to one offending instruction at the machine code level. For example, on an x86 Linux machine, a symptom of a format string attack with a %n in it will often fault on the following instruction:

```
mov     %ecx,(%eax)
```

If the fuzzer is throwing random data to the process with some format triggering characters such as %n here and there, the eax register will in many cases not contain a writable address but instead some garbage word from the stack. In this case, the instruction will raise a segmentation violation signal, SIGSEGV. If the application has a SIGSEGV signal handler, it might simply kill this process and spawn a new one. With some applications, the signal handler might even attempt to allow execution to continue within that process without restarting. With a format string vulnerability, this actually becomes possible (although extremely ill advised) due to the fact that memory *might* not have actually been corrupted before the SIGSEGV signal occurred. So what if our fuzzer does not detect this? The process does not crash and instead gracefully handles the fault through the signal handler, so there is no security issue, right? Well, keep in mind that a successful format string exploit will write to areas of memory and subsequently use those controlled memory locations to silently gain control of the process. A signal handler will not stop a precise exploit, as a precise exploit will not cause any fault at all.

Depending on the extent of your target monitoring, your fuzzer might or might not catch such situations.

## MULTISTAGE VULNERABILITIES

Exploitation is not always as simple as attacking a single weakness. Complex attacks often involve leveraging several vulnerabilities in succession to compromise a machine. Perhaps an initial flaw grants unprivileged access to a machine, and a subsequent flaw allows for privilege escalation. Fuzzing might be useful for identifying the individual flaws but will not generally be valuable for chaining together a series of minor vulnerabilities or otherwise uninteresting events to identify a multivector attack.

## SUMMARY

Although fuzzing has been around for some time, it is still not a widely understood methodology outside of the security research community. For that reason, you will likely find just as many unique definitions for fuzzing as the number of people that you ask. Now that we've defined fuzzing for our purposes, provided a brief history, and set expectations, it's time to dive into the types of fuzzers and methods they use.

# Fuzzing Methods and Fuzzer Types

"*Too many good docs are getting out of the business. Too many OB/GYNs aren't able to practice their love with women all across this country.*"

—George W. Bush, Poplar Bluff, Mo., September 6, 2004

Fuzzing defines an overall approach to vulnerability discovery. However, under the umbrella of fuzzing you will find various individual methods for how to implement the methodology. In this chapter we begin to dissect fuzzing by looking at these unique methods. We also look at different types of fuzzing that employ these methods and are leveraged against specific classes of targets. Part II of the book is dedicated to dissecting each of these fuzzer types in much greater detail.

## FUZZING METHODS

In the previous chapter, we mentioned that all fuzzers fall into one of two categories. *Mutation-based* fuzzers apply mutations on existing data samples to create test cases, and *generation-based* fuzzers create test cases from scratch by modeling the target protocol or file format. In this section we further expand these two into subcategories. There is no agreed-on list of fuzzing categories, but because this is the first book on fuzzing, we choose the following five buckets.

## PREGENERATED TEST CASES

As mentioned in the previous chapter, this is the method taken by the PROTOS framework. Test case development begins with studying a particular specification to understand all supported data structures and the acceptable value ranges for each. Hard-coded packets or files are then generated that test boundary conditions or violate the specification altogether. Those test cases can then be used to test how accurately the specification has been implemented on target systems. Creating test cases can require considerable work up front, but has the advantage of being able to be reused to uniformly test multiple implementations of the same protocol or file format.

A disadvantage to using pregenerated test cases is that fuzz testing in this manner is inherently limited. Because there is no random component, once the list of test cases is exhausted, fuzzing is complete.

## RANDOM

This method is by far the least effective, but it can be used as a quick once over to determine if the target has completely awful code. The random approach simply spews pseudo-random data at the target, hoping for the best, or the worst depending on your point of view. The simplest example of this approach is the always amusing yet sometimes effective:

```
while [ 1 ]; do cat /dev/urandom | nc -vv target port; done
```

This one-line command reads random data from the Linux urandom device and then transmits that data to a target address and port using netcat. The `while` loop ensures that the process continues until the user interrupts it.

Believe it or not, vulnerabilities affecting mission-critical software have been identified in the past using this technique. How embarrassing! The difficult part about truly random fuzzing is reversing what caused the exception in the case of a server crash. It can be a painful process tracking back how 500,000 random bytes caused a server to crash. You will want to capture the traffic you send with a sniffer to help you narrow things down. Also, expect to spend a fair amount of time in a debugger and disassembler. Smashing the stack using this technique can be a pain to debug, especially because the call stack will be corrupted. Figure 3.1 is a screen shot taken from a debugger attached to an enterprise system and network monitoring utility, which has just crashed under a random fuzz attack. Can you determine the cause of the fault? Not likely, unless you are Nostradamus. A lot more research is required to pinpoint the cause of this issue. Note that some data has been obfuscated to protect the guilty.

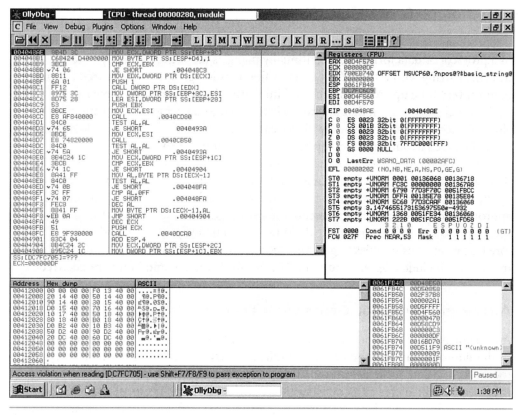

**Figure 3.1** Now what? The dilemma of a /dev/urandom fuzzer

## MANUAL PROTOCOL MUTATION TESTING

Arguably even less sophisticated than the /dev/urandom method is manual protocol testing. In manual protocol testing, there is no automated fuzzer involved. In fact, the researcher is the fuzzer. After loading up the target application, the researcher simply enters inappropriate data in an attempt to crash the server or induce some undesirable behavior. This is truly the poor man's fuzzing method, but it has certainly been used successfully in the past. The benefit to this approach, of course, is that the analyst can leverage past experience and "gut feeling" during the audit. This class of fuzzing is most often applied to Web applications.

## MUTATION OR BRUTE FORCE TESTING

When we say brute force here, we are referring to a fuzzer that starts with a valid sample of a protocol or data format and continually mangles every individual byte, word, dword, or string within that data packet or file. This is a great early approach because it requires very little up-front research and implementing a basic brute force fuzzer is relatively straightforward. All that the fuzzer is required to do is modify data and pass it along. Of course, many bells and whistles can be added for fault detection, logging, and so on, but such a tool can generally be created in a short period of time.

This is a somewhat inefficient approach, as many CPU cycles will be wasted on data that cannot be interpreted in the first place. However, that challenge is offset somewhat by the fact that the process can be fully automated. Code coverage using a brute force approach is dependent on the collection of known good packets or files that are tested. Most protocol specifications or file definitions are relatively complex and it would therefore take numerous samples to get even decent coverage. Examples of brute force file format fuzzers include FileFuzz and notSPIKEfile, for Windows and Linux, respectively.

## AUTOMATIC PROTOCOL GENERATION TESTING

Automatic protocol generation testing is a more advanced method of brute force testing. In this approach, up-front research is required to first understand and interpret the protocol specification or file definition. However, rather than creating hard-coded test cases, the researcher then creates a grammar that describes how the protocol specification works. In doing so, he identifies portions of the packet or file that are to remain static and others that represent fuzzable variables. The fuzzer then dynamically parses these templates, generates fuzz data, and sends the resulting packet or file to the target. The success of this approach is dependent on a researcher's ability to pinpoint those portions of the specification that are most likely to lead to faults in the target application during parsing. Examples of this type of fuzzing are SPIKE and SPIKEfile. Both of these fuzzing tools take SPIKE script descriptions of their target protocol or file format and use a fuzzing engine to create mangled data. The downside of this approach is the time it takes to generate your grammar or definition.

## FUZZER TYPES

We have seen the different methods or approaches to fuzzing, so now let's take a look at some specific fuzzer types. The different types of fuzzers are based on the target. Different targets are different animals and each type lends itself to its own class of fuzzer.

In this section, we take a brief look at some of these different fuzzer types. Throughout the remainder of the book we cover the specific details regarding each of these classes with regard to both background materials and specific automation and development examples.

## Local Fuzzers

In the UNIX world, `setuid` applications allow a normal user to temporarily gain elevated privileges. This makes such applications an obvious target for fuzzing, as any vulnerability in a `setuid` application will allow a user to permanently escalate privileges and execute code of his or her choosing. There are two distinct targets for fuzzing `setuid` applications. The first, command-line argument fuzzing, focuses on passing malformed arguments to the `setuid` application on the command line. The second also passes malformed arguments, but in a different way. The malformed arguments in the second case are passed through the UNIX shell environment. Now let us take a look at command line and environment variable fuzzing.

### Command-Line Fuzzers

When an application begins, it often processes command-line arguments that have been passed to it from the user. The following example, also used in Chapter 1, "Vulnerability Discovery Methodologies," demonstrates the simplest form of a command-line parameter stack overflow:

```
#include <string.h>

int main (int argc, char **argv)
{
    char buffer[10];
    strcpy(buffer, argv[1]);
}
```

If this program was indeed `setuid`, it would be of interest to a local fuzzer. The question is how security researchers find more subtle bugs in `setuid` applications to which the source is not available. You should not be surprised to hear that the simplest answer is fuzzing.

The following are useful tools for command-line fuzzers:

- *clfuzz[1] by warl0ck.* A command-line fuzzer that tests for format string and buffer overflow vulnerabilities in applications.
- *iFUZZ[2] by Adam Greene.* A command-line fuzzer that tests for format string and buffer overflow vulnerabilities in applications. Includes options for fuzzing several different arguments and can also intelligently fuzz applications when given information from their "usage" help message.

### Environment Variable Fuzzers

Another type of local fuzzing involves the environment variable vector, which also targets `setuid` applications. Consider the following application, which unsafely uses values from the user's environment:

```
#include <string.h>

int main (int argc, char **argv)
{
    char buffer[10];
    strcpy(buffer, getenv("HOME"));
}
```

There are several effective ways to fuzz environment variable usage in an application, but not many automated tools exist, despite the simplicity of the process. Many security researchers seem to have their own hacked-together scripts for this task, which could be part of the reason there are not many publicly released tools. For the most part, local environment variable fuzzers are not terribly complex to develop and often do not warrant a public software release. The following are useful tools for environment variable fuzzing:

- *Sharefuzz[3] by Dave Aitel.* The first publicly available environment variable fuzzer. It intercepts calls to the `getenv` function and returns malicious data.
- *iFUZZ[4] by Adam Greene.* Although primarily a command-line fuzzer, the iFUZZ package does also include basic environment variable fuzzing capabilities. iFUZZ uses the same method as Sharefuzz but is a little easier to customize during use.

---

[1]  http://warl0ck.metaeye.org/cb/clfuzz.tar.gz

[2]  http://fuzzing.org

[3]  http://www.immunitysec.com/resources-freesoftware.shtml

[4]  http://fuzzing.org

We discuss local fuzzing and the concept of `setuid` in more detail in Chapter 7, "Environment Variable and Argument Fuzzing," and Chapter 8, "Environment Variable and Argument Fuzzing: Automation."

### File Format Fuzzers

A large number of applications, both client and server in nature, must at some point deal with file input and output. For example, antivirus gateways often need to parse compressed files to diagnose what lies within them. Another example is an office productivity suite that needs to open a document. Both of these types of applications can be susceptible to vulnerabilities that occur when parsing maliciously crafted files.

This is where file format fuzzing comes in. A file format fuzzer will dynamically create different malformed files that are then launched using the target application. Although the specific methods used in file fuzzing are not exactly the same as other types of fuzzing, the general idea is the same. The following are useful tools for file format fuzzing:

- *FileFuzz[5] by Michael Sutton.* A Windows graphical user interface (GUI)-based file format fuzzing tool.
- *notSPIKEfile and SPIKEfile[6] by Adam Greene.* UNIX-based file fuzzing tools, not based on SPIKE and based on SPIKE, respectively.
- *PAIMEIfilefuzz[7] by Cody Pierce.* Similar to FileFuzz, another Windows GUI-based file format fuzzing tool built on top of the PaiMei reverse engineering framework. PaiMei is discussed in more detail later in the book.

File format fuzzing is dissected in more detail in Chapter 11, "File Format Fuzzing," Chapter 12, "File Format Fuzzing: Automation on UNIX," and Chapter 13, "File Format Fuzzing: Automation on Windows."

## REMOTE FUZZERS

Remote fuzzers target software that listens on a network interface. Network-enabled applications are likely the most targeted fuzzing target. With the growth of the Internet, virtually all corporations now have publicly accessible servers to deliver Web pages, e-mail, Domain Name System (DNS) resolution, and so on. A vulnerability in any such

---

[5]  http://fuzzing.org

[6]  http://fuzzing.org

[7]  https://www.openrce.org/downloads/details/208

system could provide an attacker with access to sensitive data or a launch pad for further attacks against trusted servers.

## Network Protocol Fuzzers

Network protocol fuzzers can be broken into two major categories: those that target simple protocols and those designed for complex protocols. We next present some of the common characteristics of each type.

### Simple Protocols

Simple protocols often have simple authentication or no authentication at all. They are often based on ASCII printable text as opposed to binary data. A simple protocol will not contain length or checksum fields. Additionally, there are typically not many states within the application.

An example of a simple protocol is FTP. In FTP, all control channel communications are in plain ASCII text. For authentication, only a plain text username and password are required.

### Complex Protocols

Complex protocols are typically comprised of binary data with the occasional human-readable ASCII string. Authentication might require encryption or some form of obfuscation and there might be several complex states involved.

A good example of a complex protocol is the Microsoft Remote Procedure Call (MSRPC) protocol. MSRPC is a binary protocol that requires several steps to establish a communication channel prior to transmitting data. The protocol requires length description fields and fragmentation. Overall, it is not a fun protocol to implement for fuzzing. The following are useful tools for network protocol fuzzing.

- *SPIKE[8] by Dave Aitel.* SPIKE is the first publicly released fuzzing framework. It includes pregenerated fuzzing scripts for several popular protocols and can also be used as an API.
- *Peach[9] by Michael Eddington.* A cross-platform fuzzing framework written in Python. It is very flexible and can be used to fuzz nearly any network target.

Network protocol fuzzing is discussed in more depth in Chapter 14, "Network Protocol Fuzzing," Chapter 15, "Network Protocol Fuzzing: Automation on UNIX," and Chapter 16, "Network Protocol Fuzzing: Automation on Windows."

---

[8]   http://www.immunitysec.com/resources-freesoftware.shtml

[9]   http://peachfuzz.sourceforge.net/

## Web Application Fuzzers

Web applications have become popular as a convenient way to access back-end services such as e-mail and bill paying. With the advent of Web 2.0 (whatever that really is), traditional desktop applications such as word processing are moving to the Web.[10]

When fuzzing Web applications, the researcher is primarily looking for vulnerabilities unique to Web applications such as SQL injection, Cross Site Scripting (XSS), and so on. This necessitates fuzzers capable of communicating via Hypertext Transfer Protocol (HTTP) and capturing responses for further analysis to identify the existence of vulnerabilities. The following tools are useful for Web application fuzzing:

- *WebScarab[11] by OWASP.* An open source Web application auditing suite with fuzzing capabilities.
- *SPI Fuzzer[12] by SPI Dynamics.* A commercial HTTP and Web application fuzzer included with the WebInspect vulnerability scanner.
- *Codenomicon HTTP Test Tools[13] by Codenomicon.* A commercial HTTP test suite.

Web application fuzzing is further explored in Chapter 9, "Web Application and Server Fuzzing," and Chapter 10, "Web Application and Server Fuzzing: Automation."

## Web Browser Fuzzers

Although Web browser fuzzers are technically just a special type of file format fuzzer, we feel they are deserving of their own class due to the popularity of Web-based applications. Web browser fuzzers often utilize functionality in the HTML to automate the fuzzing process. For example, the mangleme utility by lcamtuf, which was one of the first publicly available tools for browser fuzzing, utilizes the <META REFRESH> tag to continually load test cases in an automated fashion. This unique feature of Web browsers allows for a fully automated client-side fuzzer without any complex wrappers around the application. Such wrapping is a typical requirement for other client-side fuzzers.

Web browser fuzzing is not limited to HTML parsing; there are plenty of suitable targets. For example, the fuzzing tools See-Ess-Ess-Die targets the parsing of Cascading Style Sheets (CSS), and COM Raider focuses on Component Object Model (COM) objects that can be loaded into Microsoft Internet Explorer. Other fuzzable elements

---

[10] http://www.google.com/a/

[11] http://www.owasp.org/index.php/Fuzzing_with_WebScarab

[12] http://www.spidynamics.com/products/webinspect/index.html

[13] http://www.codenomicon.com/products/internet/http/

include graphics and server response headers. The following tools are useful for Web browser fuzzing:

- *mangleme[14] by lcamtuf.* The first public HTML fuzzer. This is a CGI script that repeatedly sends mangled HTML data to a browser.
- *DOM-Hanoi[15] by H.D. Moore and Aviv Raff.* A DHTML fuzzer.
- *Hamachi[16] by H.D. Moore and Aviv Raff.* Another DHTML fuzzer.
- *CSSDIE[17] by H.D. Moore, Aviv Raff, Matt Murphy, and Thierry Zoller.* A CSS fuzzer.
- *COM Raider[18] by David Zimmer.* An easy-to-use, GUI-driven COM object (ActiveX control) fuzzer.

COM and ActiveX object fuzzing is discussed in depth in Chapter 17, "Web Browser Fuzzing," and Chapter 18, "Web Browser Fuzzing: Automation." CSS and graphics file fuzzing are not specifically discussed in the context of Web browser fuzzing, but the same concepts presented in file format fuzzing chapters are applicable.

## IN-MEMORY FUZZERS

Sometimes during testing, certain obstacles hinder quick and effective fuzzing. This is when in-memory fuzzing might be useful. The basic idea is simple, but developing a proper implementation is far from trivial. One implementation approach involves freezing and taking a snapshot of a process and rapidly injecting faulty data into one of its input parsing routines. After each test case, the snapshot taken previously is restored and new data is injected. This is repeated until all of the test cases are exhausted. As with any other fuzzing method, in-memory fuzzing has advantages and disadvantages. Advantages include the following:

- *Speed.* Not only are there no network bandwidth requirements, but also any insignificant code that runs between receiving a packet off the wire and actually parsing the packet can be eliminated, thus resulting in improved testing performance.
- *Shortcuts.* Sometimes a protocol uses custom encryption or compression algorithms, or is full of checksum validation code. Instead of spending time creating a fuzzer that

---

[14] http://freshmeat.net/projects/mangleme/

[15] http://metasploit.com/users/hdm/tools/domhanoi/domhanoi.html

[16] http://metasploit.com/users/hdm/tools/hamachi/hamachi.html

[17] http://metasploit.com/users/hdm/tools/see-ess-ess-die/cssdie.html

[18] http://labs.idefense.com/software/fuzzing.php#more_comraider

can handle all of this, an in-memory fuzzer can take a snapshot at a point after decompression, decryption, or checksum validation, thus eliminating a great deal of effort.

The disadvantages of in-memory fuzzing include the following:

- *False positives.* Because raw data is injected into the process address space, there might be instances where data is injected that could never be introduced through an outside source.
- *Reproduction.* Although causing an exception might indicate an exploitable condition, the researcher will still have the task of re-creating the exception remotely outside of the process. This can be time consuming.
- *Complexity.* As we'll see in Chapter 19, "In-Memory Fuzzing," and Chapter 20, "In-Memory Fuzzing: Automation," this method of fuzzing is extremely complicated to implement.

## FUZZER FRAMEWORKS

Fuzzing frameworks can be used for fuzzing a variety of targets. A fuzzing framework is simply a generic fuzzer or fuzzer library that simplifies data representation for many types of targets. Some of the fuzzers we have already mentioned in this chapter are actually fuzzing frameworks, including SPIKE and Peach.

Typically, a fuzzing framework includes a library to produce fuzz strings, or values that commonly cause problems in parsing routines. Also typical is a set of routines for simplifying network and disk input and output. Fuzzing frameworks should also include some sort of script-like language that can be used when creating a specific fuzzer. Fuzzing frameworks are popular, but they are by no means the absolute answer. There are both pros and cons to using or designing a framework. Advantages include the following:

- *Reusability.* If a truly generic fuzzing framework is created, it can be used over and over when fuzzing different targets.
- *Community involvement.* It is much easier to get a community development effort started for a large project that can be used in multiple ways than it is to get a large group of developers to work on a small project with very narrow scope, as is the case with a protocol-specific fuzzer.

The disadvantages of fuzzing frameworks include the following:

- *Limitations.* Even with a very carefully designed framework, it is very likely that a researcher will come across a target that is just not suitable for the framework. This can be frustrating.

- *Complexity.* It is nice to be able to have a generic fuzzing interface, but it can also be time consuming to simply learn how to drive the framework. This sometimes makes it more time effective to simply reinvent the portions of the wheel that you will need for your particular target, thus ditching the framework.

- *Development time.* It is much more work to design something completely generic and reusable than it is to design a one-time-use application for a specific protocol. This work almost always translates into longer development time.

Some researchers feel strongly that frameworks are the best approach for any serious fuzzer, and others insist this is not the case and that every fuzzer should be created on a one-off basis. It is up to you as the reader to experiment with both approaches and decide for yourself.

## SUMMARY

When performing fuzz testing, you should always consider the value of applying each method discussed in this chapter. Often you will receive the best results combining various approaches, as one method could complement another.

Just as there are many different targets on which a fuzzer can focus, there are many different classes of fuzzers. As you begin to digest the basic concepts behind the various fuzzer classes, begin to imagine how you might implement some of them. This puts you in good shape to critique the implementations presented in detail later in this book.

# Data Representation and Analysis

*"My job is to, like, think beyond the immediate."*

—George W. Bush, Washington, DC, April 21, 2004

Computers use protocols in all aspects of internal and external communication. They form the basis of the structure that is necessary for data transfer and processing to occur. If we are to fuzz successfully, we must first gain an understanding of the protocols that are used by our targets. With this understanding we will then be able to target portions of the protocols most likely to cause anomalous conditions. Moreover, to access a vulnerable portion of a protocol, we might also need to provide legitimate protocol data prior to the commencement of fuzzing. Gaining knowledge of both open and proprietary protocols will inevitably lead to more efficient vulnerability discovery.

## WHAT ARE PROTOCOLS?

Protocols are necessary to facilitate communication. Sometimes protocols are defined standards and at other times they are de facto standards that are generally agreed on. Spoken communication would be an example of a protocol that uses de facto standards. Although there are no formal documented rules for speaking, it is generally understood that when one person speaks to another, the listener is silent and is then provided with the opportunity to respond. Likewise, you cannot simply walk up to another individual and start spewing out your name, address, and other vital information (nor should you in this day and age of identity theft). Instead, individual information is prefaced with *metadata*. For example, "My name is John Smith. I live at 345 Chambers Street." Certain standards and rules understood by both sending and receiving parties must be agreed on to communicate data in a meaningful way. In computing, protocols are critical. Computers are not intelligent. They do not have the luxury of intuition. Therefore, rigidly defined protocols are vital to facilitate communication and data processing.

Wikipedia defines a protocol as "a convention or standard that controls or enables the connection, communication, and data transfer between two computing endpoints."[1] Those endpoints could be two separate computers or two points within a single machine. For example, when reading data from memory, a computer must access memory on the hard drive, move it through the data bus to volatile memory, and then move it to the processor. At each point, data must take a specific form so that both the sending and receiving endpoint are able to handle the data appropriately. At the lowest level, data is nothing more than a collection of bits. It is only when perceived in context that this collection of bits has meaning. If both endpoints are unable to agree on the context, then the transferred data is meaningless.

Intermachine communication is also dependent on protocols. A commonly known example of such communication is the Internet. The Internet is a collection of numerous layered protocols. A household desktop computer sitting in the Unites States can wrap data in successive protocol layers and then transmit that data over the Internet to another desktop computer in China. Understanding the same protocols, the receiving computer can unwrap and interpret the data. In this specific scenario, the Chinese government will likely intercept the transmitted data, unwrapping and interpreting it for itself as well. It is only because the two machines involved each understand the protocols used that such communication is possible. In between the endpoints lie numerous routers that must also understand certain aspects of the protocols used to route the data properly.

Although protocols serve a common purpose, they come in various forms. Some protocols are designed to be human readable and are represented in plain text form. Other protocols are represented in binary, a format not recommended for human consumption. File formats such as those used to represent GIF images or Microsoft Excel spreadsheets are examples of binary protocols.

The individual components that comprise a protocol are generally referred to as fields. The protocol specification defines how these fields are separated and ordered. Let's take a closer look.

## PROTOCOL FIELDS

Many decisions need to be made when designing a protocol, but one of the most critical is how the protocol will be delimited or divided into distinct components. Both sending

---

[1]   http://en.wikipedia.org/wiki/Protocol_%28computing%29

and receiving machines need to be aware of how to interpret individual elements within the data, and this is defined by the protocol. Three typical approaches to addressing this challenge are fixed length fields, variable length fields, or delimited fields. Simple plain text protocols are often delimited by characters such as carriage returns. When the client or server parses a carriage return in the data received, it indicates the end of a specific command. Character-delimited fields are also commonly used in file formats such as comma-separated value (CSV) files, which are used for two-dimensional arrays of data and can be read by spreadsheet programs such as Microsoft Excel. XML is another example of a file type that uses character-delimited fields, but instead of simply using single characters to indicate the end of a field, XML leverages multiple characters to delimit the file. For example, elements are defined with both opening and closing angle brackets (< >), and the name[nd]value components of attributes within elements are separated by an equals sign (=).

Fixed length fields predefine a set number of bytes to be used by each field. This approach is commonly used in the headers of network protocols such as Ethernet, Internet Protocol (IP), Transmission Control Protocol (TCP), and User Datagram Protocol (UDP) as such headers require highly structured data that is required each and every time. For example, an Ethernet packet always begins with six bytes identifying the destination Media Access Control (MAC) address, followed by an additional six bytes defining the source MAC address.

## CHOOSING FIELDS FOR OPTIMIZATION

Another advantage of being able to mandate the size and position of certain fields is that the author of the specification can help to facilitate processor optimization by choosing intelligent byte alignments. For example, many of the fields in the IPv4 header conveniently align on 32-bit boundaries. As described in the Intel Optimization Manual in section 3.41, unaligned reads can be expensive on Pentium processors.

> A misaligned access costs three cycles on the Pentium processor family. On Pentium Pro and Pentium II processors a misaligned access that crosses a cache line boundary costs six to nine cycles. A Data Cache Unit (DCU) split is a memory access which crosses a 32-byte line boundary. Unaligned accesses which cause a DCU split stall Pentium Pro and Pentium II processors. For best performance, make sure that in data structures and arrays greater than 32 bytes that the structure or

array elements are 32-byte aligned, and that access patterns to data structure and array elements do not break the alignment rules.[2]

Conversely, some Reduced Instruction Set Computing (RISC) architectures, such as SPARC, will fail completely when performing unaligned accesses to memory by raising the fatal bus error signal.

When data is less structured, variable length fields might be desirable. This approach is commonly employed with media files. An image or video file format can be rather complex with numerous optional headers and data components. Using variable length fields provides protocol developers with flexibility, while still creating an effective protocol that uses memory efficiently. With a variable length field, rather than setting aside a fixed length of bytes for a particular data element, all of which might not be required, the field is typically prefixed with both an identifier to indicate the type of field and a size value indicating the subsequent number or bytes that comprise the remainder of the field.

## PLAIN TEXT PROTOCOLS

The term *plain text protocol* is used to refer to a protocol in which the data bytes communicated mostly fall into the printable ASCII range. This includes all numbers, capital and lowercase letters, symbols such as percent and dollar signs, as well as carriage returns (\r, hex byte 0x0D), new lines (\n, hex byte 0x0A), tabs (\t, hex byte 0x09), and spaces (hex byte 0x20).

A plain text protocol is simply one that is designed to be human readable. Plain text protocols are generally less efficient than their binary counterparts as they are more memory intensive, but there are many situations in which it is desirable to have a protocol be human readable. The control channel of File Transfer Protocol (FTP) is an example of a plain text protocol. The data transfer channel, on the other hand, is capable of transmitting binary data. FTP is used for uploading and downloading data to a remote machine. The fact that FTP control traffic is human readable allows communication to be handled manually using command-line tools.

```
C:\>nc 192.168.1.2 21
220 Microsoft FTP Service
USER Administrator
```

---

[2]  http://download.intel.com/design/intarch/manuals/24281601.pdf

```
331 Password required for Administrator.
PASS password
230 User Administrator logged in.
PWD
257 "/" is current directory.
QUIT
221
```

In the previous example, we've used the popular Netcat[3] tool to manually connect to a Microsoft FTP Server. Although there are many FTP clients available, using Netcat allows us to fully control the requests sent to the server and illustrate the plain text nature of the protocol. In this example, all bold text shows the requests sent to the server, whereas regular font represents the server responses. We can clearly see that all requests and responses are human readable. This makes it very easy to see exactly what is going on and debug any issues that might arise.

## BINARY PROTOCOLS

Binary protocols are more difficult for humans to decipher, as instead of a stream of readable text you will be looking at a stream of raw bytes. Without an understanding of the protocol, the packets will not be particularly meaningful. For fuzzing, an understanding of the protocol structure is essential if you are to target meaningful locations within the protocol.

To better illustrate how you would gain an appropriate understanding of a binary protocol to produce a fuzzer, we will examine a full-featured protocol that is currently in use by millions of people each day who turn to AOL Instant Messenger (AIM) chatting with friends, while they should be working. Specifically, we'll walk through the data packets sent and received during a logon session.

Before diving into the specifics of the AIM protocol, let's discuss some of the fundamental building blocks used in the development of binary protocols. AIM is an example of a proprietary protocol.[4] Although not officially documented, plenty of details about the structure of the protocol are available thanks to the reverse engineering efforts of others. The AIM protocol is officially known as OSCAR (for Open System for CommunicAtion in Realtime). Reverse engineering efforts have allowed for the creation

---

[3]  http://www.vulnwatch.org/netcat/

[4]  http://en.wikipedia.org/wiki/AOL_Instant_Messenger

of alternate clients such as GAIM[5] and Trillian.[6] Furthermore, some network protocol analyzers such as Wireshark are able to fully decode the packet structure. This is an important point. If you are looking to build a fuzzer that targets a proprietary protocol, never start from scratch by trying to reverse engineer the protocol. Although this might be necessary in some situations, chances are that if you're interested in the details of a protocol or file format, so are others. Start with your good friend Google and see what work others have already done for you. For file formats, try Wotsit.org, an excellent collection of official and unofficial documentation for hundreds of proprietary and open protocols.

Now let's take a look at the AIM authentication or sign on process. The first step in understanding the protocol is to capture some raw bytes and break them down a more meaningful structure. In the case of AIM, we are fortunate as Wireshark already understands the structure of the protocol. We'll skip past some of the initial handshake packets and move to the point where a user signs on. In Figure 4.1, you will see Wireshark output for the initial packet, whereby the AIM client username is sent to the AIM server. We see that the protocol is comprised of two separate layers. At a higher level we have the AOL Instant Messenger header, which identifies the type of traffic being sent. In this case, the header identifies that the packet contains data from the AIM Signon family (0x0017) and Signon subfamily (0x0006).

At a lower layer, we see the actual signon data under the AIM Signon, Sign-on heading. At this point, only the infotype (0x0001), buddyname (fuzzingiscool), and length of the buddyname in bytes (13) is sent. This is an example of variable length field being employed. Notice that the length of the buddyname is included immediately prior to the name itself. As mentioned, it is common for binary protocols to employ data blocks. The blocks begin with a size value, indicating the length of the data and then include the actual data (buddyname). Sometimes the size value includes the bytes used for the size value and at other times, as is the case here, the size describes only the data. Data blocks are an important concept for fuzzing. If you are creating a fuzzer that injects data into the data blocks, you must also take care to adjust the block size accordingly; otherwise the receiving application won't understand the remainder of the packet. Network protocol fuzzers such as SPIKE[7] are designed with this concept in mind.

---

[5]  http://gaim.sourceforge.net/

[6]  http://www.ceruleanstudios.com/

[7]  http://www.immunitysec.com/resources-freesoftware.shtml

```
No.      Time          Source              Destination              Protocol Info
    15 3.225113      192.168.1.2         205.188.153.121          AIM Signon AIM Signon,
Sign-on Username: fuzzingiscool

Frame 15 (95 bytes on wire, 95 bytes captured)
Ethernet II, Src: Intel_a4:83:57 (00:0c:f1:a4:83:57), Dst: ZyxelCom_25:d5:72
(00:13:49:25:d5:72)
Internet Protocol, Src: 192.168.1.2 (192.168.1.2), Dst: 205.188.153.121
(205.188.153.121)
Transmission Control Protocol, Src Port: 4971 (4971), Dst Port: 5190 (5190), Seq: 11,
Ack: 11, Len: 41
AOL Instant Messenger
    Command Start: 0x2a
    Channel ID: SNAC Data (0x02)
    Sequence Number: 2
    Data Field Length: 35
    FNAC: Family: AIM Signon (0x0017), Subtype: Sign-on (0x0006)
AIM Signon, Sign-on
    Infotype: 0x0001
    Buddy: fuzzingiscool
        Buddyname len: 13
        Buddy Name: fuzzingiscool

0000   00 13 49 25 d5 72 00 0c f1 a4 83 57 08 00 45 00    ..I%.r.....W..E.
0010   00 51 87 c7 40 00 80 06 49 ff c0 a8 01 02 cd bc    .Q..@...I.......
0020   99 79 13 6b 14 46 1d 02 03 3b e2 5d 3c 37 50 18    .y.k.F...;.]<7P.
0030   ff f5 50 5c 00 00 2a 02 00 02 00 23 00 17 00 06    ..P\..*....#....
0040   00 00 00 00 00 00 00 01 00 0d 66 75 7a 7a 69 6e    ..........fuzzin
0050   67 69 73 63 6f 6f 6c 00 4b 00 00 00 5a 00 00       giscool.K...Z..
```

**Figure 4.1**   AIM Signon: Username sent

In response to the initial request, as seen in Figure 4.2, the server provides a challenge value (3740020309). The AIM client uses the challenge to generate a password hash. Note that once again, we're dealing with a data block, as the challenge value is preceded by the length of the challenge in bytes.

```
No.      Time          Source              Destination           Protocol Info
    17 3.253298    205.188.153.121     192.168.1.2           AIM Signon AIM Signon,
Sign-on Reply

Frame 17 (82 bytes on wire, 82 bytes captured)
Ethernet II, Src: ZyxelCom_25:d5:72 (00:13:49:25:d5:72), Dst: Intel_a4:83:57
(00:0c:f1:a4:83:57)
Internet Protocol, Src: 205.188.153.121 (205.188.153.121), Dst: 192.168.1.2
(192.168.1.2)
Transmission Control Protocol, Src Port: 5190 (5190), Dst Port: 4971 (4971), Seq: 11,
Ack: 52, Len: 28
AOL Instant Messenger
    Command Start: 0x2a
    Channel ID: SNAC Data (0x02)
    Sequence Number: 3005
    Data Field Length: 22
    FNAC: Family: AIM Signon (0x0017), Subtype: Sign-on Reply (0x0007)
AIM Signon, Sign-on Reply
    Signon challenge length: 10
    Signon challenge: 3740020309

0000   00 0c f1 a4 83 57 00 13 49 25 d5 72 08 00 45 20   .....W..I%.r..E
0010   00 44 aa 99 40 00 61 06 46 1a cd bc 99 79 c0 a8   .D..@.a.F....y..
0020   01 02 14 46 13 6b e2 5d 3c 37 1d 02 03 64 50 18   ...F.k.]<7...dP.
0030   40 00 b2 20 00 00 2a 02 0b bd 00 16 00 17 00 07   @.. ..*.........
0040   00 00 00 00 00 00 00 0a 33 37 34 30 30 32 30 33   ........37400203
0050   30 39                                             09
```

**Figure 4.2**    AIM Signon: Server reply

Once the challenge has been received, as shown in Figure 4.3, the client responds once again with the screen name but this time also includes the hashed value of the password. Included with these logon credentials are a number of details about the client that is performing the logon, presumably to aid the server in identifying the functionality of which the client is capable. These values are submitted as name[nd]value pairs, another common data structure within binary protocols. An example of this would be the *client id string* (name), which is submitted in conjunction with the *value* of AOL Instant Messenger, version 5.5.3591/WIN32. Once again, a length value is also included to detail the size of the value field.

```
No.      Time        Source              Destination          Protocol Info
   18 3.263960    192.168.1.2         205.188.153.121      AIM Signon AIM Signon, Logon

Frame 18 (215 bytes on wire, 215 bytes captured)
Ethernet II, Src: Intel_a4:83:57 (00:0c:f1:a4:83:57), Dst: ZyxelCom_25:d5:72
(00:13:49:25:d5:72)
Internet Protocol, Src: 192.168.1.2 (192.168.1.2), Dst: 205.188.153.121 (205.188.153.121)
Transmission Control Protocol, Src Port: 4971 (4971), Dst Port: 5190 (5190), Seq: 52, Ack: 39,
Len: 161
AOL Instant Messenger
    Command Start: 0x2a
    Channel ID: SNAC Data (0x02)
    Sequence Number: 3
    Data Field Length: 155
    FNAC: Family: AIM Signon (0x0017), Subtype: Logon (0x0002)
        Family: AIM Signon (0x0017)
        Subtype: Logon (0x0002)
        FNAC Flags: 0x0000
            .... .... .... ...0 = Followed By SNAC with related information: Not set
            0... .... .... .... = Contains Version of Family this SNAC is in: Not set
        FNAC ID: 0x00000000
AIM Signon, Logon
    TLV: Screen name
        Value ID: Screen name (0x0001)
        Length: 13
        Value: fuzzingiscool
    TLV: Password Hash (MD5)
        Value ID: Password Hash (MD5) (0x0025)
        Length: 16
        Value
    TLV: Unknown
        Value ID: Unknown (0x004c)
        Length: 0
        Value
    TLV: Client id string (name, version)
        Value ID: Client id string (name, version) (0x0003)
        Length: 45
        Value: AOL Instant Messenger, version 5.5.3591/WIN32
    TLV: Client id number
    TLV: Client major version
    TLV: Client minor version
    TLV: Client lesser version
    TLV: Client build number
    TLV: Client distribution number
    TLV: Client language
    TLV: Client country
    TLV: Use SSI

0000  00 13 49 25 d5 72 00 0c f1 a4 83 57 08 00 45 00   ..I%.r.....W..E.
0010  00 c9 87 c8 40 00 80 06 49 86 c0 a8 01 02 cd bc   ....@...I.......
0020  99 79 13 6b 14 46 1d 02 03 64 e2 5d 3c 53 50 18   .y.k.F...d.]<SP.
0030  ff d9 73 de 00 00 2a 02 00 03 00 9b 00 17 00 02   ..s...*.........
```

**Figure 4.3**  AIM Signon: Logon credentials sent

## NETWORK PROTOCOLS

Both the FTP and AIM protocols detailed previously provide examples of network protocols. The Internet is all about network protocols and there is no shortage of them. We have protocols for data transfer, routing, e-mail, streaming media, instant messaging, and more types of communication than you could ever hope for. As a wise man once said, "The best thing about standards is that there are so many of them to choose from." The standards that are network protocols are no exception.

How are network protocols developed? The answer to the question depends largely on whether the protocol is open or proprietary. Proprietary protocols can be developed by a closed group within a single company to be used by specific products maintained and controlled by that same company. In a way, developers of proprietary protocols have an inherent advantage as they only need to reach a consensus among a small group of developers when agreeing on a standard. On the other hand, Internet protocols are inherently open and therefore require a consensus among many diverse groups. In general, Internet protocols are developed and maintained by the Internet Engineering Task Force (IETF).[8] The IETF has a lengthy process for publishing and obtaining feedback on proposed Internet standards, which begins with the publication of Requests for Comment (RFCs), which are public documents used to detail protocols and solicit peer review. Following appropriate debate and revision, RFCs can then be adopted by the IETF as Internet standards.

## FILE FORMATS

Like network protocols, file formats describe the structure of data and can be open or proprietary standards. To illustrate file formats, consider Microsoft Office documents. Microsoft has historically used proprietary formats for its productivity applications, such as Microsoft Office, Excel, and PowerPoint. A competing, open format known as the OpenDocument format (ODF)[9] was originally created by OpenOffice.org and later adopted by the Organization for the Advancement of Structured Information Standards (OASIS) consortium.[10] OASIS is an industry group backed by major IT vendors that works toward developing and adopting e-business standards.

In response to this move by OASIS, Microsoft first strayed from a proprietary Microsoft Office protocol format in September 2005[11] when it announced that future versions of Microsoft Office would use the new Microsoft Office Open XML format. This format is an open but competing format to ODF. Microsoft later announced the Open XML Translator project,[12] which promised tools that would handle translations between the competing XML formats.

---

[8]  http://www.ietf.org/

[9]  http://en.wikipedia.org/wiki/OpenDocument

[10]  http://www.oasis-open.org

[11]  http://www.microsoft.com/office/preview/itpro/fileoverview.mspx

[12]  http://sev.prnewswire.com/computer-electronics/20060705/SFTH05506072006-1.html

Let's compare an open plain text file format and a proprietary binary file format by comparing the same content created in both OpenOffice Writer and Microsoft Word 2003. In both cases, we'll start with a blank document, add the word *fuzzing* using the default font, and save the file. By default, OpenOffice Writer saves the file as an OpenDocument Text (*.odt) file. Opening this file in a hex editor, it appears to be a binary file. However, if we change the extension to *.zip and open it using a suitable unzip utility, we see that it is simply an archive of XML files, directories, images, and other text files as seen in the following directory listing:

```
Directory of C:\Temp\fuzzing.odt

07/18/2006  12:07 AM    <DIR>          .
07/18/2006  12:07 AM    <DIR>          ..
07/18/2006  12:07 AM    <DIR>          Configurations2
07/18/2006  04:05 AM         2,633 content.xml
07/18/2006  12:07 AM    <DIR>          META-INF
07/18/2006  04:05 AM         1,149 meta.xml
07/18/2006  04:05 AM            39 mimetype
07/18/2006  04:05 AM         7,371 settings.xml
07/18/2006  04:05 AM         8,299 styles.xml
07/18/2006  12:07 AM    <DIR>          Thumbnails
              5 File(s)        19,491 bytes
              5 Dir(s)   31,203,430,400 bytes free
```

These files all describe different portions of the content or formatting of the file. Because they are XML files, they are all human readable using any basic text editor. Looking at the Content.xml file as shown next, following a series of elements detailing namespaces and formatting details, we can clearly see in bold text toward the end of the file, the original content (*fuzzing*).

```
<?xml version="1.0" encoding="UTF-8"?>
  <office:document-content
    xmlns:office="urn:oasis:names:tc:opendocument:xmlns:office:1.0"
    xmlns:style="urn:oasis:names:tc:opendocument:xmlns:style:1.0"
    xmlns:text="urn:oasis:names:tc:opendocument:xmlns:text:1.0"
    xmlns:table="urn:oasis:names:tc:opendocument:xmlns:table:1.0"
    xmlns:draw="urn:oasis:names:tc:opendocument:xmlns:drawing:1.0"
    xmlns:fo="urn:oasis:names:tc:opendocument:xmlns:xsl-fo-compatible:1.0"
    xmlns:xlink="http://www.w3.org/1999/xlink"
    xmlns:dc="http://purl.org/dc/elements/1.1/"
    xmlns:meta="urn:oasis:names:tc:opendocument:xmlns:meta:1.0"
      xmlns:number="urn:oasis:names:tc:opendocument:xmlns:datastyle:1.0"
```

```
xmlns:svg="urn:oasis:names:tc:opendocument:xmlns:svg-compatible:1.0"
xmlns:chart="urn:oasis:names:tc:opendocument:xmlns:chart:1.0"
xmlns:dr3d="urn:oasis:names:tc:opendocument:xmlns:dr3d:1.0"
xmlns:math="http://www.w3.org/1998/Math/MathML"
xmlns:form="urn:oasis:names:tc:opendocument:xmlns:form:1.0"
xmlns:script="urn:oasis:names:tc:opendocument:xmlns:script:1.0"
xmlns:ooo="http://openoffice.org/2004/office"
xmlns:ooow="http://openoffice.org/2004/writer"
xmlns:oooc="http://openoffice.org/2004/calc"
xmlns:dom="http://www.w3.org/2001/xml-events"
xmlns:xforms="http://www.w3.org/2002/xforms"
xmlns:xsd="http://www.w3.org/2001/XMLSchema"
xmlns:xsi="http://www.w3.org/2001/XMLSchema-instance"
office:version="1.0">
<office:scripts/>
<office:font-face-decls>
  <style:font-face style:name="Tahoma1" svg:font-family="Tahoma"/>
  <style:font-face style:name="Times New Roman"
    svg:font-family="&apos;Times New Roman&apos;"
    style:font-family-generic="roman"
    style:font-pitch="variable"/>
  <style:font-face style:name="Arial"
    svg:font-family="Arial"
    style:font-family-generic="swiss"
    style:font-pitch="variable"/>
  <style:font-face style:name="Lucida Sans Unicode"
    svg:font-family="&apos;Lucida Sans Unicode&apos;"
    style:font-family-generic="system"
    style:font-pitch="variable"/>
  <style:font-face style:name="Tahoma"
    svg:font-family="Tahoma"
    style:font-family-generic="system"
    style:font-pitch="variable"/>
</office:font-face-decls>
<office:automatic-styles/>
<office:body>
  <office:text>
    <office:forms form:automatic-focus="false"
form:apply-design-mode="false"/>
    <text:sequence-decls>
      <text:sequence-decl text:display-outline-level="0"
text:name="Illustration"/>
      <text:sequence-decl text:display-outline-level="0"
text:name="Table"/>
      <text:sequence-decl text:display-outline-level="0"
text:name="Text"/>
```

```
        <text:sequence-decl text:display-outline-level="0"
text:name="Drawing"/>
        </text:sequence-decls>
      <text:p text:style-name="Standard">fuzzing</text:p>
    </office:text>
  </office:body>
</office:document-content>
```

Creating a file with the same content using Microsoft Word 2003, we end up with a single binary Word document (*.doc) file. Despite being a binary file, it is actually larger (20KB vs. 7KB) than the OpenDocument text file created previously. Opening the file in a hex editor, you will notice various human-readable strings, mixed in with bytes that appear to be gibberish. The selected snippets displayed next show the original content, the authors listed in the document properties, and other strings identifying the application used to create the content.

```
00000a00h: 66 75 7A 7A 69 6E 67 0D 00 00 00 00 00 00 00 00 ; fuzzing........
...
000024d0h: 66 75 7A 7A 69 6E 67 00 1E 00 00 00 04 00 00 00 ; fuzzing........
000024e0h: 00 00 00 00 1E 00 00 00 1C 00 00 00 4D 69 63 68 ; ...........Mich
000024f0h: 61 65 6C 2C 20 41 64 61 6D 20 61 6E 64 20 50 65 ; ael, Adam and Pe
00002500h: 64 72 61 6D 00 00 00 00 1E 00 00 00 04 00 00 00 ; dram...........
...
00002560h: 4D 69 63 72 6F 73 6F 66 74 20 4F 66 66 69 63 65 ; Microsoft Office
00002570h: 20 57 6F 72 64 00 00 00 40 00 00 00 00 00 00 00 ;  Word...@.......
```

## COMMON PROTOCOL ELEMENTS

Why is this background necessary for fuzzing? Depending on the structure of the file format or network protocol, you will have to adjust your fuzzing approach. The more you know about the data structure, the better you'll be able to focus your fuzzing on segments most likely to lead to anomalous conditions. Let's take a look at some of the common elements found within protocols.

### NAME–VALUE PAIRS

Whether dealing with binary or plain text protocols, data is often presented in name–value pairs (e.g., size=12) but this is especially true for plain text protocols. Look at the Content.xml file shown previously and you will see name–value pairs throughout the XML file. As a general rule of thumb, when dealing with name–value pairs, you are most likely to identify potential vulnerabilities by fuzzing the value portion of the pairing.

## BLOCK IDENTIFIERS

Block identifiers are values that identify the type of data being represented in binary data. They might be followed by variable or fixed length data. In the AIM example discussed previously, the AIM Signon header contained the infotype (0x0001) block header. This value defined the type of data that followed, in this case the AOL buddyname. Fuzzing can be used to identify other perhaps undocumented block identifiers that might accept additional data types that can also be fuzzed.

## BLOCK SIZES

Block sizes were described previously and generally consist of data such as name–value pairs that are preceded by one or more bytes detailing the type of field and the size of the variable length data that follows. When fuzzing, try altering the size so that it is larger or smaller than the data that follows and monitor the results. This is a common source of buffer over- and underflows. Alternately, when fuzzing data within the block, be sure that the size is adjusted accordingly to ensure that the application is able to properly identify the data.

## CHECKSUMS

Some file formats embed checksums throughout the file to help applications to identify data that might have become corrupt for some reason or another. This is not necessarily implemented as a security measure; as files can become corrupt for various reasons but it can impact fuzzing results as applications will generally abort file processing in the event of an incorrect checksum. The PNG image format is an example of a file type that takes advantage of checksums. When encountering checksums, it is vital that your fuzzer take the checksums into account and recalculate and overwrite the appropriate checksums to ensure that the target application can properly process the file.

## SUMMARY

Although files and network traffic can be fuzzed in a brute force fashion, it is much more efficient to only target those portions of the data that are most likely to lead to potentially vulnerable situations. Although such knowledge requires some up-front effort, it is generally worthwhile to put forth such effort, especially given the abundance of documentation that exists for both open and proprietary protocols. Experience will assist in identifying the best target locations within a protocol but hopefully the areas detailed in this chapter will aid in highlighting some of the more common weak spots that have led to vulnerabilities in the past. In Chapter 22, "Automated Protocol Dissection," we examine some automated techniques for dissecting protocol structure.

# Requirements for Effective Fuzzing

*"You teach a child to read, and he or her will be able to pass a literacy test."*

—George W. Bush, Townsend, TN, February 21, 2001

In previous chapters, we introduced various fuzzer classes and different approaches to fuzzing. In this chapter we discuss a variety of tips and techniques that can contribute to more effective and efficient fuzzing. Obvious factors such as planning for test reproducibility and fuzzer reusability should be considered prior to commencing with the development of a fuzzer. This will help ensure that future work can be built on top of, as opposed to in place of, current efforts. Further characteristics that increase fuzzer complexity such as process state and depth, tracking and metrics, error detection, and constraints are also discussed in this chapter. Later, in Part II of this book, we discuss a number of fuzzer targets as well as the construction of automated tools that can be used against each target. As you progress through these chapters, keep in mind the concepts explored in this chapter as they will play a role whenever we architect a new fuzzer and even more so during the construction of a fuzzing framework as discussed in Chapter 12, "File Format Fuzzing: Automation on UNIX." Even among the various commercial fuzzers sold today, none satisfy all of the requirements we're about to cover.

## REPRODUCIBILITY AND DOCUMENTATION

An obvious requirement for a fuzzing tool is the capability to reproduce the results from both individual tests and test sequences. This is crucial for communicating test results to other persons or groups. As a fuzz tester, you should be able to provide your fuzzing tool with a list of malicious test case numbers knowing that the observed target's behavior will be exactly the same between test runs. Consider the following fictitious situation: You are fuzzing a Web server's capability to handle malformed POST data and discover a potentially exploitable memory corruption condition when the 50th test case you sent that crashes the service. You restart the Web daemon and retransmit your last malicious payload, but nothing happens. Was the issue a fluke? Of course not: Computers are deterministic and have no notion of randomness. The issue must rely on some combination of inputs. Perhaps an earlier packet put the Web server in a state that later allowed the 50th test to trigger the memory corruption. We can't tell without further analysis and we can't narrow the possibilities down without the capability of replaying the entire test set in a methodical fashion.

Documentation of the various testing results is also a useful, if not mandatory, requirement during the information sharing phase. Given the rising trend of internationally outsourced development,[1] it is frequently not possible for the security tester to walk down the hall and sit with the affected product developer. Outsourcing has become so popular even computer science students have been known to take advantage of it.[2] Various barriers of communication including time zone, language, and communication medium make it ever more important to bundle as much information as possible in a clear and concise form. The burden of organized documentation should not be an entirely manual effort. A good fuzzing tool will produce and store easily parsed and referenced log information.

Think about how the individual fuzzers we discuss handle reproducibility, logging, and automated documentation. Think about how you could improve on the implementation.

## REUSABILITY

On a large scale, if we are building a file format fuzzing tool, we don't want to have to rewrite the entire tool every time we want to test a new file format. We can create some

---

[1]   http://www.outsourceworld.org/, http://money.cnn.com/2003/09/17/news/economy/outsourceworld/

[2]   "Computer Science Students Outsource Homework," http://developers.slashdot.org/developers/06/01/19/0026203.shtml

reusable features that will save us time in the future if we decide to test a different format. Sticking with our example, let's say we were motivated to construct a JPEG file format fuzzing tool to test for bugs in Microsoft Paint. Thinking ahead and knowing that we will want to reuse portions of our labor, we may decide to separate the tool set into three components as shown in Figure 5.1.

A JPEG file generator is responsible for generating an endless series of mutated JPEG files. A launching front end is responsible for looping over the generated images, each time spawning Microsoft Paint with the appropriate arguments to load the next image. Finally, an error detection engine is responsible for monitoring each instance of Microsoft Paint for exceptional conditions. The separation into three components allows us to adapt our test set to other file formats with changes only to the generator.

On a smaller scale, numerous building blocks should be portable between our fuzz testing projects. Consider, for example, an e-mail address. This basic string format is seen everywhere, including Simple Mail Transfer Protocol (SMTP) transactions, login screens, and the Voice over IP (VoIP) Session Initiation Protocol (SIP):

```
Excerpt of an SIP INVITE Transaction

49 4e 56 49 54 45 20 73 69 70 3a 72 6f 6f 74 40   INVITE sip:root@
6f 70 65 6e 72 63 65 2e 6f 72 67 20 53 49 50 2f   openrce.org SIP/
32 2e 30 0d 0a 56 69 61 3a 20 53 49 50 2f 32 2e   2.0..Via: SIP/2.
30 2f 55 44 50 20 70 61 6d 69 6e 69 4c 2e 75 6e   0/UDP voip.openr
```

In each case, it is an interesting field to fuzz because we are certain the field will be parsed and potentially separated into various components (e.g., user and domain). If

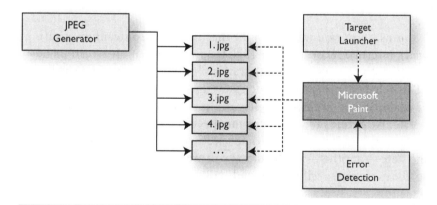

**Figure 5.1** Fictitious file format fuzzer breakdown and overview

we're going to spend the time to enumerate the possible malicious representations of an e-mail address, wouldn't it be nice if we can reuse it across all of our fuzzers?

Think about how you might abstract or modularize the individual fuzzers that we discuss to increase reusability.

## PROCESS STATE AND PROCESS DEPTH

For a solid grasp on the concepts of process state and process depth, let's pick an example most people are all too familiar with: ATM banking. Consider the simple state diagram shown in Figure 5.2.

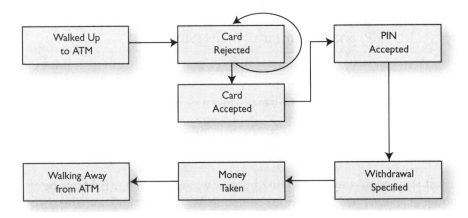

**Figure 5.2**   Contrived ATM state diagram example

In a typical ATM transaction, you walk up to the machine (ever so stealthily ensuring you weren't followed), insert your card, enter a PIN, follow a series of on-screen menus to select the amount of money you wish to withdraw, collect your money, and conclude your transaction. This same concept of state and state transitions applies to software; we'll give a specific example in a minute. Each step of the ATM transaction process can be referred to as a state. We define *process state* as the specific state a target process is in at any given time. Actions, such as inserting a card or selecting a withdrawal amount, transition you from one state to another. How far along you are in the process is referred to as *process depth*. So, for example, specifying a withdrawal amount happens at a greater depth than entering a PIN.

As a more security-relevant example consider a secure shell (SSH) server. Prior to connecting to the server it is in the *initial* state. During the authentication process, the server is in the *authentication* state. Once the server has successfully authenticated a user it is in the *authenticated* state.

Process depth is a specific measure of the number of "forward" steps required to reach a specific state. Following our SSH server example, consider the state diagram depicted in Figure 5.3.

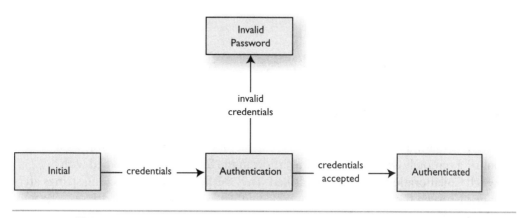

**Figure 5.3**   SSH server state diagram

The authenticated state is "deeper" in the process than the authentication state because the authentication state is a required substep of the authenticated state. The notion of process state and process depth is an important concept that can create significant complication in fuzzer design. The following example demonstrates such a complication. To fuzz the e-mail address argument of the MAIL FROM verb in an SMTP server, we have to connect to the server and issue either a HELO or EHLO command. As shown in Figure 5.4, the underlying SMTP implementation may handle the processing of the MAIL FROM command with the same function regardless of what initiation command was used.

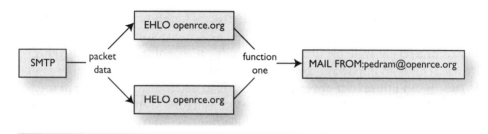

**Figure 5.4**   SMTP example state diagram 1

In Figure 5.4, function one is the only function defined to handle MAIL FROM data. Alternatively, as shown in Figure 5.5, the SMTP implementation might have two separate routines for handling MAIL FROM data depending on the chosen initiation command.

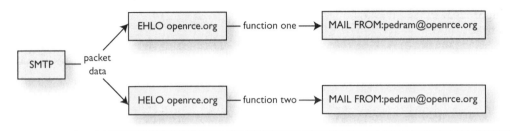

**Figure 5.5**   SMTP example state diagram 2

This is actually a real-world example. On September 7, 2006, a security advisory[3] detailing a remotely exploitable stack overflow in the SMTP server bundled with Ipswitch Collaboration Suite was published. The overflow occurs when long strings are supplied between the characters @ and : during the parsing of e-mail addresses. The vulnerable parsing routine is only reachable, however, when the connecting client begins the conversation with EHLO. When building fuzzers, be mindful of potential logic splits like this. To get complete coverage, our fuzzer will have to run through all of its e-mail address mutations twice, once through EHLO and once through HELO. What happens if there is another logic split further down the process depth path? The number of necessary iterations for complete coverage starts to increase exponentially.

Think about how you might handle variances in process depth and where logic splits might be found as we discuss various fuzzers in upcoming chapters.

## TRACKING, CODE COVERAGE, AND METRICS

*Code coverage* is a term referring to the amount of process state a fuzzer induces a target's process to reach and execute. At the time of writing, we are currently unaware of any publicly or commercially available fuzzing technology capable of tracking and logging code coverage. This is an important concept for analysts across the board. Quality assurance (QA) teams can utilize code coverage as a metric to determine confidence in the level of testing that has taken place. If you are the QA lead for a Web server product, for example, you would probably feel more comfortable shipping your product with zero

---

[3]   http://www.zerodayinitiative.com/advisories/ZDI-06-028.html

failures across 90 percent code coverage than you would with zero failures across only 25 percent code coverage. Vulnerability researchers can benefit from code coverage analysis by identifying the modifications necessary to expand their code coverage into more obscure states of their target where other eyes may not have already been. This important concept is covered in detail in Chapter 23, "Fuzzer Tracking."

Think about creative approaches to determining code coverage and the benefits that such an analysis might provide as we discuss various fuzzers in upcoming chapters. When fuzzing, people always ask, "How do I start?" Remember that it's equally important to ask, "When do I stop?"

## ERROR DETECTION

Generating and transmitting potentially malicious traffic encompasses only half of the fuzzing battle. The other half of the battle is accurately determining when an error has occurred. At the time of writing, the majority of available fuzzers are "blind" in that they have no concept of how the target reacts to transmitted tests. Some commercial solutions interweave "ping" or keepalive checks between malicious attempts as a control to determine whether or not the target is still functional. The term *ping* here is loosely used to refer to any form of transaction that should generate a known good response. Other solutions exist that build on log output analysis. This could involve monitoring ASCII text logs maintained by individual applications or querying entries in system logs such as the Windows Event Viewer as shown in Figure 5.6.

The benefit of these approaches to error detection is that they are, for the most part, easily ported between platforms and architectures. However, these approaches are severely limited with regard to the kinds of errors they are capable of detecting. Neither of these approaches, for example, can detect the case where a critical error occurs in a Microsoft Windows application but is gracefully handled by a Structured Exception Handling[4] (SEH) routine.

The next generation in error detection is the use of lightweight debug clients to detect when an exceptional condition has occurred in a target. For example, the FileFuzz tool that we discuss in Part II includes a custom, open source Microsoft Windows debug client. The one negative aspect of utilizing these types of tools is that you have to develop one for each target platform on which you are testing. For example, if you want to test three SMTP servers on Mac OS X, Microsoft Windows, and Gentoo Linux, you will likely

---

[4]  http://msdn2.microsoft.com/en-us/library/ms680657.aspx

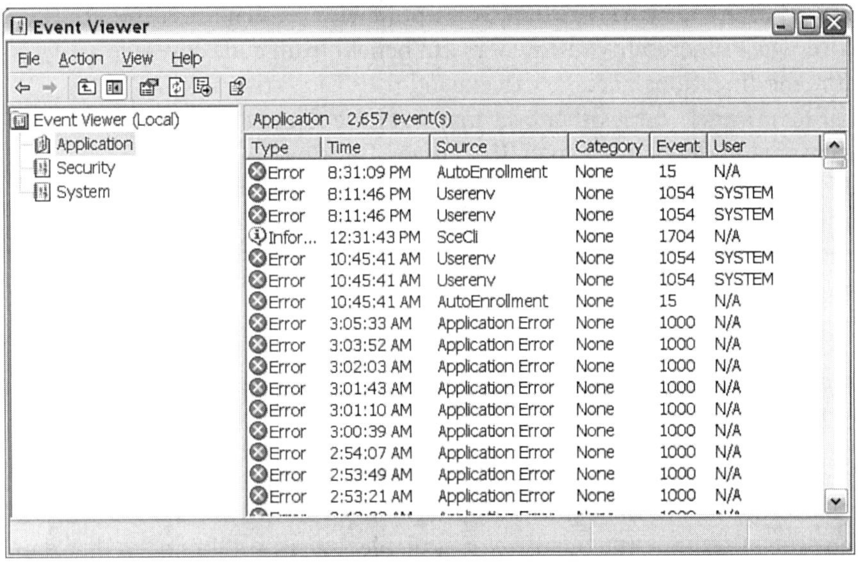

**Figure 5.6**   Example Error log from the Microsoft Windows Event Viewer

have to develop two or possibly three different monitoring clients. Furthermore, depending on your target, it might not be possible or timely to construct a debugging client. If you are testing a hardware VoIP phone, for example, you might have to fall back to control testing or log monitoring, as hardware solutions are less conducive to debugging and might require special tools.

Looking even further ahead, the panacea of error detection lies in dynamic binary instrumentation/translation[5] (DBI) platforms such as Valgrind[6] and Dynamo Rio.[7] On such platforms, it becomes possible to detect errors as they develop rather than after they trigger. At a 50,000-foot view, DBI-based debugging engines are able to very specifically analyze and instrument a target software application at a low level. Such control allows for the creation of memory leak checks, buffer overflow and underrun checks, and so on. Referring to the memory corruption example we used when discussing reproducibility, a lightweight debug client is capable of informing us when the memory corruption triggers. If you recall our example, we posed a scenario whereby a number of packets were

---

[5]   http://en.wikipedia.org/wiki/Binary_translation

[6]   Valgrind: http://valgrind.org/

[7]   Dynamo RIO: http://www.cag.lcs.mit.edu/dynamorio

sent to the target service, which crashed on receiving the 50th test case. On a platform such as Valgrind, we might be able to detect the initial memory corruption that occurred at some earlier test prior to triggering the exception. This approach can save hours and perhaps days of fuzz tuning and bug tracking.

Think about the various target monitoring approaches and which might be most applicable as we discuss various fuzzers in upcoming chapters.

## Resource Constraints

Various nontechnical factors such as budget and deadlines can impose limitations on fuzz testing. These factors must be kept in mind during the design and planning stage. You could, for example, find yourself in a last-minute, prelaunch panic because no one has even briefly examined the security of your $50-million product investment. Security is all too often an afterthought in the software development lifecycle (SDLC), taking a backseat to adding new features and meeting production deadlines. Security must be "baked in" as opposed to being "brushed on" if we ever hope to produce secure software. That involves making fundamental changes to the SDLC to ensure that security is considered at every stage of development. That said, we recognize that software is developed in the real world and not utopia where resources are plentiful and defects are scarce. As you progress through this book it is therefore equally important to mentally classify various techniques that can be applied when time and finances are limited as well as dreaming up the "ultimate" fuzzing suite. Consider also where you would implement such tools in the SDLC and who would be responsible for owning the processes.

## Summary

The main purpose of this chapter was to introduce ideas that will provoke creative thought with regard to developing a fully featured fuzzer. Revisiting the concepts outlined in this chapter can prove prudent during the development, comparison, and usage of fuzzing technologies. As various fuzzing solutions are introduced and dissected in future chapters, consider improvements that can be realized with the application of beneficial requirements such as metrics and improved error detection.

# PART II

# TARGETS AND AUTOMATION

# Automation and Data Generation

*"Our enemies are innovative and resourceful, and so are we. They never stop thinking about new ways to harm our country and our people, and neither do we."*

—George W. Bush, Washington, DC, August 5, 2004

Fuzzing is all about *automation*. The key benefit of fuzzing over alternative software testing methodologies is the high ratio of automation to manual labor. Generating individual test cases is laborious and tedious work, a category of tasks ideally suited for a computer. The core competency of a fuzzer is its ability to generate useful data, preferably with minimal human interaction. This chapter focuses on various aspects of automation including language choice, helpful building blocks, and the ever so important art of choosing appropriate fuzz values during data generation to thoroughly test target software.

## VALUE OF AUTOMATION

Although the benefits of automation might seem obvious, for clarity, we review it here from two perspectives. First, we emphasize the value in terms of human computation power and then we look at reproducibility. In the days of early computers, computation time was expensive, more expensive, in fact, than human computation time; therefore, programming on these systems was a very tedious manual process. Programmers fed tape, toggled switches, and manually entered the decimal or binary machine opcodes. As time went on, programmer talent increased in value, computation time increased in abundance, and the balance of the expense shifted. Today, this trend continues as is evident in the increasing popularity of higher level programming languages such as Java, .NET, and Python. Each of these languages sacrifices computation time to provide programmers with an easier development environment and faster development turn-around times.

On this note, although it is very feasible for a human analyst to interactively connect to a socket-based daemon and manually enter data in hopes of uncovering software flaws, a person's time is better spent on other tasks. This same argument can be compelling when comparing fuzzing to manual auditing tasks such as source code review or binary auditing. The latter methods require the time of highly skilled analysts, whereas the former, fuzzing, can more or less be conducted by anyone. In the least, automation should be used as a first step to reduce the amount of work left for highly skilled analysts capable of pinpointing discovered faults as well as focusing on alternative methodologies.

Next, we emphasize the need for reproducibility. There are two key factors that drive the importance of reproducibility:

- If we can create a reproducible testing process for one FTP server then we can easily test other versions, as well as entirely different FTP servers using the same process. Otherwise, time would be needlessly spent redesigning and reimplementing a new fuzzer for each FTP server.

- In the event that a nontrivial sequence of events triggered a fault in our target, we must be able to reproduce the entire sequence to narrow down the specific subsequence responsible for the anomaly. A human analyst firing off various test cases as he remembers them is far from scientifically reproducible.

In short, the Sisyphean task of data generation, regeneration, and fault monitoring is one best left to an automated system. Like most computing tasks, when it comes to fuzzing, we are fortunate that a number of tools and libraries already exist that we can leverage.

## HELPFUL TOOLS AND LIBRARIES

Most fuzzer developers will find themselves creating tools from scratch as is evident in the abundance of fuzzer scripts already available for public consumption.[1] Fortunately,

---

[1]   http://www.threatmind.net/secwiki/FuzzingTools

many tools and libraries can help you during the design and implementation phase of your fuzzer. This section lists a few of these tools and libraries (in alphabetical order).

## ETHEREAL[2]/WIRESHARK[3]

Wireshark (a project branch off of Ethereal)[4] is a popular open source network sniffer and protocol dissector. Although not necessarily a library you can build on, this tool will no doubt come in handy during both the research and debugging phase of fuzzer construction. Wireshark exposes a plethora of open source dissectors that also frequently come in handy as a reference. Captured traffic identified as having an available dissector is displayed as a series of field and value pairs as opposed to a block of raw bytes. Before diving into manual protocol analysis, it is always prudent to see what Wireshark has to say about it first. For a quick list of available dissectors, refer to the Wireshark subversion repository, specifically the epan\dissectors[5] directory.

## LIBDASM[6] AND LIBDISASM[7]

Both libdasm and libdisasm are freely available and open source disassembler libraries that you can embed into your tools for producing AT&T and Intel syntax disassembly from binary streams. libdasm is written in C and libdisasm is written in Perl. A Python interface is included with libdasm. Although a disassembler is not necessary for generating network traffic, it is important when automating the fault detection end of the equation. Both of these libraries are used throughout the book, specifically in Chapter 12, "File Format Fuzzing: Automation on UNIX," Chapter 19, "In-Memory Fuzzing," Chapter 20, "In-Memory Fuzzing: Automation," Chapter 23, "Fuzzer Tracking," and Chapter 24, "Intelligent Fault Detection."

---

[2] http://www.ethereal.com

[3] http://www.wireshark.org

[4] http://www.wireshark.org/faq.html#q1.2

[5] http://anonsvn.wireshark.org/wireshark/trunk/epan/dissectors/

[6] http://www.nologin.org/main.pl?action=codeView&codeId=49

[7] http://bastard.sourceforge.net/libdisasm.html

## Libnet[8]/LibnetNT[9]

Libnet is a freely available, open source, high-level API for the construction and injection of low-level network packet data. The library hides much of the complexity normally involved when generating IP and link layer traffic, all the while providing for portability across various platforms. If you are writing a network stack fuzzer, you might be interested in this library.

## LibPCAP[10]

LibPCAP and the Microsoft Windows-compatible WinPCAP[11] are freely available, open source, high-level libraries that allow for the easy construction of network capture and analysis tools across both UNIX and Microsoft Windows platforms. Many network protocol analysis tools such as the aforementioned Wireshark are built against this library.

## Metro Packet Library[12]

The Metro Packet Library is a C# library that provides an abstracted interface to working with IPv4, TCP, UDP and Internet Control Message Protocol (ICMP). The library is useful for constructing packet sniffers and network analysis tools. This library is further discussed and utilized in Chapter 16, "Network Protocol Fuzzing: Automation on Windows."

## PTrace

Debugging on UNIX platforms is accomplished for the most part with the help of the `ptrace()` (process trace) system call. A process can utilize `ptrace()` to control the register state, memory, and execution, and capture the generated signals of another process. This mechanism is used to implement the tools discussed in Chapter 8, "Environment Variable and Argument Fuzzing: Automation," and Chapter 12, "File Format Fuzzing: Automation on UNIX."

---

[8]   http://www.packetfactory.net/libnet

[9]   http://www.securityfocus.com/tools/1559

[10]   http://www.tcpdump.org

[11]   http://www.tcpdump.org/wpcap.html

[12]   http://sourceforge.net/projects/dotmetro

## PYTHON EXTENSIONS

Various Python extensions can come in handy when building fuzzers. Example extensions include Pcapy, Scapy, and PyDbg. Pcapy[13] is a Python extension that interfaces to LibPCAP / WinPCAP, enabling Python scripts to capture network traffic. Scapy[14] is a powerful and simple packet manipulation extension that can be used either interactively or as a library. Scapy is capable of both constructing and decoding a wide variety of protocols. PyDbg[15] is a pure Python Microsoft Windows 32-bit debugger that allows for easy and elegant process instrumentation. The PyDbg library is a subset of the larger PaiMei[16] reverse engineering framework, a framework that is used later in the book including in Chapters 19, 20, 23, and 24.

Some of the libraries listed here are available for use in multiple languages. Others are more limited. Your specific needs and the available libraries that can assist in accomplishing those needs are among the factors involved when deciding which language to develop your fuzzer in.

## PROGRAMMING LANGUAGE CHOICE

Many consider the choice of fuzzer programming language a religious debate and vehemently stand by their choice  no matter what the task, while others follow the philosophy of "the right tool for the right job." We tend to preach the latter.  Throughout the book, you will find source code written in a variety of languages. A conscious effort was made during the authoring of this book to include as many reusable real-world code examples as possible. No matter what your personal preference, we encourage you to consider the pros and cons of any given language choice prior to selecting it for a particular task.

At the highest level, there is one fundamental distinction in programming languages you will find yourself considering at the very start of development: interpreted versus compiled. Low-level, compiled languages such as C and C++ provide accurate and raw access to underlying components. The Libnet library previously mentioned, for example, is interfaced at this lower level. Higher level, interpreted languages such as Python and Ruby provide faster development times and the ability to make modifications without

---

[13] http://oss.coresecurity.com/projects/pcapy.html

[14] http://www.secdev.org/projects/scapy

[15] http://openrce.org/downloads/details/208/PaiMei

[16] http://openrce.org/downloads/details/208/PaiMei

requiring recompilation. Libraries that expose low-level functionality to these higher level languages typically exist. Given that the nature of a fuzzer requires flexibility versus production-quality code, you will find fuzzers written in all languages. From shell scripts to Java, from PHP to C#, depending on your given task and familiarity, one language might suit you better than another.

## DATA GENERATION AND FUZZ HEURISTICS

Implementation of *how* to generate data is only part of the solution. Equally as important is deciding *what* data to generate. For example, consider if we are constructing a fuzzer to analyze the robustness of an IMAP server. Among the many IMAP verbs and constructs that we need to examine is the Command Continuation Request (CCR), described in the following excerpt from RFC 3501:[17]

```
7.5.    Server Responses - Command Continuation Request

   The command continuation request response is indicated by a "+" token instead of a
   tag.  This form of response indicates that the server is ready to accept the
   continuation of a command from the client.  The remainder of this response is a
   line of text.

   This response is used in the AUTHENTICATE command to transmit server
   data to the client, and request additional client data.  This
   response is also used if an argument to any command is a literal.

   The client is not permitted to send the octets of the literal unless
   the server indicates that it is expected.  This permits the server
   to process commands and reject errors on a line-by-line basis.  The
   remainder of the command, including the CRLF that terminates a
   command, follows the octets of the literal.  If there are any
   additional command arguments, the literal octets are followed by a
   space and those arguments.

   Example:    C: A001 LOGIN {11}
               S: + Ready for additional command text
               C: FRED FOOBAR {7}
               S: + Ready for additional command text
               C: fat man
```

---

[17] http://www.faqs.org/rfcs/rfc3501.html

```
S: A001 OK LOGIN completed
C: A044 BLURDYBLOOP {102856}
S: A044 BAD No such command as "BLURDYBLOOP"
. . .
```

According to the RFC, any command ending in the form {number} (highlighted in bold) specifies that the remaining "number" of bytes of the command that are continued on the following line. This is a prime target for fuzzing, but what values should we use to test this field? Can all possible numeric values be tested? The target daemon likely accepts values up to the maximum 32-bit integer size of 0xFFFFFFFF (4,294,967,295). If the fuzzer can exercise one test case every second, it would take more than 136 years to complete the test! Jolting the fuzzer with a healthy dose of caffeine and increasing throughput to 100 test cases per second still requires close to 500 days for completion. At this rate the IMAP protocol might have been retired by the time we complete our testing. It's clear that the entire range cannot be examined and an intelligent subset or sampling of the possible integer values must be chosen.

The specific inclusion of potentially dangerous values in our list of fuzz strings, or fuzz data, is also known as fuzz heuristics. Let's go over a couple of categories of data types we might want to include in our intelligent library.

## INTEGER VALUES

The two extreme border (0 and 0xFFFFFFFF) test cases are obvious choices for the new and improved list of integer test cases. What else can we add? Perhaps the supplied number is used as the size parameter to a memory allocation routine. It's not uncommon for additional space to be included with the specified size to accommodate a header, footer, or terminating NULL byte, for example:

```
int size = read_ccr_size(packet);
// save space for NULL termination.
buffer = (char *) malloc(size + 1);
```

On the same token, perhaps the specified size is subtracted from prior to allocation. This case might occur if the target program knows it is not going to copy all the specified data to the newly allocated buffer. Keeping in mind that integer overflows (additions causing a wrap beyond the maximum 32-bit integer range) and integer underflows (subtractions causing a wrap under 0) might result in potential security issues down the line, it would be prudent to include near-border test cases such as 0xFFFFFFFF-1, 0xFFFFFFFF-2, 0xFFFFFFFF-3, ... , and 1, 2, 3, 4, and so on.

Similarly, a multiplier can be applied to the specified size. Consider, for example, if the supplied data is converted to Unicode. This would require the specified size to be multiplied by 2. Furthermore, an additional two bytes can be included to ensure NULL termination. For example:

```
int size = read_ccr_size(packet);
// create space for the Unicode converted buffer
// plus Unicode NULL termination (2 bytes).
buffer = (char *) malloc((size * 2) + 2);
```

To trigger an integer overflow in this and similar situations, we would also have to include the following near-border test cases: 0xFFFFFFFF/2, 0xFFFFFFFF/2-1, 0xFFFFFFFF/2-2 and so on. What about border cases around divisions by 3? Or by 4? While we're at it, how about including the previously listed near-border test cases for 16-bit integers (0xFFFF) as well? And 8-bit integers (0xFF)? Let's throw those into the list along with some other smart choices. Our list now includes:

- MAX32 – 16 <= MAX32 <= MAX32 + 16
- MAX32 / 2 – 16 <= MAX32 / 2 <= MAX32 / 2 + 16
- MAX32 / 3 – 16 <= MAX32 / 3 <= MAX32 / 3 + 16
- MAX32 / 4 – 16 <= MAX32 / 4 <= MAX32 / 4 + 16
- MAX16 – 16 <= MAX16 <= MAX16 + 16
- MAX16 / 2 – 16 <= MAX16 / 2 <= MAX16 / 2 + 16
- MAX16 / 3 – 16 <= MAX16 / 3 <= MAX16 / 3 + 16
- MAX16 / 4 – 16 <= MAX16 / 4 <= MAX16 / 4 + 16
- MAX8 – 16 <= MAX8 <= MAX8 + 16
- MAX8 / 2 – 16 <= MAX8 / 2 <= MAX8 / 2 + 16
- MAX8 / 3 – 16 <= MAX8 / 3 <= MAX8 / 3 + 16
- MAX8 / 4 – 16 <= MAX8 / 4 <= MAX8 / 4 + 16

Where MAX32 represents the maximum 32-bit integer (0xFFFFFFFF), MAX16 represents the maximum 16-bit integer (0xFFFF), MAX8 represents the maximum 8-bit integer (0xFF), and the range 16 was arbitrarily chosen as a reasonable amount. Time and result depending, you might want to increase this range. If there are hundreds of integer fields within our target protocol, each additional integer heuristic increases the overall number of test cases a hundred fold.

Take these chosen integer "heuristics" with a grain of salt. A heuristic is nothing more than a fancy way of saying "educated guessing." More advanced users can examine the target binary under a disassembler and extract potentially interesting integer values by examining cross-references to memory allocation and data copy routines. This process can also be automated, a concept that is touched on in Chapter 22, "Automated Protocol Dissection."

## THE NEED FOR A SMART DATA SET

On September 1, 2005, a security advisory titled "Novell NetMail IMAPD Command Continuation Request Heap Overflow"[18] was publicly released in coordination with the relevant vendor supplied patch. The advisory details a flaw that allows remote unauthenticated attackers to execute arbitrary code and thereby completely compromise the underlying system.

The described flaw exists in the handling of CCR as the user-specified size value is used directly as the argument to a custom memory allocation wrapper named MMalloc() as shown in the following assembly snippet:

```
; ebx is attacker controlled
00402CA2 lea ecx, [ebx+1]
00402CA5 push ecx
00402CA6 call MMalloc
```

The MMalloc() routine performs a trivial mathematical operation to the supplied value prior to allocating memory. An attacker can specify a malicious number that will result in an integer overflow and cause a small memory chunk to be allocated. The original and larger supplied value will be later used in an inline memcpy():

```
; destination is attacker allocated
00402D6E rep movsd
00402D70 mov ecx, edx
00402D72 and ecx, 3
00402D75 rep movsb
```

---

[18] http://pedram.redhive.com/advisories/novell_netmail_imapd/

This instruction sequence will copy attacker-supplied data beyond the brims of the allocated heap chunk and arbitrarily overwrite the heap, eventually leading to a complete compromise.

While Novell's patch for this issue successfully addressed this specific vector, it did not account for all possible exploit paths. Unfortunately for Novell, the IMAP daemon will convert human readable numeric forms to their integer equivalent. For example, "-1" converts to 0xFFFFFFFF, "-2" converts to 0xFFFFFFFE and so on. Therefore the following malicious request is properly handled:

```
x LOGIN {4294967295}
```

However, this one is not:

```
x LOGIN {-1}
```

This added exploit vector was subsequently discovered by an independent researcher and patched by Novell on December 22, 2006.[19]

## STRING REPETITIONS

We've covered a range of smart integers we might want to include in our fuzz data, but what about strings? Starting with the age old classic[20] "long string":

```
perl -e 'print "A"*5000'
```

There are a number of additional character sequences we want to include when fuzzing strings. We should first include other ASCII characters, such as "B." This is important, for example, when triggering heap overflows on Microsoft Windows OS due to differing behavior when heap structures are overwritten the ASCII value for "A" versus "B." Another reason this is important is that believe it or not, the authors have actually

---

[19] http://www.zerodayinitiative.com/advisories/ZDI-06-053.html

[20] If you don't believe us, see Google: http://www.google.com/search?hl=en&q=%22perl+-e+%27print+%22A%22*%22

seen production software that specifically looks for and blocks long strings of As. Evidently some vendors have caught on to the power of AAAAAAAAAAAAAAAAA.

## FIELD DELIMITERS

We will also want to include nonalphanumeric characters, including spaces and tabs. These characters are frequently used as field delimiters and terminators. Including them randomly throughout our generated fuzz strings improves our chances of partially replicating the protocol we are fuzzing and therefore increasing the amount of code being fuzzed. Consider the relatively simple HTTP protocol, for example, and the following list of nonalphanumeric characters:

```
!@#$%^&*()-_=+{}|\;:'",<.>/?~`
```

How many can you recognize as HTTP field delimiters? As a reference, take a look at the following typical HTTP server response code:

```
HTTP/1.1 200 OK
Date: Sun, 01 Oct 2006 22:46:57 GMT
Server: Apache
X-Powered-By: PHP/5.1.4-p10-gentoo
Expires: Thu, 19 Nov 1981 08:52:00 GMT
Cache-Control: no-store, no-cache, post-check=0, pre-check=0
Pragma: no-cache
Keep-Alive: timeout=15, max=93
Connection: Keep-Alive
Transfer-Encoding: chunked
Content-Type: text/html; charset=ISO-8859-1
```

The first pattern you might notice is that there are a number of newline delimited lines, represented at the byte level with the sequence 0x0d 0x0a. Each individual line further utilizes various delimiting characters. In the first line, for example, we can see that the characters space ( ), front slash (/) and dot (.) are used to split the response code. A common delimiter we see on subsequent lines is the use of the colon (:) to separate directives such as Content-Type, Server and Date from their values. Further examination reveals the use of comma (,), equal sign (=), semicolon (;), and dash (-) also being used to delimit fields.

When generating fuzz strings, it will be important for us to include varying length strings separated by various field delimiters such as those previously shown. Furthermore, increasing the length of the delimiter is important as well. Consider, for example, the critical Sendmail header processing vulnerability[21] from 2003. The vulnerability in this case required a long string of <> characters to trigger an exploitable memory corruption. Consider also the following contrived code snippet that suffers from a repeated string delimiter parsing vulnerability:

```
void parse (char *inbuf)
{
    char cpy[16];
    char *cursor;
    char *delim_index;
    int   length = 0;

    for (cursor=inbuf; *cursor; cursor++)
    {
        if (*cursor == ':')
            delim_index = cursor;
        else
            length++;
    }

    // -2 for null termination and the ':' delimiter
    if (length < sizeof(cpy) - 2)
        strcpy(cpy, inbuf);
}
```

This vulnerable parser processes a string, expecting to find a single instance of the delimiting character (colon). In the event that the delimiting character is found, a pointer to this string index is saved. Otherwise, the length variable is incremented by one. At the end of the loop the calculated length variable minus one to save space for NULL termination and minus another one to account for the found delimiter is checked against the size of the destination character buffer to ensure enough space exists for the subsequent strcpy() function call. This logic handles expected strings such as name:pedram amini correctly. Given this string, the parser would calculate the value of length as 16, determine that enough space does not exist and skip the strcpy(). What about the following case: name::::::::::::::::::::::pedram? Given this string the calculated value for length comes to 10, thereby passing the conditional check and falling into the strcpy(). However, the actual length of the string that will be used in the strcpy() is 32 and a stack overflow will be triggered.

---

[21] http://xforce.iss.net/xforce/alerts/id/advise142

## FORMAT STRINGS

Format strings are a relatively easy class of bugs to detect and the data generated by a fuzzer should account for them. Format string vulnerabilities can be revealed with any format string token, such as %d, which will display a base 10 decimal number or %08x, which will display a base 16 hexadecimal number. A better choice for a format string token to use when fuzzing is either the %s or %n tokens (or both). These tokens provide a better chance at causing a detectable error, such as a memory access violation. Most format string tokens result in a memory read from the stack and are unlikely to trigger a fault in the underlying vulnerable code. The %s token results in a higher quantity of memory reads as the stack is dereferenced in search of a NULL byte indicating a string termination. In most cases the %n token provides the greatest possibility of triggering a fault. Our list of fuzz heuristics should include long sequences of %s%n.

### THE KEY TO EXPLOITING FORMAT STRING VULNERABILITIES

Whereas all other format string tokens, including %d, %x, and %s, result in a memory read from the stack, the %n format string is unique in that it results in a memory write. This is a key requirement in exploiting format string vulnerabilities for code execution. While other injected format string tokens can be used to "leak" potentially critical information from the underlying vulnerable software, leveraging the %n token is the only method for directly writing memory through a format string. It is for this very reason that Microsoft decided to implement a control to toggle support for %n format string tokens in the printf family of functions. The API responsible for this is _set_printf_count_output(),[22] which given a nonzero value will enable %n support and given a value of zero will disable %n support. In fact, %n is utilized in production code so rarely that the default setting is to disable support for it.

## CHARACTER TRANSLATION

Another nuance to keep an eye out for is character conversions and translations, specifically with regards to character expansion. For example, the hex values 0xFE and 0xFF are expanded to four characters under UTF16. Inadequate accounting for such character expansion within parsing code is a common area where vulnerabilities can be found.

---

[22] http://msdn2.microsoft.com/en-us/library/ms175782.aspx

Character conversions might also be incorrectly implemented, especially when handling rarely seen or used border cases. Microsoft Internet Explorer, for example, was affected by such an issue during the translation from UTF-8 to Unicode.[23] The crux of the issue was that the conversion routine did not properly account for 5- and 6-byte UTF-8 characters when determining the size of the dynamic allocation for storing the converted buffer. The actual data copy routine, however, did properly handle 5- and 6-byte UTF-8 characters, thereby resulting in a heap-based buffer overflow. Our list of fuzz heuristics should include these and other similarly mischievous character sequences.

## DIRECTORY TRAVERSAL

Directory traversal vulnerabilities affect network daemons and Web applications alike. A common misconception is the belief that directory traversal vulnerabilities are limited solely to Web applications. Directory traversal vulnerabilities are indeed prolific in Web applications, however, this attack vector might appear in proprietary network protocols and other avenues as well. According to the 2006 Mitre CVE statistics, while directory traversal vulnerabilities have diminished somewhat over time, they remain the fifth most common class of vulnerability discovered in software applications.[24] These statistics capture both Web applications and traditional client/server applications. Take a look at the Open Source Vulnerability Database (OSVDB) for a sampling of the many directory traversal vulnerabilities that have reared their ugly heads over the years.[25]

Consider, for example, Computer Associates BrightStor ARCserve backup software. BrightStor exposes a custom logging interface via TCP through the caloggerd daemon. Although the protocol is undocumented, basic packet analysis reveals that the name of the log file is actually specified within the network data stream. Prefixing the supplied filename with directory traversal modifiers allows an attacker to specify an arbitrary file to which to write an arbitrary log message. As the logger daemon runs with superuser privileges, this vulnerability can be trivially exploited. On UNIX systems, for example, a new superuser can be added to the /etc/passwd file. At the time of writing this issue remains a 0day vulnerability and is scheduled for public release in July of 2007. Our list of fuzz heuristics should include directory traversal modifiers such as ../../ and ..\..\.

---

[23] http://www.zerodayinitiative.com/advisories/ZDI-06-017.html

[24] http://cwe.mitre.org/documents/vuln-trends.html#table1

[25] http://www.osvdb.com/searchdb.php?text=directory+traversal

## COMMAND INJECTION

Like directory traversal vulnerabilities, command injection vulnerabilities are typically associated with Web applications and more specifically CGI scripts. Again, it is a common misconception that these classes of bugs are isolated to Web applications as they can affect network daemons through documented and proprietary protocols. Any target, Web application, or network daemon that passes unfiltered or improperly filtered user data to API calls such as exec() or system() is potentially exposing a command injection vulnerability. Consider the following simplified Python code snippet:

```
directory = socket.recv(1024)
listing   = os.system("ls /" + directory)
socket.send(listing)
```

Under normal circumstances a system path is received by the server, the file listing under the path is determined, and the listing is sent back to the client. Due to a lack of input filtering however, certain characters can be specified that allow for additional commands to be executed. On UNIX systems these include: &&, ; and |. For example, the argument var/lib ; rm -rf / translates to ls /var/lib ; rm -rf /, a command that can cause significant problems for the administrator of the affected system. Our list of fuzz heuristics should include these characters as well.

## SUMMARY

We began this chapter discussing the need for automation as well as a brief list and description of various libraries and utilities that can be used to ease the burden of development. Some of these libraries are explained in further detail and used in the development of custom tools in Parts II and III of this book. The factors behind choosing intelligent and productive fuzz values with regards to numbers, strings, and binary sequences was a key concept covered in this chapter. This information will come into play and be expanded on in future chapters.

In the following chapters, we discuss a variety of fuzz targets, including Web applications, privileged command-line applications, network services, and more. Keep the concepts discussed in this chapter in mind while reading upcoming chapters. Make note of the various libraries and tools that can be leaned on in the development of the covered fuzzers. Consider the intelligent fuzz values discussed here and what future values you might add to the list.

# Environment Variable and Argument Fuzzing

*"This foreign policy stuff is a little frustrating."*

—George W. Bush, as quoted by the New York Daily News, April 23, 2002

Local fuzzing is arguably the simplest type of fuzzing. Although many attackers and researchers will have more impressive results exploiting remote and client-side vulnerabilities, local privilege escalation is still an important topic. Even when a remote attack is leveraged to gain access to a targeted machine, local attacks are often used as a secondary attack vector to obtain required privileges.

## INTRODUCTION TO LOCAL FUZZING

A user can introduce variables into a program in two main ways. Other than the obvious standard input device, which is usually the keyboard, command-line arguments and process-environment variables represent input vectors. We first present command-line arguments as a vector for fuzzing.

## COMMAND-LINE ARGUMENTS

Except for the most sheltered Windows user, everyone has at one time or another experienced a program that has required command-line arguments. Command-line arguments are passed into a program and addressed via the pointer argv, which is declared in the main function of C programs. The variable `argc` is also passed into the main. It holds the count of arguments that were passed to the program, plus one, because the name of the program as it was invoked is counted as an argument. Let's go through a few simple examples.

```c
int main(int argc,char *argv[])
{
int ix;
for (ix=0;ix<argc;ix++)
 printf("argv[%d] == %s\n",ix,argv[ix]);
}
```

When we try and run this a few times with varying arguments, we get the results shown in Figure 7.1.

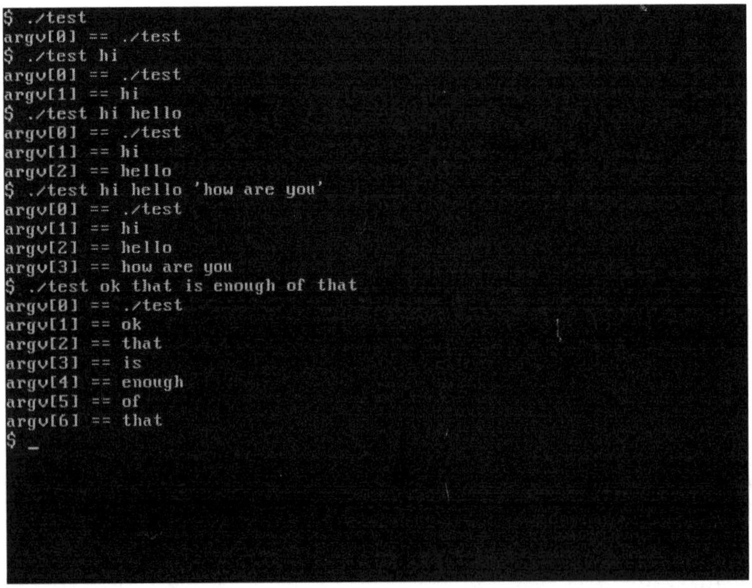

```
$ ./test
argv[0] == ./test
$ ./test hi
argv[0] == ./test
argv[1] == hi
$ ./test hi hello
argv[0] == ./test
argv[1] == hi
argv[2] == hello
$ ./test hi hello 'how are you'
argv[0] == ./test
argv[1] == hi
argv[2] == hello
argv[3] == how are you
$ ./test ok that is enough of that
argv[0] == ./test
argv[1] == ok
argv[2] == that
argv[3] == is
argv[4] == enough
argv[5] == of
argv[6] == that
$ _
```

**Figure 7.1**   A demonstration of how command-line arguments are stored

## ENVIRONMENT VARIABLES

Another way a user can introduce variables into a process is to use environment variables. Every process contains what is called an environment, which is comprised of environment variables. Environment variables are global values that define the behavior of applications. They can be set or unset by a user, but are typically set to standard values either during a software package installation or by an administrator. Most command interpreters will cause all new processes to inherit the current environment. The command.com shell is an example of a command interpreter in Windows. UNIX systems typically have multiple command interpreters such as sh, csh, ksh, and bash.

Some examples of commonly used environment variables include HOME, PATH, PS1 and USER. These values hold the home directory of the user, the current executable search path, the command prompt, and the current username, respectively. These particular variables are fairly standard; however, many other common variables, including those created by software vendors, are used only in the operation of their applications. When an application requires knowledge of a certain variable it simply uses the getenv function, which specifies the variable name as the argument. Although Windows processes have an environment in the same way the UNIX applications have environments, we focus primarily on the UNIX side of things because Windows does not have a concept of setuid applications, which can be started by an unprivileged user and gain privileges during execution. Figure 7.2 demonstrates what a typical UNIX environment might look like. You can view the current shell environment in the bash shell by typing the command set.

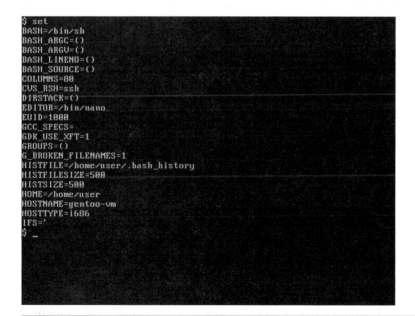

**Figure 7.2**    An example of some environment variables used by the bash shell

Each variable in this list can be manipulated by the user using the `export` command. Armed with an understanding of how command-line arguments and environment variables are used, we can now move on to the basic principles of fuzzing them.

## LOCAL FUZZING PRINCIPLES

The idea behind environment variable fuzzing and command-line fuzzing is simple: If an environment variable or command-line option contains an unexpected value, how will the application respond when that value is received? Of course, we are only interested in misbehaving privileged applications. This is because local fuzzing requires local access to the machine. Therefore, simply causing an application to crash is of limited value—you would be performing a denial-of-service attack on yourself. There could be some risk if an overflow were discovered in an environment variable that caused the system or a shared application to crash if the system were shared among multiple users. However, what we're most interested in is finding a buffer overflow in a privileged application that will allow a restricted user to elevate his or her privileges. Finding privileged targets is discussed later in this chapter in the section titled "Finding Targets."

Many applications are designed to accept command-line arguments from the user when they are invoked. The application then uses this data to determine what actions it should take. A perfect example of this is the 'su' application found on nearly all UNIX systems. When users invoke the application with no arguments, it is assumed they would like to authenticate to the root user; however, if the users specify a different username as the first argument, it is understood they would like to switch to that user instead of the root user.

Consider the following C language code, which is a simplification of how the su command might behave differently with different arguments:

```
int main(int argc,char *argv[])
{
   [...]
   if (argc >1)
    become(argv[1]);
   else
    become("root");
   [...]
}
```

Command-line arguments and environment variables are essentially just two different vectors for introducing variables into a program. The basic idea behind fuzzing these is simple. What happens when we pass bogus data to an application on the command line? Does this behavior lead to a security risk?

# FINDING TARGETS

There are usually only a handful of desirable binary targets on a system when performing local fuzzing. These programs have higher privileges when executed. On UNIX-based systems, these programs are easily recognizable, as they will have the setuid or setgid bits set.

The setuid and setgid bits indicate that when a program runs, it can acquire elevated privileges. In the case of the setuid bit, the process will have the privileges of the owner of the file, and not the person running it. In the case of the setgid bit, the process will have the privileges of the group owner of the file. For example, successful exploitation of a program that is setuid root and setgid staff might yield a shell with those permissions.

It is trivial to construct a list of setuid binaries using the find command, which is a standard tool on UNIX and UNIX-like operating systems. The following command is sufficient to dump a list of all of the setuid binaries on the system. It should be run as root to avoid file system reading errors:

```
find / -type f -perm -4000 -o -perm -2000
```

The find command is a very powerful tool that can be used to find very specific types of files, devices, and directories on a file system. In this example, we use just a few of the options the find command supports. The first argument specifies we will be searching the entire system and everything below /, the root directory. The type option tells find that we are only interested in files. This means no symbolic links, directories, or devices will be returned. The -perm options describe the permissions we are interested in. The usage of the -o option allows find to use *or* logic. If a binary has the setgid bit or the setuid bit set, it will evaluate to true and print the path for that file out. In summary, this command will find all regular files that have either the setuid bit (4) or the setgid (2) bit set. Here is a sample of the output from this command on a default Fedora Core 4 installation:

```
[root@localhost /]# find / -type f -perm -4000 -o -perm -2000
/bin/traceroute6
/bin/traceroute
/bin/mount
/bin/su
/bin/ping6
/bin/ping
/bin/umount
/usr/bin/lppasswd
```

```
/usr/bin/gtali
/usr/bin/wall
/usr/bin/chsh
/usr/bin/passwd
/usr/bin/glines
/usr/bin/gnibbles          ← everyone knows gnibbles is absolutely
/usr/bin/at                   required for a functional system...
/usr/bin/gnotravex
/usr/bin/gnobots2
/usr/bin/sudo
/usr/bin/same-gnome
/usr/bin/gataxx
/usr/bin/rcp
/usr/bin/mahjongg
/usr/bin/iagno
/usr/bin/rlogin
/usr/bin/gnotski
/usr/bin/chage
/usr/bin/lockfile
/usr/bin/write
/usr/bin/gpasswd
/usr/bin/ssh-agent
/usr/bin/crontab
/usr/bin/gnomine
/usr/bin/sudoedit
/usr/bin/chfn
/usr/bin/slocate
/usr/bin/newgrp
/usr/bin/rsh
/usr/X11R6/bin/Xorg
/usr/lib/vte/gnome-pty-helper
/usr/libexec/openssh/ssh-keysign
/usr/sbin/userhelper
/usr/sbin/userisdnctl
/usr/sbin/sendmail.sendmail
/usr/sbin/usernetctl
/usr/sbin/lockdev
/usr/sbin/utempter
/sbin/pam_timestamp_check
/sbin/netreport
/sbin/unix_chkpwd
/sbin/pwdb_chkpwd
```

## UNIX FILE PERMISSIONS EXPLAINED

In UNIX, the file permission model allows for three different types of basic access: read, write, and execute. There are also three sets of permissions for each file. They pertain to the user, the group, and those that don't fit into either (other). In any given situation, only one of these permissions is actually applied. For example, if you own a file, the set of permissions that will be used is that of the user. If you do not own the file, but are in the group that the file is owned by, the group permissions will be applied. For all other cases, the other permissions will be applied. An example follows:

```
-r-x-x-- 2 dude staff  2048 Jan  2 2002  File
```

In this example, the user *dude* owns the file. The permissions this user is allowed include read and execute access. Of course, this user owns the file, so he or she may modify these permissions in any way.

If another member of the staff group attempts to access this file, he or she will only be able to execute this file, but not read it. Attempts to read the file will fail with invalid permissions. Finally, all other users will be denied access as they do not have read, write, or execute access.

In UNIX, a special way of describing absolute file permissions exists. Under this system, permissions are represented in octal form. That is, each combination of permissions has a value from 0 to 7. The read flag has the octal value 4, the write flag has the value 2, and the execute flag has the value 1. These numbers are then added up to get the overall permission. For example, a file that allows read and write access to the user, the group, and other users would be referenced as 666. The example file owned by *dude* would be represented as 510 -user (5) = .read (4) + execute (1), group (1) = execute (1) and other (0) is null.

A fourth column represents special flags such as the setuid and setgid bits. The setuid bit is represented by a 4 and the setgid by a 2. Therefore, a file that is setuid and setgid might have 6,755 permissions. If the special flag column is left off, it is assumed to be zero, and thus would have no extended permissions.

## LOCAL FUZZING METHODS

Environment variables and command-line arguments can be provided easily by a user, and because they are almost always simple ASCII strings, it is practical to perform some basic manual testing against a target. The most trivial test might be setting your HOME variable to a long string, and then running the target to see what happens. This can be accomplished very quickly utilizing Perl, which is available by default on most UNIX systems:

```
HOME=`perl -e 'print "X"x10000'` /usr/bin/target
```

This is a very rudimentary way to test the application to see if it can handle a long HOME variable. However, this example assumes that you already knew of an application that utilizes the HOME variable. What if you don't know what variables are used by the application? How can you determine which ones are used?

## ENUMERATING ENVIRONMENT VARIABLES

At least two automatic methods determine what environment variables a program uses. If the system supports library preloading, you can hook the getenv library call. Providing a new getenv function that performs the standard getenv functionality while also logging the call to a file will effectively record all variables requested by the application. An extension of this method is described in more detail later in this chapter in the section titled "Automating Environment Variable Fuzzing."

### THE GNU DEBUGGER (GDB) METHOD

Another method we can use requires a debugger. Using GDB, one can set a breakpoint inside the getenv function and dump the first argument. An example using GDB scripting to automate this on Solaris 10 follows:

```
(08:55AM)[user@unknown:~]$gdb -q /usr/bin/id
(no debugging symbols found)...(gdb)
(gdb) break getenv
Function "getenv" not defined.
Make breakpoint pending on future shared library load? (y or [n]) y
Breakpoint 1 (getenv) pending.
(gdb) commands
Type commands for when breakpoint 1 is hit, one per line.
End with a line saying just "end".
>silent
>x/s $i0
>cont
>end
(gdb) r
```

```
Starting program: /usr/bin/id
[...]
Breakpoint 2 at 0xff2c4610
Pending breakpoint "getenv" resolved
(no debugging symbols found)...
0xff0a9064:      "LIBCTF_DECOMPRESSOR"
0xff0a9078:      "LIBCTF_DEBUG"
0xff24b940:      "LIBPROC_DEBUG"
0xff351940:      "LC_ALL"
0xff351948:      "LANG"
0xff3518d8:      "LC_CTYPE"
0xff3518e4:      "LC_NUMERIC"
0xff3518f0:      "LC_TIME"
0xff3518f8:      "LC_COLLATE"
0xff351904:      "LC_MONETARY"
0xff351910:      "LC_MESSAGES"
uid=100(user) gid=1(other)

Program exited normally.
(gdb)
```

If you are not familiar with the commands used in this GDB session, they can be summarized in a few words:

- The break command sets a breakpoint on a specified function or address. Here, we use it to cause the execution of the program to stop inside the call to getenv.

- The commands command specifies certain actions that will occur when a breakpoint is hit. In this case, we tell it to be silent and print out the value of the i0 register as a string using x/s. On SPARC, i0 is the register that holds the first argument to the function being entered.

- The next command simply continues execution so we do not have to tell it to continue after each break. We then use a shortcut for the run command to start execution of the program.

Using this method, we can immediately see the list of 11 environment variables that are requested by the /usr/bin/id program. Note that this method should work on all systems; however, you will need to change the name of the register you are dereferencing as different architectures have different mnemonics for their registers. For example, you might be printing out $eax on x86, $i0 on SPARC, and $a0 on MIPS.

Now that we have covered what variables your target will use, we will explore ways of testing them in a more automated fashion.

## AUTOMATING ENVIRONMENT VARIABLE FUZZING

Recall that we briefly mentioned using library preloading in the previous section, "Enumerating Environment Variables;" this is also useful for automated fuzzing. To retrieve the value of an environment variable, it must invoke the getenv function. If we hook the getenv function and return long strings for all calls to it, we do not even need to know a list of variables that are used; we can simply fuzz every one by intercepting all calls to getenv. This is very useful when performing a quick check for unsafe environment variable use.

The following function is a trivial implementation of the getenv function. It uses the global variable environ, which points to the start of the environment. The code simply steps through the environ array and checks to see if the value being requested is within the environ array. If it is, it returns a pointer to the value it holds; if not, it returns NULL to indicate the variable is not set:

```
extern char **environ;
char *getenv(char *variable)
{
  int ix=0;
  while (environ[ix])
    {
      if ( ! ( strncmp(string,environ[ix],strlen(string))) &&
      (environ[ix][strlen(string)] == '=')  )
      {
        printf("%s\n",environ[ix]+strlen(string)+1);
        return environ[ix]+strlen(string)+1;
      }
      ix++;
    }
```

### LIBRARY PRELOADING

The next topic we cover is library preloading. Library preloading provides an easy way to hook functions by using the operating system linker to essentially replace functions with user-supplied functions. Although the specifics vary from system to system, the general concept is the same. The user typically sets a certain environment variable to the path of a user-compiled library. The library is then loaded when the program executes. If the library contains symbols that are duplicates of the symbols in the program, they are used instead of the original symbols. When we say symbols, we are primarily referring to functions. For example, if a user builds a library with a function called strcpy, and preloads it when running a binary, the binary will call the user's version of strcpy instead of the system copy of strcpy. This has many legitimate purposes, such as wrapping calls to do profiling and auditing. It also has some uses for finding vulnerabilities. Consider the uses of wrapping or completely replacing the getenv routine; this routine is used to request environment variable values.

The following function is a simple replacement for getenv that can be used to find simple long string issues. You can force this function to override the real getenv by using library preloading:

```
#define BUFFSIZE 20000
char *getenv(char *variable)
{
    char buff[BUFFSIZE];
    memset(buff,'A',BUFFSIZE);
    buff[BUFFSIZE-1] = 0x0;
    return buff;
}
```

It is easy to see that this function returns a long string for every variable request that is made. It does not use the environ array at all as we are not concerned with returning correct values.

This method is used by Dave Aitel's GPL sharefuzz utility, which has been used to find numerous vulnerabilities in setuid applications. To initiate this trivial fuzz test, simply compile the C code into a shared library and use your operating system's library preloading functionality (assuming it has such a functionality). For Linux, this can be done in two steps as follows:

```
gcc –shared –fPIC –o my_getenv.so my_getenv.c
LD_PRELOAD=./my_getenv.so /usr/bin/target
```

When /usr/bin/target is executed, all calls to getenv will use our modified getenv function.

## DETECTING PROBLEMS

Now that you are familiar with the basic methods of local fuzzing, you will need to know how to recognize when an interesting misbehavior has occurred in your target; many times this is very obvious. For example, the program might crash and print "Segmentation Fault" or some other fatal signal message.

However, as our ultimate goal is automation, we cannot rely on the user recognizing a crash manually. For our purposes, we require a way to do this reliably and programmatically. There are at least two good ways this can be done. The simplest way is by checking the return code of the application. On modern UNIX and Linux systems, if an application terminates due to an unhandled signal, the shell return code will be equal to 128 plus the signal number. For example, a segmentation fault will cause the shell to receive a return code of 139 decimal as SIGSEGV has a value of 11. If the program terminates on an illegal instruction, the shell will receive a return code of 132 as the value of SIGILL is 4. The logic here is simple: If the shell return code of the application is 132 or 139, flag it as a possibly interesting crash.

You also might want to consider the abort signal. SIGABRT is interesting as well due to the introduction of stricter heap checking in newer versions of glibc. Abort is a signal that can be raised in a process to terminate it and dump core. Although the process might abort on heap corruption in a particular case, there are clever ways of getting around this.

Using the shell return code makes sense if you are doing your fuzzing with a hacked together shell script. However, if you are using, for example, a proper fuzzer written in C or some other language, you would want to use the wait or waitpid functions. The general method for local fuzzing in this manner is a simple fork with an execve in the child in tandem with a wait or waitpid in the parent. When used correctly, you can easily determine if the child process crashed by checking the status that is returned via wait or waitpid. A simplified snippet from iFUZZ, a local fuzzing tool, is included in the next chapter to illustrate this method.

If you are concerned about catching signals that might be handled by the application (and thus go undetected by the previous method), there is at least one alternative aside from hooking the signal routine. You will have to use the system's debugging API to attach to the process and intercept the signals it receives before a signal handler is invoked. For most UNIX operating systems, you will use ptrace for this. The general method here is a fork with a ptrace and execve in the parent in tandem with waitpid and ptrace inside the child in a loop to continuously monitor the processes' execution and intercept and pass along any signals that might occur. When waitpid returns each time in the child, it means the program has received a signal or has terminated. You will have to check the status returned by waitpid to determine which has occurred. You will also have to explicitly tell the application to continue execution and pass the signal through in most cases. This is also done using ptrace. The implementations in SPIKEfile and notSPIKEfile can be used as references for this general method. These two tools are used for file fuzzing and are explained in detail in Chapter 12, "File Format Fuzzing: Automation on UNIX." A code snippet is provided in the next chapter that demonstrates this method.

In many cases, the `ptrace` method is overkill for local fuzzing. Very few `setuid` UNIX applications make much use of signal handlers for signals like `SIGSEGV` and `SIGILL`. Also, once you start using `ptrace`, you are introducing code that will not necessarily be compatible across different operating systems and architectures. Consider this if you are designing an application that can be used on many platforms without modification.

In the next chapter, we present an implementation of a simple command-line fuzzer that was designed to compile and run on just about any UNIX system with a C compiler. The tool also includes a simple shared library fuzzer for the `getenv` hooking method.

## SUMMARY

Although there is far less glory in the discovery of local vulnerabilities, there is still value in a good privilege escalation bug. We have laid down the foundation to demonstrate various ways of automating discovering these types of vulnerabilities, and in the next chapter implement some of these methods to actually find some bugs.

# Environment Variable and Argument Fuzzing: Automation

*"Those weapons of mass destruction have got to be somewhere!"*

—George W. Bush, Washington, DC, March 24, 2004

This chapter introduces iFUZZ, a program that implements fuzzing for local applications. The main targets here are command-line arguments and environment variables in setuid UNIX programs, which were discussed in Chapter 7, "Environment Variable and Argument Fuzzing." In this chapter, we discuss the features of iFUZZ, explain the design decisions, and discuss how iFUZZ was used to uncover numerous local vulnerabilities in IBM AIX 5.3.

## FEATURES OF iFUZZ LOCAL FUZZER

iFUZZ contains several features you might have envisioned for a local fuzzer. Among these features is an engine for processing multiple target binaries automatically, the ability to output C language trigger files for easy bug reproduction, and several different methods of fuzzing, implemented somewhat modularly. One of the more convenient features of iFUZZ is that it can run on almost any UNIX or UNIX-like operating system without modification. It has found vulnerabilities on IRIX, HP-UX, QNX, MacOS X, and AIX. The guts of this fuzzer lie in the different modules for each type of fuzzing:

- *Argv fuzzer modules.* The first two modules are similar enough that they can be explained together. They fuzz the `argv[0]` and the `argv[1]` values of an executable. The basic usage of these two modules is simple: Specify a directory full of target applications and let it run. It will try using varying length strings as well as strings with format specifiers. The strings it actually uses depend on the fuzz string database, which can be supplemented with end-user-supplied strings fairly easily.

- *Single-option/multioption fuzzer modules.* This module is still what one might consider a dumb fuzzer; that is, the user doesn't provide the module with any information about the target, and it doesn't care. It is simply throwing string values at the target for each possible option. With the single-option fuzz, iFUZZ will loop from a to Z and attempt to run commands of the form:

```
./target -a FUZZSTRING
```

The value FUZZSTRING is a string taken from the internal iFUZZ fuzzing string database. This is a quick way to find simple option-related issues, but it will not find more complex issues, such as those that require multiple option values.

- getopt *fuzzer.* This module requires some information from the user. Namely, it requires the options string that the application uses with `getopt` so that it can fuzz only the options it knows the application will use. Although this can be a very time-consuming fuzz, it can also be dramatically more thorough than any of the other fuzz types. With a module like this, you can also find much more complex vulnerabilities than you might find with one of the other fuzzers. Consider, for example, an application that only triggers a buffer overflow when the debug and verbose options are set and a long `-f` argument is provided. Here is the sample output from the fictitious program in question displaying the usage:

```
$ ./sample_program
Usage:
-f <file> Input filename
-o <file> Output filename
-v  Verbose output
-d  Debug mode
-s  Silent mode
```

Based on the usage information that is printed, we can determine that the `getopt` string for this application is most likely `f:o:vds`. This means the f and o options take an argument and the v, d, and s options are just switches. How do we know this? According to the getopt man page:

> *The* options *argument is a string that specifies the option characters that are valid for this program. An option character in this string can be followed by a colon (':') to indicate that it takes a required argument. If an option character is followed by two colons ('::'), its argument is optional; this is a GNU extension.*

If we run iFUZZ in getopt fuzz mode with f:o:vds, it will not be long before we find the vulnerability we described. Because iFUZZ also randomly provides the path to an existing file as a fuzz string, you can even uncover vulnerabilities that require one of the options to be a valid file. Because of the way iFUZZ was designed, getting creative here is not difficult. You can also add some other valid strings into the string database, such as usernames, hostnames, valid X displays, and so on. The sky is the limit here and the more creative you get, the more thorough your fuzz will be.

Included within iFUZZ is also a simple preloadable getenv fuzzer. It contains an array of variables that you wish to return unmodified, but fuzzes all others. This is simply a hack-up of Dave Aitel's sharefuzz with a little extra functionality, allowing you to return data from the real environment if desired. This isn't actually a core component of iFUZZ, but more of a quick utility.

Also included is a simple getopt hooker that can be preloaded to dump the getopt options string from a targeted binary. Although useful, this is really just a one-line C program and is included only for your convenience. When using it, keep in mind that some applications use their own function to parse command-line options. For these applications, you will have to manually construct the getopt string based on the output of the usage function.

## DEVELOPMENT

Now that the features of the tool have been presented, it is time to move on to some of the implementation details. To gain a full understanding of how iFUZZ was built, we recommend downloading and reviewing the source code from fuzzing.org, but here we highlight some of the key functionality and review specific design decisions.

### DEVELOPMENT APPROACH

The approach taken with iFUZZ was to keep things modular and therefore extensible. This made it simple to nail down the basic functionality of the application without spending too much time on each different method of fuzzing up front. Each module was really an afterthought, added once the main engine was complete.

The first module that was developed after the basic engine and helper functions were complete was the argv[0] fuzzer. A test suite of several binaries known vulnerable to argv[0] overflows and format strings and some safely written applications were used on several operating systems including QNX, Linux, and AIX. This test suite was used to eliminate any small bugs and to confirm accurate results.

As a developer, you will not always have knowledge of preexisting vulnerable binaries to use as part of your test suite, so you can create some of your own sample vulnerable applications. For example, the following is the simplest way to create an application with an argv[0] format string vulnerability:

```
int main(int argc,char *argv[])
{
if (argc >1) printf(argv[1]);
exit(0);
}
```

This can be compiled and thrown into a test suite consisting of some known safe binaries to detect false negatives and false positives.

### FORMAT STRINGS AS AN ATTACK VECTOR

Format string vulnerabilities have been around for some time, yet they were once thought to be relatively harmless. In 1999, following a security audit of proftpd 1.2.opre6, Tymm Twillman posted details of an exploit to the BugTraq mailing list,[1] which would allow an attacker to overwrite memory using a format string vulnerability. The vulnerability was caused by a snprintf() function that passed user input without a format string.[2]

---

[1]  http://seclists.org/bugtraq/1999/Sep/0328.html

[2]  http://en.wikipedia.org/wiki/Format_string_attack

The next module that was implemented was the single-option fuzzer. Although still a very simple idea, it is one of the most effective when put up against many commercial UNIX systems. The design here was simple and presented no real challenges. A simple loop was used to progress through the entire alphabet, each time using the chosen character as an option to the program. The argument to that option is taken from the fuzz database.

After these simple modules were implemented, it became clear that iFUZZ would find some vulnerabilities, but not any of the more difficult ones to trigger, such as those requiring multiple options. This led to the development of the next two modules, the multiple option and the getopt fuzzers.

The design of the multiple-option fuzzer is simple; it is merely a single-option fuzzer, nested inside another single-option fuzzing loop. The maximum amount of options to be used at any one time can be specified on the command line. The more options that are specified, the deeper the loops get.

For a more effective and efficient variation on the multiple-option fuzz, the getopt fuzz was born. This is basically the same as the multiple-option fuzzer, except instead of clumsily trying all values as options, it is given a subset of values that are known to be significant to the application. Although this technically makes the fuzz less thorough, it is much quicker to run to completion, and often much quicker to find vulnerabilities.

We devised two trivial methods of catching exceptions. The first method will not pick up handled signals, but as we mentioned in the previous chapter, very few applications under UNIX will handle the signals we are interested in catching.

### Fork, Execute, and Wait Approach

A simple implementation of the fork, execute, and wait approach follows:

```
[...]
if ((pid = fork ()) != 0)
        {
            child = pid;
            waitpid (pid, &status, 0);
        if (WIFSIGNALED (status))
          {
          switch (WTERMSIG (status))
             {
               case SIGBUS:
               case SIGILL:
               case SIGABRT:
               case SIGSEGV:
                            fprintf (stderr, "CRASH ON SIGNAL #%d\n",
WTERMSIG (status));
```

```
                        break;
            default:
                        break;
        }
      }
    }
  else /* child */
    {
    execle ("/bin/program","program",NULL, environ);
    perror ("execle");
    }
[...]
```

## Fork, Ptrace/Execute, and Wait/Ptrace Approach

The following C code snippet demonstrates how one might fork off a process and monitor it for interesting signals, even if they are handled internally by the application. This is
a stripped-down example shared in both notSPIKEfile and SPIKEfile, two file fuzzing
tools that are discussed in Chapter 12, "File Format Fuzzing: Automation on UNIX."

```
  [...]
    if ( !(pid = fork ()) )
    { /* child */
     ptrace (PTRACE_TRACEME, 0, NULL, NULL);
     execve (argv[0], argv, envp);
    }
     else
    { /* parent */
     c_pid = pid;
monitor:
          waitpid (pid, &status, 0);
          if ( WIFEXITED (status) )
          { /* program exited */
              if ( !quiet )
                printf ("Process %d exited with code %d\n", pid,WEXITSTATUS
(status));
              return(ERR_OK);
          }
          else if ( WIFSIGNALED (status) )
          { /* program ended because of a signal */
           printf ("Process %d terminated by unhandled signal %d\n", pid, WTERMSIG
(status));
          return(ERR_OK);
```

```
        }
        else if ( WIFSTOPPED (status) )
        { /* program stopped because of a signal */
                if ( !quiet )
                    fprintf (stderr, "Process %d stopped due to signal %d (%s)
",pid,WSTOPSIG (status), F_signum2ascii (WSTOPSIG (status)));
        }
         switch ( WSTOPSIG (status) )
        { /* the following signals are usually all we care about */
                case SIGILL:
                case SIGBUS:
                case SIGSEGV:
                case SIGSYS:
                printf("Program got interesting signal…\n");
                    if ( (ptrace (PTRACE_CONT, pid, NULL,
                        (WSTOPSIG (status) ==SIGTRAP) ? 0 : WSTOPSIG (status))) ==
-1 )
                        {
                            perror("ptrace");
                        }
                    ptrace(PTRACE_DETACH,pid,NULL,NULL);
                    fclose(fp);
                    return(ERR_CRASH); /* it crashed */
            }
/* deliver the signal through and keep tracing */
            if ( (ptrace (PTRACE_CONT, pid, NULL,
                (WSTOPSIG (status) == SIGTRAP) ? 0 : WSTOPSIG (status))) == -1 )
        {
                perror("ptrace");
        }
    goto monitor;
    }
    return(ERR_OK);
}
```

## LANGUAGE

C is the language that was chosen for the development of iFUZZ. Although I could invent a few false reasons for choosing this, I can't hide the fact that C was used mainly because it is the language I use daily and feel the most comfortable with.

However, C clearly has some advantages outside of being my preferred language; for example, most UNIX machines, even older ones, have C compiler suites already installed on them. This is not necessarily true for languages such as a Python or Ruby. Perl might also be a candidate, as it is fairly ubiquitous among UNIX machines. However, Perl code is notoriously difficult to maintain.

The advantage of choosing a language such as Python or Perl for a project like this is mainly in the development time. With these scripting languages, development time can be dramatically reduced.

In the end, our comfort level with C and our desire to have a fuzzer that wasn't a "hack" like all of the smaller fuzzers we had done in bash and other scripting languages drove the decision to use C.

## CASE STUDY

Using iFUZZ, more than 50 local vulnerabilities were identified in IBM AIX 5.3, each with varying degrees of usefulness for a penetration tester or black hat hacker cracker. Many of these are fairly easy to find and were only hiding in argv[0] or argv[1]. However, some of the vulnerabilities were a little more interesting and "difficult" to find. When we say difficult, we don't mean that finding them requires any degree of technical skill. What we really mean is that you will need to be a little more patient when preparing your iFUZZ command-line options and waiting for iFUZZ results. The following two vulnerabilities (occurring in one setuid root binary) demonstrate the power and effectiveness of iFUZZ as a local fuzzer on a system:

- `piomkpq -A ascii -p X -d X -D x -q LONGSTRING`
- `piomkpq -A ascii -p LONGSTRING -d X -D X -q`

Although the targeted binary in this case does not present a significant threat to system security because access to the printq group is required to exploit it, it has been used as an example due to the unique requirements for triggering the vulnerabilities within it.

To find these issues, the manual page for this binary was read and a getopt string was created for iFUZZ. The getopt string used was a:A:d:D:p:q:Q:s:r:w:v:

The following output from the ls command shows the location and permissions of the binary:

```
-r-sr-x--   1 root     printq       32782 Dec 31 1969  /usr/lib/lpd/pio/etc/piomkpq*
```

After a fair amount of time running, iFUZZ came up with at least two interesting and possibly exploitable crashes in the binary. In the previous presentation of the vulnerabilities, LONGSTRING means a string of approximately 20,000 characters and X means any reasonable string, such as the string X itself. The X values must be used in conjunction with the long strings to reach the vulnerable code.

Although it is interesting to be able to find a more difficult-to-trigger vulnerability like the preceding ones, it is also fun to see how many simple bugs you can find with one pass through all the basic modules of iFUZZ. Run iFUZZ in argv[0], argv[1], or single-option mode on the setuid binaries in AIX 5.3 and you will find enough heap overflows, stack overflows, and format string issues to keep you busy for a few days. Many of the vulnerabilities have been reported to IBM and fixed since their discovery with iFUZZ, both by the authors and by other independent researchers, who most likely used similar fuzzing concepts to find them.

## BENEFITS AND ROOM FOR IMPROVEMENT

After reading this chapter, hopefully you have come away with some ideas about what is useful in iFUZZ. Equally important is that you have identified some of the weaknesses of iFUZZ. What follows are some postdevelopment observations made about iFUZZ.

- First of all, iFUZZ does not take into account the possibility of crashing the system, other than by using a few hard-coded sleep values to try to keep the load down. It would be a nice feature to be able to analyze the system load to see if this sleep time needs to be increased to keep the system from hanging or causing false negatives or false positives, which can occur under heavy load.

- It would be desirable to have a specialized option that will determine the approximate string length or absolute minimum required to trigger a crash. This is a fairly trivial feature, but would save a few moments here and there.

- Another trivial feature missing from iFUZZ is the ability to automatically locate all of the setuid and setgid binaries on the system. This is another time-saving feature.

- The ability to parse the options from a given binary would be a great feature, but is probably not trivial to implement. If the user could specify a binary, and iFUZZ could automatically determine which flags and options the application required, that would result in an intelligent and complete fuzz with minimal user interaction. Of course, this is not a trivial implementation, as many applications use many different formats. Even after a fairly complete implementation of this feature, a new application with a new style of usage function could be unparsable with the current code. That being said, it is not completely impossible to make the feature extensible so that users can add new formats for different applications they encounter.

- Something we found to be trivial to implement, yet invaluable to have, was the C code generation capability. Being able to have a C language program produced after a crash means the vulnerability can be reproduced manually in almost no time. The code generated might even be used as the basis for an exploit. This saves time for the exploit developer, especially when fuzzing a weak system with many crashes when the time of writing skeleton C programs to trigger the vulnerability begins to add up.

## SUMMARY

With such a great amount of attention being given to remote vulnerabilities, and more recently, client-side vulnerabilities, local system security remains an area filled with relatively low-hanging fruit. Through the implementation of a local fuzzer, much of this low-hanging fruit and even the more complex vulnerabilities can be uncovered with a very small time investment, proving that fuzzing can be very rewarding.

# Web Application and Server Fuzzing

*9*

*"I'm the master of low expectations."*

—George W. Bush, aboard Air Force One, June 4, 2003

We now move from local fuzzing to fuzzing in a client–server architecture. Specifically, we look at the fuzzing of Web applications and Web servers. As we discuss, fuzzing a Web application can also reveal vulnerabilities in the underlying Web server, but for simplicity, we refer to this class of fuzzing simply as Web application fuzzing going forward. Although the basic concepts remain consistent from network fuzzing, which was previously discussed, we must make a few adjustments. First, Web application inputs are numerous and often lie in nonobvious locations, so we'll need to redefine what constitutes an input vector. Second, we need to adjust our detection mechanisms to be able to capture and interpret the error messages produced by Web applications that might reveal an exploitable condition. Finally, to make Web application fuzzing practical, we need to set up an architecture that compensates for the performance hit that would be added by sending inputs over a network.

## WHAT IS WEB APPLICATION FUZZING?

Web application fuzzing is a specialized form of network protocol fuzzing. Whereas network protocol fuzzing (discussed in Chapter 14, "Network Protocol Fuzzing") mutates any type of network packet, Web application fuzzing focuses specifically on packets that conform to the HTTP specification. We chose to single out Web application fuzzing as a unique methodology due to the prevalence and importance of Web applications in the world today. Vendors are increasingly shifting to delivering software as a service over the Web, as opposed to traditional software products that are installed directly on the local computer. Web applications can be hosted either by the entity using them or by a third party. When a third party is involved, the model is often referred to as an application service provider (ASP) model.

Web applications provide a number of advantages for both software vendors and end users. They provide vendors with recurring revenue and allow updates, including security fixes, to be applied instantaneously. There's no longer the need for end users to download and apply patches due to the fact that the application is housed on a central server. From an end user's perspective, this also means less overhead in maintaining an application, as maintenance is handled by the ASP. This, however, comes at the cost of entrusting the ASP to maintain appropriate security to keep your private data from prying eyes. Therefore, Web application security should be a paramount concern.

## MICROSOFT LIVE

Microsoft is betting heavily on the growing importance of Web applications. Although its bread and butter has traditionally been GUI applications such as Microsoft Office, in November 2005, Microsoft Chairman Bill Gates announced the launch of two new Web-based applications: Windows Live and Office Live.[1] Windows Live is a collection of services for individuals, whereas Office Live targets small businesses. Microsoft will generate revenues from the services via advertisement and subscription models. The Live suite of services first emerged in November 2002 with the launch of Xbox Live, an online community and marketplace for the Xbox video game console.

The programming languages and development environments used to develop Web applications are also becoming increasingly more user friendly. As a result, many companies are now producing their own Web applications for use internally on corporate intranets and as a means for facilitating commerce and communication with partners and customers. Today, virtually any company could be considered a software developer,

---

[1]   http://news.com.com/2061-10805_3-6026895.html

regardless of size. Even a one-man shop has the ability to produce and host Web applications thanks to advances in technology. However, despite the fact that it is relatively easy to produce a Web application, it's not easy to produce a secure Web application. When development is done by a company for which building software is not a strength, the application is less likely to undergo rigorous security testing before being deployed. Unfortunately, easy-to-use and freely available applications for testing the security of Web applications has not kept pace with the technologies designed to produce the applications in the first place. One of the goals of this book is to change that. The following list provides an overview of common technologies that are employed for such development efforts.

## WEB APPLICATION TECHNOLOGIES

### CGI

Common Gateway Interface (CGI) is a standard originally developed by the National Center for Supercomputing Applications (NCSA) for the NCSA HTTPd Web server in 1993. CGI defines how data should be transferred between a Web client and an application that handles that request on behalf of a Web server.[2] Although any language can be used with CGI, it is most commonly implemented using Perl.

### PHP

Hypertext Preprocessor (PHP)[3] is a popular scripting language that is commonly used for developing Web applications. Interpreters are widely available that allow PHP to be used on most operating systems. PHP scripts can be embedded directly within HTML pages to handle portions of Web content that require dynamic generation.

### Flash

Flash was initially developed by FutureWave Software, which was acquired by Macromedia in December 1996.[4] Flash is somewhat unique among the technologies mentioned here in that it requires the installation of separate client-side software. Most other technologies mentioned simply require a Web browser.

---

[2]  http://en.wikipedia.org/wiki/Common_Gateway_Interface

[3]  http://www.php.net/

[4]  http://en.wikipedia.org/wiki/Adobe_Flash

Macromedia was able to encourage the adoption of Macromedia Flash by making the Macromedia Flash Player freely available. Flash employs a language known as ActionScript to handle most of its interactive features. Although Flash is primarily a client-side technology, Macromedia Flash Remoting does allow for interaction between the Flash Player and the Web server application.[5] Macromedia was itself acquired by Adobe Systems in 2005.[6]

### JavaScript

Netscape created JavaScript back in 1995 as a means to allow dynamic content in Web pages.[7] JavaScript can be employed as a client- or server-side technology. When used on the client side, JavaScript is embedded within the HTML delivered to the Web browser and is interpreted directly by the browser. JavaScript can also be employed as a server-side technology and is used by the Web server when creating dynamic content. Other server-side technologies such as Microsoft ASP.Net (see below) support the inclusion of JavaScript.

### Java

Java was the brainchild of James Gosling at Sun Microsystems. It began life as Oak and was originally designed to run on embedded systems. It was later adapted to be used as a Web-based technology and the name was changed to Java when it was discovered that Oak had previously been trademarked.[8] Java is a cross between a compiled and an interpreted language. Java source code is compiled into byte code, which is then interpreted by a Java Virtual Machine running on the intended platform. This approach allows Java to be platform independent. It is often used within Web browsers as a means of delivering complex and interactive applications.

### ASP.Net

.Net is a development framework as opposed to a language. It consists of a Common Language Runtime (CLR) environment that can be leveraged by many languages including Visual Basic and C#. Microsoft introduced .Net in 2002 and is counting on it to be the development platform of choice for many application

---

[5]  http://www.macromedia.com/software/flashremoting/

[6]  http://en.wikipedia.org/wiki/Macromedia

[7]  http://en.wikipedia.org/wiki/Javascript

[8]  http://en.wikipedia.org/wiki/Java_programming_language

types including web applications. It is similar to Java in that source code is compiled to an intermediary byte code known as Common Intermediate Language (CIL), which is then interpreted by a virtual machine.[9] Web applications are designed using ASP .Net, which is language independent. ASP.Net applications can be written using any .Net compatible language.

## TARGETS

Web application fuzzing can uncover vulnerabilities in the Web application itself or any of the underlying components of its infrastructure including the Web or database server that it might integrate with. Web applications cover a wide range of application types but there are common categories of applications that tend to be delivered over the Web. The following list shows such categorizations and gives a sample of vulnerabilities in specific applications that could potentially have been identified using fuzzing techniques:

- Web Mail
  
  Microsoft Outlook Web Access Cross-Site Scripting Vulnerability
  
  http://www.idefense.com/intelligence/vulnerabilities/display.php?id=261

- Discussion Boards
  
  phpBB Group phpBB Arbitrary File Disclosure Vulnerability
  
  http://www.idefense.com/intelligence/vulnerabilities/display.php?id=204

- Wikis
  
  Tikiwiki tiki-user_preferences Command Injection Vulnerability
  
  http://www.idefense.com/intelligence/vulnerabilities/display.php?id=335

- Weblogs
  
  WordPress Cookie cache_lastpostdate Variable Arbitrary PHP Code Execution
  
  http://www.osvdb.org/18672

- Enterprise Resource Planning (ERP)
  
  SAP Web Application Server sap-exiturl Header HTTP Response Splitting
  
  http://www.osvdb.org/20714

---

[9] http://en.wikipedia.org/wiki/Microsoft_.Net

- Log Analysis

  AWStats Remote Command Execution Vulnerability

  http://www.idefense.com/intelligence/vulnerabilities/display.php?id=185
- Network Monitoring

  IpSwitch WhatsUp Professional 2005 (SP1) SQL Injection Vulnerability

  http://www.idefense.com/intelligence/vulnerabilities/display.php?id=268

  Multiple Vendor Cacti Remote File Inclusion Vulnerability

  http://www.idefense.com/intelligence/vulnerabilities/display.php?id=265

This is by no means a complete listing of all types of Web applications, but it should provide an indication of the types of applications that lend themselves to delivery over the Web and a sampling of the vulnerability types to which they may be susceptible.

## METHODS

Before we can begin fuzzing a Web application, we must first set up the target environment and then select the input vectors to target. Web applications present some unique challenges on both fronts. By design, the architecture of Web applications can be deployed across multiple networked machines. Although this enables the scalability necessary when deploying such applications in a production environment, it can also create performance hits that might not be desirable during fuzzing. Beyond this, Web application inputs can be disguised in numerous ways, yet all can lead to vulnerabilities. We must therefore be rather liberal when defining inputs that can be fuzzed.

## SET UP

Fuzzing in general requires the ability to send numerous inputs to the target in quick succession. The chain of events for a single input involves producing the input locally, sending it to the target application, allowing the input to be processed by the target, and then monitoring the results. The time required to run a fuzzer is therefore determined by the slowest point in this chain. When fuzzing a local application, the bottleneck in this process tends to be CPU cycles and hard drive read/write times. Given the speed provided by modern computer hardware, such times are minimal and fuzzing is therefore a viable approach for vulnerability research.

For Web application fuzzing, the bottleneck is typically caused by the transport of network packets from the fuzzer to the target. Consider the process of loading a Web page from a remote location. When you browse a Web page, the speed with which that page renders is determined by the speed of three variables: your computer, the server(s) on which the page resides, and the Internet connection between the two. You only have control over the first of the three variables, your local machine. Therefore, when fuzzing Web applications, it is important to improve the speed of network traffic by removing the other two variables. When possible, rather than running the target application on a remote server, host it locally so that packets never have to traverse a network in the first place. Most desktop operating systems such as Windows XP[10] or Linux have built in Web servers; therefore, it is generally an option to install and configure the target application on the local machine.

A virtual machine (VM) application such as VMWare[11] or Microsoft Virtual Machine[12] can also be a helpful tool when fuzzing Web applications. Using a virtual machine, the targeted Web application can be running in a VM instance while the fuzzer is running locally. This setup provides a few advantages not achieved by running the target application locally. First, the amount of resources consumed by the target application can be better managed through the VM. This ensures that the fuzzing process will not consume all machine resources. Additionally, network traffic resulting in system crashes and denial-of-service attacks will not affect the local machine where the fuzzer is running. After all, these are the exceptions that we're trying to detect and it's difficult to do so if the machine continually locks up.

## INPUTS

Before fuzzing can begin, we must first determine the various inputs that a Web application provides as these inputs will be the targets of our fuzzing activity. That begs this question: What do we consider to be an input? It is obvious that the data fields in a Web form would be considered inputs but what about the URL itself or cookies sent to the Web server? How about headers within a Web request? The answer is that all of these constitute inputs. For our purposes, an input is considered to be anything that is sent to and interpreted by the Web server.

We'll break all possible inputs down into categories in a minute, but let's first walk through the process of making a Web request to better understand what is going on behind the scenes. Most people access a Web page using a Web browser such as Microsoft

---

[10] http://www.microsoft.com/resources/documentation/windows/xp/all/proddocs/en-us/iiiisin2.mspx

[11] http://www.vmware.com

[12] http://www.microsoft.com/windows/virtualpc/default.mspx

Internet Explorer or Mozilla Firefox. When a Web browser is employed, accessing the contents of a Web page is as simple as typing a URL into the address bar.

However, a Web browser hides much of the activity that actually takes place when requesting a Web page. To better understand all of the activity, let's request a Web page but do so manually. We can do this by using the telnet application included in most modern operating systems. Telnet connects to a host and port of your choosing and then sends and receives TCP packets. To request a page, open a console window and issue the following commands:

```
telnet www.fuzzing.org 80[Return]
GET / HTTP/1.1[Return]
Host: www.fuzzing.org[Return]
[Return]
```

Let's break down this request. First, we launch the telnet application and provide it with two parameters: the server name (fuzzing.org) and the port (80) to connect to. By default, Telnet will connect to TCP port 23. However, because we're manually sending a request to a Web server, we need to force it to use TCP port 80. The next line represents the minimal request required by the HTTP protocol. First, we inform the server of the request method that we're using (GET). Different methods are described in detail later in the chapter. We then send the path and/or Web page that we're requesting. In this case, rather than requesting a specific Web page, we're asking for the default Web page provided by the server (/). On that same line, we also let the Web server know what version of the HTTP protocol that we'd like to use (HTTP/1.1). The next header specifies the host header, which although optional in HTTP 1.0, became mandatory in HTTP 1.1.[13] When this request is submitted (note that two carriage returns are required to complete the request), the server will return a response similar to the following:

```
HTTP/1.1 200 OK
Cache-Control: private
Content-Type: text/html
Set-Cookie: PREF=ID=56173d883ba96ae9:TM=1136763507:LM=1136763507:S=W43uFkQu1vexo
Pq-; expires=Sun, 17-Jan-2038 19:14:07 GMT; path=/; domain=.google.com
Server: GWS/2.1
Transfer-Encoding: chunked
Date: Sun, 08 Jan 2006 23:38:27 GMT

<html>
```

---

[13] http://rfc.net/rfc2616.html#s14.23

```
<head>
 <meta http-equiv= "content-type" content="text/html;charset=UTF-8">
 <title>Google</title>
 <style><!-
  body,td,a,p,.h{font-family:arial,sans-serif;}
  .h{font-size: 20px;}
  .q{color:#0000cc;}
  //->
 </style>
</head>
<body bgcolor=#ffffff text=#000000 link=#0000cc vlink=#551a8b
alink=#ff0000  topmargin=3 marginheight=3>
 <center>

[snip]

 <a href=http://www.google.com/intl/en/about.html>About Google</a>
 <span id=hp style="behavior:url(#default#homepage)"></span>
 </font><p><font size=-2>&copy;2006 Google</font></p></center>
 </body>
</html>
```

The response received is the HTML source for the Web page preceded by a series of headers that provide the Web browser with additional information about the response. If you were to save the HTML portion of the response to a file and open it with a Web browser, you would see the page that is displayed when simply surfing to the URL. There might, however, be missing images, assuming that relative links were used as opposed to absolute links.

We mentioned that the previous request represented the minimum format required for an HTTP request. What other inputs can we provide to a Web server? To answer that question, we'll start by sniffing the request sent when using the Internet Explorer Web browser. Using Ethereal, we're able to uncover the following request:

```
GET / HTTP/1.1
Accept: */*
Accept-Language: en-us
Accept-Encoding: gzip, deflate
User-Agent: Mozilla/4.0 (compatible; MSIE 6.0; Windows NT 5.1; SV1; .NET CLR 1.1.4322;
.NET CLR 2.0.50727)
Host: www.google.com
Connection: Keep-Alive
Cookie:
PREF=ID=32a1c6fa8d9e9a7a:FF=4:LD=en:NR=10:TM=1130820854:LM=1135410309:S=b9I4GWDAtclpmX
BF
```

What do all of the additional headers mean? The HTTP protocol defines many headers and each has a number of acceptable values. A complete breakdown of the HTTP/1.1 protocol is available in the 176-page RFC 2616—Hypertext Transfer Protocol—HTTP/1.1.[14] Rather than attempt to summarize the entire document, we'll instead go over the sample headers encountered previously:

- `Accept: */*`

  The `Accept` header specifies media types that can be used in the response. In this case we are stating that all media types (`*/*`) are acceptable. However, we could limit responses to such media types as text/html or image/jpeg.

- `Accept-Language: en-us`

  `Accept-Language` allows the user to specify the types of natural languages that can be used in the response. In our case we've asked for a response that uses U.S. English. The proper format for language tags is defined in RFC 1766—Tags for the Identification of Languages.[15]

- `Accept-Encoding: gzip, deflate`

  Once again, we're specifying an acceptable format for the response, but this time we're defining acceptable encoding schemes. The request that we've sent indicates that the gzip[16] or deflate[17] encoding algorithms can be used.

- `User-Agent: Mozilla/4.0 (compatible; MSIE 6.0; Windows NT 5.1; SV1; .NET CLR 1.1.4322; .NET CLR 2.0.50727)`

  `User-Agent` defines the client (Web browser) used to make this request. This is important to the server as it allows for responses to be tailored to the varying functionality supported by different browsers. The user-agent listed here defines Microsoft Internet Explorer 6.0 SP2 running on Windows XP SP2.

- `Host: www.google.com`

  This header defines the host and port that is serving the requested Web page. If the port is not included, the server will assume the default port for the Web service. This field is important to the server as multiple hostnames can be served from a single IP address.

---

[14] http://rfc.net/rfc2616.html

[15] http://rfc.net/rfc1766.html

[16] http://rfc.net/rfc1952.html

[17] http://rfc.net/rfc1951.html

- Connection: Keep-Alive

  The Connection header allows the client to specify various options that are desired for the connection. A persistent connection allows multiple requests to be made without opening a separate connection for each request. Connection: close would indicate the connection should be immediately closed once the response is sent.

- Cookie: PREF=ID=32b1c6fa8e9e9a7a:FF=4:LD=en:NR=10:TM=1130820854: LM=1135410309:S=b9I4GWDAtc2pmXBF

  Cookies can be stored for a specified period of time on a computer's local hard drive or in memory, in which case they will be discarded when the current session is complete. Cookies allow a server to recognize the requestor. This enables a site to track a user's surfing habits and potentially customize the Web page for the user. If a cookie exists locally for a particular Web site, the browser will submit it to the server when the request is made.

Now that we've walked through an example request, we're in a better position to define the different inputs available for Web application fuzzing. As mentioned, any portion of the data sent in a request to a Web server can be considered an input. At a high level, this includes the request method, the request Uniform Resource Identifier (URI), the HTTP protocol version, all HTTP headers, and post data. In the following sections, we break each of the following components down and determine appropriate fuzzing variables for each:

```
[Method] [Request-URI] HTTP/[Major Version].[Minor Version]
[HTTP Headers]

[Post Data]
```

## Method

The GET and POST methods are most commonly used to request a Web page. These methods utilize name–value pairs that represent a means for requesting specific content from a Web server. Think of them as the variables in a Web request. The GET method submits name–value pairs to the Web server within the Request URI. For example, http://www.google.com/search?as_q=security&num=10 will submit a request to the Google search engine letting it know that we want to search for the word *security* (as_q=security) and have 10 results returned per page (num=10). When the GET method is used, name–value pairs are appended to the URI following the ? character and different name–value pairs are separated by the & character.

Name–value pairs can also be submitted using the POST method. When this approach is taken, name–value pairs are submitted as HTTP headers, following other standard HTTP headers. An advantage to using the POST method is that values of any size can be sent. Although the HTTP specification does not specifically limit the overall length of a URI, Web servers and Web browsers often impose a limit. Web servers will return a 414 (Request-URI Too Long) status if a URI exceeds the expected length. A downside to using the POST method is that a URI cannot be shared to direct another person to a dynamically generated page simply by forwarding the URI. For example, people often share maps and directions by forwarding the Google Maps URI that is generated following a particular search. Any guess on where the following map will lead you?

http://maps.google.com/maps?hl=en&q=1600+Pennsylvania+Ave&near=20500

As mentioned, there are a number of other methods that can be used in a Web server request. Here is a brief description of other valid methods:

- HEAD: Identical to the GET method but the server returns only the response headers and not the HTML content of the requested Web page.

- PUT: Allows a user to upload data to a Web server. Although this method is not widely supported, vulnerabilities have been discovered when the PUT method is supported but improperly implemented. For example, the security fix introduced by Microsoft Security Bulletin MS05-006[18] quietly fixed just such a vulnerability. It was discovered that unauthenticated users could upload data to a Microsoft SharePoint server using the PUT method.[19]

- DELETE: Allows the user to request a resource be deleted from the Web server. Once again, although this method is not widely implemented, testing should ensure that it is not unknowingly supported. Exposing this method improperly could allow an attacker to deny access to legitimate users by deleting resources from the Web server.

- TRACE: Allows a client to submit a request that is then echoed back to the requesting client. This can be useful when attempting to debug connectivity issues as you can see the structure of the request that actually made it to the server. In January 2003, Jeremiah Grossman of WhiteHat Security released a whitepaper entitled "Cross-Site Tracing (XST),"[20] which revealed how client-side scripting could be leveraged to allow malicious Web servers to gain access to cookie values for third-party Web servers that supported the TRACE method. Once again, testing should identify situations where the TRACE method is unknowingly supported.

---

[18] http://www.microsoft.com/technet/security/Bulletin/MS05-006.mspx

[19] http://support.microsoft.com/kb/887981

[20] http://www.cgisecurity.com/whitehat-mirror/WH-WhitePaper_XST_ebook.pdf

- CONNECT: Reserved for use with a proxy that can dynamically switch to being a tunnel.
- OPTIONS: Allows clients to query the Web server to determine the standard and proprietary methods that the server supports. It can be leveraged by vulnerability scanners to determine if potentially vulnerable methods are implemented.

The OPTIONS method could, for example, be used to determine if a Web server was running a version of Internet Information Services (IIS) that was susceptible to a serious vulnerability in WebDAV, a set of extensions to the HTTP protocol that better facilitate the publication of Web content. The vulnerability in question is detailed in MS03-007[21] (Unchecked Buffer in Windows Component Could Cause Server Compromise). When issuing a request of OPTIONS * HTTP/1.0, a server supporting the OPTIONS method will return the following responses identifying whether or not WebDAV is enabled.[22] The following server response would indicate that WebDAV is not enabled as none of the WebDAV extensions are listed in the Public header:

```
HTTP/1.1 200 OK
Server: Microsoft-IIS/5.0
Date: Mon, 17 Mar 2003 21:49:00 GMT
Public: OPTIONS, TRACE, GET, HEAD, POST
Content-Length: 0
```

This next response includes a whole host of additional headers that include extensions provided by WebDAV. Seeing that WebDAV is enabled on a server running Microsoft IIS 5.0 suggests that the server could be vulnerable to MS03-007, if the appropriate patches haven't been implemented.

```
HTTP/1.1 200 OK
Server: Microsoft-IIS/5.0
Date: Mon, 17 Mar 2003 21:49:00 GMT
Content-Length: 0
Accept-Ranges: bytes
DASL:
DAV: 1, 2
Public: OPTIONS, TRACE, GET, HEAD, DELETE, PUT, POST, COPY, MOVE, MKCOL, PROPFIND,
PROPPATCH, LOCK, UNLOCK, SEARCH
```

---

[21] http://www.microsoft.com/technet/security/bulletin/MS03-007.mspx

[22] http://www.klcconsulting.net/articles/webdav/webdav_vuln.htm

```
Allow: OPTIONS, TRACE, GET, HEAD, DELETE, PUT, POST, COPY, MOVE, MKCOL, PROPFIND,
PROPPATCH, LOCK, UNLOCK, SEARCH
Cache-Control: private
```

### *Request-URI*

After the method, the client passes the request-URI to the Web server. The purpose of the request-URI is to identify the resource (Web page) that is being requested. It can take the format of an absolute URI (e.g., http://www.target.com/page.html) or a relative URI (/page.html). Additionally, the server itself can be identified instead of a specific resource on the server. This is done using the * character and is required for the OPTIONS method.

When fuzzing the request URI, each segment of the URI can be fuzzed. Take the following relative path as an example:

```
/dir/page.html?name1=value1&name2=value2
```

It can be broken into the following components:

```
/[path]/[page].[extension]?[name]=[value]&[name]=[value]
```

Each of the separate components can and should be fuzzed. Some should be fuzzed with known values that have lead to previous vulnerabilities, whereas others should be provided random values to determine if the server gracefully handles unexpected requests. The random content should also include large volumes of data to determine if buffer overflows result when the server parses and interprets the data. We'll look at each of the components individually:

- *Path.* The most common vulnerabilities uncovered when fuzzing the path component are buffer overflows and directory traversal attacks. Buffer overflows are most likely to be identified when sending large volumes of data, and directory traversals can be uncovered by sending successive ../ character sequences. Different encoding schemes should also be employed in an effort to bypass input validation routines that might be done prior to the request being decoded.
  - *Buffer overflow example.* Macromedia JRun 4 Web Server prior to the JRun 4 Updater 5 release was susceptible to a stack-based buffer overflow when receiving an overly long path.[23] The vulnerability is triggered when the path exceeds

---

[23] http://www.idefense.com/intelligence/vulnerabilities/display.php?id=360

approximately 65,536 characters. This illustrates the need to include very large variables when fuzzing.

- *Directory traversal example.* A vulnerability in 3Com's Network Supervisor application provides a classic example of a directory traversal vulnerability.[24] The application enables a Web server that listens on TCP port 21700 and it was discovered that in Network Supervisor 5.0.2 and earlier a simple URL containing successive `../` sequences would allow a user to break out of the webroot directory. It should be noted that vulnerabilities such as this are actually vulnerabilities in the server as opposed to the application.

- *Page.* Fuzzing for common page names might reveal sensitive pages that are not properly secured or once again, lead to buffer overflow vulnerabilities.

  - *Buffer overflow example.* Microsoft IIS 4.0 suffered from a stack-based buffer overflow when overly long requests were made to files with .htr, .stm, and .idc file extensions. This vulnerability was detailed in Microsoft Security Bulletin MS99-019[25] and led to a host of public exploits.

  - *Information leakage example.* The 3Com OfficeConnect Wireless 11g Access Point contained a vulnerability whereby sensitive Web pages could be accessed on the Web-based administrative interface without having to provide appropriate authentication credentials.[26] Therefore, requesting a page such as `/main/config.bin` would reveal the contents of the page as opposed to a login prompt, and include information including the administrative username and password. Nikto[27] is an example of an application that searches for this type of vulnerability by sending repeated requests to a Web server to uncover common and possibly unsecured Web pages.

- *Extension.* As with local files, Web pages typically have file extensions identifying the technology to produce the page. Examples of Web page extensions include *.html (HyperText Markup Language), *.asp (Active Server Page), or *.php (Hypertext Preprocessor). Vulnerabilities have been uncovered in Web servers when requests are made for pages with unknown extensions.

- *Name.* Fuzzing common name components could lead to the discovery of undocumented variables that can be passed to the server. Alternately, sending unexpected

---

[24] http://www.idefense.com/intelligence/vulnerabilities/display.php?id=300

[25] http://www.microsoft.com/technet/security/bulletin/MS99-019.mspx

[26] http://www.idefense.com/intelligence/vulnerabilities/display.php?id=188

[27] http://www.cirt.net/code/nikto.shtml

variables might cause the application to malfunction if it doesn't have adequate error handling.

- *Value.* The appropriate approach to fuzzing the value component is dependent on the variable type expected by the Web application. For example, if the name–value pair in question for the legitimate request was `length=50` it would seem logical to fuzz the value component with overly large or small numerical values. For example, what happens if the length submitted is smaller that than the actual length of the data? What happens when the value is zero or even negative? Perhaps a value larger than what the application is designed to handle will cause an application crash or an integer overflow. Fuzzing can be used to find these answers. If the value component expects string content, try sending unexpected string values to see if the application handles them gracefully. Last but not least, fill the value component with increasingly large amounts of data to see if a buffer overflow or crash results.

- *Separator.* Even characters as seemingly benign as the separators between the various components (/, =, &, ., :, etc.) should be targeted for fuzzing. These characters are parsed by the Web server or application, and improper error handling could lead to exploitable conditions if the server is unable to handle unexpected values.

### Protocol

Numeric variables can be used to fuzz the HTTP protocol version to submit supported and unsupported HTTP protocol versions, which could uncover server vulnerabilities. The most current stable HTTP protocol version is HTTP/1.1. The HTTP protocol is divided into a major and minor version (`HTTP/[major].[minor]`).

### Headers

Any and all request headers can and should be fuzzed. Request headers adhere to the following format:

```
[Header name]: [Header value]
```

Therefore, there are three possible variables to be fuzzed: the name, the value, and the separator (`:`). Names should be fuzzed with known legitimate values to determine if the Web application supports undocumented headers. A listing of headers that adhere to the various HTTP protocols can be found in the following RFCs:

- RFC 1945–Hypertext Transfer Protocol—HTTP/1.0[28]
- RFC 2616–Hypertext Transfer Protocol—HTTP/1.1[29]

Values can be fuzzed to determine if the application can gracefully handle unexpected values.

---

**HEAP OVERFLOW EXAMPLE**

In January 2006, iDefense Labs published details of a remotely exploitable heap overflow vulnerability in Novell SUSE Linux Enterprise Server 9.[30] The vulnerability could be triggered simply by submitting a POST request with a negative value in the Content-Length header. An example of a request that would trigger the overflow is shown here:

```
POST / HTTP/1.0
Content-Length: -900

[Data to overwrite the heap]
```

---

### Cookies

Cookies are stored locally and are submitted as an HTTP header when a request is sent to a Web server for which a cookie was previously saved. The format for a cookie is as follows:

```
Cookie: [Name1]=[Value1]; [Name2]=[Value2] ...
```

Once again, the name, value, and separators should be fuzzed. As with other values, fuzzed values should be influenced by the type of variable that would be submitted in a legitimate request.

---

[28] http://rfc.net/rfc1945.html

[29] http://rfc.net/rfc2616.html

[30] http://labs.idefense.com/intelligence/vulnerabilities/display.php?id=371

## Post Data

As mentioned previously, name–value pairs can be submitted to the Web server either within the request URI using the GET method or as separate HTTP headers using the POST method. Post data is sent in the following format:

```
[Name1]=[Value1]&[Name2]=[Value2]
```

### BUFFER OVERFLOW EXAMPLE

Greg MacManus of iDefense Labs discovered a buffer overflow vulnerability in the Web server included with the popular Linksys WRT54G wireless router.[31] He found that sending a POST request to the apply.cgi page with a content length longer than 10,000 bytes would result in an exploitable buffer overflow. Although such a vulnerability would typically be difficult to exploit on an embedded Web server, the open source nature of the firmware for the device and the availability of modified firmware with development tools aided in the development of proof of concept exploit code.

## Identifying Inputs

We now know the structure of requests made to Web applications and the various components of those requests that can be considered as individual input variables and therefore potential targets for fuzzing. The next step is conducting reconnaissance to identify all of the different legitimate input values. This can be done either manually or in an automated fashion. Regardless of the approach, we want to make our coverage as complete as possible. When studying the application, our goal should be to document all of the following inputs:

- Web pages
- Directories
- Methods supported by pages
- Web forms
  - Name–value pairs
  - Hidden fields

---

[31] http://www.idefense.com/intelligence/vulnerabilities/display.php?id=305

- Headers
- Cookies

The simplest and least efficient means of identifying the aforementioned inputs involves simply surfing the Web page using a Web browser and viewing the page source. Within the source you can look for the inputs included in Web forms. Be sure and look for hidden fields (input type="hidden") as lazy application developers sometimes use hidden fields as a means of implementing security through obscurity. They might assume that you won't test such fields as they're not readily visible on the page. This is obviously an extremely weak control as hidden fields can always be viewed within the page source.

When identifying inputs using a Web browser, you will not be able to see the request/response headers. For example, you won't see the structure of cookies being passed to the application server as these are included in the HTTP headers and are automatically passed by the browser. To view the raw HTTP requests you can always employ a network protocol analyzer such as Wireshark.[32]

Even with a Web browser and a sniffer, manually identifying all possible inputs for a Web application is impractical once the application exceeds more than a few Web pages. Fortunately, tracing through a Web application can be automated using a Web spider. A Web spider (or Web crawler) is an application that identifies all hyperlinks within a Web page, traverses those links, finds additional hyperlinks, and continues the process until all possible Web pages have been visited. Along the way, it can document information that is of importance to a security researcher such as the inputs mentioned earlier. Fortunately, there are many free or open source spiders that have excellent functionality. A simple, yet powerful Web spider is the wget[33] utility. Although originally designed for the UNIX operating system, ports of wget are also available for the win32 platform.[34] Another free spider that we would recommend is included within WebScarab.[35] The WebScarab project is collection of tools provided by the Open Web Application Security Project (OWASP) that are useful when analyzing Web applications. Among the many WebScarab utilities is a spider that can be leveraged to automatically identify URLs throughout the application. Another useful WebScarab tool is a proxy server that comes in handy during manual page audits. If you set up your Web browser to utilize the

---

[32] http://wireshark.org/

[33] http://www.gnu.org/software/wget/

[34] http://gnuwin32.sourceforge.net/packages/wget.htm

[35] http://www.owasp.org/software/webscarab.html

WebScarab proxy, it will record all raw requests/responses as you surf the application. It even includes a very basic Web fuzzer, but in the next chapter, we discuss how to build a more powerful one.

## VULNERABILITIES

Web applications are susceptible to a wide variety of vulnerabilities, all of which can be identified through fuzzing. The following list highlights standard vulnerability classifications:

- *Denial-of-service (DoS):* DoS attacks on Web applications present a significant threat. Although a DoS attack will not provide an attacker with access to a target, denying access to a site that is the external portal to your corporation and perhaps a source of income can cause substantial financial damage.

- *Cross-site scripting (XSS).* According to Mitre, in 2006, XSS vulnerabilities accounted for 21.5 percent of new vulnerabilities discovered.[36] That makes XSS vulnerabilities the most prevalent, not just among Web applications, but among all applications. XSS vulnerabilities were once considered to be more of a nuisance than a security threat, but that has all changed with the explosive growth of phishing attacks. XSS holes provide an attacker with the ability to control client-side actions in a Web browser and are therefore a valuable tool for those conducting such attacks.

- *SQL injection:* Of Web application vulnerabilities, SQL injection is not only one of the most prevalent weaknesses, but also one of the most critical. The 2006 Mitre statistics indicate that SQL injection claimed the number two spot, accounting for 14 percent of new vulnerabilities. The prevalence is driven both by the growth in dynamic Web sites powered by relational databases but also by insecure SQL coding practices that are still taught in the majority of textbooks. Some mistakenly believe that SQL injection is limited to an attack that provides an avenue to read database records and is therefore purely a confidentiality risk. With the advent of the powerful stored procedures supported by most relational databases, SQL injection is a far greater risk that can lead to the full compromise of a trusted back-end system.

- *Directory traversal/Weak access control*: Directory traversal attacks were once relatively common but are now fortunately a dying breed. Weak access controls on the other hand remain a threat, as it doesn't take much for a developer to forget about a

---

[36] http://cwe.mitre.org/documents/vuln-trends.html#table1

restricted page or directory and fail to apply appropriate access controls. This is one of the many reasons that Web applications should be continually audited not just prior to their release into the production environment but also throughout their lifetime. A once secure Web application can suddenly be left wide open by a mistaken configuration change on the server that removes or weakens access controls.

- *Weak authentication:* There are no shortage of authentication schemes to choose from and all can be insecure if not implemented properly. Weak passwords are vulnerable to brute force attacks and passing credentials in clear text leaves them vulnerable to capture on the wire. Although these mistakes are typically easy to detect with basic due diligence, the greater challenge comes when understanding the business logic of the application to ensure that developers have not mistakenly left an entry way into the application that can bypass the authentication controls.

- *Weak session management.* Given that HTTP is a stateless protocol, some form of state management is necessary to be able to differentiate among concurrent users and not require input authentication credentials on each and every page. Whether unique session tokens are passed via cookies, within the URI, or in the page data itself is less important than how they are structured and secured. Cookies should be sufficiently random and of a size that makes brute force attacks impractical. Additionally, they must expire frequently enough to guard against replay attacks.

- *Buffer overflow.* Buffer overflow attacks are less common in Web applications than desktop and server applications. This can be credited primarily to the languages generally used for Web application development such as C# or Java, which have memory management controls that lessen the risk of buffer overflows. That is not to say, however, that buffer overflows should be ignored when fuzzing. It is quite possible that the application passes user-supplied input to a separate application written in C or C++ that is susceptible to an overflow. Beyond that, keep in mind when fuzzing that you have at least two targets: the Web application and the Web server. Web servers, on the other hand, are often written in languages susceptible to buffer overflows.

- *Improperly supported HTTP methods.* In general, Web applications handle GET and POST requests. As discussed previously, however, there are numerous other RFC-compliant and third-party methods. If not properly implemented, they can allow an attacker to manipulate data on the server or obtain valuable information for subsequent attacks. Fuzzing should therefore be used to identify all supported methods to determine if they are appropriately implemented.

- *Remote command execution.* Web servers might simply pass user-supplied inputs to other applications or the operating system itself. If these inputs are not appropriately validated they can provide an attacker with the ability to directly execute commands on the target system. PHP and Perl applications have traditionally been especially prone to such attacks.

- *Remote code injection.* Once again, this vulnerability tends to plague PHP applications. A poor coding practice that is seen far too often involves allowing unsanitized user input to be passed to a method such as `include()` or `require()`, which allows for the inclusion of PHP code from local or remote locations. When user input is blindly passed to such methods, it allows attackers to inject their own PHP code into the target application. PHP file inclusion vulnerabilities claimed the number three spot in Mitre's 2006 statistics with 9.5 percent of new vulnerabilities.

- *Vulnerable libraries.* Developers often mistakenly trust third-party libraries that are included in an application. Any code included in a Web application, whether written from scratch or precompiled and obtained from a third party, is potentially vulnerable code and must undergo the same level of scrutiny when testing for security defects. At a minimum, vulnerability archives should be checked to ensure that included libraries don't have known vulnerabilities. Beyond that, they should be subjected to the same level of fuzzing and other security tests as home-grown code.

- *HTTP response splitting.* HTTP response splitting first gained widespread recognition with the release of the Sanctum Inc. whitepaper "Divide and Conquer."[37] This attack is made possible when a user has the ability to inject a CRLF sequence into the response headers. This in turn provides the attacker with the ability to craft the response provided by the Web server and can lead to a variety of attacks including Web proxy and browser cache poisoning.

- *Cross Site Request Forgery (CSRF).* CSRF attacks are difficult to protect against and represent a growing threat. When a victim has an active session a CSRF vulnerability exists if an attacker can cause the victim to perform some action simply by convincing the victim to click on a link, perhaps in an e-mail message. For example, at a bank Web site a request to transfer funds might be done by submitting a Web form that includes the account information and the amount to transfer. Only the owner of that account can make the transfer, as that is the only person that has the ability to login with his or her credentials. However, if that individual is already logged in and unknowingly clicks on a link that forwards that same Web form data to the bank Web site that same transfer could occur without the victim's knowledge. To protect against CSRF attacks, Web sites often require that the user reauthenticate or perform some manual task prior to performing a sensitive action such as transferring funds. Web sites are also beginning to implement nonce (one time) values in web forms in order to validate the source of the form.

---

[37] http://www.packetstormsecurity.org/papers/general/whitepaper_httpresponse.pdf

Although this is not a complete list of all possible Web application vulnerabilities, it illustrates that Web applications are susceptible to a wide range of vulnerabilities. It also demonstrates that while some of the same vulnerabilities that affect local applications also affect Web applications, many attacks are specific to the Web application world. For the purpose of discovering Web application vulnerabilities through fuzzing, inputs must be submitted via HTTP and different mechanisms must be used for detecting errors when compared to fuzzing local applications. For a more complete list of Web application threats, we recommend the Web Application Security Consortium's Threat Classification project.[38]

## DETECTION

Detecting exceptions when fuzzing Web applications is one of the more significant challenges for this class of fuzzing. It does us little good if we leave a Web fuzzer running overnight and find that the application has crashed due to one of the more than 10,000 requests that it received. We would know that a vulnerable condition exists, but we would have no way of re-creating it. Therefore, it is important to look at the following data, which can be used to identify potentially vulnerable conditions:

- *HTTP Status codes.* When a Web server responds to a request, it includes a three-digit code to identify the status of the request. A complete list of status codes can be found in section 10 of RFC 2616–Hypertext Transfer Protocol—HTTP/1.1.[39] These status codes can provide clues as to which fuzzed requests require further investigation. For example, a series of 500 Internal Server Errors might suggest that previous fuzzed requests have caused the server to malfunction. Alternately, a 401 Unauthorized error suggests that a requested page exists, but is password protected.

- *Web server error messages.* The Web application might be designed to display an error message directly in the page content. Using regular expressions to parse through the HTML included in the response can reveal such messages.

- *Dropped connections.* Should one of the fuzzed inputs cause the Web server to freeze or crash, it is likely that subsequent requests will not be able to successfully connect to the server. Therefore, fuzzing tools should maintain log files to record when a broken pipe or failed connection has occurred. When reviewing the log files and identifying a string of bad connection attempts, look to one of the requests immediately preceding the log entries to identify the culprit.

---

[38] http://www.webappsec.org/projects/threat/

[39] http://rfc.net/rfc2616.html

- *Log files.* Most Web servers can be configured to log various types of errors. Once again, these logs can provide clues as to which fuzzing requests are causing problems that could lead to an exploitable condition. The challenge with log files is that they can't be directly tied to the request that caused the error. One option to help tie requests to error logs is to synchronize the clocks of both the attacking and target machines and look at the timestamps of both the requests and the log entries, although this will only narrow the list of possible culprits. It is not accurate enough to definitively tie a fuzz request to the error that it caused.
- *Event logs.* Event logs are similar to Web server logs in that they are not directly tied to the requests that caused them but can be correlated to a certain extent via time-stamps. Event logs are used by Microsoft Windows operating systems and can be accessed using the Event Viewer application.
- *Debuggers.* The best way to identify handled and unhandled exceptions is to attach the target application to a debugger prior to fuzzing. Error handling might prevent obvious signs of many errors caused by fuzzing, but these can generally be detected using a debugger. It is important to look for handled as well as unhandled exceptions as certain types of errors such as null pointer dereferences and format strings might cause handled exceptions but could be made into exploitable vulnerabilities given appropriate input values. As always, the biggest challenge is in determining which request caused the exception. Debuggers however have limited effectiveness when fuzzing web applications as they can detect server exceptions but not exceptions at the application layer.

## SUMMARY

In this chapter, we have defined Web application and Web server fuzzing and learned how it can be used to uncover vulnerabilities in Web applications. This required gaining a thorough understanding of how Web browsers submit requests and how Web servers respond to them. From this knowledge we were able to identify all of the subtle inputs that can be controlled and manipulated by the end user. It is these inputs that can be fuzzed to uncover vulnerabilities with appropriate monitoring to identify potential exceptions. In the next chapter we will build a Web application fuzzer to automate the processes that have been discussed thus far.

# Web Application and Server Fuzzing: Automation

*"The most important thing is for us to find Osama bin Laden. It is our number one priority and we will not rest until we find him."*

—George W. Bush, Washington, DC, September 13, 2001

*"I don't know where bin Laden is. I have no idea and really don't care. It's not that important. It's not our priority."*

—George W. Bush, Washington, DC, March 13, 2002

Now that we've discussed how Web applications could be fuzzed, it's time to put our theories to the test. In this chapter, we take what we learned in the background chapter and apply it by developing WebFuzz, a graphical Web application fuzzer. We start by planning the design of the application and identifying any unique challenges that we'll face. We can then move onto the selection of an appropriate development platform and begin building the fuzzer. Once development is complete, our work won't yet be done. When building a vulnerability discovery tool you should never consider development complete until you've used it to find vulnerabilities. You wouldn't build a car without test driving it would you? We'll therefore walk through a number of different classes of known Web application vulnerabilities to determine if WebFuzz would be able to uncover them.

## WEB APPLICATION FUZZERS

The concept of Web application fuzzing is not new. Various fuzzers exist and the list is continuing to grow. Here is a listing of some popular freeware and commercial Web application fuzzers:

- *SPIKE Proxy.*[1] Developed by Dave Aitel, SPIKE Proxy is a browser-based Web fuzzer written in Python. It acts as a proxy, capturing Web browser requests, and then allows you to run a series of predefined audits against a target Web site in an effort to identify various vulnerabilities such as SQL injection, buffer overflows, and XSS. Being built on an open source framework, SPIKE Proxy can be further extended to fuzz various targets. SPIKE Proxy isn't exclusively a fuzzer; rather it is a combination of a vulnerability scanner and a fuzzer. Figure 10.1 displays a screenshot of SPIKE Proxy.

- *WebScarab.*[2] The Open Web Application Security Project (OWASP) makes available various tools for testing the security of Web applications including WebScarab. Although more of an overall Web application security-testing tool, WebScarab does contain a basic fuzzer for injecting fuzzed values into application parameters.

- *SPI Fuzzer.*[3] SPI Fuzzer is a component of the SPI Toolkit, which is itself part of the WebInspect application. WebInspect is a commercial tool developed by SPI Dynamics, designed to provide a comprehensive set of tools for testing Web applications.

- *Codenomicon HTTP Test Tools.*[4] Codenomicon produces commercial fuzzing test suites for just about every protocol imaginable, including HTTP.

- *beSTORM.*[5] Like Codenomicon, Beyond Security has built a business around the development of commercial fuzzers. beSTORM is a fuzzer that can handle various Internet protocols, including HTTP.

WebFuzz was inspired by the commercial tool SPI Fuzzer. SPI Fuzzer is a simple but well-designed graphical Web application fuzzer that provides a user with complete control over the raw HTTP requests that are used for fuzzing. It requires a basic knowledge

---

[1]  http://www.immunitysec.com/resources-freesoftware.shtml

[2]  http://www.owasp.org/index.php/Category:OWASP_WebScarab_Project

[3]  http://www.spidynamics.com/products/webinspect/toolkit.html

[4]  http://www.codenomicon.com/products/internet/http/

[5]  http://www.beyondsecurity.com/BeStorm_Info.htm

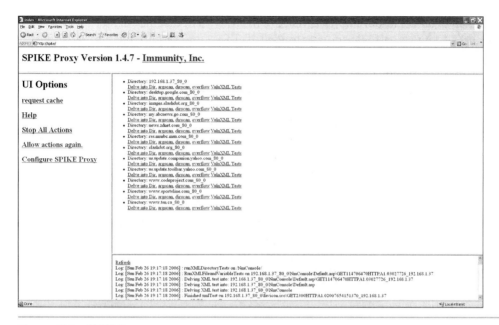

**Figure 10.1** SPIKE Proxy

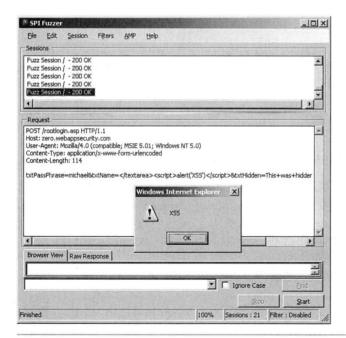

**Figure 10.2** SPI Fuzzer

of the HTTP protocol to develop tests that are likely to yield results. Such knowledge is also required to interpret the responses to identify those that require further investigation. Figure 10.2 shows SPI Fuzzer.

The primary downside to SPI Fuzzer is that fact that it is only available as a component of a rather expensive commercial application. We have built on the lessons learned from SPI Fuzzer to create a limited but open source alternative to meet our specific needs in WebFuzz. As with most fuzzers, WebFuzz is not a point-and-click, walk away and all the work is done for you security tool. It is simply a tool to automate what would otherwise need to be done manually. It is up to you as the end user to leverage it to develop meaningful tests and interpret the results. It should also be seen as a starting point, not a final solution.

As with all of the tools developed for this book, WebFuzz is an open source application. It therefore provides a framework that can and should be built on. We encourage you to add functionality and fix bugs, but most important, we hope that you will share your improvements with the rest of the world. The remainder of this chapter details the development of WebFuzz and walks through various case studies to demonstrate its capabilities and limitations. WebFuzz can be downloaded from this book's Web site at www.fuzzing.org.

## FEATURES

Before we dive into building our own fuzzer, let's first consider what we learned in the last chapter about how the HTTP protocol functions and use that knowledge to determine the features that our fuzzer will require.

## REQUESTS

Let's start at the beginning. You can't fuzz a Web application unless you have a way to send it requests. In general, we use a Web browser when communicating with a Web server. After all, it knows how to speak the lingo (HTTP) and takes care of all the messy details in putting together an HTTP request. When fuzzing, however, we want the messy details. We want to be able to roll up our sleeves and alter every aspect of the request. For this reason, we have chosen to expose the raw request to the end user and allow for any portion of it to be fuzzed.

Figure 10.3 displays a basic WebFuzz request. The request consists of the following fields:

- *Host.* The name or IP address of the target machine is a required field. We can't fuzz a Web application without letting WebFuzz know where to send the request. This is not a fuzzable field.

- *Port.* While Web applications run on TCP port 80 by default, they can just as easily run on any TCP port. It is actually common for Web applications designed to provide Web-based administration consoles to run on an alternate port to not interfere with the main Web server. As with the hostname, the port field exists to tell WebFuzz where to send the request and is not a fuzzable field.

- *Timeout.* Because we're purposely sending nonstandard Web requests, it won't be uncommon for the target application not to respond in a timely fashion, if at all. We have therefore included a user-definable timeout value measured in milliseconds. When recording the resulting response for a request that timed out, it will be important that we record that fact as it could indicate that our request has knocked the target offline, resulting in a potential DoS vulnerability.

- *Request Headers.* This is where the rubber hits the road. When using a Web browser, the end user has control over the target host, port, and request URI, but not all of the various headers. We have intentionally kept all components of the request in a single writable text field because we want the end user to be able to control every aspect of the request. The request can be built manually by simply typing the desired request into the Request Headers field. Alternately, if you prefer a point-and-click solution, headers can also be pieced together using the list of standard headers provided in the context menu as shown in Figure 10.3. One last option allows for the Default Headers to be selected from the context menu if a basic request of the default Web page is desired.

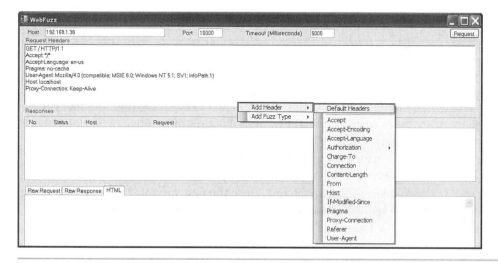

**Figure 10.3**   WebFuzz request

## FUZZ VARIABLES

We refer to fuzz variables as the areas within the request that will be replaced by fuzz data. As discussed, the user has full control over the raw request sent to the Web server. Therefore, fuzz variables are added directly to the raw request and are identified by variable names enclosed in square brackets (e.g., [Overflow]). When designing the functions to create fuzz variables we have chosen to divide them into two basic types: static lists or generated variables. Static lists are fuzz variables pulled from a predefined list of data. An example of a static list would be fuzz data used to identify XSS vulnerabilities. A predefined list of various inputs that could lead to XSS vulnerabilities (e.g., <script>alert('XSS')</script>) is compiled and the data is injected one line at a time into the request. The static lists are intentionally maintained as external ASCII text files so that users can modify the variables without needing to recompile the application. Generated fuzz variables, on the other hand, are built from predefined algorithms that might allow for input from the user. The Overflow variable is an example of a generated fuzz variable. An overflow allows the user to define the text used for the overflow, its length, and the number of times that it is repeated. Figure 10.4 illustrates the default pop-up window that allows the inputs for the overflow variable to be altered.

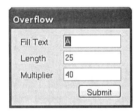

**Figure 10.4**    Overflow fuzz variable

To be efficient, we might wish to define multiple fuzz variables within a single request. Although there are times when you might want to dynamically change two or more variables at the same time (e.g., a length value along with the content that it describes), for the sake of simplicity we have chosen to handle only one variable at a time, but it is possible to include multiple fuzz variables in a single request. WebFuzz will handle the first encountered fuzz variable and ignore the rest. Once the first variable has been completely fuzzed, it will be removed from the raw request so that WebFuzz can move on to subsequent variables. The following WebFuzz request demonstrates a request designed to identify a number of common vulnerabilities in one shot.

```
[Methods] /file.php?var1=[XSS][SQL]&var2=[Format] HTTP/1.1
Accept: */*
Accept-Language: en-us
User-Agent: Mozilla/4.0
Host: [Overflow]
Proxy-Connection: Keep-Alive
```

## RESPONSES

WebFuzz captures and archives all resulting responses in a raw format. By capturing the full raw response, we have the flexibility to display the responses in various formats. Specifically, we enable the user to display raw results or view the HTML within a Web browser control. Figure 10.5 shows a raw response and Figure 10.6 shows the same data within a Web browser. This is important, as clues to existing vulnerabilities can arrive in various forms. For example, the headers might include a status code (e.g., 500 – Internal Error) suggesting that a DoS has occurred. Alternately, the Web page itself might display a customer error message suggesting that SQL injection is possible. In this case, the error will be easier to see when a browser interprets the HTML.

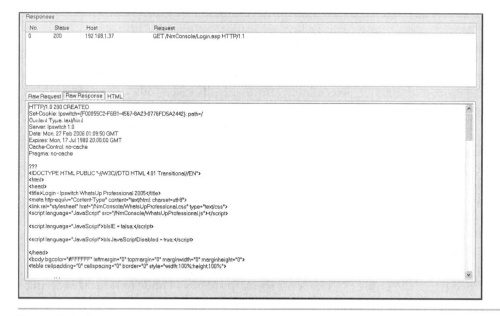

**Figure 10.5** Raw response

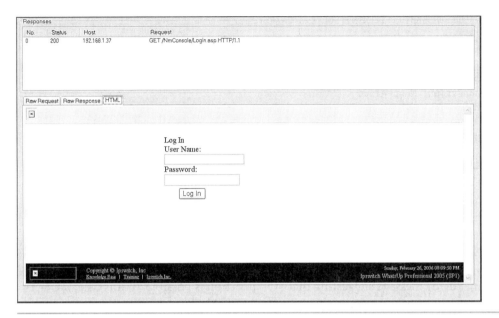

**Figure 10.6**   HTML formatted response

## NECESSARY BACKGROUND INFORMATION

HTTP provides some unique challenges both in terms of determining how best to monitor traffic and more important, in determining how to identify exceptions when they occur. Next, we'll pull back the curtains to determine what is going on behind the Web browser.

### IDENTIFYING REQUESTS

WebFuzz requires the user to build a raw HTTP request, but how do you identify appropriate requests for a given Web application? What Web pages exist? What variables can those pages receive and how should the variables be passed? In the last chapter, we discussed how inputs could be identified manually or through the use of sniffers, spiders, and proxies. Before we continue, we'd like to introduce a Web browser plug-in that can come in handy when working with WebFuzz and needing to identify the raw request for a single Web page. The LiveHTTPHeaders project[6] provides a handy tool for identifying raw HTTP requests within Mozilla-based Web browsers. Figure 10.7 shows

---

[6]   http://livehttpheaders.mozdev.org/

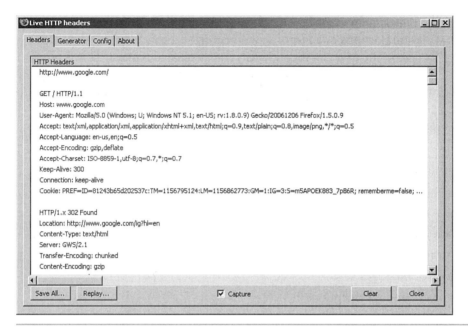

**Figure 10.7**   LiveHTTPHeaders

LiveHTTPHeaders being used to display all requests and their associated responses in the Firefox sidebar. A nice advantage of using this approach is that a request can be captured and then cut and pasted directly into WebFuzz to streamline the creation of a fuzzed request. Various other browser plug-ins exist, such as Tamper Data[7] or Firebug,[8] which are also Firefox extensions, or Fiddler,[9] a browser add-on for Internet Explorer, but LiveHTTPHeaders is a favorite due to its simplicity.

## DETECTION

As discussed previously, the response sent back from the targeted application can provide various clues about the impact of the initial fuzzed request. WebFuzz is designed to provide the user with detection data, but it is up to the user to interpret the responses.

---

[7]   https://addons.mozilla.org/firefox/966/

[8]   http://www.getfirebug.com/

[9]   http://www.fiddlertool.com

Although it's not realistic to manually review in detail all responses from the Web server, the hope is that certain portions of a response will highlight the fact that an anomalous condition has occurred. The user can then identify the associated request. This is possible because all responses, in both a raw and HTML format, can be viewed in conjunction with the associated request simply by selecting the appropriate tab from the Responses window.

When running WebFuzz, the following pieces of information might indicate the existence of a vulnerable condition:

- HTML status codes
- Error messages embedded in the response
- User input embedded in the response
- Performance degradation
- Request timeouts
- WebFuzz error messages
- Handled or unhandled exceptions

Let's look at each of these pieces of information individually to better understand why they might be helpful in identifying vulnerabilities.

### HTML Status Codes

We already mentioned that HTML status codes are a vital piece of information, as they provide a quick visual indication of the success or failure of the initial request. Therefore, WebFuzz parses the raw response to identify the status code, which is then separately displayed in a table detailing all responses. With this information, the user can quickly identify responses that should be reviewed in greater detail.

### Error Messages Embedded in the Response

Web servers by design can include error messages in dynamically generated Web pages. This is especially true if a Web server is incorrectly launched in a production environment with debugging functionality enabled. A classic example of an error message that says too much is an authentication error that states something like "password incorrect" as opposed to "username or password incorrect." When brute forcing the login screen for a Web application, the first message will let you know that the username exists but the password is incorrect. This reduces the unknown variables from two (username and password) to one (password) and greatly increases the odds of being able to gain access. Application error messages can also be particularly useful when identifying SQL injection attacks.

### User Input Embedded in the Response

When dynamically generated Web pages contain user-supplied data, it is possible that XSS vulnerabilities exist. Web application designers need to filter user input to ensure that such attacks aren't possible, but improper filtering is a very common problem. Therefore, identifying data in the HTML response that was provided by WebFuzz is an indication the application should be tested for XSS vulnerabilities.

### Performance Degradation

Although a flat-out application crash makes a DoS attack easy to spot, such vulnerabilities are typically more subtle. Often, performance degradation will indicate that the application might be vulnerable to DoS attacks. A request timeout is one way to identify performance degradation, but performance monitors should also be used during fuzzing to identify issues such as excessive CPU or memory usage.

### Request Timeouts

As mentioned, request timeouts should not be ignored, as they might indicate a temporary or permanent DoS condition.

### WebFuzz Error Messages

WebFuzz has its own error handling and will pop up error messages when certain functions fail to execute. For example, if the target server goes offline due to a previous fuzz request, WebFuzz might issue an error message indicating that it cannot connect to the target. This could mean that a DoS attack has occurred.

### Handled or Unhandled Exceptions

When fuzzing Web applications, it is possible to uncover vulnerabilities in both the application itself and the Web server on which it is running. It is therefore also important to be monitoring the status of the server. Although responses returned by the Web server provide insight into potential vulnerabilities, they do not tell the full story. It is quite likely that fuzzed requests will cause handled and unhandled exceptions that could lead to exploitable conditions if the inputs were altered slightly. It is therefore recommended that the targeted Web server have a separate debugger attached during fuzzing to identify such exceptions. Other tools discussed in this book such as FileFuzz and COMRaider include built-in debugging functionality. However, this is not required for Web fuzzing, as WebFuzz does not need to repeatedly launch and kill an application. This time we are sending a series of fuzzed requests to a single Web application that continues to run and respond to all requests barring input that causes a DoS condition.

## DEVELOPMENT

Okay, enough theory; now it's time for the fun stuff. Let's roll up our sleeves and build a Web application fuzzer.

## APPROACH

In designing WebFuzz, our goal was to create a user-friendly tool for fuzzing Web applications. As our target audience is expected to have a reasonable understanding of HTTP, it was not necessary to create a point-and-click solution. Instead, we wanted to design a tool that provided end users with maximum flexibility over request structure. We also wanted to deliver response data in a means that simplified the detection of potential vulnerabilities.

## LANGUAGE SELECTION

To make WebFuzz user friendly, it made sense to build a GUI application. C# was selected as the development language for two primary reasons. First, C# allowed us to design a reasonably professional-looking GUI with minimal effort. Second, C# provides a number of classes to assist with sending/receiving network traffic. A downside to using C# is that we're primarily tied to the Windows platform. However, when fuzzing Web applications, we're not necessarily fuzzing targets running on the same machine as the fuzzer. Therefore, designing a Windows tool does not limit us to fuzzing only Windows-based targets.

## DESIGN

It's not possible to dissect every piece of code without putting the reader to sleep. However, the main functionality for our fuzzer is contained within a few basic classes and we'll now highlight key functionality in each of those classes. Remember that full source code for all of the applications presented in this book is available on the book's website.

### TcpClient Class

C# provides a WebClient class that includes functions for handling HTTP requests and responses. It encapsulates much of the code needed to generate and handle the necessary network traffic and can greatly streamline application development. It even comes with functions to handle much of the functionality required by WebFuzz, such as accessing the headers in the HTTP response. At a slightly lower level, C# provides the HttpWebRequest and HttpWebResponse classes. These classes require a little more coding effort but also expose more advanced functionality such as the ability to use proxies. Which of these slick classes did we use with WebFuzz? The answer is none. Instead we chose to use the TcpClient class, which is designed for any type of TCP traffic, not just HTTP. As such, it lacks the canned functionality of the other Web classes. Why would we do such a thing? Are we sadistic and enjoy writing unnecessary lines of code? No, it was just a necessary evil.

A major challenge when writing fuzzers is that you're trying to do things in a way that they're not supposed to be done. Therefore, standard classes and functions might not suit your needs. For our purposes we want complete control over the raw HTTP request and unfortunately, the various Web classes do not provide us with that level of granularity. Consider, for example, the following code:

```
WebClient wclFuzz = new WebClient();
wclFuzz.Headers.Add("blah", "blah");

Stream data = wclFuzz.OpenRead("http:// www.fuzzing.org");
StreamReader reader = new StreamReader(data);

data.Close();
reader.Close();
```

This simple code sample is all that is required to send a custom Web request using the WebClient class. We have created a basic GET request and have added only one custom header (blah: blah). However, when sniffing the actual traffic generated we find that the following request was sent:

```
GET / HTTP/1.1
blah: blah
Host: www.fuzzing.org
Connection: Keep-Alive
```

You will note that in the actual request, two additional headers were added, Host and Connection. It is for this reason that we're unable to use the classes that are generally desirable. We need to sacrifice ease of use to go to a lower level and gain complete control over the process. In our case, we'll use the TcpClient class for the networking component of WebFuzz.

### Asynchronous Sockets

Networking can be done using asynchronous or synchronous sockets. Although asynchronous sockets require a bit of extra work, their use within WebFuzz was a deliberate decision as the choice better handles the anticipated network problems that are likely when using a fuzzer.

Synchronous sockets are blocking. This means that when a request or response is encountered, the main thread will stop and wait for that communication to complete before proceeding. With a fuzzer we are deliberately trying to cause anomalous conditions, some of which might cause performance degradation or take the target application offline completely. We wouldn't want WebFuzz to become nonresponsive while waiting for communication that might never occur. Asynchronous sockets allow us to avoid this problem as they are nonblocking. Asynchronous sockets launch a separate thread to handle the communication that will invoke a callback function to signal when the communication is complete. This allows other events to continue uninterrupted.

Let's walk through the networking code in WebFuzz to better understand the concept of asynchronous sockets:

```
TcpClient client;
NetworkStream stream;
ClientState cs;

try
{
   client = new TcpClient();
   client.Connect(reqHost, Convert.ToInt32(tbxPort.Text));
   stream = client.GetStream();
   cs = new ClientState(stream, reqBytes);
}
catch (SocketException ex)
{
   MessageBox.Show(ex.Message, "Error", MessageBoxButtons.OK,
     MessageBoxIcon.Error);
   return;
}
catch (System.IO.IOException ex)
{
   MessageBox.Show(ex.Message, "Error", MessageBoxButtons.OK,
     MessageBoxIcon.Error);
   return;
}
IAsyncResult result = stream.BeginWrite(cs.ByteBuffer, 0,
   cs.ByteBuffer.Length, new AsyncCallback(OnWriteComplete), cs);

result.AsyncWaitHandle.WaitOne();
```

After creating a typical TCPClient and NetworkStream we invoke the BeginWrite() method of the stream. The BeginWrite() method takes the following five arguments:[10]

- byte[] array. A buffer that contains the data to write to the network stream.
- int offset. The location in the buffer to begin sending data.
- int numBytes. The maximum number of bytes to write.
- AsyncCallback userCallback. The callback method that will be invoked when communication is complete.
- object stateObject. An object to distinguish this asynchronous write request from other such requests.

AsyncWaitHandle.WaitOne() causes the listening thread to be blocked until the request has been successfully sent. At that point, the callback function will be invoked as follows:

```
public static void OnWriteComplete(IAsyncResult ar)
{
   try
   {
      ClientState cs = (ClientState)ar.AsyncState;
      cs.NetStream.EndWrite(ar);
   }
   catch (System.ObjectDisposedException ex)
   {
      MessageBox.Show(ex.Message, "Error", MessageBoxButtons.OK,
        MessageBoxIcon.Error);
   }
}
```

When we have finished writing our request to the network stream, we are then able to receive the result back from the server:

```
try
{
   result = stream.BeginRead(cs.ByteBuffer, cs.TotalBytes,
   cs.ByteBuffer.Length - cs.TotalBytes,
   new AsyncCallback(OnReadComplete), cs);
}
catch (System.IO.IOException ex)
{
```

---

[10] http://msdn.microsoft.com/library/en-us/cpref/html/frlrfsystemiofilestreamclassbeginwritetopic.asp

```
      MessageBox.Show(ex.Message, "Error", MessageBoxButtons.OK,
        MessageBoxIcon.Error);
      ReadDone.Close();
      return;
  }
```

At this point, we once again use an asynchronous socket, but this time it is used to receive the response back from the target application. We now invoke the BeginRead() method, which takes the same arguments as the BeginWrite() method, but this time around, we are using OnReadComplete() as our callback method:

```
public void OnReadComplete(IAsyncResult ar)
{
   readTimeout.Elapsed += new ElapsedEventHandler(OnTimedEvent);
   readTimeout.Interval = Convert.ToInt32(tbxTimeout.Text);
   readTimeout.Enabled = true;

   ClientState cs = (ClientState)ar.AsyncState;
   int bytesRcvd;

   try
   {
      bytesRcvd = cs.NetStream.EndRead(ar);
   }
   catch (System.IO.IOException ex)
   {
      MessageBox.Show(ex.Message, "Error", MessageBoxButtons.OK,
        MessageBoxIcon.Error);
      return;
   }
   catch (System.ObjectDisposedException ex)
   {
      return;
   }

   cs.AppendResponse(Encoding.ASCII.GetString(cs.ByteBuffer,
     cs.TotalBytes, bytesRcvd));
   cs.AddToTotalBytes(bytesRcvd);

   if (bytesRcvd != 0)
   {
      cs.NetStream.BeginRead(cs.ByteBuffer, cs.TotalBytes,
      cs.ByteBuffer.Length - cs.TotalBytes,
                new AsyncCallback(OnReadComplete), cs);
   }
```

```
    else
    {
        readTimeout.Enabled = false;
        if (ReadDone.Set() == false)
            ReadDone.Set();
    }
}
```

We begin `OnReadComplete()` by creating a timer (`readTimeout`) that will call `ReadDone.Set()` if the user-defined timeout is reached. This allows us to ensure that the thread does not live indefinitely if the read fails to complete and provides the end user with a means of controlling the timeout length. We then append the response received to our buffer. At that point, we need to decide if we should continue waiting for further data. We do this by determining if more than zero bytes were received. If that's the case, we do it all over again by once again invoking `BeginRead()`. If not, we kill the thread and move on.

### Generating Requests

Before we ever send a request, we must first determine what to send. This is obviously taken from the Request Headers window where the user creates the request, but each fuzz variable [XXX] must be replaced by the actual fuzz data. This process kicks off once the user clicks the Request button within the `btnRequest_Click()` method:

```
if (rawRequest.Contains("[") != true || rawRequest.Contains("]") != true)
        rawRequest = "[None]" + rawRequest;
while (rawRequest.Contains("[") && rawRequest.Contains("]"))
{
    fuzz = rawRequest.Substring(rawRequest.IndexOf('[' ) + 1, (rawRequest.IndexOf(']')
- rawRequest.IndexOf('[')) - 1);
```

When we generate requests, we begin a loop that will continue to parse the user-supplied data so long as fuzz variables are encountered in the request. We then move onto a case statement that will determine what is to be done with each fuzz variable.

```
int arrayCount = 0;
int arrayEnd = 0;
Read fuzzText = null;
WebFuzz.Generate fuzzGenerate = null;
ArrayList fuzzArray = null;
string replaceString = "";
```

```
string[] fuzzVariables = { "SQL", "XSS", "Methods", "Overflow", "Traversal", "Format"
};

switch (fuzz)
{
    case "SQL":
        fuzzText = new Read("sqlinjection.txt");
        fuzzArray = fuzzText.readFile();
        arrayEnd = fuzzArray.Count;
        replaceString = "[SQL]";
        break;
    case "XSS":
        fuzzText = new Read("xssinjection.txt");
        fuzzArray = fuzzText.readFile();
        arrayEnd = fuzzArray.Count;
        replaceString = "[XSS]";
        break;
    case "Methods":
        fuzzText = new Read("methods.txt");
        fuzzArray = fuzzText.readFile();
        arrayEnd = fuzzArray.Count;
        replaceString = "[Methods]";
        break;
    case "Overflow":
        fuzzGenerate= new WebFuzz.Overflow(overflowFill, overflowLength,
        overflowMultiplier);
        fuzzArray = fuzzGenerate.buildArray();
        arrayEnd = fuzzArray.Count;
        replaceString = "[Overflow]";
        break;
    case "Traversal":
        fuzzGenerate= new WebFuzz.Overflow("../", 1, 10);
        fuzzArray = fuzzGenerate.buildArray();
        arrayEnd = fuzzArray.Count;
        replaceString = "[Traversal]";
        break;
    case "Format":
        fuzzGenerate= new WebFuzz.Overflow("%n", 1, 10);
        fuzzArray = fuzzGenerate.buildArray();
        arrayEnd = fuzzArray.Count;
        replaceString = "[Format]";
        break;
    case "None":
        ArrayList nullValueArrayList = new ArrayList();
        nullValueArrayList.Add("");
        fuzzArray = nullValueArrayList;
```

```
      arrayEnd = fuzzArray.Count;
      replaceString = "[None]";
      break;
   default:
      arrayEnd = 1;
      break;
```

Those fuzz variables, which come from a static list (SQL, XSS, and Methods), create a new Read() class and pass the constructor the name of the ASCII text file that contains the fuzz variables. Generated variables (Overflow, Traversal, and Format) on the other hand, instantiate a new Generate() class and pass in the string to be repeated, the total size of the string, and the number of times that the string is to be repeated.

### Receiving Responses

As responses are received, WebFuzz archives the request, raw response, HTML response, hostname, and path by adding them to individual string arrays. Additionally, identifying information including the status code, hostname, and request are added to a ListView control. This way, when the fuzzing is complete you can simply click on the appropriate response in the ListView control and full details will be displayed in a series of tabbed RichTextBox and WebBrowser controls.

```
rtbRequestRaw.Text = reqString;
rtbResponseRaw.Text = dataReceived;
wbrResponse.DocumentText = html;

string path = getPath(reqString);

lvwResponses.Items.Add(lvwResponses.Items.Count.ToString());
lvwResponses.Items[lvwResponses.Items.Count - 1].SubItems.Add(status);
lvwResponses.Items[lvwResponses.Items.Count - 1].SubItems.Add(reqHost);
lvwResponses.Items[lvwResponses.Items.Count - 1].SubItems.Add
   (requestString.Substring(0, requestString.IndexOf("\r\n")));

lvwResponses.Refresh();

requestsRaw[lvwResponses.Items.Count - 1] = reqString;
responsesRaw[lvwResponses.Items.Count - 1] = dataReceived;
responsesHtml[lvwResponses.Items.Count - 1] = html;
responsesHost[lvwResponses.Items.Count - 1] = reqHost;
responsesPath[lvwResponses.Items.Count - 1] = path;
```

As mentioned, WebFuzz is not a point-and-click vulnerability scanner. Rather, it is a tool designed to allow a knowledgeable individual to fuzz targeted portions of an HTTP request. Full source code and binaries for the tool are available at www.fuzzing.org.

## CASE STUDIES

Now that we have a basic understanding of how and why WebFuzz was built, it's time to move on to more important things. It's time to see if it actually works.

### DIRECTORY TRAVERSAL

A directory traversal exists when a user is able to break out of the Web root directory and access files and folders that are not meant to be delivered via the Web application. This type of vulnerability poses a confidentiality risk but can also be escalated to result in a complete system compromise depending on the files that can the accessed. Consider, for example, a situation whereby a directory traversal would allow an attacker to obtain a password file. Even if the file were encrypted, it might present the opportunity to crack the passwords offline after it has been retrieved so that the attacker can return at a later time and connect to the server using valid authentication credentials.

Traversals generally involve sending a series of ../ characters to traverse to a higher level directory. The traversal characters are also often URL encoded to bypass basic detection filters. If directories are browsable this might be all that is required but it is generally also necessary to append the name of an existing file. When testing for a directory traversal attack, it is advisable to append the name of a file that will by default exist on the target server. For example, on a Windows system, boot.ini or win.ini are good choices as they are ASCII files that are easily recognizable when encountered and exist on all modern Windows operating systems.

Let's start by looking at a simple directory traversal attack in Trend Micro Control Manager[11] that is caused by improper input validation in the IMAGE parameter in the rptserver.asp page. We'll use WebFuzz to send a get request to the rptserver.asp page but we'll replace the legitimate IMAGE parameter with the [Traversal] fuzz variable followed by a known file, in this case, win.ini. We can see from the results shown in Figure 10.8 that the directory traversal is indeed exposed after a single traversal.

---

[11] http://www.idefense.com/intelligence/vulnerabilities/display.php?id=352

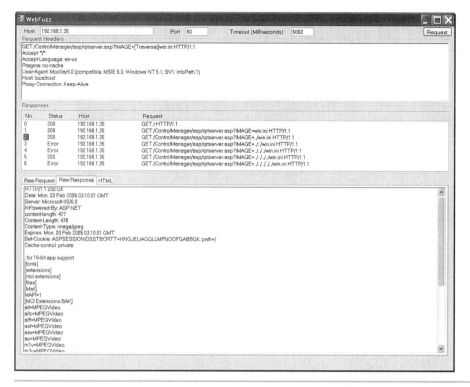

**Figure 10.8**  Trend Micro Control Manager directory traversal

Let's try another example, but this time, we'll throw in a little twist. A vulnerability in Ipswitch Imail Web Calendaring[12] showed us that to find a directory traversal, sometimes you must also ask for something that isn't there. In this case, it was discovered that a directory traversal vulnerability existed when the traversal was passed to a nonexistent JSP page. Once again, let's put WebFuzz to the test (see Figure 10.9).

To test this particular vulnerability, we'll pass a GET method to the server that requests the nonexistent blah.jsp Web page, followed by the traversal and ultimately the common boot.ini file. Figure 10.9 shows us that it takes a few requests but after five traversal sequences...you guessed it, the vulnerability is revealed.

---

[12] http://www.idefense.com/intelligence/vulnerabilities/display.php?id=242

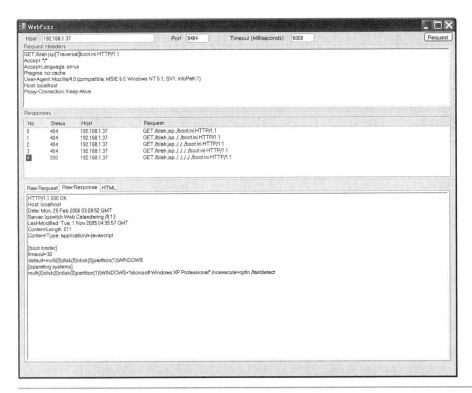

**Figure 10.9**    Ipswitch Imail Web Calendaring directory traversal

## OVERFLOW

Although relatively rare in the Web application world, buffer overflows can exist in Web applications or servers just as they do in console or GUI applications and they exist for the same reason: User-supplied input is not appropriately filtered, allowing data of an unexpected length to overflow a fixed size buffer. Overflows are particularly dangerous as they might lead to arbitrary code execution. However, when fuzzing, the most likely indicator that an overflow has occurred will be the fact that the application has crashed following a request containing an overly long string. By attaching a debugger to the target during fuzzing, it will be possible to determine if the overflow is limited to a DoS attack or could be extended to allow for remote code execution.

To illustrate the use of WebFuzz in detecting overflow vulnerabilities, we'll use a simple example. What could be simpler that an overflow in PMSoftware's Simple Web

Server?[13] In this case, all we need to do is send a long GET request to the server. We'll therefore send the following request, which includes an overflow fuzz variable:

```
GET /[Overflow] HTTP/1.1
```

At first, nothing happens other than a 404 – Page Not Found error but as can be seen in Figure 10.10, following request number 10, WebFuzz no longer receives a response of any kind. Why?

The answer is soon revealed when we look at the server where Simple Web Server was running, as the pop-up message shown in Figure 10.11 is displayed.

This is not a good sign (at least not for Simple Web Server). When the error message is closed, so too is the application. Yes indeed, at the very least, we have a DoS attack. Do

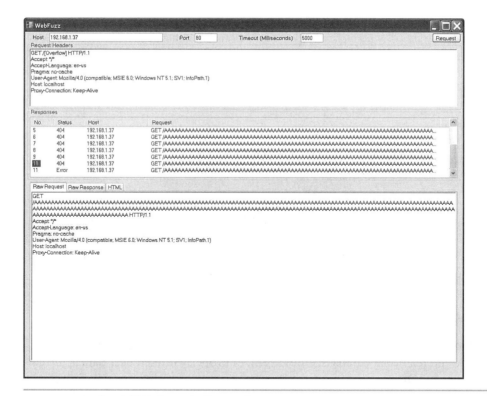

**Figure 10.10**   Simple Web Server buffer overflow

---

[13] http://secunia.com/advisories/15000/

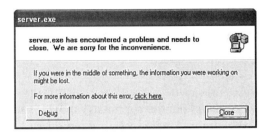

**Figure 10.11**   Simple Web Server error message

```
Registers (FPU)                              <   <   <
EAX 00000001
ECX 7C91056D ntdll.7C91056D
EDX 00880000
EBX 00000000
ESP 0012FDD0 ASCII "AAAAAAAAAAAAAAAAAAAA"
EBP 0012FE2C
ESI 000001DC
EDI 00880758
EIP 41414141
C 0   ES 0023 32bit 0(FFFFFFFF)
P 1   CS 001B 32bit 0(FFFFFFFF)
A 0   SS 0023 32bit 0(FFFFFFFF)
Z 0   DS 0023 32bit 0(FFFFFFFF)
S 0   FS 003B 32bit 7FFDF000(FFF)
T 0   GS 0000 NULL
D 0
O 0   LastErr ERROR_SUCCESS (00000000)
EFL 00000206 (NO,NB,NE,A,NS,PE,GE,G)
ST0 empty -??? FFFF 00700070 00700070
ST1 empty -??? FFFF 00F000F0 00F000F0
ST2 empty -??? FFFF 00000000 002C006F
ST3 empty -??? FFFF 00000000 005F00ED
ST4 empty -??? FFFF 0F0566FB 8F6698F5
ST5 empty 1.0000000000000000000
ST6 empty 1.0000000000000000000
ST7 empty 1.0000000000000000000
                  3 2 1 0    E S P U O Z D I
FST 4000  Cond 1 0 0 0  Err 0 0 0 0 0 0 0 0  (EQ)
FCW 027F  Prec NEAR,53  Mask   1 1 1 1 1 1
```

**Figure 10.12**   Simple Web Server overflow

we have the potential for code execution as well? The answer lies in Figure 10.12, where the attached debugger shows that EIP is controlled and therefore code execution will be possible. If you're new to buffer overflows, don't get too excited. This is a best case scenario. It's not often that the fruit is hanging quite this low.

## SQL INJECTION

SQL injection attacks occur when user-supplied data can influence SQL requests reaching the back-end relational database. Once again, improperly filtered user data is the culprit. When fuzzing, application error messages provide a strong clue that SQL injection could be possible.

A SQL injection attack in the username field at the login screen for Ipswitch Whatsup Professional (SP1)[14] allowed attackers to bypass security altogether by changing the Administrator password. But how do we find it? Using LiveHTTPHeaders, we're able to easily see that the username and password parameters are passed to the Login.asp page via a POST request as shown here:

```
POST /NmConsole/Login.asp HTTP/1.1
Host: localhost
User-Agent: Mozilla/5.0 (Windows; U; Windows NT 5.1; en-US; rv:1.8.0.1) Gecko/20060111
Firefox/1.5.0.1
Accept:
text/xml,application/xml,application/xhtml+xml,text/html;q=0.9,text/plain;q=0.8,image/
png,*/*;q=0.5
Accept-Language: en-us,en;q=0.5
Accept-Encoding: gzip,deflate
Accept-Charset: ISO-8859-1,utf-8;q=0.7,*;q=0.7
Keep-Alive: 300
Connection: keep-alive
Referer: http://localhost/NmConsole/Login.asp
Cookie: Ipswitch={A481461B-2EC6-40AE-B362-46B31959F6D1}
Content-Type: application/x-www-form-urlencoded
Content-Length: 81

bIsJavaScriptDisabled=false&sUserName=xxx&sPassword=yyy&btnLogIn=Log+In
```

Now that we know the proper format of the request, we can put together a fuzz request such as the following:

```
POST /NmConsole/Login.asp HTTP/1.1
Host: localhost

bIsJavaScriptDisabled=false&sUserName=[SQL]&sPassword=&btnLogIn=Log+In
```

The standard error message for a failed login attempt is the following: *There was an error while attempting to login: Invalid user name.* However, when we run WebFuzz, we find that alternate error messages such as the one shown in Figure 10.13 are displayed in certain responses. You can clearly see from the content of the error message that user-supplied data appears to be getting submitted to the database.

---

[14] http://www.idefense.com/intelligence/vulnerabilities/display.php?id=268

**Figure 10.13**    Ipswitch Whatsup Professional (SP1) error message

However, this is not a straightforward SQL injection attack. Common authentication bypass techniques such as ` or 1=1`[15] do not work here so we'll have to actually craft a legitimate UPDATE query to change the administrator password. At this point we need details of the database schema to issue tailored SQL injection attacks that are specific to the target, but where can we obtain such information? A quick Google search reveals the answer. First, Ipswitch provides the schema itself for download.[16]

That's great, but it still requires some effort to come up with a meaningful query and we're busy building fuzzers. Not to worry: Ipswitch is kind enough to provide us with the query that we're looking for. The Ipswitch knowledge base[17] actually provides us with the following command that will reset the password for the Admin user to its default value:

```
osql -E -D WhatsUp -Q "UPDATE WebUser SET sPassword=DEFAULT WHERE sUserName='Admin'"
```

Ipswitch provided this query to be used from a command-line tool to help out administrators who had accidentally locked themselves out of the application after forgetting their password. What they didn't realize is that the same query works equally well with our SQL injection attack. Looks like the knowledge base Q and A section should have read as follows:

**Question/Problem:** I forgot the password for the default admin user in the Web interface. How can I reset it?

**Answer/Solution:** Find a SQL injection vulnerability and issue the following command. . .

---

[15] http://www.securiteam.com/securityreviews/5DP0N1P76E.html

[16] http://www.ipswitch.com/support/whatsup_professional/guides/WhatsUpDBSchema.zip

[17] http://support.ipswitch.com/kb/WP-20041122-DM01.htm

## XSS SCRIPTING

XSS is everywhere. According to Mitre, in 2006, 21.5 percent of all new vulnerabilities involved XSS[18] and you don't need to look hard to find them. In fact sla.ckers.org maintains an ever-growing XSS wall of shame[19] in their forums and it's disappointing to see the number of large corporations that make an appearance on the list.

As with most Web application vulnerabilities, XSS is made possible because of improper input validation. The vulnerable application accepts user input and embeds it within dynamic page content without any filtering. As such, an attacker can inject client-side script such as JavaScript into the requested page. This in turn can allow the attacker to control the contents of the displayed Web page or perform actions on behalf of the victim.

To walk through an XSS fuzzing example, we'll start with a known vulnerable Web page. SPI Dynamics hosts a vulnerable Web application at http://zero.webappsecurity.com, shown in Figure 10.14, for the purpose of testing WebInspect, their Web application

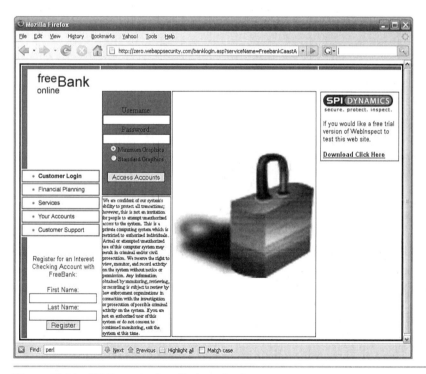

**Figure 10.14** SPI Dynamics Free Bank application

---

[18] http://cwe.mitre.org/documents/vuln-trends.html#table1

[19] http://sla.ckers.org/forum/read.php?3,44

scanner. The default login page contains two Web forms. One is a login form that posts to the `login1.asp` page, and the other posts data to the `rootlogin.asp` page. It is this second form that contains an XSS vulnerability. Of the input fields in this form, the contents of the `txtName` field, which is labeled as Last Name, will be echoed back in the requested `rootlogin.asp` page. As the user input is displayed without any validation, the application is vulnerable to an XSS attack.

A common way to test for the existence of XSS is to input a simple JavaScript code snippet with an alert function that will result in a popup window. This is a quick and dirty test that results in a simple visual queue that leaves no doubt that client-side JavaScript can be injected into the target page. Therefore, we'll submit the following request to test for XSS on the page:

```
POST /rootlogin.asp HTTP/1.1
Host: zero.webappsecurity.com
User-Agent: Mozilla/5.0 (Windows; U; Windows NT 5.1; en-US; rv:1.8.1.1) Gecko/20061204
Firefox/2.0.0.1
Accept:
text/xml,application/xml,application/xhtml+xml,text/html;q=0.9,text/plain;q=0.8,image/
png,*/*;q=0.5
Accept-Language: en-us,en;q=0.5
Accept-Encoding: gzip,deflate
Accept-Charset: ISO-8859-1,utf-8;q=0.7,*;q=0.7
Keep-Alive: 300
Connection: keep-alive
Referer: http://zero.webappsecurity.com
Content-Type: application/x-www-form-urlencoded
Content-Length: 72
txtPassPhrase=first&txtName=<script>alert('Does fuzzing
work?')</script>&txtHidden=This+was+hidden+from+the+user
```

As can be seen in Figure 10.15, this results in a pop-up window being displayed on the page. However, when it comes to fuzzing, this isn't a practical detection mechanism as it would require that we sit and watch for results. The greatest advantage of fuzzing is that it can be automated so that we can walk away and have results when we return.

Fortunately, given that we can inject code into the page, we have numerous options. What about injecting JavaScript that would 'phone home' when successful? That would work, but we can take an even more simplistic approach. Client side script doesn't have to be JavaScript, it can be any scripting language that the browser is capable of interpreting. How about HTML? It's a client side scripting language and it's less likely to be filtered via blacklists than JavaScript so in one way it provides a stronger XSS test. An HTML IMG tag gives us a very simple 'phone home' capability. All that we need to do is

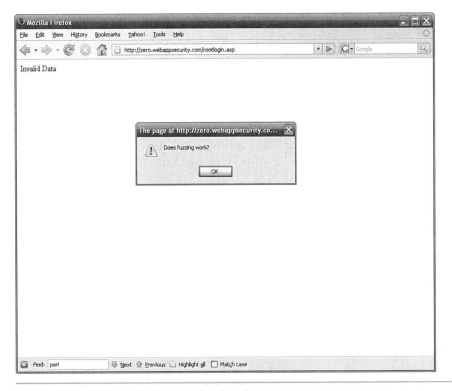

**Figure 10.15** A Cross Site Scripting Attack in Action

use our fuzzer to inject an HTML IMG tag which requests a fake page from a local web server. When the fuzzing is complete, we check the server logs and if we see the request, voila! We know that the target is vulnerable to XSS. Let's give it a try. First off, we need to add an appropriate fuzz variable to WebFuzz. This is why WebFuzz was designed to pull fuzz variables from plain text files. Adding new variables is simple and doesn't require recompiling the application. In order to conduct the test, we'll add the following line to the xssinjection.txt file.

```
%3Cimg+src%3D%27http%3A%2F%2Flocalhost%2Fblah%27%3E
```

This is simply a URL encoded version of the following image request, which attempts to retrieve a fake page from our local web server.

```
<img src='http://localhost/blah'>
```

When we check our Web server log files, what do we see?

```
#Software: Microsoft Internet Information Services 5.1
#Version: 1.0
#Date: 2007-01-31 00:57:34
#Fields: time c-ip cs-method cs-uri-stem sc-status
00:57:34 127.0.0.1 GET /xss 404
```

Busted! The 404 – Page Not Found log entry was made when WebFuzz injected the image request into the `rootlogin.asp` page, proof positive that the page has an XSS vulnerability.

## BENEFITS AND ROOM FOR IMPROVEMENT

The benefits provided by WebFuzz stem from the level of control provided to the end user. Namely, the user can completely control every aspect of the request. However, this comes at the price of needing to have a reasonable understanding of HTTP to put together a meaningful request that is likely to bear fruit. One area where the request portion of the tool could be improved is in allowing for more complex combinations of fuzz variables. For example, dependent variables could be added so that more than one variable is added at a time with the value of one being driven by the value of the other.

There is also plenty of room to further automate WebFuzz to allow for complete coverage of the entire application. This could be greatly enhanced by adding spidering functionality, which would be run initially to identify all possible requests and their structure. Porting the functionality in WebFuzz to a Web browser extension would also be valuable as it would allow for specific requests to be fuzzed as they're encountered while surfing the Web. Finally, we foresee an opportunity to further automate the detection of responses that identify potential vulnerabilities. For example, a parsing engine could run over the raw responses and look for identifiers such as user-supplied data in the response that could indicate the existence of XSS vulnerabilities.

Well, we got the ball rolling but it's in your court now. Make the application better and share your improvements with the world by resubmitting them to us so that we can roll them into future versions.

## SUMMARY

Web applications present some unique challenges but they are definitely appropriate targets for fuzzing. Hopefully, we've demonstrated the value of using fuzzing to uncover vulnerabilities in your Web applications before releasing them to production. WebFuzz is only a proof of concept but even in its raw state it is capable of uncovering vulnerabilities. We encourage you to take the source code for WebFuzz and build it into an even more effective tool.

# File Format Fuzzing

File format fuzzing is a specialized fuzzing method with specifically defined targets. These targets are usually client-side applications. Examples include media players, Web browsers, and office productivity suites. However, targets can also be servers, such as antivirus gateway scanners, spam filters, and even regular e-mail servers. The end goal of file format fuzzing is to find an exploitable flaw in the way that an application parses a certain type of file.

An impressive number of client-side file format parsing vulnerabilities were uncovered in 2005 and 2006, many by nefarious parties as a number of 0day exploits were discovered in the wild prior to the typical vulnerability disclosure process. The eEye security research group does an excellent job detailing such exposures in their Zero-Day Tracker.[1] There are a number of factors indicating that the majority of these discoveries were uncovered through file format fuzzing. This class of bugs is far from extinct, making file format fuzzing a very interesting and "hot" topic.

In this chapter, we present various methods of approaching file fuzzing, as well as talk about the different ways certain targets will accept input. Finally, we demonstrate some

---

[1]  http://research.eeye.com/html/alerts/zeroday/

common vulnerabilities a file fuzzer will encounter and suggest ways of detecting such vulnerabilities in practice. The first step of course, is to choose a suitable target.

## TARGETS

Just like traditional types of fuzzing, many different types of vulnerabilities can be found with file format fuzzing. There are also many different types of exploitation scenarios. For example, some situations will require an attacker to send a malicious file to a user and have him or her open it manually. Other situations will only require a user browsing to an attacker-controlled Web page. Finally, some situations can be triggered by simply sending a malicious e-mail through a mail server or antivirus gateway. This last scenario was the case with the Microsoft Exchange TNEF vulnerability mentioned in Table 11.1 along with other file format vulnerability examples.

**Table 11.1**  Common Types of Vulnerable Applications and Examples of Previously Discovered File Format Vulnerabilities

| Application Category | Vulnerability Name | Advisory |
| --- | --- | --- |
| Office productivity suites | Microsoft HLINK.DLL Hyperlink Object Library Buffer Overflow Vulnerability | http://www.tippingpoint.com/security/advisories/TSRT-06-10.html |
| Antivirus scanners | Kaspersky Anti-Virus Engine CHM File Parser Buffer Overflow Vulnerability | http://www.idefense.com/intelligence/vulnerabilities/display.php?id=318 |
| Media players | Winamp m3u Parsing Stack Overflow Vulnerability | http://www.idefense.com/intelligence/vulnerabilities/display.php?id=377 |
| Web browsers | Vulnerability in Vector Markup Language Could Allow Remote Code Execution | http://www.microsoft.com/technet/security/Bulletin/MS06-055.mspx |
| Archiving utilities | WinZip MIME Parsing Buffer Overflow Vulnerability | http://www.idefense.com/intelligence/vulnerabilities/display.php?id=76 |
| E-mail servers | Microsoft Exchange TNEF Decoding Vulnerability | http://www.microsoft.com/technet/security/Bulletin/MS06-003.mspx |

You will find that most targets will fit into one of these categories. Some applications fit into several categories by way of their secondary functions. For example, many antivirus scanners will also include libraries to decompress files, allowing them to act as archiving utilities. There are also some content scanners that claim to analyze image files for pornographic content. These programs can also be considered as image viewers![2] It is not uncommon for applications to share common libraries, in which case a single vulnerability can affect multiple applications. Consider, for example, the vulnerability detailed in Microsoft Security Bulletin MS06-055, which affects both Internet Explorer and Outlook.

## METHODS

File format fuzzing is different than other types of fuzzing in that it is typically performed entirely on one host. When conducting Web application or network protocol fuzzing, you will most likely have at least two systems, a target system and a system on which your fuzzer will run. The increased performance achieved by being able to fuzz on a single machine makes file format fuzzing a particularly attractive approach for vulnerability discovery.

With network-based fuzzing, it is often evident when an interesting condition has occurred in the target application. In many cases, the server will shut down or crash outright and no longer be reachable. With file format fuzzing, mainly when fuzzing client-side applications, the fuzzer will be continually restarting and killing the target application so a crash might not be recognizable to the fuzzer without proper monitoring. This is an area where file format fuzzing is more complex than network fuzzing. With file format fuzzing, the fuzzer will generally have to monitor the target application for exceptions with each execution. This is generally accomplished by using a debugging library to dynamically monitor handled and unhandled exceptions in the target application, logging the results for later review. At the 50,000-foot view, a typical file fuzzer will follow these steps:

1. Prepare a test case, either via mutation or generation (more on this later).
2. Launch the target application and instruct it to load the test case.
3. Monitor the target application for faults, typically with a debugger.
4. In the event a fault is uncovered, log the finding. Alternatively, if after some period of time no fault is uncovered, manually kill the target application.
5. Repeat.

---

[2] http://www.clearswift.com/solutions/porn_filters.aspx

File format fuzzing can be implemented via both generation and mutation methods. Although both methods have been very effective in our experiences, the mutation or "brute force" method is definitely the simpler to implement. The generation method or "intelligent brute force" fuzzing, although more time consuming to implement, will uncover vulnerabilities that would otherwise not be found using the more primitive brute force approach.

## BRUTE FORCE OR MUTATION-BASED FUZZING

With the brute force fuzzing method, you need to first collect several different samples of your target file type. The more different files you can find, the more thorough your test will be. The fuzzer then acts on these files, creating mutations of them and sending them through the target applications parser. These mutations can take any form, depending on the method you choose for your fuzzer. One method you can use is to replace data byte for byte. For example, progress through the file and replace each byte with 0xff. You could also do this for multiple bytes, such as for two- and four-byte ranges. You can also insert data into the file as opposed to just overwriting bytes. This is a useful method when testing string values. However, when inserting data into the file, be aware that you might be upsetting offsets within the file. This can severely disrupt code coverage, as some parsers will quickly detect an invalid file and exit.

Checksums can also foil brute force parsers. Due to the fact that any byte change will invalidate the checksum, it is quite likely that the parsing application will gracefully exit, providing an error message before a potentially vulnerable piece of code can ever be reached. The solution for these problems is to either switch to intelligent fuzzing, which is discussed in the next section, or as an alternative approach, disable the checks within the target software. Disabling the software checks is not a trivial task and generally requires the efforts of a reverse engineer.

Why is this method simple to use once it is implemented? That's easy. The end user doesn't need to have any knowledge of the file format and how it works. Provided they can find a few sample files using a popular search engine, or by searching their local system, they are essentially done with their research until the fuzzer finds something interesting.

There are a few drawbacks this fuzzing approach. First, it is a very inefficient approach and can therefore take some time to complete fuzzing on a single file. Take, for example, a basic Microsoft Word document. Even a blank document will be approximately 20KB in size. To fuzz each byte once would require creating and launching 20,480 separate files. Assuming 2 seconds per file, it would take more than 11 hours to complete and that's only for trying a single byte value. What about the other 254 possibilities? This issue can be sidestepped somewhat through the usage of a multithreaded fuzzer, but it does illustrate the inefficiency of pure mutation fuzzing. Another way to streamline this fuzzing approach is to solely concentrate on areas of the file that are more likely to yield desired results, such as file and field headers.

The primary drawback to brute force fuzzing is the fact that there will almost always be a large piece of functionality that will be missed, unless you have somehow managed to gather a sample file set containing each and every possible feature. Most file formats are very complex and contain a multitude of permutations. When measuring code coverage, you will find that throwing a few sample files at an application will not exercise the application as thoroughly as if the user truly understands the file format and has manually prepared some of the information about the file type. This thoroughness issue is addressed with the generation approach to file fuzzing, which we have termed intelligent brute force fuzzing.

## INTELLIGENT BRUTE FORCE OR GENERATION-BASED FUZZING

With intelligent brute force fuzzing, you must first put some effort into actually researching the file specifications. An intelligent fuzzer is still a fuzzing engine, and thus is still conducting a brute force attack. However, it will rely on configuration files from the user, making the process more intelligent. These files usually contain metadata describing the language of the file types. Think of these templates as lists of data structures, their positions relative to each other, and their possible values. On an implementation level, these can be represented in many different formats.

If a file format without any public documentation is chosen for testing, you, as the researcher, will have to conduct further research on the format specification before building a template. This might require reverse engineering on your part, but always start with your good friend Google to see if someone else has done the work for you. Several Web sites, such as Wotsit's Format,[3] serve as an excellent archive of official and unofficial file format documentation. An alternate but complementary approach involves comparing samples of the file type to reveal some patterns and profile some of the data types being used. Remember that the effectiveness of an intelligent fuzz is directly related to your understanding of the file format and your ability to describe it in a generic way to the fuzzer you are using. We show a sample implementation of an intelligent brute force fuzzer later on in the book when building SPIKEfile in Chapter 12, "File Format Fuzzing: Automation on UNIX."

---

[3]  http://www.wotsit.org

Once a target and method have been determined, the next step is to research appropriate input vectors for the chosen target.

## INPUTS

With a target application selected, the next step is to enumerate the supported file types and extensions as well as the different vectors for getting those files parsed. Available format specifications should also be collected and reviewed. Even in cases where you only intend to perform a simple brute force test, it is still useful to have knowledge of the file formats you have as possible candidates. Focusing on the more complex file types can be lucrative, as implementing a proper parser will be more difficult, and therefore the chances of discovering a vulnerability arguably increase.

Let's consider an example and see how we might gather inputs. The archive utility WinRAR[4] is a popular archive utility that is freely available. An easy way to tell what files WinRAR will handle is to simply browse the WinRAR Web site. On the main WinRAR page, you will find a list of supported file types. These include zip, rar, tar, gz, ace, uue, and several others.

Now that you have a list of the file types that WinRAR will handle, you must pick a target. Sometimes, the best way to pick a target is to look up information about each file type, and go with the one that is most complex. The assumption here is that complexity often leads to coding mistakes. For example, a file type that uses a number of length tagged values and user-supplied offsets might be more appealing than a simpler file type that is based on static offsets and static length fields. Of course, there are plenty of exceptions to this rule as you will find once you get some fuzzing under your belt. Ideally, the fuzzer will eventually target every possible file type; the first one chosen is not necessarily important, however it is always a nice payoff to find interesting behavior in your first set of fuzz tests for a particular application.

## VULNERABILITIES

When parsing malformed files, a poorly coded application can be susceptible to a number of different classes of vulnerabilities. This section discusses some of these vulnerability classifications:

---

[4]   http://www.rarlab.com

- DoS (crash or hang)
- Integer handling problems
- Simple stack/heap overflows
- Logic errors
- Format strings
- Race conditions

## DENIAL OF SERVICE

Although DoS issues are not very interesting in client-side applications, you need to keep in mind that we can also target server applications that must remain available for security and productivity purposes. This includes, of course, e-mail servers and content filters. Some of the most common causes of DoS issues in file parsing code in our experience have been out of bound reads, infinite loops, and NULL pointer dereferences.

A common error leading to infinite loops is trusting offset values in files that specify the locations of other blocks within the file. If the application does not make sure this offset is forward in relation to the current block, an infinite loop can occur causing the application to repeatedly process the same block or blocks ad infinitum. There have been several instances of this type of problem in ClamAV in the past.[5]

## INTEGER HANDLING PROBLEMS

Integer overflows and "signedness" issues are very common in binary file parsing. Some of the most common issues we have seen resemble the following pseudo-code:

```
[...]
[1] size            = read32_from_file();
[2] allocation_size = size+1;
[3] buffer          = malloc(allocation_size);
[4] for (ix = 0; ix < size; ix++)
[5]     buffer[ix] = read8_from_file();
[...]
```

---

[5] http://idefense.com/intelligence/vulnerabilities/display.php?id=333

This example demonstrates a typical integer overflow that results in a memory corruption. If the file specifies the maximum unsigned 32-bit integer (0xFFFFFFFF) for the value size, then on line [2] allocation_size gets assigned as zero due to an integer wrap. On line [3], the code will result in a memory allocation call with a size of zero. The pointer buffer at this stage will points to an underallocated memory chunk. On lines [4] and [5], the application loops and copies a large amount of data, bounded by the original value for size, into the allocated buffer, resulting in a memory corruption.

This particular situation will not always be exploitable. Its exploitability is dependent on how the application uses the heap. Simply overwriting memory on the heap is not always enough to gain control of the application. Some operation must occur causing the overwritten heap data to be used. In some cases, integer overflows like these will cause a non-heap-related crash before heap memory is used.

This is, of course, just one example of how integers can be used incorrectly while parsing binary data. We have seen integers misused in many different ways, including the often simpler signed to unsigned comparison error. The following code snippet demonstrates the logic behind this type of vulnerability:

```
[0] #define MAX_ITEMS 512

[...]

[1] char buff[MAX_ITEMS]
[2] int size;

[...]

[3] size = read32_from_file();
[4] if (size > MAX_ITEMS)
[5]     { printf("Too many items\n");return -1; }
[6] readx_from_file(size,buff);

[...]

/* readx_from_file: read 'size' bytes from file into buff */
[7] void readx_from_file(unsigned int size, char *buff)
{
[...]
}
```

This code will allow a stack-based overflow to occur if the value size is a negative number. This is because in the comparison at [4], both size (as defined on [1]) and MAX_ITEMS (as defined on [0]) are treated as signed numbers and, for example, -1 is less than 512. Later on, when size is used for copy boundaries in the function at [7], it is treated as unsigned. The value -1, for example, now is interpreted as 42949672954294967295. Of course, the exploitability of this is not guaranteed, but in many cases depending on how the `readx_from_file` function is implemented, this will be exploitable by targeting variables and saved registers on the stack.

## SIMPLE STACK AND HEAP OVERFLOWS

The issues here are well understood and have been seen many times in the past. A typical scenario goes like this: A fixed size buffer is allocated, whether it be on the stack or on the heap. Later, no bounds checking is performed when copying in oversized data from the file. In some cases, there is some attempt at bounds checking, but it is done incorrectly. When the copy occurs, memory is corrupted, often leading to arbitrary code execution. For more details regarding these vulnerability classes, "The Shellcoder's Handbook: Discovering and Exploiting Security Holes"[6] serves as an excellent reference.

## LOGIC ERRORS

Depending on the design of the file format, exploitable logic errors might be possible. Although we have not personally discovered any logic errors during file format vulnerability research, a perfect example of this class of vulnerabilities is the Microsoft WMF vulnerability addressed in MS06-001.[7] The vulnerability was not due to a typical overflow. In fact, it did not require any type of memory corruption, yet it allowed an attacker to directly execute user-supplied position-independent code.

## FORMAT STRINGS

Although format string vulnerabilities are mostly extinct, especially in open source software, they are worth mentioning. When we say mostly extinct, we say that because not all programmers can be as security aware as the folks at US-CERT, who recommend that to secure your software, you should Not Use the "%n" Format String Specifier.[8]

---

[6]  ISBN-10: 0764544683

[7]  http://www.microsoft.com/technet/security/Bulletin/MS06-001.mspx

[8]  https://buildsecurityin.us-cert.gov/daisy/bsi/articles/knowledge/guidelines/340.html

But seriously, in our personal experiences, we have actually found several format string-related issues while file fuzzing. Some were discovered in Adobe[9] and RealNetworks[10] products. A lot of the fun in exploiting format string issues comes from being able to use the vulnerability to leak memory to aid exploitation. Unfortunately, with client-side attacks using malformed files, you rarely are afforded this opportunity.

## RACE CONDITIONS

Although people don't typically think of file format vulnerabilities occurring due to race conditions, there have been a few that do and there are probably many more to come. The main targets for this type of vulnerability are complex multithreaded applications. We hate to target just one product in specific, but Microsoft Internet Explorer is the first application that comes to mind here. Vulnerabilities caused by Internet Explorer using uninitialized memory and using memory that is in use by another thread will probably continue to be discovered.

## DETECTION

When fuzzing file formats you will typically be spawning many instances of the target application. Some will hang indefinitely and have to be killed, some will crash, and some will exit cleanly on their own. The challenge lies in determining when a handled or unhandled exception has occurred and when that exception is exploitable. A fuzzer can utilize several sources of information to find out more information about a process:

- *Event logs.* Event logs are used by Microsoft Windows operating systems and can be accessed using the Event Viewer application. They are not terribly useful for our purposes, as it is difficult to correlate an event log entry with a specific process when we are launching hundreds during a fuzz session.

- *Debuggers.* The best way to identify unhandled and handled exceptions is to attach a debugger to the target application prior to fuzzing. Error handling will prevent obvious signs of many errors caused by fuzzing but these can generally be detected using a debugger. There are more advanced techniques than applying a debugger for fault detection, some of which are touched on in Chapter 24, "Intelligent Fault Detection."

---

[9]  http://labs.idefense.com/intelligence/vulnerabilities/display.php?id=163

[10]  http://labs.idefense.com/intelligence/vulnerabilities/display.php?id=311

- *Return codes.* Capturing and testing the return code of the application, although not always as accurate or informative as using a debugger, can be a very quick and dirty way to determine why an application ended. Under UNIX at least, it is possible to determine which signal caused an application to terminate via the return code.

- *Debugging API.* Instead of leveraging a third-party debugger, it is often feasible and effective to implement some rudimentary debugging features into the fuzzer itself. For example, all we will be interested in knowing about a process is the reason it terminated, what the current instruction was, the register state, and possibly the values in a few memory regions like at the stack pointer or with respect to some register. This is often trivial to implement, and is invaluable in terms of time saving when analyzing crashes for exploitability. In later chapters, we explore this option and present a simple and reusable debugger creation framework on the Microsoft Windows platform named PyDbg, part of the PaiMei[11] reverse engineering framework.

Once a given test case has been determined to cause a fault, make sure to save the information that was gathered by whatever fault monitoring method you choose in addition to the actual file that triggered the crash. Saving test case metadata in your records is important as well. For example, if the fuzzer was fuzzing the 8th variable field in the file and it was using the 42nd fuzz value, the file might be named file-8-42. In some cases, we might want to drop a core file and save that as well. This can be done if the fuzzer is catching signals using a debugging API. Specific implementation details regarding this can be found in the next two chapters.

## SUMMARY

Although file format fuzzing is a narrowly defined fuzzing method, there are plenty of targets and numerous attack vectors. We have discussed not only the more traditional client-side file format vulnerabilities, but even some "true remote" scenarios, such as antivirus gateways and mail servers. As more and more emphasis is placed on preventing and detecting network-based attacks over TCP/IP, file format exploits still remain as a valuable weapon to penetrate internal network segments.

Now that you know what type of vulnerabilities you are looking for, what applications you are targeting, and exactly how you are trying to fuzz them, it is time to explore some implementations of file format fuzzing tools.

---

[11] http://www.openrce.org/downloads/details/208

# File Format Fuzzing: Automation on UNIX

*"I'm the commander—see, I don't need to explain—I do not need to explain why I say things. That's the interesting thing about being president."*

—George W. Bush, as quoted in Bob Woodward's *Bush at War*

File format vulnerabilities can be exploited both client-side, as is the case with Web browsers and office suites, as well as server-side, as is the case with e-mail scanning antivirus gateways, for example. With regards to client-side exploitation, widespread usage of the affected client is directly related to the severity of the issue. An HTML parsing vulnerability affecting Microsoft Internet Explorer, for example, is among the most coveted file format vulnerabilities as far as severity is concerned. Adversely, client-side vulnerabilities limited to the UNIX platform are not as interesting due to limited exposure.

Nevertheless, in this chapter we introduce two fuzzers, notSPIKEfile and SPIKEfile, that implement mutation-based and generation-based file format fuzzing, respectively. We take a look at both the features and shortcomings of both tools. Then, diving further into the development process, we present the approach taken when developing the tools and present key code snippets. We also go over some basic UNIX concepts such as interesting and uninteresting signals and zombie processes. Finally, we cover the basic usage of the tool and explain the reasoning behind the chosen programming language used.

## notSPIKEfile AND SPIKEfile

The two tools developed to demonstrate file fuzzing on UNIX are named SPIKEfile and notSPIKEfile. As the names imply, they are based on SPIKE[1] and not based on SPIKE, respectively. The following list summarizes some of the key features provided in the implementations:

- Integrated minimal debugger capable of detecting handled and unhandled signals and dumping both memory and register state.
- Fully automatic fuzzing with user-specified delay before killing targeted process.
- Two distinct databases of fuzz heuristics for targeting binary or ASCII printable data types.
- Easily extensible fuzz heuristic database seeded with values historically known to cause problems.

### What's Missing?

There are several features that are missing from notSPIKEfile and SPIKEfile that could be useful to someone using the tools. What follows is a quick summary of these missing features:

- *Portability.* Because the integrated debugger was created to work on x86 and uses Linux ptrace, it will not work out of the box on other architectures or operating systems. However, adding compatibility would be fairly trivial, provided the availability of other debugging and disassembling libraries.
- *Intelligent load monitoring.* Although the user can specify how many processes to fuzz at once, it is currently completely up to the user to determine if system load is too high.

Clearly there were some compromises made during the development process, as demonstrated by the missing features. The author of the tool will utilize an age-old cover-up by stating that the improvements are left as "an exercise for the reader." Let's take a look at the development process undertaken during the construction of these tools.

---

[1]   http://www.immunityinc.com/resources-freesoftware.shtml

# DEVELOPMENT APPROACH

The focus of this chapter is not how to use a fuzzer, but rather how to implement one. This section describes the design and development details of file format fuzzers under Linux. In the realm of file fuzzer development, we can make the safe assumption that our fuzzer will be executing on the same system as the target. Our design includes three distinct functional components.

## EXCEPTION DETECTION ENGINE

This portion of code is responsible for determining when the target has demonstrated some undefined and potentially insecure behavior. How can this be done? There are two basic approaches. The first, which is fairly simple, involves simply monitoring any signals that are received by the application. This allows the fuzzer to detect, for example, buffer overflows that result in an invalid memory reference. This approach, of course, will not capture behavior such as metacharacter injection or logic flaws. For example, consider an application that passes a partially attacker-supplied value through to the UNIX system function. This would allow an attacker to execute arbitrary programs by using shell metacharacters, but would not cause any type of memory access violation. Although there are vulnerabilities that will allow an attacker to compromise host security that don't involve memory corruption at all, a decision was made that we are not interested in such bugs, as the implementation of detecting such things would be more painful to develop than the payoff would be worth.

For those wishing to explore logic bugs such as these, a good approach would be to hook C library (LIBC) functions and monitor for fuzzer-supplied values being passed unsafely to calls such as open, creat, system, and so on.

For our design, we decided on simply detecting signals using the system's ptrace debugging interface. Although it is trivial to determine that a signal has caused an application to terminate by simply waiting for the application to return, it requires a little more work to detect signals that are handled internally by the application. It is because of this that the approach taken for the exception detection engine relies heavily on the system's debugging interface, in this case, the ptrace system call.

## EXCEPTION REPORTING (EXCEPTION DETECTION)

On discovering an exception, a good fuzzer should report useful information about what exactly happened. In the least, the signal that occurred should be reported. Ideally further details such as the offending instruction, CPU register states, and a stack dump would also be included in the report. Both of the fuzzers implemented in this chapter are capable of producing such detailed reports. To obtain this desired low-level information, we must employ the help of the `ptrace` system call to gather it. We must also leverage a library to disassemble instructions if we intend to report them to the user. The library should be capable of converting a buffer of arbitrary data into the string representation of x86 instructions. The library chosen was libdisasm[2] because it works well, exposes a simple interface, and appears to be the preferred choice of the Google search engine, which listed it above all others. To really seal the deal, libdisasm includes examples that we can cut and paste from, making our life that much easier.

## CORE FUZZING ENGINE

This is the heart of the file format fuzzer as it controls the decisions on what malformed data to use and where to insert it. The code that does this for notSPIKEfile is different than the code for SPIKEfile because SPIKEfile leverages the already existent SPIKE code to implement this functionality. Rest assured, however, that they are fairly similar.

As you no doubt have already guessed, SPIKEfile utilizes the same fuzzing engine as SPIKE. The fuzzing engine requires a template, referred to as a SPIKE script, which describes the format of the file. SPIKE then "intelligently" produces variations on that format using combinations of valid and invalid data.

In notSPIKEfile, the fuzzing engine is much more limited. The user must provide the fuzzer with a valid target file. The engine then mutates various parts of that file using a database of fuzz values. These values are split into two types that are referred to as binary and string. Binary values can be of any length and have any value, but are typically used to represent the size of common integer fields. String values are, as the name implies, merely strings. These can contain long or short strings, strings with format specifiers, and all sorts of other exceptional values such as file paths, URLs, and any other type of distinct string you can think of. For a complete list of these types of values, see the SPIKE and notSPIKEfile source, but to get you started, Table 12.1 offers a brief list and a short explanation for several effective fuzz strings. This is nowhere near an exhaustive list, but it should help you get an idea about what types of inputs you need to consider.

---

[2]   http://bastard.sourceforge.net/libdisasm.html

**Table 12.1**    Some Common Fuzz Strings and Their Significance

| String | Significance |
| --- | --- |
| "A"x10000 | Long string, could cause buffer overflow |
| "%n%n"x5000 | Long string with percent signs, could cause buffer overflow or trigger format string vulnerability |
| HTTP:// + "A"x10000 | Valid URL format, could trigger buffer overflow in URL parsing code |
| "A"x5000 + "@" + "A"5000 | Valid e-mail address format, could trigger buffer overflow in e-mail address parsing code |
| 0x20000000,0x40000000, 0x80000000,0xffffffff | A few of the many integers that might trigger an integer overflow. You can get very creative here. Think of code that does `malloc(user_count*sizeof (struct blah))`; Also consider code that might increment or decrement integers without checking for overflows or underflows. |
| "../"x5000 + "AAAA" | Could trigger overflow in path or URL address parsing code |

There is really no limit to the amount of fuzz strings you can use. The important thing to remember, though, is that any type of value that might require special parsing or might create an exceptional condition should be well represented. The difference in missing and finding a bug with your fuzzer might be due to something as simple as appending .html to the end of a large fuzz string.

In the next section, we explore some of the more interesting and relevant code excerpts from both SPIKEfile and notSPIKEfile.

## MEANINGFUL CODE SNIPPETS

Much of the core functionality is shared between both of the fuzzing tools being dissected here. For example, let's begin by highlighting the basic method for forking off and tracing a child process. The following code excerpt is written in the C language and used by both fuzzers:

```
[...]
    if ( !(pid = fork ()) )
    { /* child */
        ptrace (PTRACE_TRACEME, 0, NULL, NULL);
        execve (argv[0], argv, envp);
    }
    else
    { /* parent */
```

```
          c_pid = pid;
monitor:
          waitpid (pid, &status, 0);
          if ( WIFEXITED (status) )
          { /* program exited */
               if ( !quiet )
          printf ("Process %d exited with code %d\n", pid,WEXITSTATUS (status));
               return(ERR_OK);
          }
          else if ( WIFSIGNALED (status) )
          { /* program ended because of a signal */
          printf ("Process %d terminated by unhandled signal %d\n", pid, WTERMSIG
(status));
          return(ERR_OK);
          }
          else if ( WIFSTOPPED (status) )
          { /* program stopped because of a signal */
               if ( !quiet )
                fprintf (stderr, "Process %d stopped due to signal %d (%s) ",
pid,WSTOPSIG (status), F_signum2ascii (WSTOPSIG (status)));
          }
          switch ( WSTOPSIG (status) )
          { /* the following signals are usually all we care about */
               case SIGILL:
               case SIGBUS:
               case SIGSEGV:
               case SIGSYS:
                    printf("Program got interesting signal…\n");
                    if ( (ptrace (PTRACE_CONT, pid, NULL,(WSTOPSIG (status) ==SIGTRAP)
? 0 : WSTOPSIG (status))) == -1 )
                    {
                            perror("ptrace");
                    }
                    ptrace(PTRACE_DETACH,pid,NULL,NULL);
                    fclose(fp);
                    return(ERR_CRASH); /* it crashed */
          }
/* deliver the signal through and keep tracing */
          if ( (ptrace (PTRACE_CONT, pid, NULL,(WSTOPSIG (status) == SIGTRAP) ? 0 :
WSTOPSIG (status))) == -1 )
          {
               perror("ptrace");
          }
          goto monitor;
     }
     return(ERR_OK);
}
```

The main process, or parent, begins by forking off a new process for the target. The new process, or child, uses the ptrace call to indicate that it will be traced by its parent by issuing the PTRACE_TRACEME request. The child then continues on to execute the target knowing that its parent, like any good parent, will watch over it should the desire to do anything inappropriate arises.

As the parent process, the fuzzer is able to receive all signals that are destined for the child process because the child used the PTRACE_TRACEME request. The parent even receives a signal on any call to the exec family of functions. The parent loop is straightforward yet powerful. The fuzzer loops to receive every signal that is destined for the child. The fuzzer then behaves differently depending on the signal and the status of the child.

For example, if the process is stopped, this means that the program has not exited, but it has received a signal and is waiting for the parent's discretion in allowing it to continue. If the signal is one indicative of a memory corruption issue, the fuzzer passes the signal through to the child, assuming it will kill the process and then report the results. If the signal is harmless in nature or is just plain uninteresting, the fuzzer passes it through to the application without any concern for monitoring.

The fuzzer also checks if the child process has actually terminated, another nonintersecting situation. What if the program crashed, you might ask? Shouldn't we be very interested? Well, because we are intercepting all of the interesting signals before the application actually terminates, we know that this program terminated due to either natural behavior or due to an uninteresting signal. This highlights how important it is that you understand which signals are interesting to you. Some people might consider a floating point exception interesting if they are looking for DoS vulnerabilities. Others might be interested only in true memory corruption issues. Still others might look for abort signals, which have come to be an indicator for heap corruption in newer versions of GLIBC. It has been shown that in some circumstances these heap corruption checks can by worked around to execute arbitrary code.[3]

After seeing the code responsible for handling certain signals, there might be some question as to why we handle certain signals differently than others. What follows is an explanation of UNIX signals in the context of vulnerability research.

## Usually Interesting UNIX Signals

Table 12.2 provides a list of signals that a vulnerability researcher might consider interesting during fuzzing, along with an explanation of why they are interesting.

---

[3] http://www.packetstormsecurity.org/papers/attack/MallocMaleficarum.txt

**Table 12.2**   Interesting Signals When Conducting Fuzzing Under UNIX

| Interesting Signal Name | Meaning |
| --- | --- |
| SIGSEGV | Invalid memory reference. The most common result of successful fuzzing. |
| SIGILL | Illegal instruction. This is a possible side effect of memory corruption, but relatively rare. It often results from the program counter becoming corrupted and landing in the middle of data or in between instructions. |
| SIGSYS | Bad system call. This is also a possible side effect of memory corruption, but relatively rare (actually, very rare). This can happen for the same reasons as SIGILL. |
| SIGBUS | Bus error. Often due to some form of memory corruption. Results from accessing memory incorrectly. More common with RISC machines due to their alignment requirements. On most RISC implementations, unaligned stores and loads will generate SIGBUS. |
| SIGABRT | Generated by the abort function call. This is often interesting because GLIBC will abort when it detects heap corruption. |

## NOT SO INTERESTING UNIX SIGNALS

In contrast to Table 12.2, Table 12.3 describes signals that commonly occur during fuzzing, but are generally not interesting to a vulnerability researcher.

**Table 12.3**   Uninteresting Signals When Conducting Fuzzing Under UNIX

| Uninteresting Signal Name | Meaning |
| --- | --- |
| SIGCHLD | A child process has exited. |
| SIGKILL, SIGTERM | Process was killed. |
| SIGFPE | Floating point exception, such as divide by zero. |
| SIGALRM | A timer expired. |

Now that we have introduced SIGCHLD, it is an appropriate time to discuss the handling of a common scenario caused by not properly handling this signal. The next section explains what a zombie process is and how to properly handle child processes so that zombie processes are not created.

## Zombie Processes

A zombie process is a process that has been forked from a parent process and has completed execution (i.e., exited) but its parent has not retrieved its status by calling either wait or waitpid. When this happens, information about the completed process is retained in the kernel indefinitely, until the parent process requests it. At that time, the information is released and the process is truly complete. The general life span of a process forked from our fuzzer is illustrated in Figure 12.1.

When writing a fuzzer that is spawning children using fork, one has to be sure that the parent receives all of the processes completions using wait or waitpid. If you miss a process completion, you will end up with zombie processes.

Earlier versions of notSPIKEfile had some bugs that over time led to the count of active processes slowly decreasing until the fuzz reached a deadlocked state. For example, assume the user specified to fuzz the application using eight processes at a time. As time went on, the active processes slowly dwindled down to just one. This was due to two careless errors on the author's part. The original design relied entirely on the SIGCHLD signal, which is sent to the process when a child process has completed. Using this design, however, some SIGCHLD signals were being missed. There were also several

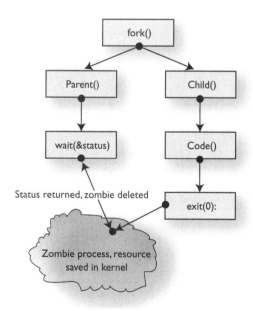

**Figure 12.1**    The lifetime of a forked process

places that the author carelessly failed to decrement the active processes count when child processes completed, which led to a gradual slowdown of the fuzzing process. Oops!

Once noticed, these bugs were trivial to address. All wait and waitpid calls that could cause problems when blocking were changed to be nonblocking using the WNOHANG flag. After they return, the status that is returned is checked to see if a process did indeed complete. If so, the active processes count is always decremented.

With SPIKEfile, there is no option to launch multiple applications at once, which greatly simplified the design and implementation. We did not need to worry about missing SIGCHLD signals because there would only be one coming back at a time.

Because SPIKEfile is based on SPIKE, we only needed to add a file or two into it so that it could handle file input and output instead of just network input and output. By taking a quick look at how SPIKE functioned for TCP/IP, it was simple to hack together file support. The following code is the trivial addition of filestuff.c:

```c
#include <stdio.h>
#include <sys/types.h>
#include <sys/stat.h>
#include <fcntl.h>
#include "filestuff.h"
#include "spike.h"

extern struct spike *current_spike;

int
spike_fileopen (const char *file)
{
  int fd;
  if ((fd =
       open (file, O_CREAT | O_TRUNC | O_WRONLY,
             S_IRWXU | S_IRWXG | S_IRWXO)) == -1)
    perror ("fileopen::open");
  return current_spike->fd = fd;
  current_spike->proto = 69; /* 69==file,0-68 are reserved by the ISO fuzzing standard
*/
}

int
spike_filewrite (uint32 size, unsigned char *inbuffer)
{
  if (write (current_spike->fd, inbuffer, size) != size)
    {
      perror ("filewrite::write");
```

```
        return -1;
    }
  return 1;
}

void
spike_close_file ()
{
  if (current_spike->fd != -1)
    {
      close (current_spike->fd);
      current_spike->fd = -1;
    }
}
```

By adding this file to the Makefile, anyone who has used SPIKE can now use it just as easily with files as an endpoint. If you are interested in seeing exactly what files were added to SPIKE, Table 12.4 provides that information.

**Table 12.4**  List of Changes Made to SPIKE to Create SPIKEfile

| Filename | Purpose |
| --- | --- |
| filestuff.c | Contains routines to open and write files. |
| util.c | Contains a lot of the shared code between notSPIKEfile and SPIKEfile. It contains `ptrace` wrappers, the main `F_execmon` function, and some other useful functions. |
| generic_file_fuzz.c | This is the main SPIKEfile source. It contains the `main` function. |
| include/filestuff.h | A header file for filestuff.c. |
| Libdisasm | The library used to disassemble x86 instructions when something crashes. |

## USAGE NOTES

If you plan to use SPIKEfile or notSPIKEfile with an application that cannot be launched directly, you need to work around it in some way. Good examples of these types of applications include Adobe Acrobat Reader and RealNetworks RealPlayer.

Normally, with these applications, the program you actually run is a shell script wrapper. The shell script sets up the environment so that the true binary can run properly. This is done mainly so that the applications can include copies of their own shared libraries. Including their own copies of common shared libraries allows the product to be more portable. Although this is done as a courtesy to the user to make things easier, for our purposes, it makes things a little more annoying. For example, if we specify the shell script as the file to fuzz, we will not be attached to the actual binary as it runs, we will be attached to an instance of the shell. This will make our signal catching worthless. Here is an example of how to get around this for Acrobat Reader and RealPlayer. The idea is similar for all other applications like it.

## ADOBE ACROBAT

For Acrobat, you must simply first run acroread using the –DEBUG option. This will drop you to a shell with the correct environment set to directly invoke the real acroread binary, which is often in $PREFIX/Adobe/Acrobat7.0/Reader/intellinux/bin/acroread. Although this isn't documented and there is no usage function, we were able to determine this information by simply reading the acroread shell script. You can now fuzz this binary with no problems. This method was used along with notSPIKEfile to discover the Adobe Acrobat Reader UnixAppOpenFilePerform Buffer Overflow Vulnerability.[4]

## REALNETWORKS REALPLAYER

As shown by the following output, the realplay command is actually a shell script. We also see that the real binary application is called realplay.bin.

```
user@host RealPlayer $ file realplay realplay.bin
realplay:     Bourne shell script text executable
realplay.bin: ELF 32-bit LSB executable, Intel 80386, version 1 (SYSV), for GNU/Linux
2.2.5, dynamically linked (uses shared libs), stripped
```

For RealPlayer, you only need to set the shell environment variable HELIX_PATH to the path of the RealPlayer installation. You can then fuzz the binary realplay.bin directly, which is included with RealPlayer. This information was determined by simply reading the realplay shell script file. Using this method along with notSPIKEfile, the RealNetworks RealPlayer/HelixPlayer RealPix Format String Vulnerability[5] was discovered.

---

[4]  http://www.idefense.com/intelligence/vulnerabilities/display.php?id=279

[5]  http://www.idefense.com/intelligence/vulnerabilities/display.php?id=311

# CASE STUDY: REALPLAYER REALPIX FORMAT STRING VULNERABILITY

We now describe how notSPIKEfile was used to discover a vulnerability in RealPlayer that was patched in September 2005. The first step is to arbitrarily choose a file format that RealPlayer supports. Of course in this case, the RealPix format was chosen. After a great deal of Googling, several sample RealPix files were compiled and used as base files for notSPIKEfile fuzzing. One such stripped-down example follows:

```
<imfl>
    <head title="RealPix(tm) Sample Effects"
    author="Jay Slagle"
    copyright="(c)1998 RealNetworks, Inc."
    timeformat="dd:hh:mm:ss.xyz"
    duration="46"
    bitrate="12000"
    width="256"
    height="256"
    url="http://www.real.com"
    aspect="true"/>
</imfl>⁶
```

This is a barebones example of a very minimal RealPlayer file. If you load this in RealPlayer, nothing will display, as it only contains a header. We will be running this through notSPIKEfile to test the header parsing code for bugs. We use the following command to start the fuzzing.

```
user@host $ export HELIX_PATH=/opt/RealPlayer/
user@host $ ./notSPIKEfile -t 3 -d 1 -m 3 -r 0- -S -s SIGKILL -o FUZZY-sample1.rp
sample1.rp "/opt/RealPlay/realplay.bin %FILENAME%"
[...]
user@host $
```

We tell the tool to let each invocation of RealPlayer last three seconds using the -t option. We also tell it to wait one second between the time it kills an idle process and the time it starts a new one using the -d option. We specify the launching of three concurrent instances of realplayer using the -m options, and tell the tool to fuzz the whole file

---

⁶ http://service.real.com/help/library/guides/realpix/htmfiles/tags.htm

starting at byte zero using the -r option. We also specify string fuzzing mode using -S and specify the SIGKILL signal to terminate idle processes using the -s option. Finally, we tell the tool a format for fuzzed file names and specify the filename of our sample file, sample1.rp, and tell the tool how to execute RealPlayer so that it parses our file. We are ready to go! The output from notSPIKEfile suggests we have found some sort of a vulnerability by reporting several crashes.

We list the files in the current directory and see that the file FUZZY-sample1.rp-0x28ab156b-dump.txt has been created. When we view this file, we see a verbose report created to summarize the process state at the time of the crash. We also see the name of the file that caused the crash. In this case, it has been saved as 12288-FUZZY-sample1.rp. This file can be used to re-create the crash. When viewing the file, we get a good tip as to what the issue might be. The files contents are as follows:

```
<imfl>
    <head title="RealPix(tm) Sample Effects"
      author="Jay Slagle"
      copyright="(c)1998 RealNetworks, Inc."
      timeformat="%n%n%n%n%n%n%n%n%n%n%n%ndd:hh:mm:ss.xyz"
      duration="46"
      bitrate="12000"
      width="256"
      height="256"
      url="http://www.real.com"
      aspect="true"/>
</imfl>
```

Due to the presence of the %n characters, we immediately suspect a format string vulnerability as the cause of the crash. Our suspicions are confirmed when we launch the RealPlayer binary in GDB.

```
user@host ~/notSPIKEfile $ gdb -q /opt/RealPlayer/realplay.bin
Using host libthread_db library "/lib/tls/libthread_db.so.1".
(gdb) r 12288-FUZZY-sample1.rp
Starting program: /opt/RealPlayer/realplay.bin 12288-FUZZY-sample1.rp

Program received signal SIGSEGV, Segmentation fault.
0xb7e53e67 in vfprintf () from /lib/tls/libc.so.6
(gdb) x/i $pc
0xb7e53e67 <vfprintf+13719>:    mov     %ecx,(%eax)
```

We have indeed discovered a format string vulnerability in RealPlayer, in the handling of the `timeformat` option. It is now left as an exercise for you to create an exploit for the vulnerability.

## LANGUAGE

These tools were written in C for several logical reasons. First, like salt and pepper, C and Linux always have and always will work well with another. Every modern Linux distribution has a C compiler and probably always will due to the fact that the Linux kernel is written in C. There are no special libraries required to expose the `ptrace` interface to our application, and we have all of the freedom to perform the tasks that we need.

Another reason the tools were written in C is because SPIKE is written in C. Because at least one of the tools uses the SPIKE code extensively, and because these two tools ideally needed to share some code, such as the exception handling and reporting, it would have been foolish to implement the common functionality in two different languages.

## SUMMARY

With reliable tools to fuzz file formats, client-side vulnerability discovery becomes just a matter of choosing a target and being patient. Whether you choose to write your own fuzzer or extend someone else's, the time invested is well worth it.

# File Format Fuzzing: Automation on Windows

*"It's in our country's interests to find those who would do harm to us and get them out of harm's way."*

—George W. Bush, Washington, DC, April 28, 2005

In the previous chapter, we looked into automating file format fuzzing on the UNIX platform. We'll now switch to uncovering file format vulnerabilities within Windows applications. Although the overall concept remains consistent, there are important differences that we'll attempt to highlight. First off, Windows programming by nature lends itself to graphical tool design so we'll stray from the command-line applications presented in the last chapter and build a fancy GUI for the script kiddies. We also spend time identifying appropriate file formats to target which is an important decision when working in the Windows environment, given the heavy reliance within Windows on default applications for given file types. Finally, we present a solution for the ever-present challenge of detecting exploitable conditions.

## WINDOWS FILE FORMAT VULNERABILITIES

Although file format vulnerabilities can also affect servers, they are more likely to affect client-side applications. The emergence of file format vulnerabilities has marked a trend toward the importance of client-side vulnerabilities. Network administrators have over time focused resources on protecting the corporate network from network-level vulnerabilities. At the same time, software vendors have awakened to the threats posed by server vulnerabilities and these efforts have, in combination, led to a decrease in critical server-side vulnerabilities in popular applications and operating systems, which have in the past led to fast spreading worms that caused significant damage. The same cannot be said, however, for trends occurring on the client side. In the past couple of years we have seen an increase in client-side vulnerabilities that lend themselves to targeted attacks as well as phishing and identity theft.

File format vulnerabilities pose a unique risk to enterprises. Although such vulnerabilities do not lend themselves to fast spreading worms or instant network compromise, they are in many ways more difficult to protect against. The Internet, by design, promotes the sharing of information. The Web is filled with movies, images, music, and documents that make it a vast source of information and entertainment. All of that content requires that files be openly and freely shared. We have not historically considered files such as pictures or spreadsheets to be malicious as they are not themselves executable. As discussed previously, however, they can lead to exploitation when interpreted by a vulnerable application. How do we then protect against this threat? Should network administrators block all content at the firewall? The Web would be a very boring place if it was only text based. Do we really want to go back to the days of surfing the Web with a text-based browser such as Lynx? Of course not, but we do need to be aware of the threat posed by file format vulnerabilities.

The Windows platform is particularly impacted by file format vulnerabilities due to its user-friendly nature. File types are associated with applications that will handle them by default. This allows users to watch a movie or read a document simply by double-clicking on the file. It isn't even necessary to know what applications are capable of rendering specific file types to view or listen to them. Imagine the risk posed by a file format vulnerabilities discovered in applications that run by default on the Windows operating system. Millions of end users are immediately impacted. The following sidebar lists some of the more significant file format vulnerabilities that have impacted Microsoft Windows.

## SIGNIFICANT FILE FORMAT VULNERABILITIES AFFECTING MICROSOFT WINDOWS

**MS04-028 - Buffer Overrun in JPEG Processing (GDI+) Could Allow Code Execution**

In September 2004, Microsoft issued a security bulletin detailing a buffer overflow vulnerability that occurred when the GDI+ graphics device interface rendered JPEG images containing comments with an invalid size. Comments in JPEG files are prefaced by 0xFFFE byte values followed by a two-byte size for the subsequent comment. The minimum valid size for a comment is two bytes as the comment size includes the two bytes used by the size value itself. It was discovered that a size value of zero or one would lead to an exploitable heap overflow due to an integer underflow. This vulnerability affected numerous Windows applications as the GDI+ library (gdiplus.dll) is leveraged by multiple applications. Following the release of the security bulletin, public exploit code quickly emerged.

### MS05-009 - Vulnerability in PNG Processing Could Allow Remote Code Execution

Many vendors, including Microsoft, turned out to have applications vulnerable to buffer overflows that could occur when rendering Portable Network Graphics (PNG) images containing large tRNS chunks, which are used for image transparency. This vulnerability affected Windows Messenger and MSN Messenger and led to Microsoft blocking vulnerable clients from accessing their instant messaging network until the appropriate patch was applied.

### MS06-001 - Vulnerability in Graphics Rendering Engine Could Allow Remote Code Execution

During the 2005 holiday season reports began emerging about Web sites that were hosting malicious Windows Meta File (WMF) files that could lead to code execution when the pages were viewed with Internet Explorer. Microsoft was subsequently forced to release an out-of-cycle patch for the issue early in 2006 due to the level of exploitation that was occurring. The vulnerability turned out to have been caused by a design error. WMF files include records that allow for arguments to be passed to certain Windows Graphics Device Interface (GDI) library calls. One of the calls, Escape, and its subcommand SETABORTPROC, actually allowed arbitrary executable code to be called. It would later be reported that details of the vulnerability had been sold underground for $4,000.[1]

### Excel Vulnerability Auction on eBay

On December 8, 2005, an auction was posted by "fearwall" on eBay offering details of a vulnerability in Microsoft Excel.[2] The posting garnered significant media attention and was quickly pulled by eBay, which cited a policy against promoting illegal activity[3] as the reason for removing the auction.

---

[1] http://www.securityfocus.com/brief/126

[2] http://www.osvdb.org/blog/?p=71

[3] http://www.theregister.co.uk/2005/12/10/ebay_pulls_excel_vulnerability_auction/

FileFuzz was created to automate the process of identifying file format vulnerabilities. The goals for FileFuzz are threefold. First, the application should be intuitive and user friendly. Second, it should automate both the creation of fuzzed files and execution of the applications designed to interpret them. Third, it should incorporate debugging functionality to ensure that both handled and unhandled exceptions are identified. To satisfy those goals, we chose to design the application using the Microsoft .NET platform. This allowed us to build a graphical front end using C#, while some back-end components such as the debugger were written in C. A screenshot of the GUI can be seen in Figure 13.1.

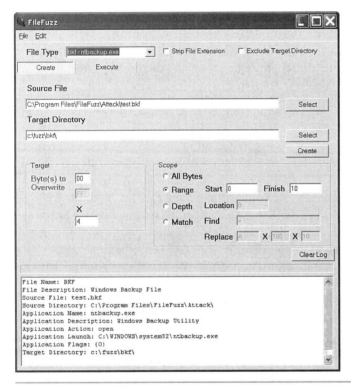

**Figure 13.1    FileFuzz**

## FEATURES

FileFuzz is designed to identify file format vulnerabilities and does so by following a simple but effective brute force approach. In a nutshell, FileFuzz mangles properly formatted files, launches them within applications designed to interpret those files, and watches to see if any problems occur. It might not be pretty, but it works. When developing FileFuzz, we were amazed at just how easy it was to find potentially exploitable conditions within file formats.

FileFuzz goes through three distinct phases. First, it creates the files that are to be fuzzed. It does this by taking a legitimate user-supplied file and based on the directives provided, makes a calculated succession of mutations and saves the resulting files. Second, one by one, the mutated files are launched within the target application. The files are launched repeatedly and the resulting process is ultimately killed based on a user-defined timeout. Finally, built-in debugging functionality monitors the processes to identify handled and unhandled exceptions that might occur. When such events are identified, they are recorded and reported to the end user. Each of these phases is presented in further detail next.

## FILE CREATION

FileFuzz takes a brute force approach to fuzzing. This means that we need the ability to read from a valid file, overwrite specific segments of that file, and save the altered file so that it can be read by the application responsible for interpreting the file. This process must be automated as it will be repeated hundreds or thousands of times.

FileFuzz allows for four separate approaches (All Bytes, Range, Depth, and Match) to file mutation that can be divided into the following categories

- Binary files
- Breadth
-   All bytes
-   Range
- Depth
- ASCII text files
-   Match

As can be seen, FileFuzz is capable of handling both binary and ASCII text file formats. Within binary files, we take two separate approaches, namely breadth and depth. To differentiate between breadth and depth, we'll use the analogy of drilling for oil. If you're searching for oil in a large geographic area you can't simply start by drilling. You must first use various techniques to identify those locations that are most likely to contain the treasure that you're looking for. Perhaps you study maps, analyze rock formations, or use ground-penetrating radar. Regardless of the approach, once you find those interesting locations, you can start drilling test holes to see which are the most promising.

With file format fuzzing, we take a similar approach. First we use breadth to find the interesting locations and then we use depth to determine if we've struck black gold. Breadth refers to covering either all bytes within the file or a specific range. Separate files are created by consecutively changing byte values within the range to a predefined value until the entire range has been covered. Once that has been completed, the files are launched one after the other to determine if the changes result in any exception.

Occasionally we get lucky and need to go no further. Sometimes at this point, exceptions result that are clearly interesting and it is obvious that the end user has control over the crash, as the value of the mutation that was introduced is clearly visible in the registers. More often than not, it's not this easy. A crash will occur and the location might be interesting, but it's not clear from the register values if the end user will have any means of controlling the crash. In this case, we then move onto depth. Once interesting byte locations have been identified within the file, we then focus on these locations and use depth to try all possible byte values for that location. When we look at the resulting crashes we can get a sense of the degree to which we can control that crash. If the exception location and resister values are consistent regardless of the byte values provided, we have no control over that exception. If, however, the crash occurs at different locations or the register values continually change, it is then clear that we have at least some influence over the resulting exception based on the values that we use when mutating the file.

FileFuzz also accommodates ASCII text files. It does this by allowing the end user to first select a string that identifies the location to overwrite and then requests three separate inputs to determine the input used to mutate the file. The end user must provide a string value, its length, and the number of times that it is to be multiplied. Let's look at an example. In general, ASCII text files such as *.ini files contain name–value pairs in the following format:

```
name = value
```

Typically, we want to overwrite the value. Let's assume that we want to overwrite the value with a succession of A characters in multiples of 10. In this case, we would first set the Find value to the = character, as this identifies the start of the value. We would then set the Replace value to A X 10 X 10. This will create 10 mutated files with overwritten values for each instance where an = character is found. The resulting 10 files will contain from 10 to 100 A characters in the value location.

## APPLICATION EXECUTION

Once the fuzzed files have been created, we need to launch them within the target application. For example, if we had mutated *.doc files, we would then want to launch them within Microsoft Word. File Fuzz uses the `CreateProcess()` function from the Windows API to do this, so we can use FileFuzz to launch the application so long as we can determine how the same application would be launched from a command prompt, including necessary flags that might be passed to the application. We provide detail on how to identify this information later in the chapter.

In file format fuzzing, we need to launch the same application over and over hundreds or perhaps thousands of times. If we were to leave all of the previously executed processes running, we would quickly run out of available memory. Therefore, the execution phase isn't complete until the process is also killed after a predefined interval. We allow the end user to control this, by including a Milliseconds field under the Execute tab that identifies the amount of time that the process will be allowed to run before being forcibly killed if necessary.

## EXCEPTION DETECTION

As mentioned in previous chapters, detection is a key component to fuzzing. What good is it to run a fuzzer overnight and wake up to find that you have indeed been able to crash the application but you have no idea which of the 10,000 inputs caused the crash? You're no closer to the answer than you were before you started. File format fuzzing provides many options for detecting exceptions but one stands out. For starters, you could go very low tech and simply watch the fuzzing process to identify error windows or perhaps an application or system crash. If you like watching paint dry, this is the approach for you. If you'd prefer to step it up a notch, you could check the log files to determine if a problem has occurred. This would include both application log files and system log files such as those maintained by the Windows Event Viewer. The problem with this approach is that the input (fuzz file) is not associated with the output (log event). The only way to tie the two together would be through the use of timestamps, which is imperfect at best.

As with most types of fuzzing, the best approach for identifying exceptions is to use a debugger. The advantage of a debugger is that it will identify both handled and unhandled exceptions. Windows has strong exception handling and can often recover from the fuzzed files that it reads. However, it is important to identify these situations, as a small change to the file at the location in question could end up creating an unrecoverable or exploitable condition.

The use of a debugger when conducting file format fuzzing is not quite as straightforward as it is for other types of fuzzing. We cannot in this case manually attach a debugger to the targeted application and let the fuzzer run. This is because the fuzzer is constantly launching and killing the target application. In doing so, it also kills the debugger. For this reason, we need to leverage a debugging API and build the debugger directly into our fuzzer. This way the fuzzer can execute the target application, attach a debugger itself, and then kill the application. In doing so, the fuzzer will monitor for exceptions each time the target application is launched.

For FileFuzz, we created crash.exe, which is actually a stand-alone debugger that is executed by the GUI application and in turn launches the target application. It is a completely stand-alone command-line application and as FileFuzz is an open source project, you are free to leverage crash.exe for your own fuzzing projects.

## Saved Audits

An audit in FileFuzz can be conducted manually by selecting the target to fuzz and identifying how the fuzzed files should be generated and stored. Alternately, a previously saved audit can be used to fill in all necessary fields to start fuzzing right away. The application comes with a number of canned audits that can be accessed from the File Types drop-down menu on the main screen. However, end users can also create their own saved audits and add them to the drop-down menu without needing to recompile the application. This is possible as the menu is dynamically generated at runtime by parsing the targets.xml file. The structure of an individual audit is shown in the following example:

```
<test>
   <name>jpg - iexplore.exe</name>
   <file>
   <fileName>JPG</fileName>
      <fileDescription>JPEG Image</fileDescription>
   </file>
   <source>
      <sourceFile>gradient.jpg</sourceFile>
      <sourceDir>C:\WINDOWS\Help\Tours\htmlTour\</sourceDir>
   </source>
   <app>
      <appName>iexplore.exe</appName>
      <appDescription>Internet Explorer</appDescription>
       <appAction>open</appAction>
      <appLaunch>"C:\Program Files\Internet Explorer\iexplore.exe"</appLaunch>
      <appFlags>{0}</appFlags>
```

```
   </app>
   <target>
      <targetDir>c:\fuzz\jpg\</targetDir>
   </target>
</test>
```

The inclusion of a dynamically generated drop-down menu was an intentional design decision. Although FileFuzz is an open source application, it is assumed that most users will not have the programming experience or the interest in extending functionality through additional coding. The approach of using a dynamic menu allows the majority of end users to extend functionality in a relatively user-friendly manner. The structure of the XML file illustrates an important point: Make your applications as intuitive and user friendly as possible. Although documentation is a key component of the development process, don't expect users to turn to documentation as a first step. Users expect intuitive applications and want to start using them out of the box.

Look at the preceding XML file. The descriptive XML tags are self-explanatory. An end user could add an audit simply by adding and customizing an additional <test> block. Although creating intuitive applications is not a legitimate excuse for ignoring documentation, it is an important design concept. Modern programming languages allow for user-friendly applications as they take care of the low-level code such as networking or graphical display. Invest the time saved in making an application that provides a better experience for the end user. Just because you're designing a security application doesn't mean that you should need a PhD to operate it.

## NECESSARY BACKGROUND INFORMATION

Windows and UNIX file format fuzzing have the same basic fundamentals, but the importance of default applications in the Windows environment can increase the risk posed by this class of vulnerabilities. Before building our fuzzer we'll therefore spend some time investigating this issue to better understand how to identify high risk targets.

### IDENTIFYING TARGETS

Microsoft Windows allows users to assign default applications to specific file types. This enhances the usability of the operating system by allowing an application to automatically be launched when a file is double-clicked. This is an important point to keep in mind when identifying file formats to target. There's minimal risk if a buffer overflow is found in an application that is unlikely to ever be used to view a particular file type, but there is significant risk when the same vulnerability is discovered in an application that opens a commonly traded file by default. Take, for example, an overflow in the JPEG image format. Like all graphic formats, there are many applications available that are capable of rendering the image, but only one that is associated with the file type by default on a given operating system. On Windows XP, the default JPEG viewer is Windows Picture and Fax Viewer. Therefore, an overflow discovered in Windows Picture and Fax Viewer carries with it much greater risk than the same overflow in a freeware picture viewer obtained from Download.com. Why? If a default Windows application is found to be vulnerable, millions of machines are immediately vulnerable.

## Windows Explorer

How do we figure out which applications will render a particular file type within the Windows environment? A simple approach would be to simply double-click on the file and see which application is launched. This is fine for a quick check, but it doesn't help us to determine the exact instructions that were executed to launch the application. These instructions are important to us when fuzzing, as we need a way to automate the continual execution of the target application. Rapid double-clicking just doesn't cut it when you have a few thousand files to fuzz.

Windows Explorer is a quick and simple way to identify applications associated with file types and to identify the command-line arguments used to launch the application. Let's use Explorer to prove that JPEG files are associated with Windows Picture and Fax Viewer. More important, let's identify how we could repeatedly launch fuzzed JPEG files within FileFuzz to identify vulnerabilities.

The first step requires selecting Tools[el]Folder Options from the Windows Explorer menu. From there, we want to select the File Types tab. This displays the screen shown in Figure 13.2.

This screen alone is a wealth of information. Scrolling through the Registered file types list shows us virtually all of the file extensions that are associated with particular applications. These file types make for good fuzzing targets as vulnerabilities identified in the default applications could be exploited simply by sending a file to a victim and convincing them to double-click on the file. Although this isn't trivial, spam e-mail has proven that end users are already trigger-happy when it comes to their mouse clicks, so it represents a reasonable exploitation scenario.

At this point, thanks to the Opens with label, we already know the application associated with the JPEG file type, but we don't know how the operating system actually launches that application. Fortunately, we're just a few mouse clicks away from that vital information.

When handling file types, Windows includes the concept of actions. Actions allow for the file to be opened in a different way or with a different application, given unique command-line options. For our purposes, we want to know how Windows opens JPEG files,

**Figure 13.2**   Windows Explorer Folder Options dialog box

**Figure 13.3**   Windows Explorer Edit File Type dialog box

**Figure 13.4**   Windows Explorer Editing Action for Type dialog box

so we focus on the Open Action. As shown in Figure 13.3, highlighting Open and clicking the Edit button will reveal the answer.

At last! Windows reveals the secret that we've been searching for. In the Application used to perform action field, shown in Figure 13.4, we see that Windows Picture and Fax Viewer isn't an executable application after all. In fact, it's a dynamic-link library (DLL) launched using rundll32.exe. The full command-line argument for launching an image in Windows Picture and Fax Viewer is shown here.

```
rundll32.exe C:\WINDOWS\system32\shimgvw.dll,ImageView_Fullscreen %1
```

Not only is Windows Picture and Fax Viewer not an executable as we might have expected, but we can see that Windows also expects the ImageView_Fullscreen argument to be supplied. If you were to run this line from a command prompt and replace the %1 with the name of a legitimate JPEG file, you would see that sure enough, the file is rendered within Windows Picture and Fax Viewer as expected. This is a key concept. If we can determine the appropriate command-line arguments to render a file within a given application, we can then use FileFuzz to test for vulnerabilities. We can now take that same command line and copy it into the Application and Arguments fields under the Execute tab within FileFuzz. The only necessary change is that we must change the %1, which represents the target file, to a {0}, as this is the format that FileFuzz expects.

A word of advice: Windows can be very picky when it comes to things such as spaces and quotation marks within command-line arguments. Be sure to copy the command exactly to avoid some painful debugging later on.

### Windows Registry

Although Windows Explorer can reveal the association between a particular file type and the application that it is associated with 90 percent of the time, we have encountered situations in which an association exists but it is not shown in Windows Explorer. Take, for example, the *.cbo file type. CBO files are used by the Microsoft Interactive Training application that is included by default on certain distributions of Windows XP, such as those packaged with many Dell machines. If you have a machine that includes Microsoft Interactive Training, you will notice that the CBO file type is not included in the Windows Explorer File Types list, yet within Windows Explorer a CBO file is displayed with a pencil icon and does indeed launch the Microsoft Interactive Training application when double-clicked. What gives? How do we determine the command-line arguments for launching a file type that doesn't appear in Windows Explorer? For this, we need to turn to the Windows registry. First check the value of the default field of the \HKEY_CLASSES_ROOT\.xxx registry key, where xxx is the associated file extension. This value provides us with the name of the application used to launch the file type. Next, identify the HKEY_CLASSES_ROOT\ registry key that corresponds to that same descriptive name. Within the …\shell\open\command key, you'll find details of command-line arguments used to launch the application associated with the mystery file extension.

## DEVELOPMENT

Now that we have a primer on the unique aspects of file format fuzzing on the Windows platform, it's time to build a fuzzer. We break down the thought process that we went through when designing FileFuzz and then conclude by using FileFuzz to identify the much hyped JPEG GDI+ vulnerability detailed in  Microsoft Security Bulletin MS04-028.

### APPROACH

In creating FileFuzz, we sought to develop a user-friendly, graphical application that would allow an end user to perform fuzzing without learning a series of command-line arguments. We wanted to produce a point-and-click application that was as intuitive as possible. Our goal was also to produce a tool that was specifically geared toward the nuances of file format fuzzing on the Windows platform, so cross-platform functionality was not a necessary feature.

## LANGUAGE SELECTION

Given the design goals, we once again chose the .Net platform for our development. This allowed us to create a GUI front end with minimal effort, freeing our time to focus on the functional aspect of the project. The GUI and all file creation functionality were done using C#. For the debugging functionality we switched to C as it allowed us to more easily and directly interact with the Windows API. The .NET platform accommodated this design decision as it allows for projects to contain multiple programming languages so long as they're all compatible with the .NET Framework.

## DESIGN

We've had enough discussion about how we would design FileFuzz. Now it's time to walk through specific portions of the implementation. It isn't practical to describe every section of code, but we highlight a few of the more important segments. For a complete understanding of how FileFuzz is designed, we encourage you to download the source code from www.fuzzing.org.

### File Creation

FileFuzz needed to be able to accommodate any Windows file format and we realized that different approaches would be required for both binary and ASCII text files. The Read.cs file contains all of the code for reading the valid files, and Write.cs handles the creation of the fuzzed files.

### Reading from Source Files

FileFuzz takes a brute force approach to fuzzing so we start by reading known good files. The data from the legitimate file is read and stored for subsequent mutation when creating fuzz files. Fortunately, the .NET Framework makes tasks such as reading from files relatively painless. We took separate approaches when reading and creating binary and ASCII text files. For our purposes, we leveraged the `BinaryReader` class for reading binary files and storing the data in a byte array. Reading ASCII text files is very similar to reading binary files but for that we leveraged the `StreamReader` class. Additionally, we store the result in a string variable as opposed to a byte array. The constructor for the `Read` class can be seen next.

```
private BinaryReader brSourceFile;
private StreamReader arSourceFile;
public byte [] sourceArray;
public string sourceString;
```

```
private int sourceCount;
private string sourceFile;

public Read(string fileName)
{
    sourceFile = fileName;
    sourceArray = null;
    sourceString = null;
    sourceCount = 0;
}
```

sourceArray will be used to hold the byte array for binary files that we read, whereas sourceString will be used to hold the contents of an ASCII text file.

### Writing to Fuzz Files

Now that the files have been read, we need to mutate them and save the resulting files to launch them within the target application. As mentioned, FileFuzz divides file creation into the following four types, based on the approach used to perform file mutation:

- All bytes
- Range
- Depth
- Match

We handle all of the different approaches within a single Write class but overload the constructors to handle each of the different scenarios. For binary file types we use the BinaryWriter class to write the new byte array to a file that will be used to fuzz the target application during the execution phase. Building ASCII text files, on the other hand, takes advantage of the StreamWriter class for writing string variables to disk.

### Application Execution

The code responsible for starting the process of executing the target application is found in the Main.cs file, as shown in the next code segment. However, when you look at it you realize that it's relatively simple because the code is not actually responsible for launching the target application itself; rather, it is responsible for launching the built-in debugger, which in turn handles the execution of the target application. The crash.exe debugger is discussed in detail later.

We start by instantiating a new instance of the Process class. Within the executeApp() function, we then initiate a loop to launch each of the previously created fuzz files. During each pass of the loop, we set the attributes for the process to create, including the name of the process to execute, which, as mentioned, will always be crash.exe regardless of what is being fuzzed, as the command-line application crash.exe will in turn launch the target application. At this point, control is handed to crash.exe and the results are eventually returned by crash.exe through standard output and standard error and displayed in the rtbLog rich text box, which serves as the main output window for FileFuzz.

```
Process proc = new Process();

public Execute(int startFileInput, int finishFileInput, string targetDirectoryInput,
string fileExtensionInput, int applicationTimerInput, string executeAppNameInput,
string executeAppArgsInput)
{
   startFile = startFileInput;
   finishFile = finishFileInput;
   targetDirectory = targetDirectoryInput;
   fileExtension = fileExtensionInput;
   applicationTimer = applicationTimerInput;
   executeAppName = executeAppNameInput;
   executeAppArgs = executeAppArgsInput;
   procCount = startFile;
}

public void executeApp()
{
   bool exceptionFound = false;

   //Initialize progress bar
   if (this.pbrStart != null)
   {
      this.pbrStart(startFile, finishFile);
   }

   while (procCount <= finishFile)
   {
      proc.StartInfo.CreateNoWindow = true;
      proc.StartInfo.UseShellExecute = false;
      proc.StartInfo.RedirectStandardOutput = true;
      proc.StartInfo.RedirectStandardError = true;
      proc.StartInfo.FileName = "crash.exe";
proc.StartInfo.Arguments = executeAppName + " " + applicationTimer + " " +
String.Format(executeAppArgs,  @targetDirectory + procCount.ToString() +
fileExtension);
      proc.Start();
      //Update progress bar
      if (this.pbrUpdate != null)
```

```
        {
            this.pbrUpdate(procCount);
        }
        //Update counter
        if (this.tbxUpdate != null)
        {
            this.tbxUpdate(procCount);
        }
        proc.WaitForExit();

        //Write std output to rich text box log
        if (this.rtbLog != null && (proc.ExitCode == -1 || proc.ExitCode == 1))
        {
            this.rtbLog(proc.StandardOutput.ReadToEnd());
            this.rtbLog(proc.StandardError.ReadToEnd());
            exceptionFound = true;
        }
        procCount++;
    }
    //Clear the progress bar
    if (this.pbrStart != null)
    {
        this.pbrStart(0, 0);
    }
    //Clear the counter
    if (this.tbxUpdate != null)
    {
        this.tbxUpdate(0);
    }
    if (exceptionFound == false)
        this.rtbLog("No excpetions found\n\n");
    exceptionFound = false;
}
```

## Exception Detection

As mentioned, FileFuzz includes debugging functionality in the form of crash.exe, a stand-alone debugger written in C that leverages the debugging functions built into the Windows API. It also leverages libdasm, which is an open source library that helps with interpreting disassembly code. As can be seen in the next code segment, first a check is completed to ensure that crash.exe has been passed at least three arguments. For use in FileFuzz, those arguments are the name and path of the application being fuzzed, the wait time before forcibly killing the target application, and finally additional command-line arguments plus the name of the fuzzed file to interpret. Following this, the wait time value is converted from a string type to an integer and the full command-line argument is created and stored in a character array. Then, the target application is launched using the CreateProcess command, with the DEBUG_PROCESS flag set.

```
if (argc < 4)
{
   fprintf(stderr, "[!] Usage: crash <path to app> <milliseconds> <arg1>
     [arg2 arg3 argn]\n\n");
   return -1;
}

// convert wait time from string to integer.
if ((wait_time = atoi(argv[2])) == 0)
{
   fprintf(stderr, "[!] Milliseconds argument unrecognized: %s\n\n", argv[2]);
   return -1;
}

// create the command line string for the call to CreateProcess().
strcpy(command_line, argv[1]);

for (i = 3; i < argc; i++)
{
   strcat(command_line, " ");
   strcat(command_line, argv[i]);
}

//
// launch the target process.
//

ret = CreateProcess(NULL,     // target file name.
  command_line,               // command line options.
  NULL,                       // process attributes.
  NULL,                       // thread attributes.
  FALSE,                      // handles are not inherited.
  DEBUG_PROCESS,              // debug the target process and all spawned children.
  NULL,                       // use our current environment.
  NULL,                       // use our current working directory.
  &si,                        // pointer to STARTUPINFO structure.
  &pi);                       // pointer to PROCESS_INFORMATION structure.

   printf("[*] %s\n", GetCommandLine());   //Print the command line
```

```
if (!ret)
{
    fprintf(stderr, "[!] CreateProcess() failed: %d\n\n", GetLastError());
    return -1;
}
```

At this point, it is now possible for crash.exe to monitor for and record exceptions. In the next code segment, we see that so long as the timeout has not yet expired, we are monitoring for debug events. When one is encountered, we obtain the handle to the thread in question and determine the type of exception that has occurred. Using a case statement we look for three types of exceptions that are of interest: memory access violations, divide by zero errors, and stack overflows. We then print out pertinent debugging information that will assist the end user in determining if the exception is worthy of further analysis. Leveraging the libdasm library, we decode the location where the exception occurred, the offending opcode, and the values of the registers at the time of the crash.

```
while (GetTickCount() - start_time < wait_time)
{
    if (WaitForDebugEvent(&dbg, 100))
    {
        // we are only interested in debug events.
        if (dbg.dwDebugEventCode != EXCEPTION_DEBUG_EVENT)
        {
            ContinueDebugEvent(dbg.dwProcessId, dbg.dwThreadId, DBG_CONTINUE);
            continue;
        }

        // get a handle to the offending thread.
        if ((thread = OpenThread(THREAD_ALL_ACCESS, FALSE, dbg.dwThreadId)) == NULL)
        {
            fprintf(stderr, "[!] OpenThread() failed: %d\n\n", GetLastError());
            return -1;
        }

        // get the context of the offending thread.
        context.ContextFlags = CONTEXT_FULL;

        if (GetThreadContext(thread, &context) == 0)
        {
            fprintf(stderr, "[!] GetThreadContext() failed: %d\n\n", GetLastError());
            return -1;
        }
```

```
        // examine the exception code.
        switch (dbg.u.Exception.ExceptionRecord.ExceptionCode)
        {
            case EXCEPTION_ACCESS_VIOLATION:
                exception = TRUE;
                printf("[*] Access Violation\n");
                break;
            case EXCEPTION_INT_DIVIDE_BY_ZERO:
                exception = TRUE;
                printf("[*] Divide by Zero\n");
                break;
            case EXCEPTION_STACK_OVERFLOW:
                exception = TRUE;
                printf("[*] Stack Overflow\n");
                break;
            default:
                ContinueDebugEvent(dbg.dwProcessId, dbg.dwThreadId, DBG_CONTINUE);
        }

        // if an exception occurred, print more information.
        if (exception)
        {
            // open a handle to the target process.
            if ((process = OpenProcess(PROCESS_ALL_ACCESS, FALSE, dbg.dwProcessId)) ==
NULL)
            {
                fprintf(stderr, "[!] OpenProcess() failed: %d\n\n", GetLastError());
                return -1;
            }

            // grab some memory at EIP for disassembly.
            ReadProcessMemory(process, (void *)context.Eip, &inst_buf, 32, NULL);

            // decode the instruction into a string.
            get_instruction(&inst, inst_buf, MODE_32);
            get_instruction_string(&inst, FORMAT_INTEL, 0,
inst_string,sizeof(inst_string));

            // print the exception to screen.
            printf("[*] Exception caught at %08x %s\n", context.Eip, inst_string);
            printf("[*] EAX:%08x EBX:%08x ECX:%08x EDX:%08x\n", context.Eax, context.Ebx,
                context.Ecx, context.Edx);
            printf("[*] ESI:%08x EDI:%08x ESP:%08x EBP:%08x\n\n", context.Esi,
context.Edi,
                context.Esp, context.Ebp);
```

```
        return 1;
    }

  }
}
```

The exception details identified by crash.exe are returned to the GUI and displayed for the end user. Hopefully this information will provide a quick visual queue to the end user to help in identifying important crashes. Crashes that would lend themselves to further investigation would include exceptions occurring in opcode instructions that would allow shellcode to obtain control of the flow of code execution and where registers either contain user-controlled or user-influenced input.

## CASE STUDY

Now that we've developed a file format fuzzer, we'll test it against a known vulnerability to validate our design. Much of our interest in file format vulnerabilities was spurred by the release of Microsoft released Security Bulletin MS04-028 – "Buffer Overrun in JPEG Processing (GDI+) Could Allow Code Execution."[4] That bulletin garnered a great deal of attention as it shed light on just how damaging client-side vulnerabilities could be. Here was an exploitable buffer overflow in a number of popular client-side applications that were installed by default and affected a massive user base. The result was the quick emergence of public exploits that, although relying on some social engineering, lent themselves to both targeted attacks and indiscriminate phishing and identity theft.

The vulnerability itself resided in the gdiplus.dll library, which was used by a plethora of applications including Microsoft Office, Internet Explorer, and Windows Explorer. The JPEG format allows for comments to be embedded within the image itself. Comments are preceded by the 0xFFFE byte sequence, followed by a 16-bit word value indicating the total size of the comment. The size includes the two bytes used for the size and the header ends with the comment itself.

Would FileFuzz have been able to identify this vulnerability? Let's find out. We'll start with a legitimate image file and then add a comment either manually or using an image editor. If you choose to duplicate this example for yourself, be sure that you're using a vulnerable version of Windows. Our results were produced using Windows XP SP1. When creating the test file, we'll use a very simple image, in our case, a 1 x 1 white pixel. Why so simple? As mentioned, brute force fuzzing is inefficient. We want to focus on the

---

[4]  http://www.microsoft.com/technet/security/Bulletin/MS04-028.mspx

image headers, not the image itself, so we stick to using an image that is pretty much nonexistent. As a result, we end up with a file that is only 631 bytes in size and we can therefore brute force all bytes in a reasonable time frame. After adding the comment "fuzz" when we look at the file using a hex editor, we see the byte sequence shown next.

```
0000009eh: FF FE 00 06 66 75 7A 7A                        ; ÿþ..fuzz

Breakdown:
FF FE                   Comment preface
00 06                   Length of comments in bytes
66 75 7A 7A             ASCII value of 'fuzz'
```

Before we can start fuzzing, we want to find out which Windows XP application is responsible for rendering JPEG images by default. Fortunately, we already determined earlier in the chapter that Windows Picture and Fax Viewer is responsible for this task and uses the following command-line arguments to launch the JPEG image (see Figure 13.5):

```
rundll32.exe C:\WINDOWS\system32\shimgvw.dll,ImageView_Fullscreen %1
```

At this point, we can launch FileFuzz and begin the fuzzing process. FileFuzz has a built-in audit for JPEG files that can be accessed from the File Type drop-down menu, but to demonstrate the functionality of FileFuzz, we'll start from scratch.

We begin in the Create tab and set the appropriate options to generate a series of altered JPEG files, based on the legitimate JPEG file with an embedded comment that we created earlier. We'll set all options on the Create tab to the following values:

- *Source file.* C:\Program Files\FileFuzz\Attack\test.jpg. Legitimate JPEG file
- *Target directory.* C:\fuzz\jpg\. Target directory where generated fuzz files are to be stored.
- *Byte(s) to overwrite.* 00 x 2. According details of the vulnerability,[5] the overflow will occur if we set the length value of the vulnerability to 0x00 or 0x01. It isn't possible for the comment to be zero or one byte in length due to this fact that the two-byte size is included in the overall length. We'll therefore fuzz the file with a word value of 0x0000 in the hopes that we'll trigger the overflow by overwriting the comment size value.
- *Scope.* Range = 150-170. In the test file that we created, the size value begins at byte 160. To be safe we'll fuzz a range of bytes from 150 to 170.

---

[5]  http://www.securityfocus.com/archive/1/375204

The final settings can be seen in Figure 13.5.

Once all of the settings are in place, we click Create to generate the files. Now it's time to move to the Execute tab. Here we need to tell FileFuzz how to launch Windows Picture and Fax Viewer. The settings for the Execute tab values will be as follows:

- *Application.* rundll32.exe. As Windows Picture and Fax Viewer is actually a DLL, the application that we use is run32.exe, which will be used to launch the DLL file.

- *Arguments.* C:\WINDOWS\system32\shimgvw.dll,ImageView_Fullscreen {0}. The arguments passed include the full location of Windows Picture and Fax Viewer (shimgvw,dll), the ImageView_FullScreen argument, and {0}, which is a placeholder for the name of the fuzzed file that will be opened.

- *Start file.* 150. The first file that we created.

- *Finish file.* 170. The last file that we created.

- *Milliseconds.* 2000. The length of time that Windows Picture and Fax Viewer will be permitted to run before it is forcibly closed.

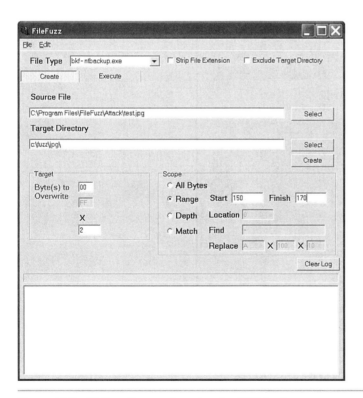

**Figure 13.5**  FileFuzz Create tab settings for JPEG fuzzing

The appropriate settings can be seen in Figure 13.6.

At this point, we're ready to go. On clicking Execute, we see Windows Picture and Fax Viewer repeatedly launch and exit. This will happen 21 times as our 21 fuzz files are opened and interpreted. When the smoke clears we see that FileFuzz detected a few exceptions. However, the one that we're interested in occurs when 160.jpg was launched as shown in the following sample output. This is of interest as byte 160 is the start of the JPEG comment size and file 160.jpg has overwritten the original value with 0x0000.

```
[*] "crash.exe" rundll32.exe 2000
C:\WINDOWS\system32\shimgvw.dll,ImageView_Fullscreen c:\fuzz\jpg\160.jpg
[*] Access Violation
[*] Exception caught at 70e15599 rep movsd
[*] EAX:fffffffe EBX:00904560 ECX:3ffffe3c EDX:fffffffe
[*] ESI:0090b07e EDI:0090c000 ESP:00aaf428 EBP:00aaf43400
```

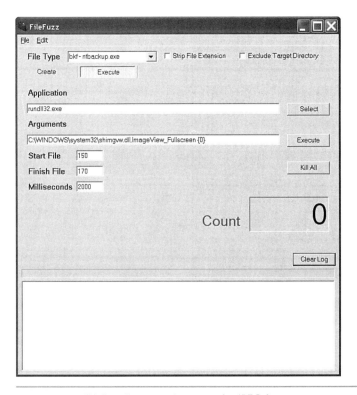

**Figure 13.6**   FileFuzz Execute tab settings for JPEG fuzzing

## BENEFITS AND ROOM FOR IMPROVEMENT

FileFuzz provides basic functionality for taking a brute force approach to fuzzing file for-mats. With its GUI and built-in debugging capabilities it allows for a quick and dirty audit using a known good file as a starting point. That said, there's plenty of room for improvement.

For starters, more comprehensive audit capabilities could be developed. As it stands, only one audit can be performed at a time. For example, when taking a breadth approach with a binary file type, only a single sweep across the byte range with a single byte value (e.g., 0xFFFFFFFF) can be performed at one time. If another value is then to be run, the process must be rerun using the new value. A more comprehensive audit function could allow for multiple values to be selected or perhaps ranges of values that would all be tested. Perhaps some intelligent capabilities could be added to first take a breadth approach and then switch to a depth approach automatically once byte locations have been identified that revealed more than a specific number or type of exceptions.

FileFuzz was intentionally designed as a brute force fuzzer, as file format fuzzing lends itself to this more simplistic approach. However, that's not to say that intelligent fuzzing capabilities couldn't also be added. Perhaps a new Create – Intelligent tab could be added in addition to the existing Create tab, which would then become a Create – Brute Force tab. This new tab would include an entirely new set of intelligent fuzzing capabilities that would require the end user to develop a template for the structure of a particular file type rather than use an existing file as a starting point. This approach would require more up-front effort by the user but would also allow him or her to better identify spe-cific areas of the file that are to be fuzzed and how they should be fuzzed. The template would likely be created after studying specification documents for the targeted file for-mat but FileFuzz could also contain built-in sample templates.

Intelligent exception handling would help to weed out many of the exceptions that are unlikely to lead to exploitable conditions. By embedding rules that are applied when analyzing the crash.exe output, certain exceptions could be omitted based on factors such as the opcodes at the memory location of the crash, register values, or condition of the stack. Alternately, rather than omitting certain results, perhaps it would be better to highlight those that show more promise.

In short, there's plenty of room for improvement. Our goal is simply to get the ball rolling. The rest is up to you.

## SUMMARY

File format vulnerabilities have plagued Microsoft during the past couple of years. Whether the vulnerabilities have appeared in media files or Office documents, they've appeared in bunches and are being used by attackers. That's not to say that Microsoft is the only vendor to struggle with this class of vulnerabilities, only that they continue to be the favorite target of bug hunters. Hopefully with the recent attention drawn to file-format vulnerabilities, software vendors will add fuzzing to their development lifecycle to catch these vulnerabilities prior to production.

# Network Protocol Fuzzing

Fuzzing was born at the University of Wisconsin with the introduction of random arguments to command-line `setuid` UNIX utilities. Despite this initial association the term *fuzzing* today is typically thought of as applying to network protocols, and for good reason. Network protocol fuzzing is the most interesting fuzzing transport for security researchers as the discovered vulnerabilities carry the highest criticality. A remotely exploitable vulnerability that does not require valid credentials to reach or any interaction from a target user to exploit is the epitome of discoveries, the gold medal if you will.

Client-side vulnerabilities, affecting Microsoft Internet Explorer, for example, are typically leveraged in the creation of bot nets. Nefarious actors cast a wide net hoping to catch as many fish as they can. For the most part, these captured fish are personal desktop computers sitting on broadband connections. A server-side vulnerability in a network daemon can be equally as useful for the construction of bot nets, but leveraging these vulnerabilities in this fashion is a waste of potential. From an attacker's perspective, owning software such as a back-end database or enterprise Web server provides a great opportunity for data theft as well as a trusted platform from which to conduct further attacks. In this chapter we introduce network protocol fuzzing and present some of the unique characteristics and challenges posed by this popular fuzzing classification. Along the way we'll explore a number of network protocol vulnerabilities.

## WHAT IS NETWORK PROTOCOL FUZZING?

As with other types of fuzzing, network protocol fuzzing requires identifying the attack surface, mutating or generating error-inducing fuzz values, transmitting those fuzz values to a target, and monitoring that target for faults. Quite simply, if your fuzzer communicates with its target over some form of socket, then it is a network protocol fuzzer.

The socket communication component of network-based fuzzing poses an interesting nuance in that it creates a bottleneck on our testing throughput. Comparing the transport speed for file format, command-line argument, and environment variable fuzzing to that of the network is like racing an Aston Martin DB9 with a Geo Metro.

Existing network protocol fuzzers tend to come in two flavors. Some are generic frameworks capable of fuzzing a variety of protocols. Tools such as SPIKE[1] and ProtoFuzz, a fuzzer we build from scratch in Chapter 16, "Network Protocol Fuzzing: Automation on Windows," fall into this category. SPIKE is the most well known fuzzer and is described in greater detail in the next chapter. The other variety of network protocol fuzzers includes those designed to target a specific protocol. Examples of this category include ircfuzz,[2] dhcpfuzz,[3] and Infigo FTPStress Fuzzer.[4] You can guess what protocols each of these mentioned fuzzers is designed to target straight from the name. Protocol specific fuzzers tend to be small targeted scripts or applications, whereas frameworks are generally larger development efforts. We discuss the values of creating and using fuzzing frameworks as opposed to specific stand-alone tools in Chapter 21, "Fuzzing Frameworks." Next, let's take a look at some example network protocol fuzzing targets.

### MICROSOFT CATCHES A VIRUS

For most nonparanoid schizophrenic citizens of the world, the new millennium was a time to celebrate. We enjoyed the biggest New Year's Eve parties in history, survived the Y2K scare, and saw that the world didn't come to an end. Unfortunately for Microsoft, the new millennium brought with it the beginning of several years in which major server-side vulnerabilities would be discovered across the most popular Microsoft products. Many of these issues, as it turned out, would

---

[1]   http://www.immunitysec.com/resources-freesoftware.shtml

[2]   http://www.digitaldwarf.be/products/ircfuzz.c

[3]   http://www.digitaldwarf.be/products/dhcpfuzz.pl

[4]   http://www.infigo.hr/en/in_focus/tools

see the rapid development and public release of exploit code. Additionally, a number of these vulnerabilities would be leveraged by fast spreading malicious code, resulting in substantial financial damage for corporations worldwide and serving as a wake up call to system administrators everywhere.

Let's take a look at some of the notable Microsoft-affecting worms and the vulnerabilities they exploited to spread across the globe. The reputation damage caused by these worms was one of the direct catalysts behind Microsoft's establishment of the Trustworthy Computing Initiative launched in 2002,[5] which fundamentally changed the way that Microsoft addressed security throughout the software development lifecycle.

- *Code Red.* A buffer overflow in an IIS Web server Internet Server Application Programming Interface (ISAPI) extension was disclosed on June 18, 2001.[6] Despite the availability of a patch for nearly a month, a worm was discovered on July 13, 2001, which exploited the flaw to deface Web sites on vulnerable servers with the message "HELLO! Welcome to http://www.worm.com! Hacked By Chinese!" After infection, the worm slept for 20 to 27 days and then attempted to launch a DoS attack against various fixed IP addresses, including the IP address of whitehouse.gov.

- *Slammer.* The SQL slammer worm exploited two separate vulnerabilities, identified by Microsoft Security Bulletins MS02-039[7] and MS02-061,[8] in Microsoft SQL Server and Desktop Engine. When it first emerged on January 25, 2003, it took about ten minutes to infect its 75,000 initial victims.[9] The buffer overflow exploit by the worm (MS02-039) had been disclosed and patched by Microsoft some six months prior, but plenty of vulnerable servers were and still are available.

- *Blaster.* On August 11, 2003, 18-year-old Jeffrey Lee Parson shared his creation with the world: a worm[10] that took advantage of a DCOM remote procedure call (RPC) buffer overflow in Windows XP and Windows 2000.[11] Once again,

---

5  http://www.microsoft.com/mscorp/twc/2007review.mspx

6  http://research.eeye.com/html/advisories/published/AD20010618.html

7  http://www.microsoft.com/technet/security/bulletin/MS02-039.mspx

8  http://www.microsoft.com/technet/security/bulletin/MS02-061.mspx

9  http://en.wikipedia.org/wiki/SQL_slammer_worm

10  http://en.wikipedia.org/wiki/Blaster_worm

11  http://www.microsoft.com/technet/security/bulletin/MS03-026.mspx

patches had already been available. The worm included functionality to perform a distributed DoS attack via a SYN flood against windowsupdate.com. For his efforts, Parson was rewarded with 18 months in prison, three years of supervised release, and 100 hours of community service.[12]

This list is far from comprehensive but illustrates some of the more significant historical Microsoft server-side vulnerabilities that led to fast spreading worms. Any of the network vulnerabilities could potentially have been discovered through network fuzzing.

## TARGETS

There are thousands of targets to choose from that could expose remotely exploitable network protocol parsing vulnerabilities. In Table 14.1, we provide a small sample of known network vulnerabilities to highlight some common target categories.

Table 14.1   Common Types of Vulnerable Applications and Examples of Previously Discovered File Format Vulnerabilities

| Application Category | Vulnerability Name | Advisory |
| --- | --- | --- |
| Mail servers | Sendmail Remote Signal Handling Vulnerability | http://xforce.iss.net/xforce/alerts/id/216 |
| Database servers | MySQL Authentication Bypass Vulnerability | http://archives.neohapsis.com/ archives/vulnwatch/2004-q3/0001.html |
| RPC-based services | RPC DCOM Buffer Overflow Vulnerability | http://www.microsoft.com/technet/ security/bulletin/MS03-026.mspx |
| Remote access services | OpenSSH Remote Challenge Vulnerability | http://bvlive01.iss.net/issEn/delivery/ xforce/alertdetail.jsp?oid=20584 |
| Media servers | RealServer ../ DESCRIBE Vulnerability | http://www.service.real.com/help/ faq/security/rootexploit082203.html |
| Backup servers | CA BrightStor ARCserve Backup Message Engine Buffer Overflow Vulnerability | http://www.zerodayinitiative.com/ advisories/ZDI-07-003.html |

---

[12] http://weblog.infoworld.com/techwatch/archives/001035.html

These six categories make up a good collection of target pools. However, any application or service that accepts incoming connections could be a potential target. This includes hardware appliances, network printers, PDAs, cell phones, and so on. Any software that has the capability to accept network traffic can be audited using network fuzzing techniques.

For a more thorough understanding of typical targets, we present examples for each of the seven layers defined in the Open Systems Interconnection Basic Reference Model (OSI model),[13] shown in Figure 14.1. Although never implemented directly in any single networking technology, the OSI model is commonly used as a point of reference when dissecting networked technologies to illustrate where particular functionality falls in comparison to other networking layers. In theory, network protocol fuzzing can target any of the seven OSI layers. In practice you will find fuzzers targeting all but Layer 1, the physical layer. As each layer is presented, a historical vulnerability relevant to that layer is provided for further clarity.

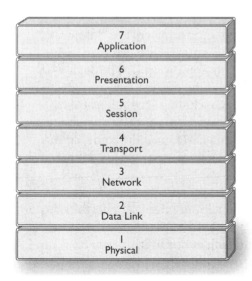

**Figure 14.1**   Open Systems Interconnection (OSI) model

---

[13] http://en.wikipedia.org/wiki/Osi_model

## LAYER 2: DATA LINK LAYER

Relevant technologies at the data link layer include Ethernet frames and 802.11 frames. Layer 2 vulnerabilities are interesting because often the handling of this low-level networking layer is implemented within the operating system kernel. An example of a recent Layer 2 vulnerability was identified by Mitre in CVE-2006-3507.[14] In this vulnerability, an attacker can compromise an AirPort wireless-enabled Mac OS system due to the existence of multiple stack-based buffer overflows. The overflows occur within the context of the kernel and although nontrivial, can be leveraged to completely compromise the affected system. An interesting requirement here is that the attacker must be within range of the wireless network he or she is targeting. If you are ever connected over public wireless in a coffee shop and your Mac OS system goes down, it might be prudent to scan the room and hold the nearest patron holding a laptop hostage for questioning.

---

**APPLEGATE**

At the 2006 Black Hat briefings in Las Vegas, security researchers Jon "Johnny Cache" Ellch and David Maynor stirred up quite a controversy when they released a video demonstrating a remote compromise of an Apple Macbook through a supposed vulnerability in its wireless drivers.[15] The ensuing media frenzy included no shortage of mudslinging from all involved parties, including accusations from Apple that the researchers had never shared adequate details of the vulnerability to allow them to validate the claim. The Apple faithful also joined the battle, crying foul as it appeared that the vulnerability exploited a third-party driver, not one written by Apple developers.

In the end, Apple released a series of patches, including CVE-2006-3507, but continues to maintain that the vulnerabilities came from internal audits initiated as a result of the Black Hat demonstration. Credit for discovering the flaws was never given to Maynor or Ellch. The only sure thing in this overly dramatized chain of events is that we'll likely never know the truth.

---

[14] http://cve.mitre.org/cgi-bin/cvename.cgi?name=CVE-2006-3507

[15] http://blog.washingtonpost.com/securityfix/2006/08/hijacking_a_macbook_in_60_seco.html

## LAYER 3: NETWORK LAYER

Layer 3, the network layer, includes IP and Internet Control Message Protocol (ICMP). Although the most common implementations of TCP/IP have been well tested over the years, vulnerabilities can still be found at this layer. It is also worth mentioning that Windows Vista contains a completely rewritten network stack, indicating that it might be a good target for fuzzing. A recent vulnerability in TCP/IP is described in MS06-032, "Vulnerability in TCP/IP Could Allow Remote Code Execution."[16] The vulnerability manifests in the kernel due to improper parsing of IP version 4 source routing options. This improper handling leads to a buffer overflow that can be exploited by remote attackers to gain kernel-level access.

## LAYER 4: TRANSPORT LAYER

One layer up in the model is Layer 4, the transport layer, which includes TCP and UDP. As mentioned previously, most TCP/IP implementations are well tested, but there have been issues in this layer in the past. A great example of a vulnerability at this level is the old "winnuke" attack that utilized out-of-band TCP packets.[17] The winnuke attack was arguably the simplest remote kernel DoS attack ever seen. All that was required to remotely crash an affected system was to transmit a TCP packet with the TCP urgent pointer set. This pointer can be set easily using any socket API by simply specifying the packet as containing out-of-band data.

## LAYER 5: SESSION LAYER

The session layer, Layer 5 in the OSI model, houses two particularly problematic protocols, both of which implement remote procedure calls. These technologies are DCE/RPC (Microsoft's MSRPC) and ONC RPC, also known as Sun RPC. The two protocols are implementations for Windows and UNIX systems, respectively. Numerous critical vulnerabilities have been exposed through these technologies in the past. Among the most significant was patched in Microsoft Security Bulletin MS04-011[18] and was used by the Sasser[19] worm to spread in the wild. The vulnerability was in the lsass.exe binary, which

---

[16] http://www.microsoft.com/technet/security/Bulletin/MS06-032.mspx

[17] http://support.microsoft.com/default.aspx?scid=kb;[LN];168747

[18] http://www.microsoft.com/technet/security/bulletin/MS04-011.mspx

[19] http://en.wikipedia.org/wiki/Sasser_worm

exposed RPC endpoints registered by default on all modern versions of the Windows operating system. Specifically, the vulnerability occurred due to a buffer overflow in the DsRolerUpgradeDownlevelServer function and could be exploited remotely.

## LAYER 6: PRESENTATION LAYER

A good example of a Layer 6 technology that lends itself well to fuzzing is XDR, the eXternal Data Representation used in Sun RPC. Across the XDR-related vulnerabilities that have been discovered in the past, a particularly good example is the xdr_array integer overflow discovered by Neel Mehta.[20] At the core of this discovery was the abuse of an integer overflow. If an attacker specified a large number of entries for an array, an undersized buffer could be allocated, subsequently written to, and overflowed. This memory corruption can be leveraged by attackers to compromise the underlying system.

## LAYER 7: APPLICATION LAYER

Layer 7, the application layer, the most commonly thought of and targeted OSI layer with regards to network protocol fuzzing. This layer is the home for common protocols such as FTP, SMTP, HTTP, DNS, and many other standardized and proprietary protocols. Historically more vulnerabilities have been discovered at this layer than at any other. Layer 7 is the most often fuzzed layer because there are so many different implementations for common protocols.

The focus of remainder of this chapter is mostly on Layer 7, but it is important to remember that software at any layer can have implementation problems and should never be ignored when performing a thorough audit of a target.

## METHODS

The available fuzzing methods are for the most part identical to the methods presented in Chapter 11, "File Format Fuzzing." At a high level, we can approach both file format and network fuzzing using either a brute force or intelligent methodology. However, there are several differences in these approaches when applied to network-based fuzzing.

---

[20] http://bvlive01.iss.net/issEn/delivery/xforce/alertdetail.jsp?oid=20823

## BRUTE FORCE OR MUTATION-BASED FUZZING

In the context of file format fuzzing, brute force fuzzing requires the fuzz tester to acquire valid samples of the targeted file format. The fuzzer application then mutates these files in various ways, presenting each test case to a target application. In the context of network fuzzing, the fuzz tester generally uses a sniffer to capture valid protocol traffic, either statically up front or dynamically at runtime. The fuzzer then mutates the captured data and fires it off at the target. This, of course, is not always as trivial as it might sound. Consider, for example, any protocol that implements basic protections against replay attacks. In such situations, simple brute force fuzzing will not be effective for anything other than session initialization code, such as the authentication process.

Another example where a simple mutation-based fuzzer will fail is when attempting to fuzz a protocol that embeds checksums. Unless the checksum fields are dynamically updated by the fuzzer, transmitted data might be dropped by the target software prior to performing any in-depth parsing. Test cases are wasted in these situations. Mutation-based fuzzing works well in the file fuzzing arena, but in general, the next fuzzing method applies better to network protocol fuzzing.

## INTELLIGENT BRUTE FORCE OR GENERATION-BASED FUZZING

With intelligent brute force fuzzing, you must first put some effort into actually researching the protocol specifications. An intelligent fuzzer is still a fuzzing engine, and thus is still conducting a brute force attack. However, it will rely on configuration files from the user, making the process more intelligent. These files usually contain metadata describing the language of the protocol.

When fuzzing a trivial network protocol, such as the control channel in FTP, intelligent fuzzing is often the best the way to go. A simple grammar describing each protocol verb (USER, PASS, CWD, etc.) and descriptions of the data types for each verb argument will allow for a fairly thorough test. Generation-based fuzzer development can build on an existing framework, such as PEACH,[21] or be built from scratch. In the latter case, a protocol-specific fuzzer is being developed that, for the most part, cannot be repurposed to target other protocols. With this approach, any notion of generic design is thrown away, simplifying the design and implementation process.

There are several tools available publicly that target a single protocol, but many testing tools remain private as they can be seen essentially as a loaded weapon. That is to say, when an author releases a generic fuzzer, whether it is mutation or generation based, the

---

[21] http://peachfuzz.sourceforge.net/

end user still needs to apply some research on his or her end to find vulnerabilities. With a protocol-specific fuzzer, all that is required is a target. If an end user runs that fuzzer against the same target the author did, the same bugs will be uncovered, at which point the tool will be of little value to the original author. This is not entirely true if new targets can be found that the fuzzer hasn't yet been tested against, which use the same protocol. The decision to release such a tool all boils down to personal beliefs about the ethics and ideals of bug killing and research sharing.

## MODIFIED CLIENT MUTATION FUZZING

One of the common criticisms of fuzz testing is that with increasing complexity the developed fuzzer starts to approach the complexity of developing an entire client. So why not work backward? A special class of fuzzing not previously mentioned, this method refers to a technique where the source code (when available) of the client half of the client–server exchange is modified to create a fuzzer. In essence, instead of implementing an entire protocol in a fuzzer, the fuzzer is embedded into an application that already speaks the desired language. This is advantageous in that the fuzzer has access to existing routines required for generating valid protocol data and minimizes the required efforts on behalf of the fuzzer developer.

Although we are unaware of any publicly released fuzzing tools that take this approach, several exploits have been developed in this fashion. One such example is the sshutuptheo[22] OpenSSH exploit written by GOBBLES to take advantage of a preauthentication integer overflow in the popular SSH server.

This approach is especially advantageous for complex protocols like SSH. However, the developer must be aware of any limitations the client might have that will affect code coverage. For example, if SSH is chosen and the client chosen only supports SSH version 1, there will be no code coverage for SSH version 2 specifics. Another disadvantage, of course, is that a legitimate client might have to be heavily modified to cover many test cases.

## FAULT DETECTION

Fault detection is a critical component of the fuzzing process, which is why Chapter 24, "Intelligent Fault Detection," is entirely dedicated to its discussion. Although advanced fault detection methods won't be covered until that chapter, let's take a look at some

---

[21] http://online.securityfocus.com/data/vulnerabilities/exploits/sshutuptheo.tar.gz

basic techniques as they applies to network protocol fuzzing. The difficulty of detecting faults during network fuzzing is completely variable depending on the target. For example, consider a network daemon that crashes and stops receiving connections after any fault. Clearly, this is great behavior from a rudimentary fault detection standpoint. When the server goes down, simply assume that the last test case caused it to go down. This can be done completely by the fuzzer with no help from a software agent or manual inspection on the target host.

Let us consider another scenario where the targeted application is able to handle faults, or spawns a separate process and maintains the listening socket on its own. In theory, we can trigger an exploitable vulnerability and never know, unless, of course, we apply some form of deeper inspection on the target host. It is safe to assume that during most fuzz testing we have access to the target host. Let's take a look at some basic approaches we can take toward conducting fault detection on the target host.

## Manual (Debugger Based)

Given local access to a machine, the simplest way to monitor exceptions is to attach a debugger to a process. The debugger can detect when an exception is raised, allowing the user to determine what actions to take. Ollydbg, Windbg, IDA, and GDB are all adequate for this task. The problem here becomes correlating which test case or test cause sequence caused the behavior.

## Automatic (Agent Based)

Consider a design where the manual debugging process is replaced. Instead of using a debugging application, the fuzz tester has written a debugging agent specific to the target platform that runs on the target. This agent has two jobs. The first job is to monitor for exceptions in the target process. The second job is to communicate with the fuzzer on the remote system. This allows an easy correlation of data to fault detection. The downside to this approach is that the developer will need to create an agent for each platform that will be tested. Again, this concept is dissected in further detail in Chapter 24.

## Other Sources

Although debuggers will likely be your most valuable tool for detecting exceptions when conducting network fuzzing, don't ignore other clues that might be available. Application and operating system logs might provide information on problems that have occurred. As with manually attaching a debugger to the application, the challenge here is to correlate the problem with the responsible fuzz case. Also, be sure to monitor the system for performance degradation, which could indicate hidden issues. This could include increased CPU utilization or perhaps memory exhaustion. A test case that causes an infinite loop might never trigger an exception, but at the same time effectively results in a DoS. The point here is simple: Although debuggers are fantastic tools for uncovering vulnerabilities, you shouldn't ignore other helpful clues.

## SUMMARY

Network protocol fuzzing is perhaps the best known and most widely utilized transport of fuzzing and there are many different ways to go about performing it. Its popularity is caused by a combination of factors, not the least of which is the fact that it can be used to uncover high-risk, remote, preauthentication vulnerabilities. Beyond this, it is a mature type of fuzzing and as such a number of publicly available tools exist to aid security researchers. Armed with the knowledge of a few common approaches to network fuzzing, it's time to move on to the implementation of a network-based fuzzer.

# Network Protocol Fuzzing: Automation on UNIX

*"I think we agree, the past is over."*

—George W. Bush, on his meeting with John McCain, *Dallas Morning News*, May 10, 2000

Although Microsoft Windows dominates in the desktop arena, UNIX systems still hold the majority market share as the server platform of choice. The Apache Web server, for example, largely run on UNIX systems, maintains an almost 30 point lead over Microsoft IIS according to the latest NetCraft survey.[1] Vulnerabilities affecting popular UNIX services are highly critical and have far-reaching impacts. The bulk of the Internet runs on UNIX-based DNS, mail, and Web services. Consider, for example, that the dis covery of a flaw in the Berkeley Internet Name Domain (BIND) DNS server could be leveraged to disrupt large portions of Internet communications. Although it can't be known for sure what percentage of past discovered vulnerabilities were found via fuzzing, one can most definitely assume that many were discovered with the assistance of a fuzzer.

In this chapter, we do not develop a custom UNIX-based fuzzer from scratch. Instead, we present and utilize the usable scripting interface provided by the SPIKE fuzzing framework, an open source fuzzer mentioned throughout this book. Because we do not focus on the actual coding of a fuzzing framework development in this chapter, we instead provide a walkthrough of a fuzz test of a closed source application from start to finish using SPIKE.

---

[1] http://news.netcraft.com/archives/2007/02/23/march_2007_web_server_survey.html

# FUZZING WITH **SPIKE**

To demonstrate the fuzzing process with SPIKE, let's walk through a complete example from start to finish, beginning with the choosing of a target, researching the target protocol, describing the protocol within a SPIKE script, and then setting the fuzzer loose.

## CHOOSING THE TARGET

For the purposes of our example, we are looking to choose a target with the following desirable characteristics:

- The target software should be commonly used.
- The target software should be easily acquired by way of a demo or evaluation.
- The target software should use a protocol that is either publicly documented or trivially reversed.

There are many possibilities, but for the purposes of this example we choose Novell NetMail,[2] an enterprise e-mail and calendaring system that implements a number of documented protocols and meets all of our desired criteria. Specifically, we target the NetMail Networked Messaging Application Protocol (NMAP). This NMAP is not to be confused with Nmap,[3] the ubiquitous network scanning and reconnaissance tool. What exactly is NetMail NMAP? We didn't know off the top of our heads, so thankfully Novell is eager to share the following definition:

> The acronym NMAP stands for Networked Messaging Application Protocol. This is a text-based IP protocol, registered with the Internet Assigned Numbers Authority (IANA) at port 689, that NIMS agents use to communicate. When combined with the distributed nature of NDS eDirectory, the protocol allows NIMS agents running on different servers (even different platforms) to operate as if they were on the same server. Instead of replacing a server with a bigger server when the demand for messaging services increase, NMAP allows additional servers to be added to the "cluster." RFC-style documentation of the NMAP protocol is provided with every version of NIMS.[4]

---

[2]  http://www.novell.com/products/netmail/

[3]  http://insecure.org/nmap/

[4]  http://support.novell.com/techcenter/articles/ana20000303.html

NMAP appears to be a Novell-developed proprietary text-based protocol built on top of TCP. Targeting a proprietary protocol has pros and cons. On the down side, our developed fuzzer won't see any usage outside of this vendor. On the up side, however, a custom protocol means there is no availability of long-standing, tried and true parsing libraries. The vendor must have written the protocol parser in-house, less eyes have reviewed the code, and therefore it might contain a larger number of vulnerabilities.

Novell is kind enough to offer free 90-day evaluation copies of NetMail through its Web site,[5] so it's easy enough to download and install the target software in a lab environment. After installing, we bring the software up to date using the patches made available by Novell. This is a critical step to to ensure we don't rediscover any old bugs (if we find any at all). It's rather disheartening to figure out you missed this step one week into an audit. The next step is to examine the NMAP protocol in detail.

## Reversing the Protocol

Before we can describe the NMAP protocol to a SPIKE we obviously need to understand it ourselves. There are a number of approaches to handling this step. Perhaps the most obvious is to monitor legitimate NMAP traffic in our lab environment. This approach is actually a bit harder than you might assume. When dealing with complex enterprise software it is sometimes difficult to generate the traffic you are looking for. Another approach is to build on the work of others. It never hurts to ask Google what others know about any given protocol. It's also always a good idea to see if a protocol decoder exists in the open source Wireshark (formerly Ethereal) sniffer. Jump over to the Wireshark Subversion repository, specifically the epan\dissectors[6] directory, and see if your protocol can be found.

Another, and the least frequently available method, is to simply talk to the NMAP daemon itself and see if it will provide us with any information. To do so, we first need to determine what ports the application uses to communicate with clients. Assuming the documentation didn't overtly state that NMAP binds to TCP port 689, we can figure this out manually with the help of the Microsoft TCPView[7] (formerly of Sys Internals) tool. Simply launching the TCPView program immediately reveals that nmapd.exe is listening on TCP port 689. We can connect to the daemon using a basic TCP connection tool such as netcat[8] or even the Windows telnet command. Taking a wild guess, we issue the

---

[5] http://download.novell.com/index.jsp

[6] http://anonsvn.wireshark.org/wireshark/trunk/

[7] http://www.microsoft.com/technet/sysinternals/Networking/TcpView.mspx

[8] http://www.vulnwatch.org/netcat/

command HELP and to our pleasant surprise we are provided with a list of commands that the daemon will accept.

Not too shabby for a few moments' work. Taking things a step further with the information we have gathered, we load the nmapd.exe binary into our favorite disassembler, IDA Pro. Press Shift + F12 to browse through the strings database as shown in Figure 15.1. We can then locate what appears to be the help response as shown in the figure, starting with the ASCII text "1000." We sort the strings database now by the content of the string rather than the address of the string and then scroll to the lines that start with "1000." It is here we find all of the commands supported by the NMAP server and their expected syntax.

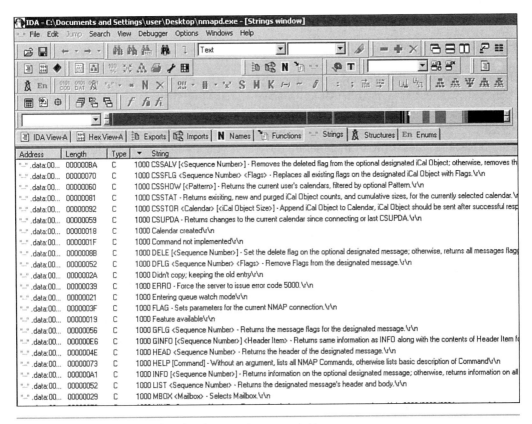

**Figure 15.1**   A list of strings found in the nmapd.exe executable

After reviewing the various commands and their described syntax, the notation for the help output becomes clear. Although some of the command's arguments are not consistent with this method, for the most part, the following prototype is used:

- `<argument>`. This argument is required. If it is not specified, the command will fail.
- `[argument]`. This argument is optional.
- `{CONSTANT1|CONSTANT2|CONSTANT3}`. This argument is required and must be taken from a set of constant strings for the command to succeed. Each possible value is separated by the pipe character `|`.

Also, any string that is not inside angle brackets should be treated as a literal string. Any string that is inside angle brackets should be treated as a variable. These same rules also apply in commands where the syntax description is nested. For example, the PASS command is described as follows:

```
PASS {SYS | USER <Username>} <Password>
```

The prototype specifies that this command will always be followed by either the string literal SYS or USER. Because the variable Username is in angle brackets after the literal USER, it is required, but only when the USER literal is chosen. If the SYS literal is chosen, then the Username argument is not required. Finally, the variable Password is always required as the last argument to the command. The protocol for the PASS command is probably the most complex command in this protocol, which isn't saying much. As it turns out, we picked a very friendly protocol to fuzz.

Because our example command deals with authentication, we can immediately guess that this daemon requires authentication for at least some of its functionality. This might or might not be interesting to a fuzz tester, depending on the scope of the test. For example, for a small team of researchers in a rush to meet a deadline and test only the most critical states of the application (preauthentication), postauthentication commands will most likely be ignored. However, for a thorough test focusing on all states of the program, the fuzzer will need to make sure they authenticate correctly after they have exhausted the preauthentication state.

Assuming we are interested in fuzzing postauthentication states, we must determine how to successfully log in. We can see there are several different ways to log in. A user can log in using the commands USER and then PASS separately, as in the FTP protocol. Optionally, a user can specify his or her username inside the PASS command. A third type of authentication allows other NMAP agents to authenticate themselves using the SYS directive in the PASS command instead of the USER directive.

By taking some time to look at the other commands and their conveniently verbose descriptions that we found using IDA, we can start to understand the workings of the protocol. In the lowest common denominator, every command begins with a single ASCII string, which we refer to as the *verb*. This tells the daemon what action we are requesting. For each command, the next component is a *space delimiter*. After the space, each command requires either a newline (if the verb requires no arguments) or verb-specific *arguments*. The format of the arguments can be gleaned from the strings we have located in IDA.

Armed with this basic information about the NMAP protocol we can now start building our SPIKE NMAP fuzzer.

# SPIKE 101

SPIKE is briefly covered among other available fuzzing frameworks in Chapter 21, "Fuzzing Frameworks," but here, we'll take a look at it in depth. Because we will be using SPIKE to fuzz this protocol, it is important that we are familiar with how SPIKE's fuzzing engine and its generic scriptable line-based TCP fuzzer work.

## FUZZ ENGINE

SPIKE works by iterating through variables and fuzz strings. Think of variables as fields in a protocol such as usernames, passwords, commands, and so on. These variables and their placement in the data stream will be specific to each target. Fuzz strings are a library of different strings and binary data that can potentially trigger a fault, and members of the fuzz string library are carefully chosen based on past experience with specific sequences that have caused issues for other software. For example, consider a very basic fuzz string such as an ASCII string of 64,000 consecutive A characters. This fuzz string might replace a username variable in a protocol to trigger a preauthentication buffer overflow. Keep in mind that the term fuzz "string" is a bit misleading. A fuzz string can be of any data type, even something such as an XDR-encoded array of binary data.

## GENERIC LINE-BASED TCP FUZZER

The fuzzer we will be building here is known as the generic line-based TCP fuzzer. The code for this application is in line_send_tcp.c within the SPIKE source code package. This fuzzer is a very simple yet powerful wrapper around SPIKE. It will process a SPIKE script and fuzz every variable in that script, repeatedly connecting to the host for each new fuzz attempt. The variables are fuzzed in order of their placement in the fuzz script.

This means that in most protocols with authentication, authentication-related information is tested first by SPIKE.

The way the scripting language is implemented allows the person writing the script to directly call SPIKE API functions. To give you a basic understanding of how you will write a script, here are some of the functions you will likely be calling:

- `s_string(char * instring)`. This will add a fixed string to the SPIKE. It will never be changed.
- `s_string_variable(unsigned char *variable)`. This will add a variable string to the SPIKE. This string will thus be replaced with fuzz strings when the variable in question is being processed.
- `s_binary(char * instring)`. Adds binary data to a SPIKE. It will never be changed.
- `s_xdr_string(unsigned char *astring)`. This will add an XDR-style string to a SPIKE. That is, it will include a 4-byte length tag and will be padded with zeros to a multiple of 4. This will never be changed.
- `s_int_variable(int defaultvalue, int type)`. This adds an integer to the SPIKE.

For calls to `s_int_variable()`, the type value can be one of the following:

- *Binary Big Endian.* Most significant bit (MSB) integer, 4 bytes.
- *ASCII.* An ASCII format signed decimal number.
- *One byte.* One byte integer.
- *Binary Little Endian Half Word.* Least significant bit (LSB) integer, 2 bytes.
- *Binary Big Endian Half Word.* MSB integer, 2 bytes.
- *Zero X ASCII Hex.* An ASCII format hex number with 0x prepended.
- *ASCII Hex.* An ASCII format hex number.
- *ASCII Unsigned.* An ASCII format unsigned decimal number.
- *Intel Endian Word.* LSB integer, 4 bytes.

Because we are not using a C preprocessor when we use SPIKE as a scripting host, we need to know integer values for the type. The following excerpt from SPIKE/SPIKE/include/listener.h shows their defined values:

```
#define BINARYBIGENDIAN 1
#define ASCII           2
#define ONEBYTE         3
#define BINARYLITTLEENDIANHALFWORD 4
#define BINARYBIGENDIANHALFWORD 5
```

```
#define ZEROXASCIIHEX 6
#define ASCIIHEX      7
#define ASCIIUNSIGNED 8
#define INTELENDIANWORD 9
```

The SPIKE functionality discussed up to this point is sufficient for our development of an NMAP fuzzer. However, let's explore SPIKE's main contribution to the fuzzing field, block-based protocol representation.

## BLOCK-BASED PROTOCOL MODELING

Although we have chosen a simple text-based protocol with which to work, SPIKE does support more complex protocols with its block-based fuzzing capabilities. Using block-based fuzzing allows dynamic creation of packets with valid field lengths. Consider, for example, a protocol with a packet structure that prefixes a username field with the length of the specified username. We would like our fuzzer to automatically update that length field while we are fuzzing the username. This insures that our fuzz strings get correctly passed through the username parser. The s_block_start() and s_block_end() functions allow you model such protocols and are declared as:

```
int s_block_start(char *blockname)
int s_block_end(char * blockname)
```

To use these effectively, you simply put them before and after the field to be measured. Then, when the actual length must be inserted into the data stream, you use one of several blocksize functions. They are similar to the integer fields discussed previously and are verbosely named. Note that some of these blocksizes are variables, which means there will be a round of fuzzing performed with invalid blocksizes. The decision to fuzz or not to fuzz the length fields is up to you. What follows is a nearly complete list of all of the different types of blocksizes that can be used in SPIKE.

```
s_blocksize_signed_string_variable(char * instring, int size)
s_blocksize_unsigned_string_variable(char * instring, int size)
s_blocksize_asciihex_variable(char * blockname)
s_binary_block_size_word_bigendian(char *blockname)
s_binary_block_size_word_bigendian_variable(char *blockname)
s_binary_block_size_halfword_bigendian(char * blockname)
s_binary_block_size_halfword_bigendian_variable(char *blockname)
s_binary_block_size_byte(char * blockname)
```

```
s_binary_block_size_byte_variable(char * blockname)
s_binary_block_size_byte_plus(char * blockname, long plus)
s_binary_block_size_word_bigendian_plussome(char *blockname, long some)
s_binary_block_size_intel_halfword(char *blockname)
s_binary_block_size_intel_halfword_variable(char *blockname)
s_binary_block_size_intel_halfword_plus_variable(char *blockname,long plus)
s_binary_block_size_intel_halfword_plus(char *blockname,long plus)
s_binary_block_size_byte_mult(char * blockname, float mult)
s_binary_block_size_halfword_bigendian_mult(char * blockname, float mult)
s_binary_block_size_word_bigendian_mult(char *blockname, float mult)
s_binary_block_size_intel_word(char *blockname)
s_binary_block_size_intel_word_variable(char *blockname)
s_binary_block_size_intel_word_plus(char *blockname,long some)
s_binary_block_size_word_intel_mult_plus(char *blockname, long some, float mult)
s_binary_block_size_intel_halfword_mult(char *blockname,float mult)
s_blocksize_unsigned_string_variable(char * instring, int size)
s_blocksize_asciihex_variable(char * blockname)
```

# ADDITIONAL SPIKE FEATURES

SPIKE is not just a fuzzer, but rather a full-fledged fuzzing framework containing a huge API of useful functions that can help simplify the creation of custom fuzzers. It also includes a large collection of protocol- and application-specific fuzzers and fuzzing scripts. Here are some other things SPIKE provides, aside from the SPIKE engine and the communications code.

## PROTOCOL-SPECIFIC FUZZERS

SPIKE includes a small collection of prewritten protocol-specific fuzzers. They are described as follows:

- HTTP fuzzer
- Microsoft RPC fuzzer
- X11 fuzzer
- Citrix fuzzer
- Sun RPC fuzzer

For the most part, these fuzzers serve best only as examples of how to use SPIKE. This is due to the fact that they have been around for some time and run against pretty much every target you are likely interested in.

## PROTOCOL-SPECIFIC FUZZ SCRIPTS

Also included with SPIKE are scripts that can be plugged into one of the many generic fuzzers within SPIKE. They are as follows:

- CIFS
- FTP
- H.323
- IMAP
- Oracle
- Microsoft SQL
- PPTP
- SMTP
- SSL
- POP3

## GENERIC SCRIPT-BASED FUZZERS

As previously mentioned, there are several generic fuzzers within SPIKE that will take scripts as input. The following generic fuzzers can be found in SPIKE:

- TCP listen (client-side) fuzzer
- TCP/UDP send fuzzers
- Line-buffered TCP send fuzzer

# WRITING THE SPIKE NMAP FUZZER SCRIPT

Switching gears back to our NetMail target, the following example SPIKE script is built purely from the knowledge gleaned through the HELP output message and the string listings from IDA Pro. This fuzz script begins by fuzzing the actual authentication command itself, looking for possible preauthentication bugs. If provided with a correct username and password, the fuzz script will then continue to fuzz postauthentication commands.

```
s_string_variable("PASS");
s_string(" ");
s_string_variable("USER");
s_string(" ");
s_string_variable("devel_user");
s_string(" ");
s_string_variable("secretpassword");
s_string("\r\n");

s_string("QCREA ");
s_string_variable("test");
s_string("\r\n");

s_string("CREA ");
s_string_variable("inbox");
s_string("\r\n");

s_string("MBOX ");
s_string_variable("test");
s_string("\r\n");

s_string("LIST ");
s_string_variable("0");
s_string("\r\n");

s_string("GINFO ");
s_string_variable("0");
s_string(" ");
s_string_variable("test");
s_string("\r\n");

s_string("SEARCH BODY ");
s_string_variable("test");
s_string("\r\n");

s_string("DFLG ");
s_string_variable("0");
s_string(" ");
s_string_variable("SEEN");
s_string("\r\n");

s_string("CSCREA ");
s_string_variable("test");
s_string("\r\n");

s_string("CSOPEN ");
s_string_variable("test");
s_string("\r\n");
```

```
s_string("CSFIND ");
s_string_variable("0");
s_string(" ");
s_string_variable("0");
s_string(" ");
s_string_variable("0");
s_string("\r\n");

s_string("BRAW ");
s_string_variable("0");
s_string(" ");
s_string_variable("0");
s_string(" ");
s_string_variable("0");
s_string("\r\n");
```

To proceed, we attach a debugger of our choice to the NMAP process on the target system and run our developed script through SPIKE. We use SPIKE's generic line-based TCP fuzzer to execute our script named nmap.spk with the following command-line options:

```
./line_send_tcp 192.168.1.2 689 nmap.spk 0 0
```

Just a few moments after starting the process, our fuzzer uncovers an exploitable stack overflow! The NMAP daemon is shown in its vulnerable state through the OllyDbg debugger in Figure 15.2.

The top right pane in Figure 15.2 displays the register values at the time of the crash. The registers EBP (stack frame pointer), EBX, ESI, EDI, and most importantly EIP (the instruction pointer) have all been overwritten with the hex value 0x41 or ASCII character A. The bottom right pane displays the stack frame, which as we can see has clearly been overwritten with a long string of A characters. The top left pane typically displays the list of instructions being executed, but it is currently blank due to the fact that the instruction pointer is at the address 0x41414141. No pages of memory are mapped to this address and therefore there is nothing to display in the disassembly window. Next, we must track down which exact verb–argument pair caused this crash so that we can reproduce it and maybe even write an exploit for it.

There are several ways this can be done. One of the simplest ways takes advantage of a feature built into SPIKE. SPIKE will often crash if it cannot connect to the target. By examining the last output from SPIKE before it crashed we can determine which test case caused the crash in NetMail NMAP. However, as we are attached with our debugger, the target process will not crash but instead hang, and SPIKE's crashing "feature" will not

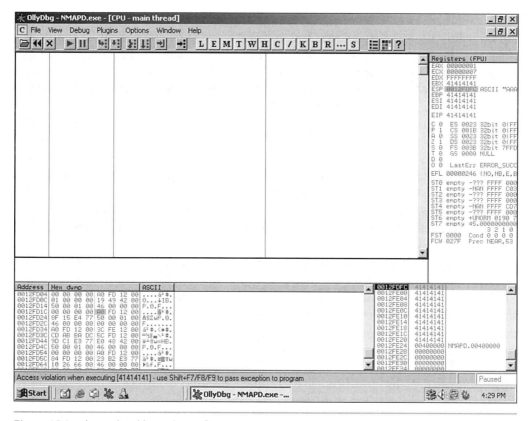

**Figure 15.2**   An exploitable stack overflow in nmapd.exe

manifest. So, for reproduction purposes, we restart the process, allow it to run unmonitored (without a debugger attached), and count on SPIKE crashing alongside the defeated NMAP daemon. We run the test again and wait, again observing a crash in NMAP and subsequently a crash in SPIKE with the following output:

```
-snip-
Fuzzing Variable 5:1
Read first line
Variablesize= 5004

Fuzzing Variable 5:2
Couldn't tcp connect to target
Segmentation fault
-snip-
```

This approach is most definitely the most rudimentary technique in tracking down the rogue test case that triggered the fault in NMAP. A slightly more scientific approach could involve monitoring all network traffic with a sniffer. NMAP will crash and no longer be able to respond to requests. SPIKE, on the other hand, will continue transmitting test cases. By locating the last transmission that solicited a response, we can determine which test case likely triggered the fault.

Back to our primitive back-tracking technique, the last successful transmission from SPIKE is advertised in the line "Fuzzing Variable 5:1." This tells us that the last successful connection was on fuzz variable 5. The last fuzz string sent to the process was fuzz string 1. To determine which fuzz variable is fuzz variable 5, we simply load up our SPIKE script and start counting lines that contain the word "variable" starting from 0. We end up on the argument to the CREA command, a verb available only postauthentication. Next we must determine what value was used for fuzz string 1, the argument to this CREA command.

There are several ways of going about this. One is to use a sniffer, as mentioned earlier. Another approach we can take is adding a printf() function call to the line_send_tcp.c fuzzing program, instructing the application to print out the current fuzz string, then simply rerunning the fuzzer. Using either of these methods, we find that the offending string is simply "CREA <longstring>". In no time we can re-create this postauthentication crash. All that is needed is for a user to log in and send a malicious CREA command argument. That wasn't so hard: a small time investment for a remote vulnerability. It makes you wonder why more vendors don't apply this form of testing prior to stamping a seal of approval on their software. If we want to continue fuzzing NMAP, we can simply remove the section in our SPIKE script that pertains to the CREA command so that we don't keep killing our target with an already known issue.

## SUMMARY

When considering writing your own fuzzer, it is always important that you first evaluate both existing fuzzers and fuzzing framework. For a simple target, such as the NMAP protocol, little would be gained by developing a fuzzer from scratch. With just a few hours of work, we can craft a set of SPIKE scripts that exercise the NMAP daemon's code effectively. Keep in mind, however, that the quality of your results will mirror the amount of time put into developing the fuzzer. In this particular case, we went with the absolute minimum. We chose to log in, make a few command requests, and log out. There are dozens of other functions to be found in NMAP that can be added to your scripts for further testing.

# Network Protocol Fuzzing: Automation on Windows

*"I couldn't imagine somebody like Osama bin Laden understanding the joy of Hanukkah."*

—George W. Bush, White House Menorah lighting ceremony, Washington, DC, December 10, 2001

Although UNIX systems might dominate in the server room, there are more installations of the Microsoft Windows operating system worldwide, which make it an equally coveted attack target. Vulnerabilities affecting the Windows desktop are frequently leveraged in the creation of the many bot nets in existence today. Consider the Slammer worm,[1] which exploits a buffer overflow in Microsoft SQL Server, as a demonstration of the power of a network enabled Windows vulnerability. The vulnerability was addressed in Microsoft Security Bulletin MS02-039[2] on July 24, 2002 and the Slammer worm surfaced on January 25, 2003. The worm has virtually no payload; it simply utilizes the infected host to scan for and spread to other infected machines.[3] Despite its lack of payload, the aggressive scanning generated enough traffic to cause disruption of the Internet, credit card processing, and in some cases cell phone network availability. What is most interesting is that even after four years, the Slammer worm is still among the top five most seen

---

[1]  http://www.cert.org/advisories/CA-2003-04.html

[2]  http://www.microsoft.com/technet/security/bulletin/MS02-039.mspx

[3]  http://pedram.openrce.org/__research/slammer/slammer.txt

traffic-generating events.[4, 5] Clearly an exposed network vulnerability in Windows has far-reaching implications.

In the previous chapter, we leveraged an existing fuzzer framework, SPIKE, to build a protocol fuzzer in a UNIX environment that targeted the Novell NetMail NMAP daemon. In this chapter, we take a different approach by walking through the construction of a simple Windows-based, GUI-enabled, and user-friendly fuzzer from start to finish. Although the final product, named ProtoFuzz, will only offer basic functionality, it serves as a good platform for expansion and provides a different perspective on fuzzer creation. We kick off the process with a discussion of the desired feature set.

## FEATURES

Before we can dive into development, we must first take a step back and consider the features that we both require and desire. At the most basic level, a protocol fuzzer simply transmits mutated packets at a target. So long as the fuzzer has the ability to generate and send data packets, it fits the bill. It would, however, also be nice if we could arm ProtoFuzz with the ability to understand the structure of the packets that we want to fuzz. Let's expand on these basic requirements.

### PACKET STRUCTURE

Before our fuzzer can send a data packet, it needs to understand how to build one. Existing fuzzers take one of three basic approaches when it comes to assembling packets for fuzzing:

- *Crafted test suites.* Both the PROTOS Test Suite[6] and its commercial sister, Codenomicon,[7] hard-code the structure of data packets used for fuzzing. Building test suites such as these is a time-consuming task, as it requires analyzing a protocol specification and then developing perhaps thousands of hard-coded test cases.

- *Generation fuzzers.* As we saw in the previous chapter, tools such as SPIKE require that the user build a template that describes the structure of the data packet. The

---

[4]   http://isc.sans.org/portreport.html?sort=targets

[5]   http://atlas.arbor.net/

[6]   http://www.ee.oulu.fi/research/ouspg/protos/

[7]   http://www.codenomicon.com/products/

fuzzer is then responsible for generating and transmitting individual test cases at runtime.

- *Mutation fuzzers.* Rather than building a packet from scratch, an alternate approach is to begin with a known good packet and then successively mutate portions of the packet. Although every byte within the packet could be mutated in a brute force fashion, this would not generally be appropriate for protocol fuzzing, as that approach would be inefficient and produce an abundance of packets that don't adhere to network protocols and might not even be routed to the target. This approach can be revised slightly by stealing a trick from the protocol template approach. The fuzzer begins with a known good packet, then the user creates a template from that packet by identifying portions of data that should be targeted for fuzzing. This is the approach that will be leveraged by ProtoFuzz.

No single approach is superior to the others and each will be better suited to various situations. Packet mutation was selected for ProtoFuzz due to its simplicity. Starting with a known good packet that can be captured from observed network traffic permits the user to begin fuzzing almost immediately without the need for excessive groundwork researching the protocol and building generation templates.

## CAPTURING DATA

Because packet mutation has been chosen as the fuzzing approach, it would be prudent for ProtoFuzz to be able to capture network data in promiscuous mode, just like a sniffer. We'll build a network protocol analyzer into ProtoFuzz so that it will be able to capture traffic to and from our target application and we'll then select individual packets to fuzz. To implement this capability, we'll leverage an existing packet capture library as detailed in the "Development" section.

## PARSING DATA

Although not absolutely essential, beyond capturing data, we want ProtoFuzz to be able to present the contents of captured packets in an easy-to-digest format. This will assist the user in identifying portions of the packet that are appropriate for fuzzing. Network packet data is nothing more than a series of bytes that follow a defined pattern. Displaying the data in a human-readable format requires leveraging a capture library capable of understanding packet structure and breaking it down into the various protocol headers and data segments that construct the data stream. Most people are familiar with the presentation format used by Wireshark, so we'll use that as the basis of our display format. Figure 16.1 displays a simple TCP packet captured by Wireshark.

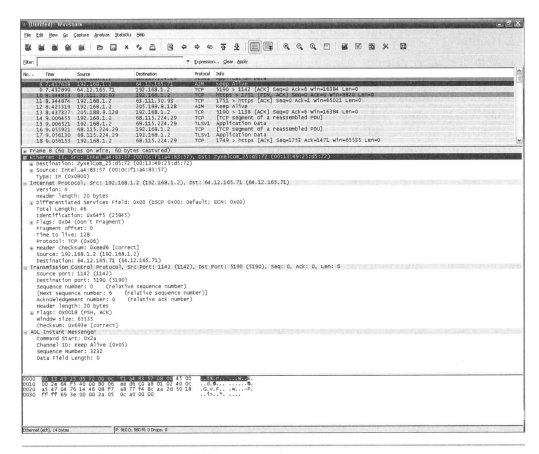

**Figure 16.1** Wireshark parsing an AIM keep alive packet

This specific screen shot from Wireshark shows the display segmented into three panes. The top pane lists the individually captured packets. Selecting one of these packets loads the contents of that packet into the bottom two panes. The middle pane shows the deconstruction of the packet into its individual fields. In this case we can see that Wireshark is familiar with the AOL Instant Messenger protocol, as it has successfully decoded the entire data segment of the TCP packet. Finally, the bottom pane displays the raw hex and ASCII bytes of the selected packet.

## FUZZ VARIABLES

Once network data is observed and captured, we want to allow the user to identify portions of it that are to be mutated for fuzzing. To do this, we'll use a very simple format that encloses portions of the hexadecimal representation of the packet with opening and closing tags. Different tags will be used to represent different types of runtime fuzz variables. This simple format will both allow the user to visually identify fuzz variables and allow ProtoFuzz to identify areas that are to be replaced with fuzz data while parsing the packet structure. We'll use the following tags:

- [XX] *Brute force.* Bytes enclosed by square brackets will be fuzzed using all possible byte values. Therefore, a single byte will be fuzzed 256 times, whereas a word value (2 bytes) would be fuzzed 65,536 times.
- <XX> *Strings.* Bytes can also be fuzzed by the hexadecimal representation of predefined variable-length strings from a user-controlled text file (Strings.txt). This type of fuzzing would typically be done in the data portions of packets as opposed to header fields, which require a defined structure.

The following template illustrates a TCP packet with both brute force and string fuzz variables.

```
00 0C F1 A4 83 57 00 13 49 25 D5 72 08 00 45 00 00 28<B0 3B>00 00 FE 06
89 40 C0 A8 01 01 C0 A8 01 02 08 A6 0B 35 14 9E E1 9F 9F 33 69 E5 50 11
10 00 09 4E 00 00 01 00 5E 00 00[16]
```

## SENDING DATA

Protocol libraries typically take two different approaches when sending data. First, they might have a series of functions that allow you to set certain pieces of data such as the target IP and MAC addresses. However, the majority of the packet structure is built for you, based on the appropriate RFC. A .NET Framework class such as HttpRequest would be an example of such a class. This class allows you to define properties such as the method and URL, but most HTTP headers and all Ethernet, TCP, and IP headers would be created for you. An alternate approach is to create a raw data packet whereby individual bytes are specified and it is up to the programmer to ensure that the packets follow the structure defined in the appropriate RFC. Although the second approach requires more work on the part of the researcher, providing a more granular level of control will provide the ability to fuzz protocol headers as well as the data segments.

# Necessary Background Information

Before we discuss how ProtoFuzz was developed, we should first highlight a few important pieces of background information.

## Detection

As with any type of fuzzing, detecting faults in the target application is critical to uncovering vulnerabilities. There is no perfect way to do this, but some approaches are certainly better than others. One hurdle in protocol fuzzing is that unlike file fuzzing, for example, the fuzzer and target application will likely be separated across two systems. When fuzzing network protocols, attaching a debugger to the target application is a good starting point that allows you to pinpoint both handled and unhandled exceptions that might not otherwise be identified. When using a debugger you will still face the challenge of correlating fuzz packets to the exceptions that they create. Although not foolproof, a workaround for this would involve sending some form of probe after each packet to ensure that the target is still responsive. For example, you could send a ping request to the target and ensure that a reply is received before sending the next fuzz packet. This is far from perfect as an exception could have occurred that would not affect the target's ability to reply to the ping. However, you can customize the probe for the target in question.

### Performance Degradation

In addition to fault monitoring, we can also monitor the target application for performance degradation. Consider, for example, a malformed data packet that causes an infinite loop within the application logic of the target. No actual fault is generated in this situation, but we do have a DoS condition. Running performance monitors on the target machine such as the Performance Logs and Alerts or System Monitor snap-ins available for Microsoft Management Console can help identify such situations.

### Request Timeouts and Unexpected Responses

Not all transmitted fuzz packets will elicit a response. However, for those that do, it's important to monitor for the response to ensure that the target application is still properly functioning. This could be taken one step further to also parse the contents of the response packet. That way you would be able to not only identify when responses aren't received, but additionally identify responses that contain unexpected data.

## PROTOCOL DRIVER

Many packet capture libraries require the use of a custom protocol driver. The Metro Packet Library[8] selected for ProtoFuzz includes `ndisprot.inf`, a sample Network Driver Interface Specification (NDIS) protocol driver supplied by Microsoft as part of their Driver Development Kit. NDIS is effectively an API for network adapters that provides applications with the ability to send and receive raw Ethernet packets. Before ProtoFuzz can be used, this driver must be manually installed and started, which can be done from the command line by running `net start ndisprot`. One downside to using a library that requires a custom driver such as this is the fact that the driver might not be able to handle all types of network adapters. In the case of Metro, the driver will not work, for example, with a wireless adapter.

## DEVELOPMENT

There are already a number of protocol fuzzers that work perfectly well. If we're going to create a new one, to avoid building a "me too" project, it will need to offer something that others don't. Given that many existing fuzzers run from the command line, we aim to differentiate ProtoFuzz with the following goals:

- *Intuitive.* Use of ProtoFuzz should not require a long learning curve. An end user should be able to figure out the basics of the tool without wrestling with a manual or remembering convoluted command-line options.

- *Ease of use.* ProtoFuzz should be immediately functional once it's started. Rather than require that the user build cumbersome templates to define the structure of a data packet, we'll leverage the structure of previously captured data packets to build fuzzing templates.

- *Access to all protocol layers.* Some network fuzzers focus on data within the packet as opposed to the protocol headers themselves. ProtoFuzz should be able to fuzz any and all portions of a packet from the Ethernet header down to the TCP/UDP data.

Our goal in producing ProtoFuzz is certainly not to replace existing tools. Rather, it is an effort to construct a basic platform for network fuzzing from a Windows environment that will serve as both a learning tool and as an open source effort available for extension by any interested parties.

---

[8]  http://sourceforge.net/projects/dotmetro/

## LANGUAGE SELECTION

As with FileFuzz, our Windows-based file format fuzzing tool, we turned to C# and the Microsoft .NET Framework for the construction of this GUI-driven network protocol fuzzer. The .NET platform handles much of the heavy lifting when it comes to developing GUI applications, allowing you to focus on the business logic of the application, or in our case, the business-breaking logic. .NET applications do require users to install the .NET Framework as a prerequisite. However, the growing prevalence of .NET-based applications is turning this into a minor inconvenience as most systems will already have the library available.

## PACKET CAPTURE LIBRARY

One of the key decisions in the construction of our network protocol fuzzer is the selection of a suitable packet capture library. This library is responsible for three core components: capturing, parsing, and transmitting packets. Although it would certainly be possible to build this functionality from scratch, it is not generally advisable given that a number a robust, open source packet capture libraries already exist.

The fact that we've chosen to develop ProtoFuzz on a Windows platform automatically limits our choices in this area. Typically, the library of choice for Microsoft Windows would be WinPcap,[9] an excellent packet capture library that originated when Piero Viano ported libpcap to Windows as part of his graduate thesis. WinPcap has been around for many years now as an open source project and as such has evolved into a strong code base that supports most major protocols. In fact, it is a prerequisite for many commercial and open source applications that need to work with data packets such as Wireshark (previously known as Ethereal) and Core Impact.[10] The WinPcap Web site lists more than 100 tools that leverage the library for packet capture functionality, and that's just the ones that they know about!

Although WinPcap was considered for ProtoFuzz, the decision to use C# for the development language limited the ease of working with the popular library. WinPcap is written in C and although there have been a handful of attempts to write wrappers to simplify the use of WinPcap from a C# application, we have yet to see a comprehensive project that incorporates all WinPcap functionality. PacketX,[11] a COM class library that

---

[9]   http://www.winpcap.org/

[10]  http://www.coresecurity.com/products/coreimpact/index.php

[11]  http://www.beesync.com/packetx/index.html

provides a wrapper for WinPcap was also considered for this project but was ultimately vetoed due to the fact that it is a commercial library, and when writing this book, we wanted to make every effort to leverage freely distributable libraries.

After a fair bit of searching, we were pleased to stumble across the Metro Packet Library. Although not as robust as WinPcap, this library is written entirely in C#, comes with strong tutorials and documentation, and was more than adequate for the basic fuzzer that we sought to create. The one weakness that Metro suffers from is limited parsing capabilities. It has classes designed to recognize all high-level packet headers—Ethernet, TCP, UDP, ICMP, IPv4, and Address Resolution Protocol (ARP)—but it does not yet have classes designed to understand data within the packets below these headers. Once again, given the modest goals of ProtoFuzz, this was not a major concern and given that Metro is an open source project, we always have the option of extending current classes to develop any needed functionality.

## DESIGN

Enough with the theory; it's time to code. As always, all of the source code for ProtoFuzz is available from the www.fuzzing.org Web site. We won't go through all portions of the code but in the following sections we highlight some of the more important code segments.

### Network Adapter

We want ProtoFuzz to be able to capture the traffic that will be used to generate fuzz templates. To do that, the user must first select the network adapter that will be placed in promiscuous mode to sniff traffic. Rather than require that users provide an adapter name or identifier that they've discovered manually, we'd like to present them with a simple drop-down menu from which they can select any of the active network adapters on the system. Fortunately, Metro provides classes to make this a relatively simple process, as shown in the following code excerpt:

```
private const string DRIVER_NAME = @"\\.\ndisprot";
NdisProtocolDriverInterface driver = new NdisProtocolDriverInterface();

try
{
   driver.OpenDevice (DRIVER_NAME);
}
catch (SystemException ex)
{
   string error = ex.Message;
```

```
    error += "\n";
    error += "Please ensure that you have correctly installed the " +
        DRIVER_NAME + " device driver.";
    error += "Also, make sure it has been started.";
    error += "You can start the driver by typing \"net start " +
        DRIVER_NAME.Substring(DRIVER_NAME.LastIndexOf("\\") + 1) +
        "\" at a command prompt.";
    error += "To stop it again, type \"net stop " +
        DRIVER_NAME.Substring(DRIVER_NAME.LastIndexOf("\\") + 1) +
        "\" in a command prompt.";
    error += "\n";
    error += "Press 'OK' to continue...";
    MessageBox.Show(error, "Error", MessageBoxButtons.OK,
        MessageBoxIcon.Error);
    return;
}

foreach (NetworkAdapter adapter in driver.Adapters)
{
    cbxAdapters.Items.Add(adapter.AdapterName);
    if (cbxAdapters.Items.Count > 0)
        cbxAdapters.SelectedIndex = 0;
}
```

First, we instantiate a new `NdisProtocolDriverInterface` and then call the `OpenDevice()` function using the `ndisprot` network adapter, which the user should already have manually installed. If the adapter is not available, a `SystemException` will be caught and the user will be instructed to install and start the adapter. Once this successfully completes, we then have a `NetworkAdapter` array containing information on all available network adapters. With this, we use a simple `foreach` loop to iterate through the array and add the `AdapterName` property to the combo box control.

### Capturing Data

Once we've opened an adapter, we can now place it in promiscuous mode and begin to capture traffic:

```
try
{
    maxPackets = Convert.ToInt32(tbxPackets.Text);

    capturedPackets = new byte[maxPackets][];

    driver.BindAdapter(driver.Adapters[cbxAdapters.SelectedIndex]);
```

```
    ThreadStart packets = new ThreadStart(capturePacket);
    captureThread = new Thread(packets);
    captureThread.Start();
}
catch (IndexOutOfRangeException ex)
{
    MessageBox.Show(ex.Message +
    "\nYou must select a valid network adapter.",
    "Error", MessageBoxButtons.OK, MessageBoxIcon.Error);
}
```

We begin by creating a two-dimensional array (`capturedPackets`), containing an array of captured packets that in turn contain an array of the bytes within that packet. We then call the `BindAdapter()` function to bind the selected network adapter to the previously instantiated `NdisProtocolDriverInterface` (`driver`). At this point we then call `capturePacket` in a separate thread. It is important to launch a separate thread for this so that the GUI doesn't lock up while packets are being captured.

```
private void capturePacket()
{
    while (packetCount < maxPackets)
    {
        byte[] packet = driver.RecievePacket();
        capturedPackets[packetCount] = packet;
        packetCount++;
    }

}
```

To obtain the byte array for a captured packet, we simply call the `ReceivePacket()` function. From there, we need only to add them to the `capturedPackets` array.

### Parsing Data

Parsing data is a two-step process as we display captured packets in two separate ways. In keeping with the layout used by Wireshark, when a user selects a captured packet, a summary of the packet contents is displayed in a TreeView control, and all raw bytes are displayed in a RichTextBox control at the same time. This way, the user has a clean and easy-to-understand overview but still has control over individual bytes for fuzzing. We've attempted to tie the two windows together by highlighting the associated raw bytes in red text when a line item from the TreeView is selected. The full layout of ProtoFuzz with a captured packet is shown in Figure 16.2.

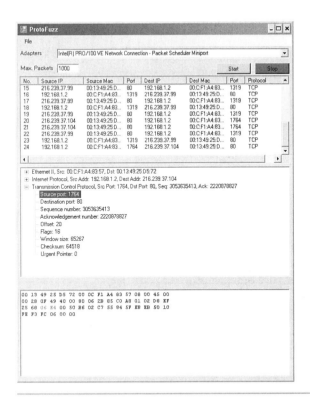

**Figure 16.2**   ProtoFuzz displays a captured packet

The summary view of a captured packet is shown in the middle TreeView pane. The code to create the TreeView is contained within the `packetTvwDecode()` function, which has separate code blocks for parsing each of the following headers: Ethernet, TCP, UDP, IP, ARP, and ICMP. For simplicity, the following code segment illustrates parsing only the Ethernet headers:

```
Ethernet802_3 ethernet = new Ethernet802_3(capPacket);

strSourceMacAddress = ethernet.SourceMACAddress.ToString();
strDestMacAddress = ethernet.DestinationMACAddress.ToString();
strEthernet = "Ethernet II, Src: " + strSourceMacAddress +
   ", Dst: " + strDestMacAddress;
strSrcMac = "Source: " + strSourceMacAddress;
strDstMac = "Destination: " + strDestMacAddress;
strEthernetType = "Type: " + ethernet.NetworkProtocol.ToString();
strData = "Data: " + ethernet.Data.ToString();
```

```
TreeNode nodeEthernet = tvwDecode.Nodes.Add(strEthernet);
TreeNode nodeEthernetDstMac = nodeEthernet.Nodes.Add(strDstMac);
TreeNode nodeEthernetSrcMac = nodeEthernet.Nodes.Add(strSrcMac);
TreeNode nodeType = nodeEthernet.Nodes.Add(strEthernetType);
TreeNode nodeData = nodeEthernet.Nodes.Add(strData);
```

As can be seen, the `Ethernet802_3` class is instantiated with the byte array from capPacket provided to the constructor and each of the nodes displayed in the TreeView is simply a property of the class. The following code segment is a basic loop that displays the raw packet bytes in a grid pattern. The loop prints 16 bytes per row.

```
static string PrintData(byte [] packet)
{

    string sData = null;

    int nPosition = 0, nColumns = 16;
    for (int i = 0; i < packet.Length;  i++)
    {
        if (nPosition >= nColumns)
        {
            nPosition = 1;
            sData += "\n";
        }
        else
            nPosition++;

        byte nByte = (byte) packet.GetValue(i);
        if (nByte < 16)
            sData += "0";

        sData += nByte.ToString("X", oCulture.NumberFormat) + " ";
    }
    sData += "\n";
    return (sData);
}
```

### Fuzz Variables

Fuzz variables are represented by bytes enclosed in either square brackets ([]) for brute force fuzzing or angle brackets (<>) for string-based fuzzing. When sending the packet, the code simply reads the raw packets and looks for enclosing brackets. When these fuzz variables are encountered, the original data is replaced with fuzz data before the packet is sent.

### Hexadecimal Encoding and Decoding

One final concern is encoding and decoding hexadecimal representations of bytes that are used to display the contents of captured data packets. The .NET Framework provides the ToString("X") function for converting a byte array into a hexadecimal string, but it does not provide similar functionality for converting a string into a byte array.[12] For this reason, the HexEncoding class was added, much of which was borrowed from "Converting Hexadecimal String to/from Byte Array in C#" at www.codeproject.com.

## Case Study

Now that we've built a network fuzzer, it's time to ensure that it works. ProtoFuzz is a single-shot tool that takes a packet and mutates it repeatedly before sending it to the target. It is not capable of sending a series of initial packets designed to place the target, for example, into a vulnerable state before sending the packet that causes the crash. Consider, for example, a buffer overflow in an SMTP server that occurs in the RCPT TO command as shown here:

```
220 smtp.example.com ESMTP
HELO mail.heaven.org
250 smtp.example.com Hello smtp.example.com
MAIL FROM:god@heaven.org
250 2.1.0 god@heaven.org... Sender ok
RCPT TO:[Ax1000]
```

In this example, we would need to send a number of the requests to the SMTP server. We would need to establish the initial TCP connection and then send one request each for the HELO, MAIL FROM, and RCPT TO commands as indicated in bold text. The initial requests are necessary to place the server in state where it is ready to receive the RCPT TO command and the long string that will ultimately lead to the overflow. A vulnerability such as this is better suited to a tool such as SPIKE, which allows for scripts to be created that define packets structure and allow for multiple requests to be sent.

---

[12] http://www.codeproject.com/csharp/hexencoding.asp

ProtoFuzz is better suited to a situation where you simply want to capture a packet in transit, select a particular portion of data, and begin fuzzing immediately. Perhaps you are dealing with a proprietary protocol and don't have adequate information to generate a script detailing the structure of the protocol. Alternately, you might simply want to do a quick test without taking the time to describe the protocol to the fuzzer.

A stack overflow vulnerability in Hewlett-Packard's Mercury LoadRunner was disclosed by TippingPoint's Zero Day Initiative (ZDI), which suits our needs.[13] The overflow occurs in an agent that binds to TCP port 54345 and listens for incoming connections. The agent does not require any form of authentication before accepting packets and we therefore have the single-shot vulnerability that we're looking for. Furthermore, the protocol used by the agent is proprietary and inadequate details are provided in the security advisory to allow us to build a proof of concept exploit from scratch. All that the advisory tells us is that the overflow is triggered by an overly long value in the server_ip_name field. We'll therefore use ProtoFuzz to capture legitimate traffic, identify the server_ip_name field, and mutate the packet accordingly.

Once we have Mercury LoadRunner installed and configured appropriately, we can begin searching for a transaction that might contain the vulnerability. When sniffing traffic, we identify the following packet, which contains a combination of binary and ASCII readable text and clearly contains the server_ip_name field that we're looking for.

```
0070   2b 5b b6 00 00 05 b2 00   00 00 07 00 00 00 12 6d    +[...... .......m
0080   65 72 63 75 72 79 32 3b   31 33 30 34 3b 31 33 30    ercury2; 1304;130
0090   30 00 00 00 00 05 88 28   2d 73 65 72 76 65 72 5f    0......( -server_
00a0   69 70 5f 6e 61 6d 65 3d                              ip_name=
```

With the packet captured, we next highlight the value contained in the server_ip_name field, right-click, and select Fuzz → Strings. This will enclose the selected bytes in angle brackets (<>). When ProtoFuzz parses the captured packet, it will replace the identified bytes with each value supplied in the Strings.txt file. Therefore, to trigger the overflow, we'll need to experiment with adding successively larger strings to the file. Separate fuzz packets will be sent for each line in the Strings.txt file.

While fuzz data is being sent to our target, it is important that we monitor for exceptions. Magentproc.exe is the application that binds to TCP port 54345, so we'll attach a debugger to that process and begin fuzzing. Once the crash is triggered, the output from OllyDbg can be seen in the following code segment:

---

[13] http://www.zerodayinitiative.com/advisories/ZDI-07-007.html

```
Registers
EAX 00000000
ECX 41414141
EDX 00C20658
EBX 00E263BC
ESP 00DCE7F0
EBP 41414141
ESI 00E2549C
EDI 00661221 two_way_.00661221
EIP 41414141

Stack
00DCE7F0    00000000
00DCE7F4    41414141
00DCE7F8    41414141
00DCE7FC    41414141
00DCE800    41414141
00DCE804    41414141
00DCE808    41414141
00DCE80C    41414141
00DCE810    41414141
00DCE814    41414141
```

Similar to the NetMail case study from the last chapter, this is a clear example of a remotely exploitable stack overflow. The fact that the service requires no authentication certainly increases the risk posed by this vulnerability in a popular quality assurance testing tool.

## BENEFITS AND ROOM FOR IMPROVEMENT

At present, ProtoFuzz is not capable of handling data blocks in which a series of bytes are preceded by the size of the data. In this situation, fuzzing the data bytes requires a parallel update to the size of the data block for the packet to remain valid. This capability would greatly extend the functionality of ProtoFuzz and would be fairly simple to implement.

ProtoFuzz also does not presently provide probing functionality to determine if during fuzzing the target host remains available. As mentioned earlier in the chapter, probe packets could be sent following a fuzz packet to determine the health of the target application. Fuzzing could be halted if the target is unresponsive as further test cases would be falling on deaf ears. This feature would also assist the end user when trying to correlate the fuzz packet(s) responsible for causing anomalous behavior in the target. ProtoFuzz can also benefit from an extension allowing it to handle complex request–response pairs. Rather than simply being able to send fuzz packets, ProtoFuzz could put the target in a particular state prior to fuzzing by first sending known good packets and waiting for the appropriate responses and even parsing and interpreting their contents.

Fault detection could be further improved by designing a remote agent that resides on the target machine to monitor the state of the target application. This agent could then communicate with ProtoFuzz and halt fuzzing when a fault is detected. This can assist in directly identifying which packet caused the fault.

## SUMMARY

ProtoFuzz has a long development laundry list before it can seize the label of being a robust fuzzer. However, it serves its purpose in demonstrating a basic framework for network protocol fuzzing that can easily be extended for specific targets. A key factor in building this network fuzzer was finding a library that can handle capturing, parsing, and transmission of raw packets. Avoid libraries that do not allow raw packets to be assembled unless you are creating a fuzzer for specific network protocols that do not require accessing all packet headers. For our purposes, the Metro library provided a strong base for ProtoFuzz and the .NET Framework allowed us to build it with an intuitive GUI front end. We encourage you to build on ProtoFuzz and take it in different directions.

# Web Browser Fuzzing

*"One of the common denominators I have found is that expectations rise above that which is expected."*

—George W. Bush, Los Angeles, September 27, 2000

Client-side vulnerabilities have quickly moved into the spotlight as they are being heavily leveraged by attackers to facilitate phishing attacks, identity theft, and the creation of large bot networks (botnets). Vulnerabilities in Web browsers offer a target-rich environment for such attacks as a weakness in popular browsers results in the exposure of millions of unsuspecting victims. Client-side attacks always require some form of social engineering, as the attacker must first coerce a potential victim to visit a malicious Web page. Often this process can be facilitated with spam e-mail or by leveraging an additional vulnerability in a popular Web site. Combine this with the fact that individual users on the Internet typically have minimal knowledge of computer security and it's not surprising that many attackers are shifting their focus to client-side vulnerabilities.

In many ways, 2006 was the year when browser bugs moved to the forefront. Vulnerabilities were discovered affecting all of the popular Web browsers, including Microsoft Internet Explorer and Mozilla Firefox. Flaws were discovered in the parsing of malformed HTML tags; JavaScript; native image files such as JPG, GIF, and PNG; CSS; and ActiveX controls. Dozens of critical ActiveX vulnerabilities were discovered affecting both default installations of the Microsoft Windows operating system and applications of third-party vendors. Additionally, hundreds of noncritical ActiveX vulnerabilities were discovered. Although security researchers have shown interest in ActiveX and COM auditing in the past, 2006 was clearly the year that the interest peaked. A strong factor in this large spike in ActiveX control vulnerabilities was the public availability of new, user-friendly ActiveX auditing tools. In this chapter we address how fuzzing can be used to uncover Web browser vulnerabilities. If history is a guide, there will be plenty of additional browser bugs to uncover.

## WHAT IS WEB BROWSER FUZZING?

Originally designed solely for surfing the Web and parsing HTML pages, Web browsers have evolved into the computer equivalent of a Swiss army knife. Modern browsers are capable of handling dynamic HTML, style sheets, multiple scripting languages, Java applets, Really Simple Syndication (RSS) feeds, FTP connections, and more. A plethora of extensions and plug-ins are available that transform the Web browser into a very flexible application. This flexibility allows companies like Google to repurpose a number of common desktop applications to the Web. Unfortunately for the end user, the added functionality also increases the attack surface area. Not surprisingly, as more and more functionality is crammed into Web browsers, more and more vulnerabilities are being discovered.

### MONTH OF BROWSER BUGS

In July 2006, H.D. Moore announced the "Month of Browser Bugs"[1] (MoBB). Throughout the month of July, H.D. released a new browser-based vulnerability each day until, by month's end, he had released details of 31 vulnerabilities. Although the majority of the vulnerabilities affected Microsoft's Internet Explorer, all major Web browsers were represented, including Safari, Mozilla, Opera, and Konqurer.[2] Most of the vulnerabilities only resulted in a DoS by crashing the Web browser due to issues such as a null pointer dereference. Although these vulnerabilities were of minimal severity, shortly before the MoBB, Skywing and skape (a contributor to the Metasploit project along with H.D. Moore) had revealed details of a design flaw in the chaining of unhandled exception filters in Internet Explorer, which could leverage otherwise unexploitable vulnerabilities to cause full

---

[1]   http://browserfun.blogspot.com/

[2]   http://osvdb.org/blog/?p=127

code execution under certain conditions.[3] This had the potential to increase the risk of some of the vulnerabilities released during the MoBB. Although some disagreed with the approach of revealing details of vulnerabilities prior to patches being available, it certainly opened people's eyes to the prevalence of Web browser vulnerabilities and the risk posed by them.

## TARGETS

Every time a study is released revealing that Firefox is a more secure browser than Internet Explorer, a new and equally biased report is released showing the opposite result. From a research perspective, it's a moot point. All Web browsers have severe vulnerabilities, and fuzzing is an effective method for identifying them. As with any piece of software, the more popular the application, the more people will be directly affected by the vulnerability. Although statistics change all the time, regardless of the source that you use, you're likely to find Internet Explorer with the lion's share of end users and Firefox remains a strong second-place contender. Naturally, Internet Explorer's popularity stems from the fact that it is included by default in an operating system that powers the majority of the world's PCs. Despite this fact, Firefox continues to give Internet Explorer a run for its money. Other Web browsers such as Netscape, Opera, Safari, and Konqueror, typically account for a small overall percentage of users and combined, come in a distant third place.

## METHODS

When fuzzing Web browsers we have two choices to make. First we must decide on an approach to conduct the fuzzing, and we must then determine the portion of the browser on which to focus our attention. Given the ever increasing functionality of Web browsers, obtaining complete code coverage can be a daunting task. Expect to use multiple tools and approaches to conduct a comprehensive audit.

### APPROACHES

When fuzzing Web browsers, there are a few basic approaches we can take and the individual approach used will depend on the portion of the browser we are fuzzing. In general, we have the following options available to us:

---

[3]  http://www.uninformed.org/?v=4&a=5&t=sumry

- *Refresh HTML pages.* In this scenario, the fuzzed Web pages are generated by a Web server, which also includes a means of causing the page to refresh at regular intervals. This can be accomplished using various means such as a refresh HTTP-EQUIV META tag or some client-side scripting. When the page is refreshed, a new version of the page is served up with new fuzzed content. Mangleme,[4] a fuzzing utility designed to uncover HTML parsing flaws in Web browsers, for example, includes the following line in the HEAD portion of each fuzzed Web page:

```
<META HTTP-EQUIV=\"Refresh\" content=\"0;URL=mangle.cgi\">
```

This tag will cause the mangleme page to refresh immediately and redirect to the mangle.cgi, where a new mangled page is awaiting the Web browser. The following client-side JavaScript could be used to accomplish a similar goal, refreshing a page after 2,000 milliseconds:

```
<HTML>
  <HEAD>
  <SCRIPT LANGUAGE="JavaScript">
    <!-
      var time = null
      function move() {
        window.location = 'http://localhost/fuzz'
      }
    //->
  </SCRIPT>
  </HEAD>
  <BODY ONLOAD="timer=setTimeout('move()',2000)">
    [Page Content]
  </BODY>
</HTML>
```

- *Load pages.* Fuzzing can be done solely on the client side by directly loading a fuzzed page into the Web browser. Using command-line options, the targeted Web browser can be directed to open up a fuzzed Web page that exists on the local machine. For example, the following command would directly open the file fuzz.html in Internet Explorer:

```
C:\>"C:\Program Files\Internet Explorer\iexplore.exe" C:\temp\fuzz.html
```

---

[4]  http://freshmeat.net/projects/mangleme/

- *Target individual browser objects.* In certain situations it's possible to conduct browser-based fuzzing without launching the browser at all. This can be done when our target is a browser object and the browser is simply the vehicle for accessing that object. For example, we can fuzz an ActiveX control, which can be remotely accessed by a malicious Web site if the object is marked as "safe for scripting." In this situation, it is not necessary to launch the ActiveX control from within the browser to determine if it is vulnerable. COMRaider,[5] designed by David Zimmer, targets ActiveX controls using this approach.

## INPUTS

As with other targets, fuzzing Web browsers requires that we identify different types of user input. Once again, we must step outside of our preconceived notions of what constitutes input. In the case of a Web browser, the attacker is the Web server delivering the content that is in turn interpreted by the browser. Therefore, anything delivered by the server constitutes input, not just the HTML code.

### HTML Headers

The first piece of data received by the browser is the HTML headers. Although not directly displayed by the browser, headers contain important information that can affect the behavior of the Web browser and how it displays the subsequent content.

An example of this type of vulnerability can be seen in CVE-2003-0113,[6] which was contained in Microsoft Security Bulletin MS03-015.[7] Jouko Pynnönen discovered that due to improper bounds checking within urlmon.dll, long values in the Content-type and Content-encoding headers[8] could lead to a stack-based buffer overflow. It was found that numerous versions of Internet Explorer 5.x and 6.x were vulnerable to this type of attack.

### HTML Tags

The content of the page itself is delivered to the browser in a series of HTML tags. Technically, a browser is capable of displaying various types of markup languages such

---

[5]  http://labs.idefense.com/software/fuzzing.php#more_COMRaider

[6]  http://cve.mitre.org/cgi-bin/cvename.cgi?name=CAN-2003-0113

[7]  http://www.microsoft.com/technet/security/bulletin/MS03-015.mspx

[8]  http://downloads.securityfocus.com/vulnerabilities/exploits/urlmon-ex.pl

as, HTML, XML, and XHTML, but for our purposes we collectively refer to Web page content simply as HTML.

HTML has become an increasingly complex standard as it has evolved to extend functionality. Add to this the many proprietary tags used by specific Web browsers and the multiple markup languages that Web browsers are capable of interpreting and you begin to see the many opportunities for exceptions when designing a Web browser. These programming errors can in turn often be identified via fuzzing.

HTML has a relatively simple structure. There are a number of HTML standards and to identify the appropriate standard to which the Web page should adhere, a properly formatted Web page should begin with a Document Type Declaration (DTD). The following DTD would, for example, inform the browser that the page should adhere to HTML 4.01:

```
<!DOCTYPE html PUBLIC "-//W3C//DTD HTML 4.01//EN"
"http://www.w3.org/TR/html4/strict.dtd">
```

When we think of HTML, we typically think of the tags that define the content of the document. These tags are known as the elements and generally consist of opening and closing tags. In addition to the tags themselves, elements can also have attributes and content. The following HTML element illustrates a font element:

```
<font color="red">Fuzz</font>
```

In this particular element `color` represents an attribute of the `font` element, and the word `Fuzz` is the content of that same element. Although this is pretty basic stuff, it is important to note that all components of the HTML code are legitimate targets for fuzzing. The Web browser is designed to parse and interpret the HTML code and if the code is in an unexpected format, the developer might not have provided appropriate error handling for an anomalous piece of HTML.

Mangleme was designed to uncover vulnerabilities in the way that Web browsers interpret malformed HTML tags and it led to the discovery of CVE-2004-1050,[9] which was addressed in Microsoft Security Bulletin MS04-040.[10] Ned and Berend-Jan Wever used mangleme to discover that overly long `SRC` or `NAME` attributes in the `IFRAME`, `FRAME`, and `EMBED` elements could lead to a heap-based buffer overflow. They subsequently

---

[9]   http://cve.mitre.org/cgi-bin/cvename.cgi?name=CAN-2004-1050

[10]   http://www.microsoft.com/technet/security/bulletin/ms04-040.mspx

released full public exploit code[11] for this issue. Other utilities designed to fuzz HTML structure within Web browsers include the DOM-Hanoi[12] and Hamachi[13] utilities developed by H.D. Moore and Aviv Raff.

### XML Tags

XML is a general markup language derived from Standardized General Markup Language (SGML) and is a commonly used to transfer data via HTTP. Standardized implementations of XML have been developed to define thousands of data formats such as RSS, Application Vulnerability Description Language (AVDL), Scalable Vector Graphics (SVG), and so on. As with HTML, modern Web browsers are able to parse and interpret the XML elements and their associated attributes and content. As such, if the browser encounters unexpected data while interpreting the elements, it might lead to an unhandled exception. Vector Markup Language (VML) is an XML specification used to define vector graphics. Vulnerabilities have been discovered in libraries used by Internet Explorer and Outlook, caused by an inability to handle certain malformed VML tags. On September 19, 2006, Microsoft released Security Advisory 925568,[14] detailing a stack-based buffer overflow in the Vector Graphics Rendering engine (vgx.dll) that could result in remote code execution. The advisory was released following evidence of active exploitation, causing Microsoft to release an out-of-cycle patch seven days later.[15] An integer overflow in the same library was later disclosed and patched in January 2007.[16]

### ActiveX Controls

ActiveX controls represent a proprietary Microsoft technology built on Microsoft's COM, to provide reusable software components.[17] Web developers often embed ActiveX controls to allow for extended functionality that would not necessarily be permitted by a typical Web application. A major drawback to using ActiveX controls is that their proprietary nature limits their use to the Internet Explorer Web browser and the Windows operating system. They are, however, widely used on many Web sites. ActiveX controls

---

[11] http://downloads.securityfocus.com/vulnerabilities/exploits/InternetExploiter.txt

[12] http://metasploit.com/users/hdm/tools/domhanoi/domhanoi.html

[13] http://metasploit.com/users/hdm/tools/hamachi/hamachi.html

[14] http://www.microsoft.com/technet/security/advisory/925568.mspx

[15] http://www.microsoft.com/technet/security/Bulletin/MS06-055.mspx

[16] http://labs.idefense.com/intelligence/vulnerabilities/display.php?id=462

[17] http://en.wikipedia.org/wiki/ActiveX_Control

are very powerful and once they are trusted; they have full access to the operating system and as such should never be run unless they come from a trusted source.

Numerous vulnerabilities have been discovered in ActiveX controls included with the Windows operating system or third-party software packages. If these controls are marked as "safe for initialization" and "safe for scripting," they can be accessed by a remote Web server and can therefore be leveraged to compromise the target machine.[18] This creates a dangerous situation, as a user might initially install an ActiveX control from a trusted source, but if it is later discovered to contain a vulnerability, such as a buffer overflow, that same trusted control could be leveraged by a malicious Web site.

COMRaider is an excellent wizard-driven fuzzing tool that can be used to identify potentially vulnerable ActiveX controls on a target system. Furthermore, it can filter the fuzzed ActiveX controls to target only those that could be accessed by a malicious Web

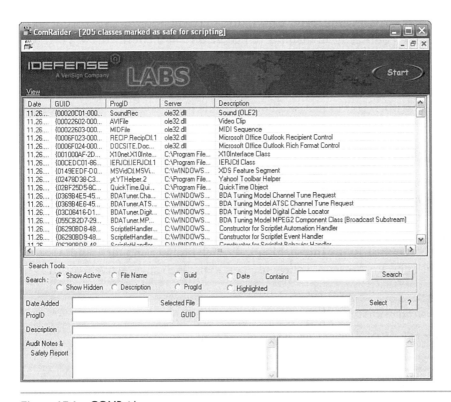

**Figure 17.1**    COMRaider

---

[18] http://msdn.microsoft.com/workshop/components/activex/safety.asp

server as this dramatically increases the risk posed by a vulnerability. COMRaider is useful for conducting a complete audit of all ActiveX controls on a given system. It will first identify all ActiveX controls and their associated methods and inputs. It will then successively fuzz all selected ActiveX controls. COMRaider has a built-in debugger and is therefore capable of identifying handled and unhandled exceptions. COMRaider also includes distributed auditing capabilities, allowing a team to share results from past audits. Figure 17.1 displays a listing produced by COMRaider after auditing a full system for all ActiveX controls marked as safe for scripting.

AxMan[19] is another freely available ActiveX fuzzer. AxMan was designed by H.D. Moore and was used to discover the majority of the ActiveX vulnerabilities released during the July 2006 Month of Browser Bugs.[20]

### *Cascading Style Sheets*

CSSDIE[21] is a CSS fuzzer that was created by H.D. Moore, Matt Murphy, Aviv Raff, and Thierry Zoller and was used during the Month of Browser Bugs to reveal a memory corruption issue in the Opera browser.[22] It was discovered that setting the CSS background property of a DHTML element to an overly long URL would lead to a client-side DoS that causes the browser to crash.

Other CSS-based issues have led to a variety of vulnerabilities such as CVE-2005-4089, addressed in MS06-021,[23] which allowed an attacker to bypass cross-domain restrictions in Internet Explorer. This was possible because sites could use the `@import` directive to download files from other domains that were not proper CSS files. Matan Gillon of hacker.co.il demonstrated how this vulnerability could be leveraged to peer into someone's Google Desktop Search (GDS) results.[24] Although the attack no longer works due to changes made by Google, it was an excellent example of how a simple Internet Explorer vulnerability could be combined with the functionality of other applications (in this case GDS) to perform a relatively complex attack. In a CSS, the format of a particular element is defined within a set of curly braces with the property and value separated by a colon. For example, an anchor tag could be defined as a `{color: white}`. When a file other than a CSS was imported using the `@import` directive, Internet

---

[19] http://metasploit.com/users/hdm/tools/axman/

[20] http://browserfun.blogspot.com/2006/08/axman-activex-fuzzer.html

[21] http://metasploit.com/users/hdm/tools/see-ess-ess-die/cssdie.html

[22] http://browserfun.blogspot.com/2006/07/mobb-26-opera-css-background.html

[23] http://www.microsoft.com/technet/security/Bulletin/MS06-021.mspx

[24] http://www.hacker.co.il/security/ie/css_import.html

Explorer would attempt to interpret the file as a CSS and anything in the file following an opening curly brace could subsequently be retrieved using the `cssText` property. Matan was able to leverage this attack to steal the unique GDS key for a user visiting a Web page by first importing the Google News page as a CSS file, with a query of "}{". This caused the query results to be included in the `cssText` property, from which the user's unique GDS key could be obtained. From there, it was possible for the attacker to then import results from the user's local GDS using another `@import` directive and this time, peer into the local GDS index.

### Client-Side Script

Web browsers leverage various client-side scripting languages to create dynamic content on a Web page. Although JavaScript is the most common client-side scripting language, there are others such as VBScript, Jscript,[25] and ECMAScript.[26] The world of client-side scripting languages is an incestuous one, as many of the languages are derived from one another. ECMAScript, for example, is just a standardized version of JavaScript, and JScript is simply a Microsoft implementation of JavaScript. These scripting languages offer powerful capabilities for Web sites, but have also led to a multitude of security issues.

Exploits involving the use of client-side scripting languages don't typically exploit vulnerabilities in the scripting engines but rather are simply using the scripting language to access another vulnerable component such as an ActiveX control. That is not to say that vulnerabilities don't exist in the scripting engines. Memory corruption issues are relatively common, such as the null reference caused in Internet Explorer using JavaScript to iterate over a native function.[27] The Month of Browser Bugs demonstrated this vulnerability using the following single line of JavaScript code:

```
for (var i in window.alert) { var a = 1; }
```

A vulnerability in the FireFox JavaScript engine discovered by Azafran led to an information leakage issue that would allow a malicious Web site to remotely retrieve the contents of arbitrary heap memory.[28] The vulnerability was caused by the `replace()` function handled lambda expressions. Although an attacker could not control the memory that was received, it could contain sensitive information such as passwords.

---

[25] http://en.wikipedia.org/wiki/Jscript

[26] http://en.wikipedia.org/wiki/Ecmascript

[27] http://browserfun.blogspot.com/2006/07/mobb-25-native-function-iterator.html

[28] http://www.mozilla.org/security/announce/2005/mfsa2005-33.html

## HEAP FILLS

Typically, client-side scripting languages are not used as an attack vector; rather they are used to facilitate the exploitation of a separate vulnerable browser component. Exploitation of browser vulnerabilities resulting from memory corruption or usage of dangling pointers, for example, are usually exploited with the assistance of a client-side scripting language. JavaScript can be used for various tasks during exploitation, and it is often leveraged during heap-based overflows. It is the obvious choice due to its widespread use and cross-platform availability. Consider that you have discovered a bug resulting in a series of dereferences under your control. Assume in the following example you have complete control of the register EAX:

```
MOV EAX, [EAX]
CALL [EAX+4]
```

Most values for EAX will cause this pair of instructions to result in an access violation and crash the browser. To successfully redirect control flow, our supplied address must be a valid pointer to a pointer to valid code, hardly something we can easily and reliably find in a regular process space. We can, however, use JavaScript to successively allocate large blocks of heap data and manipulate the memory space into something a little more attacker friendly. Client-side JavaScript is therefore often used to fill the heap with a NOP sled and shellcode to increase the chances of hitting the shellcode when landing in the heap. A NOP represents a No OPeration in assembly code and is simply an operation or series of operations that effectively do nothing. When execution is transferred to a NOP sled, execution will continue iterating through the NOP sled without altering registers or other memory locations. Berend-Jan Wever (a.k.a. SkyLined) developed a popular heap spraying technique with his Internet Exploiter code,[29] which used a value of 0x0D to spray the heap. The selection of this value is important, as it can have dual meaning. First, it can represent a 5-byte NOP-like instruction equivalent to OR EAX, 0D0D0D0D. Alternatively, it can be a self-referential pointer, pointing to a valid memory address. How it is interpreted is dependent on the context in which it is referenced.

---

[29] http://www.milw0rm.com/exploits/930

Consider the screen shot from the OllyDbg Heap Vis[30] plug-in shown in Figure 17.2.[31] The screen shot demonstrates how the plug-in can be used to explore and help visualize Internet Explorer memory state at the time of heap-fill-based exploitation.

The on-top right window pane from the screen shot labeled "Heap Vis" shows the list of allocated heap blocks. The highlighted entry is of an approximately 500Kb block starting at address 0x0D0A0020. This is the heap block that contains

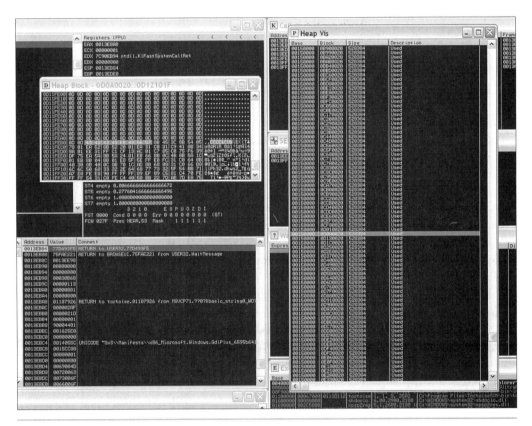

**Figure 17.2**   OllyDbg Heap Vis of SkyLined's Heap Fill in action

---

[30] http://www.openrce.org/downloads/details/1

[31] http://pedram.openrce.org/images/olly_heap_vis/skylined_ie_heap_fill.gif

the address 0x0D0D0D0D. The on-top left window pane from the screen shot labeled "Heap Block – 0D0A0020..0D12101F" shows the contents of the highlighted block specifically at the end of the 0x0D string repetition and at the start of some embedded shellcode. Following our two-line dereference example, assume that we set the value of EAX to 0x0D0D0D0D. The first dereference MOV EAX, [EAX] results in EAX maintaining the same value as the bytes contained at the target address are all 0x0Ds. The next instruction CALL [EAX+4] results in a transfer of control to the address 0x0D0D0D11, which falls into the middle of a long sequence of 0x0Ds. This sequence is executed by the processor as the NOP equivalent instructions until the shellcode is reached, as shown in the screen shot. The selected value of 0x0D0D0D0D for heap spraying leverages the fact that heap fills generally start from lower addresses and grow to higher addresses. Selecting an address that begins with a zero means less time must be dedicated to filling the heap before the target address is reached. Alternatively a higher value such as 0x44444444 will take a longer time to reach with a heap fill and increases the chances that a targeted user will kill the browser prior to successful exploitation.

To further drive the point home consider the following two "bad" choices: 0x01010101, which translates to ADD [ECX], EAX, and 0x0A0A0A0A, which translates to OR CL, [EDX]. The former example will likely fail due to an invalid write address contained within the register ECX and the latter example will likely fail due to an invalid read address contained within the register EDX. As another good example, consider 0x05050505, which translates to ADD EAX, 0x05050505. This sequence is used in some publicly seen exploits.

### Flash

Although Adobe Flash Player represents a third-party Web browser add-on as opposed to built-in browser functionality, it has been so widely adopted that the majority of Web browsers today have some version of Flash Player installed. Binary Flash files typically have an .swf extension and can be opened as stand-alone files but are more typically incorporated as objects in Web pages that are downloaded by the browser and then launched within Flash Player. Given the binary nature of Flash files, one of two alternate approaches can be taken when fuzzing. A known good .swf file could be fuzzed as described in Chapter 11, "File Format Fuzzing," Chapter 12, "File Format Fuzzing: Automation on UNIX," and Chapter 13, "File Format Fuzzing: Automation on Windows," which detail techniques for file format fuzzing. In November 2005, eEye released details of a memory access vulnerability in Macromedia Flash 6 and 7. Although it is not known how this vulnerability was discovered, fuzzing seems to be a likely candidate for the approach taken. Alternately, Flash files could be coded using ActionScript, a scripting language used by Flash for the manipulation of data and content at runtime.[32] Fuzzing could then be used to mutate the various ActionScript methods, prior to compiling the binary Flash files. In October 2006, Rapid7 released a security advisory detailing how the `XML.addRequestHeader()` method could be used to add arbitrary HTTP headers to a request made by the Flash object.[33] This in turn could be used to perform arbitrary HTTP requests via an HTTP request splitting technique.

### URLs

Sometimes the URL itself can lead to vulnerabilities. Following the release of MS06-042,[34] eEye discovered that the newly issued patches for that bulletin had also introduced a heap overflow vulnerability. They discovered that when an overly long URL was passed to Internet Explorer, if the target Web site indicated GZIP or deflate encoding that an overflow could occur when a `lstrcpynA()` call attempted to copy up to a 2,084-byte URL into a 260-byte buffer.[35] An attack using this vulnerability would only require that a user click on a supplied URL assuming that they were using a vulnerable version of Internet Explorer.

## VULNERABILITIES

Although client-side vulnerabilities require at least some social engineering to facilitate a successful attack, they still pose significant risk due to the types of attacks that they can lead to.

- *DoS.* Many Web browser vulnerabilities simply lead to a DoS attack that causes the browser to crash or become unresponsive. This typically occurs due to an infinite loop or memory corruption that cannot be further exploited. In the grand scheme of things, a client-side DoS attack is fairly minor. Although it can be a nuisance to restart your Web browser every time it crashes, it does not cause any permanent damage. Unlike server-side DoS attacks, client-side DoS attacks only have a single victim.

---

[32] http://en.wikipedia.org/wiki/Actionscript

[33] http://www.rapid7.com/advisories/R7-0026.jsp

[34] http://www.microsoft.com/technet/security/bulletin/ms06-042.mspx

[35] http://research.eeye.com/html/advisories/published/AD20060824.html

- *Buffer overflow.* Buffer overflows are relatively common Web browser vulnerabilities. They can be triggered by virtually any of the input vectors mentioned previously and are particularly dangerous, as they might lead to code execution.

- *Remote command execution.* Command execution vulnerabilities typically take advantage of existing functionality that was not designed to allow for remote code execution but allows it to occur nonetheless. For example, Albert Puigsech Galicia discovered that an attacker could inject FTP commands directly into an FTP URI, which would cause Internet Explorer 6.x and earlier versions to execute the FTP commands simply by convincing a user to click the link.[36] This vulnerability could, for example, be used to download files to the user's computer. It was further discovered that this same vulnerability could be leveraged to cause the browser to send e-mail messages. Microsoft addressed this vulnerability in MS06-042.

- *Cross-domain restriction bypass.* Web browsers have controls that prohibit a particular Web site from accessing content from another site. This is an important restriction, otherwise any site could, for example, obtain the cookies from other sites, which often contain session IDs. Numerous vulnerabilities have emerged that allow a site to break out of this domain restriction. The GDS vulnerability mentioned previously would be an example of one such issue.

- *Bypassing security zones.* Internet Explorer enforces security according to the zone from which the content originated. Documents originating from the Internet are generally considered to be untrusted and therefore have greater restrictions imposed on them. Alternately, files opened up locally are considered to be trusted and are granted greater privileges. In February 2005, Jouko Pynnönen released an advisory detailing how specially encoded URLs could be used to trick Internet Explorer into interpreting remote files as having been opened from the local zone.[37] This, in turn, could allow an attacker to include malicious script within a downloaded file that would execute an attacker-supplied exploit. Microsoft addressed this vulnerability in security bulletin MS05-14.[38]

- *Address bar spoofing.* Phishing has become a serious problem as increasing numbers of criminals attempt to obtain private information such as credit card numbers from unsuspecting Web surfers. Whereas most phishing attacks simply leverage social

---

[36] http://osvdb.org/displayvuln.php?osvdb_id=12299

[37] http://jouko.iki.fi/adv/zonespoof.html

[38] http://www.microsoft.com/technet/security/bulletin/ms05-014.mspx

engineering, some of the more sophisticated attacks leverage Web browser vulnerabilities to aid in making the phishing site appear to be legitimate. Vulnerabilities that allow for the address bar to be spoofed are of value to phishers as they allow a fake Web page to appear as though it is hosted at a legitimate site. Unfortunately, there have been several of these vulnerabilities in all major Web browsers.

## DETECTION

When fuzzing Web browsers, it is important that parallel efforts be made to identify non-obvious errors. There is no single place to look for errors. Instead, it is worthwhile to investigate a number of alternate sources.

- *Event logs.* If you're fuzzing a browser in a Windows environment, don't overlook the Event Viewer. Internet Explorer 7.0 has actually added a separate Internet Explorer log to the Event Viewer. If you're targeting an earlier version of Internet Explorer or an alternate browser, entries might be included in the application log. Although far from comprehensive, it is an easy source to check and might contain useful data.

- *Performance monitors.* Memory corruption issues or infinite loops are likely to result in performance degradation of the target Web browser. Performance monitoring tools can assist in identifying such conditions. Be sure, however, to use a dedicated machine when fuzzing to ensure that other factors are not causing the performance degradation.

- *Debuggers.* By far the most useful detection tool for Web browser fuzzing will be a third-party debugger attached to the browser that you are targeting. This will allow you to identify both handled and unhandled exceptions and will also assist in determining if memory corruption issues are likely to be exploitable.

## SUMMARY

Although client-side vulnerabilities were once overlooked, the advent of phishing attacks is forcing us to take a closer look at them in terms of the risk that they pose. A single vulnerable browser on your corporate network could be a gateway for an attacker. Client-side attacks require at least some social engineering, but this is a relatively minor hurdle. Web browser vulnerabilities also make for excellent attack vectors during targeted attacks. In this chapter, we introduced a number of existing Web browser fuzzing utilities. Next, we'll take what we've learned here to build our own fuzzer for Web browsers.

# Web Browser Fuzzing: Automation

*"Natural gas is hemispheric. I like to call it hemispheric in nature because it is a product that we can find in our neighborhoods."*

—George W. Bush, Washington, DC, December 20, 2000

In Chapter 17, "Web Browser Fuzzing," we discussed a number of web browser aspects along with their "fuzzability." An increased interest in browser fuzzing has led to the creation of a number of fuzzing tools and an even greater number of vulnerabilities affecting the most popular browsers in use today, such as Mozilla Firefox and Microsoft Internet Explorer. In this chapter, we cover the requirements for constructing an ActiveX fuzzer. Even though exploitation is limited to Internet Explorer, and a few ActiveX fuzzers already exist, this testing vector was chosen for further discussion among the others because it is the most interesting and complicated. The limitation to Internet Explorer is not entirely discouraging, either, as Microsoft's browser still holds the majority of the Web user market share. This chapter begins with a synopsis of the history of ActiveX technology and then dives directly into the development of an ActiveX fuzzing tool.

## COMPONENT OBJECT MODEL BACKGROUND

Microsoft COM is an ambitious software technology originally introduced in the early 1990s that aims to provide a universal protocol for software interoperability.

Standardized client–server communications allow software written in a variety of languages that support COM to exchange data with one another both locally, on the same system, and remotely between different systems. COM is widely in use today and has had a vital history, generating a number of acronyms (and confusion) along the way.

## HISTORY IN A NUTSHELL

The earliest ancestor to COM can be traced back to Dynamic Data Exchange (DDE), a technology still used in the Windows operating system today. You can find DDE in action through shell file extensions, the clipbook viewer (NetDDE), and Microsoft Hearts (also NetDDE). In 1991, Microsoft unveiled Object Linking and Embedding (OLE). Whereas DDE is limited to pure data exchange, OLE is capable of embedding document types within one another. OLE client–server intercommunication occurs within system libraries through the usage of virtual function tables (VTBLs).

The introduction of COM followed OLE, which was later followed by the release of OLE 2, a new generation of OLE built on top of COM instead of VTBLs. This technology was renamed ActiveX in 1996. Later that year, Microsoft released Distributed COM (DCOM) as an extension to COM and a response to the Common Object Request Broker Architecture[1] (CORBA). Distributed Computing Environment/Remote Procedure Calls[2] (DCE/RPC) is the underlying RPC mechanism behind DCOM. The addition of DCOM further extended the flexibility of COM, as it allows software developers to expose functionality over mediums such as the Internet without providing access to the underlying code.

The most recent event in the history of COM came with the introduction of COM+, which was released with the Windows 2000 operating system. COM+ provides the additional benefit of "component farms" managed with the Microsoft Transaction Server bundled with Windows 2000. Like DCOM, COM+ components can also be distributed and additionally allow for reuse without the need to unload the component from memory.

## OBJECTS AND INTERFACES

The COM architecture defines both objects and interfaces. An *object*, such as an ActiveX control, describes its functionality by defining and implementing an *interface*. Software can then query a COM object to determine what interfaces and functionality it might

---

[1]  http://en.wikipedia.org/wiki/Corba

[2]  http://en.wikipedia.org/wiki/DCE/RPC

expose. Each COM object is assigned a unique 128-bit identifier known as a class ID (CLSID). Furthermore, each COM interface is also assigned a unique 128-bit identifier known as an interface ID (IID). Example COM interfaces include IStream, IDispatch, and IObjectSafety. These interfaces and all others derive from a base interface known as IUnknown.

In addition to a CLSID, objects can optionally specify a program ID (ProgID) for identification. A ProgID is a human-readable string that is much more convenient for referencing an object. Consider the following aliases, for example:

- 000208D5-0000-0000-C000-000000000046

- Excel.Application

Both the CLSID and ProgID are defined in the registry and can be used in place of one another. Beware, however, that ProgIDs are not guaranteed to be unique.

## ACTIVEX

ActiveX is the only COM technology pertinent to our topic at hand—Web browser fuzzing. Similar to Java applets, ActiveX controls have broader access to the operating system and are used to develop a multitude of extensions that are otherwise unavailable to the browser. ActiveX components are widespread and can be found bundled with many software packages as well as distributed directly over the Web. Example products and services that might rely on ActiveX technology include online virus scanners, Web conferencing and telephony, instant messengers, online games, and more.

Microsoft Internet Explorer is the only browser that natively supports ActiveX and implements the standard Document Object Model (DOM) to handle instantiation, parameter, and method invocation. The following examples are provided for reference and demonstration:

**Pure DOM**
```
<object classid = "clsid:F08DF954-8592-11D1-B16A-00C0F0283628"
        id      = "Slider1"
        width   = "100"
        height  = "50">
  <param name="BorderStyle"  value="1" />
  <param name="MousePointer" value="0" />
  <param name="Enabled"      value="1" />
  <param name="Min"          value="0" />
  <param name="Max"          value="10" />
</object>
```

```
Slider1.method(arg, arg, arg)
```

**Outdated Embed**
```
<embed type   = "application/x-oleobject"
       name   = "foo"
       align  = "baseline"
       border = "0"
       width  = "200"
       height = "300"
       clsid  = "{8E27C92B-1264-101C-8A2F-040224009C02}">
```

```
foo.method(arg, arg, arg)
```

**Javascript / Jscript**
```
<script type="javascript">
  function call_function()
  {
    obj = new ActiveXObject('AcroPDF.PDF');
    obj.property = "value";
    obj.method(arg, arg, arg);
  }

  call_function();
</script>
```

**Visual Basic**
```
<object classid = 'clsid:38EE5CEE-4B62-11D3-854F-00A0C9C898E7'
        id       = 'target' >
</object>

<script language='vbscript'>
  'Wscript.echo typename(target)
  'Sub SelectAndActivateButton ( ByVal lButton As Long )
  arg1=2147483647
  target.property = arg1
  target.method arg1
</script>
```

In addition to loading controls directly in the browser, an ActiveX control can be loaded and interfaced with directly as a standard COM object. Loading a control directly can be advantageous to our fuzzer as it eliminates the intermediary steps of generating and loading browser code into Internet Explorer.

Microsoft COM programming and internals is a vast subject with entire books dedicated to the subject. For further information on COM, visit the Microsoft COM Web site[3] for a high-level overview and the MSDN article "The Component Object Model: A Technical Overview"[4] for a low-level overview.

In the next section, we dive directly into the development of an ActiveX fuzzer, revealing further pertinent details of COM technology along the way.

## FUZZER DEVELOPMENT

A number of languages are suitable for developing an ActiveX fuzzer. This is evident in that a plethora of programming languages is used in the implementation of various ActiveX fuzzers today. COMRaider[5] is built mostly in Visual Basic with a few sprinkles of C++. AxMan[6] is developed as a hybrid of C++, JavaScript, and HTML. We model our fuzzer after the same general approach taken by both of these fuzzers:

- Enumerate all loadable ActiveX controls.
- Enumerate accessible methods and properties for each ActiveX control.
- Parse the type library to determine method parameter types.
- Generate fuzz test cases.
- Execute fuzz test cases while monitoring for anomalies.

Unlike our predecessors, we implemented our fuzzer entirely in a single language, Python. The choice of language might initially strike you as odd and even unfeasible. However, developing in Python is indeed possible, as modern distributions include a number of modules that expose the underlying Windows API. Various modules that we rely on for interfacing with COM include win32api, win32com, pythoncom, and win32con. (If you are interested in further details regarding Python programming in the Windows environment, refer to the aptly titled "Python Programming on Win32"[7] written by Mark Hammond, the actual developer of a number of the modules we leverage to bridge Python into the world of COM.) Figures 18.1 and 18.2 are screen shots from PythonWin's COM and type library browsers respectively, showing high-level access to low-level COM information.

---

[3]  http://www.microsoft.com/com/default.mspx

[4]  http://msdn2.microsoft.com/en-us/library/ms809980.aspx

[5]  https://labs.idefense.com/software/fuzzing.php#more_comraider

[6]  http://metasploit.com/users/hdm/tools/axman/

[7]  http://www.oreilly.com/catalog/pythonwin32/

**Figure 18.1**    PythonWin COM browser

**Figure 18.2**    PythonWin type library browser

As a programmatic example, consider the following snippet that will spawn an instance of Microsoft Excel and make it visible by setting the Boolean property Visible:

```
import win32com.client
xl = win32com.client.Dispatch("Excel.Application")
xl.Visible = 1
```

We'll next dive straight into more examples by examining how to enumerate all load-able ActiveX controls. The code snippets presented in the remainder of this chapter are excerpts from a full-featured COM fuzzer available for download from the official Web site for this book (http://www.fuzzing.org).

## ENUMERATING LOADABLE ACTIVEX CONTROLS

Our first developmental task is to enumerate all COM objects available on the target system. The entire list of COM objects is published in the Windows registry[8] under the key HKEY_LOCAL_MACHINE (HKLM) and the subkey SOFTWARE\Classes. We can access this key using the standard Windows registry access API:[9]

```
import win32api, win32con
import pythoncom, win32com.client
from win32com.axscript import axscript

try:
    classes_key = win32api.RegOpenKey( \
        win32con.HKEY_LOCAL_MACHINE,   \
        "SOFTWARE\\Classes")
except win32api.error:
    print "Problem opening key HKLM\\SOFTWARE\\Classes"
```

The first three lines in this snippet are responsible for importing the necessary functionality to access the registry as well as interfacing with COM objects. Once open, the key is enumerated in search of valid class CLSIDs. If a CLSID is found, then the entry is saved to a list that is later used.

```
skey_index = 0
clsid_list = []

while True:
    try:
        skey = win32api.RegEnumKey(classes_key, skey_index)
    except win32api.error:
        print "End of keys"
        break
```

---

[8] http://en.wikipedia.org/wiki/Windows_registry

[9] http://msdn.microsoft.com/library/default.asp?url=/library/en-us/sysinfo/base/registry_functions.asp

```
progid = skey

try:
    skey = win32api.RegOpenKey(win32con.HKEY_LOCAL_MACHINE, \
        "SOFTWARE\\Classes\\%s\\CLSID" % progid)
except win32api.error:
    print "Couldn't get CLSID key...skipping"
    skey_index += 1
    continue

try:
    clsid = win32api.RegQueryValueEx(skey, None)[0]
except win32api.error:
    print "Couldn't get CLSID value...skipping"
    skey_index += 1
    continue

clsid_list.append((progid, clsid))
skey_index += 1
```

Combined, these snippets generate a list of tuples describing every available COM object on the system. Security testing of COM objects is usually limited to controls accessible to Internet Explorer. This is due to the fact that the most popular ActiveX exploitation technique by far is for an attacker to host a malicious Web site and coerce users with the vulnerable component into visiting the page. As only some of these controls are accessible in Internet Explorer, our second task is to cull the inaccessible ones out of our list. Internet Explorer will load an ActiveX control without warning if any of the following three criteria are met:[10]

- The control is marked "Safe for Scripting" in the Windows Registry.
- The control is marked "Safe for Initialization" in the Windows Registry.
- The control implements the IObjectSafety COM interface

The Windows registry contains a Component Categories key that lists subkeys for each of the categories implemented by the installed components. The two we are looking for are CATID_SafeForScripting and CATID_SafeForInitializing. The following routines will determine if a given CLSID is marked as accessible in Internet Explorer in the registry:

---

[10] http://msdn.microsoft.com/workshop/components/activex/safety.asp

```
def is_safe_for_scripting (clsid):
    try:
        key = win32api.RegOpenKey(win32con.HKEY_CLASSES_ROOT, \
            "CLSID\\%s\\Implemented Categories" % clsid)
    except win32api.error:
        return False

    skey_index = 0
    while True:
        try:
            skey = win32api.RegEnumKey(key, skey_index)
        except:
            break

        # CATID_SafeForScripting
        if skey == "{7DD95801-9882-11CF-9FA9-00AA006C42C4}":
            return True

        skey_index += 1

    return False

def is_safe_for_init (clsid):
    try:
        key = win32api.RegOpenKey(win32con.HKEY_CLASSES_ROOT, \
            "CLSID\\%s\\Implemented Categories" % clsid)
    except win32api.error:
        return False

    skey_index = 0
    while True:
        try:
            skey = win32api.RegEnumKey(key, skey_index)
        except:
            break

        # CATID_SafeForInitializing
        if skey == "{7DD95802-9882-11CF-9FA9-00AA006C42C4}":
            return True

        skey_index += 1

    return False
```

In addition to the registry, an ActiveX control can mark itself as safe to Internet Explorer by implementing the IObjectSafety interface. To determine if a given ActiveX control implements the IObjectSafety interface it must first be instantiated and then queried. The following routine will determine if a given control implements the IObjectSafety interface and is therefore accessible to Internet Explorer:

```
def is_iobject_safety (clsid):
    try:
        unknown = pythoncom.CoCreateInstance(clsid, \
            None,                                  \
            pythoncom.CLSCTX_INPROC_SERVER,        \
            pythoncom.IID_IUnknown)
    except:
        return False

    try:
        objsafe = unknown.QueryInterface(axscript.IID_IObjectSafety)
    except:
        return False

    return True
```

To finalize our list of loadable ActiveX controls we must make a final consideration. Microsoft supplies a mechanism for kill bitting[11] or preventing individual CLSIDs from loading in Internet Explorer through the registry key HKLM\Software\Microsoft\Internet Explorer\ActiveX Compatibility\<CLSID of ActiveX Control>. Each CLSID that contains an entry in this registry location must be culled out of our list. The following function can be used to determine if a given CLSID has been disabled in this manner:

```
def is_kill_bitted (clsid):
    try:
        key = win32api.RegOpenKey(win32con.HKEY_LOCAL_MACHINE, \
            "SOFTWARE\\Microsoft\\Internet Explorer"           \
            "\\ActiveX Compatibility\\%s" % clsid)
    except win32api.error:
        return False
```

---

[11] http://support.microsoft.com/kb/240797

```
try:
    (compat_flags, typ) = win32api.RegQueryValueEx(key, \
        "Compatibility Flags")
except win32api.error:
    return False

if typ != win32con.REG_DWORD:
    return False

if compat_flags & 0x400:
    return True
else:
    return False

return False
```

With our list of ActiveX controls made, and checked twice, to determine which controls might be naughty, we must next examine the exposed properties and methods.

## PROPERTIES, METHODS, PARAMETERS, AND TYPES

The ability to systematically generate a list of target controls is convenient, but this is where our ActiveX fuzzing gets really elegant. A description of every property and method exposed by a COM object is embedded directly within it. Furthermore, the types for both properties and method parameters are also described. This COM feature is just as exciting to us as fuzzer developers as it is to software developers who first hear of it. The ability to programmatically enumerate the attack surface of an ActiveX control allows us to create intelligent fuzzers that know what kind of data a specific method might be expecting. That way we don't waste time supplying a string when an integer is expected.

In the world of COM, data is passed through a structure known as a VARIANT. The VARIANT data structure supports a number of data types including integers, floats, strings, dates, Booleans, other COM objects, and any array of these. PythonCOM provides an abstraction layer hiding many of these details for us. Table 18.1 shows the mapping between some native Python types and their VARIANT equivalent.

**Table 18.1**    PythonCOM VARIANT translation

| Python Object Type | VARIANT Type |
|---|---|
| Integer | VT_I4 |
| String | VT_BSTR |
| Float | VT_R8 |
| None | VT_NLL |
| True/False | VT_BOOL |

The pythoncom module provides the LoadTypeLib() routine for parsing a type library directly from a binary COM object. Everything we need to know about the properties and methods of a COM object is accessible through the loaded type library. As an example, let's walk through the type library for the Adobe Acrobat PDF control shown previously in Figure 18.2. This ActiveX control is bundled with Adobe's Acrobat Reader and is accessible to Internet Explorer as it is marked both safe for scripting and safe for initialization. The following snippet demonstrates how to load the type library for this code and additionally applies some Python trickery to create a mapping of VARIANT names:

```
adobe = r"C:\Program Files\Common Files" \
        r"\Adobe\Acrobat\ActiveX\AcroPDF.dll"

tlb = pythoncom.LoadTypeLib(adobe)

VTS = {}
for vt in [x for x in pythoncom.__dict__.keys() if x.count("VT_")]:
    VTS[eval("pythoncom.%s"%vt)] = vt
```

The generated VARIANT name map is used solely for demonstrative purposes, as we will later see. A type library can define multiple types, and the count to loop through can be retrieved by calling GetTypeInfoCount(). In our example there are three types as shown in the first column of Figure 18.2. The following example shows how to loop through the various types and print their names:

```
for pos in xrange(tlb.GetTypeInfoCount()):
    name = tlb.GetDocumentation(pos)[0]
    print name
```

There are three types defined within the Acrobat control. Let's take a closer look at the one highlighted in Figure 18.2, IAcroAXDocShim. Like most counting in programming the position count starts at zero, meaning the index to our desired type is two and not three. In the following block of code, the type info and attributes are pulled from the previously defined type library and then used to enumerate the properties under this specific type:

```
info = tlb.GetTypeInfo(2)
attr = info.GetTypeAttr()

print "properties:"
for i in xrange(attr.cVars):
    id    = info.GetVarDesc(i)[0]
    names = info.GetNames(id)
    print "\t", names[0]
```

The cVars attribute variable specifies the number of properties (or variables) defined under the type. This count is used to loop through and print the name for each property. Enumerating the methods, parameters, and parameter types is equally simple as can be seen in the following code excerpt:

```
print "methods:"
for i in xrange(attr.cFuncs):
    desc  = info.GetFuncDesc(i)

    if desc.wFuncFlags:
        continue

    id    = desc.memid
    names = info.GetNames(id)
    print "\t%s()" % names[0]

    i = 0
    for name in names[1:]:
        print "\t%s, %s" % (name, VTS[desc.args[i][0]])
        i += 1
```

In this case, the cFuncs attribute variable specifies the number of methods defined under this type. The methods are enumerated, skipping over those where wFuncFlags is set. This flag specifies that the method is restricted (inaccessible) and is therefore not a good fuzzing candidate. The GetNames() routine returns the name of method as well as the names for each of the parameters to the method. The method name is printed and then the remainder of the list, names[1:], is traversed to access the parameters. The function description originally returned by the call to GetFuncDesc() contains a list of VARIANT types for each parameter (or argument). The VARIANT type is represented as an integer that we convert into a name by indexing the VARIANT map we generated previously.

The end result of executing this script against this script on the IAcroAXDocShim interface to the Adobe Acrobat PDF ActiveX control follows:

```
properties:
methods:
    src()
    LoadFile()
        fileName, VT_BSTR
    setShowToolbar()
        On, VT_BOOL
    gotoFirstPage()
    gotoLastPage()
    gotoNextPage()
    gotoPreviousPage()
    setCurrentPage()
        n, VT_I4
    goForwardStack()
    goBackwardStack()
    setPageMode()
        pageMode, VT_BSTR
    setLayoutMode()
        layoutMode, VT_BSTR
    setNamedDest()
        namedDest, VT_BSTR
    Print()
    printWithDialog()
    setZoom()
        percent, VT_R4
    setZoomScroll()
        percent, VT_R4
        left, VT_R4
        top, VT_R4
    setView()
        viewMode, VT_BSTR
    setViewScroll()
        viewMode, VT_BSTR
        offset, VT_R4
```

```
setViewRect()
      left, VT_R4
      top, VT_R4
      width, VT_R4
      height, VT_R4
printPages()
      from, VT_I4
      to, VT_I4
printPagesFit()
      from, VT_I4
      to, VT_I4
      shrinkToFit, VT_BOOL
printAll()
printAllFit()
      shrinkToFit, VT_BOOL
setShowScrollbars()
      On, VT_BOOL
GetVersions()
setCurrentHightlight()
      a, VT_I4
      b, VT_I4
      c, VT_I4
      d, VT_I4
setCurrentHighlight()
      a, VT_I4
      b, VT_I4
      c, VT_I4
      d, VT_I4
postMessage()
      strArray, VT_VARIANT
messageHandler()
```

In the printed results, we can see that there are 39 methods (functions) and no properties defined within this type. The list of parameters and types for each method was successfully enumerated and displayed. This information is critical in the development of an intelligent fuzzer and should be used in the generation of test cases to ensure that each variable is fuzzed accordingly. For example, consider fuzzing a short integer (VT_I2) versus a long integer (VT_I4). Instead of considering both of these types as a generic integer, precious time can be saved by fuzzing the short within its valid range of 0 through 0xFFFF (65,535) instead of the valid range of a full-sized integer (long) that extends from 0 to 0xFFFFFFFF (4,294,967,295).

At this point, we have covered the necessary steps for enumerating each property, method, and parameter for every Internet Explorer accessible ActiveX control on a given system. The next step is to choose appropriate fuzz heuristics and start testing.

## FUZZING AND MONITORING

Chapter 6, "Automation and Data Generation," covered the importance of choosing intelligent string and integer fuzz values. The chosen fuzz heuristics were designed to maximize the possibility of inducing error. The majority of the fuzzers and test cases described in this book are in fact designed to uncover low-level faults, such as buffer overflows, rather than logical issues, such as accessing restricted resources. Directory traversal modifiers are an example heuristic geared toward discovering such security vulnerabilities. There is extra prudence in searching for behavioral violations when fuzzing ActiveX controls as researchers frequently discover controls that simply should never have been accessible through Internet Explorer.

Consider, for example, the WinZip FileView ActiveX Control Unsafe Method Exposure Vulnerability.[12] In this case, the ActiveX control with ProgID WZFILEVIEW.FileViewCtrl.61 was distributed as safe for scripting, allowing a malicious Web site to load the control into the browser and leverage its exposed functionality. More specifically, the methods `ExecCmdForAllSelected` and `ExecCmdForFolder` allow the caller to copy, move, delete, and execute files from arbitrary locations including network shares, FTP directories, and Web directories. This provides a trivial vector for attackers to download and run an arbitrary executable without any warning by simply hosting a malicious Web site. WinZip issued a fix for this issue by removing the safe for scripting setting and additionally setting a kill bit for the specific control.

In addition to the typical fuzz heuristics previously used, valid file paths, commands, and URLs should be included with fuzz data to help uncover bugs similar to the WinZip FileView vulnerability. The fuzz monitor must, of course, contain the necessary capabilities to determine if any of the supplied resources were successfully accessed. This concept is dissected in further detail later.

Once a suitable list of fuzz data has been generated, the next step is to create a series of test cases. One approach to handling this task is to construct an HTML page that embeds the target ActiveX control using any one of the previously listed methods, and then calls a target method with fuzzed parameters. A separate file can be generated for each test and then individual test cases can be loaded in Internet Explorer. Alternatively, the target control can be loaded and tested directly. Following our previous examples, this Python snippet will instantiate the Adobe Acrobat PDF ActiveX control and access two of its exposed methods:

```
adobe = win32com.client.Dispatch("AcroPDF.PDF.1")
print adobe.GetVersions()
adobe.LoadFile("c:\\test.pdf")
```

---

[12] http://www.zerodayinitiative.com/advisories/ZDI-06-040.html

The first line in this snippet is responsible for actually creating an instance of the Adobe COM object accessible through the variable named adobe. Once created, the object can be interfaced with very naturally. The second line prints the results of a call to the routine GetVersions() and the third line causes the control to load a PDF file into the Acrobat Reader viewer. Expanding on this example to fuzz other methods, parameters, and controls is a simple matter.

The remaining piece to the puzzle is the monitoring portion of the fuzzer. In addition to the Python COM modules, we utilize the PaiMei[13] reverse engineering library to implement a debugger-based fuzz monitor. This library is used extensively in later chapters where it is covered in more depth. In essence, a lightweight debugger is created that wraps the execution of the target ActiveX controls. In the event a low-level vulnerability such as a buffer overflow is discovered, the debugger is engaged and the specifics of the fault are recorded. The PaiMei library also exposes functionality for hooking API calls. This feature is used to monitor for behavioral issues. By observing the arguments to Microsoft library calls such as CreateFile()[14] and CreateProcess(),[15] we can determine if the target ActiveX control has successfully accessed a resource it shouldn't. Reviewing the specifics of the API hooking functionality is left as an exercise for the reader.

On a final note, it is worthwhile to examine the names of exposed properties and methods with simple regular expressions searches. If you come across methods with names such as GetURL(), DownloadFile(), Execute(), and so on, you might want to give them some personal attention immediately.

## Summary

In this chapter, we explored the history of Microsoft's COM technology and outlined the requirements for an ActiveX control to be accessible from the Internet Explorer Web browser. The necessary Python COM interfaces were examined, as well as the specific steps necessary for enumerating accessible ActiveX controls and their properties, methods, parameters, and parameter types. The reviewed code snippets from this chapter are excerpts from a full-featured COM fuzzer available for download from the official Web site for this book (http://www.fuzzing.org).

---

[13] https://www.openrce.org/downloads/details/208/PaiMei

[14] http://msdn.microsoft.com/library/default.asp?url=/library/en-us/fileio/fs/createfile.asp

[15] http://msdn.microsoft.com/library/default.asp?url=/library/en-us/dllproc/base/createprocess.asp

# In-Memory Fuzzing

*"It is white."*

—George W. Bush, after being asked by a child in Britain what the White House was like, July 19, 2001

In this chapter, we introduce the notion of *in-memory fuzzing,* a novel approach to fuzzing that has received little public attention and for which no full-featured proof of concept tools have yet been publicly released. In essence, this technique aims to transition fuzzing from the familiar client–server (or client–target) model, to a target-only model residing solely in memory. Although technically this is a more complex approach that requires strong low-level knowledge of assembly language, process memory layout, and process instrumentation, there are a number of benefits to the technique that we outline prior to jumping into any specific implementation details.

In previous chapters, we made a concerted effort to provide an unbiased view from both the UNIX and Windows perspective. Due to the complex scope of this fuzzing technique, we limit our focus in this chapter to a single platform. We chose Microsoft Windows as the platform of focus for a number of reasons. First, this fuzzing technique is better applied against closed source targets, as binary software distributions are more popular on the Windows platform than on UNIX. Second, Windows exposes rich and powerful debugging APIs for process instrumentation. That is not to say that debugging APIs are unavailable on UNIX platforms, but we are of the opinion that they are simply not as robust. The general ideas and approaches discussed here can, of course, be adopted to apply across various platforms.

## IN-MEMORY FUZZING: WHAT AND WHY?

Every method of fuzzing we've discussed so far has required the generation and transmission of data over expected channels. In Chapter 11, "File Format Fuzzing," Chapter 12, "File Format Fuzzing: Automation on UNIX," and Chapter 13, "File Format Fuzzing: Automation on Windows," mutated files were loaded directly by the application. In Chapter 14, "Network Protocol Fuzzing," Chapter 15, "Network Protocol Fuzzing: Automation on UNIX," and Chapter 16, "Network Protocol Fuzzing: Automation on Windows," fuzz data was transmitted over network sockets to target services. Both situations require that we represent a whole file or a complete protocol to the target, even if we are interested only in fuzzing a specific field. Also in both situations, we were largely unaware and indifferent to what underlying code was executed in response to our inputs.

In-memory fuzzing is an altogether different animal. Instead of focusing on a specific protocol or file format, we focus instead on the actual underlying code. We are shifting our focus from data inputs to the functions and individual assembly instructions responsible for parsing data inputs. In this manner we skip the expected data communications channel and instead focus on either mutating or generating data within the memory of the target application.

When is this beneficial? Consider the situation where you are fuzzing a closed source network daemon that implements a complex packet encryption or obfuscation scheme. To successfully fuzz this target it is first necessary to completely reverse engineer and reproduce the obfuscation scheme. This is a prime candidate for in-memory fuzzing. Instead of focusing unnecessarily on the protocol encapsulation, we peer into the memory space of the target application looking for interesting points, for example, after the received network data has been deobfuscated. As another example, consider the situation where we wish to test the robustness of a specific function. Say that through some reverse engineering efforts we have pinned down an e-mail parsing routine that takes a single string argument, an e-mail address, and parses it in some fashion. We could generate and transmit network packets or test files containing mutated e-mail addresses, but with in-memory fuzzing we can focus our efforts by directly fuzzing the target routine.

These concepts are further clarified throughout the remainder of this chapter as well as the next one. First, however, we need to cover some background information.

## NECESSARY BACKGROUND INFORMATION

Before we continue any further, let's run through a crash course of the Microsoft Windows memory model, briefly discussing the general layout and properties of the memory space of a typical Windows process. We'll touch on a number of complex and detailed subject matter areas in this section that we encourage you to delve into further.

As some of this material tends to be quite dry, feel free to skip through to the overview and proceed directly to the diagram at the end if you so choose.

Since Windows 95, the Windows operating system has been built on the flat memory model, which on a 32-bit platform provides a total of 4GB of addressable memory. The 4GB address range, by default, is divided in half. The bottom half (0x00000000–0x7FFFFFFF) is reserved for user space and the top half (0x80000000–0xFFFFFFFF) is reserved for kernel space. This split can be optionally changed to 3:1 (through the /3GB boot.ini setting[1]), 3GB for user space and 1GB for the kernel, for improved performance in memory-intensive applications such as Oracle's database. The flat memory model, as opposed to the segmented memory model, commonly uses a single memory segment for referencing program code and data. The segmented memory model, on the other hand, utilizes multiple segments for referencing various memory locations. The main advantages of the flat memory model versus the segmented memory model are drastic performance gains and decreased complexity from the programmer's viewpoint as there is no need for segment selection and switching. Even further simplifying the world for programmers, the Windows operating system manages memory via virtual addressing. In essence, the virtual memory model presents each running process with its own 4GB virtual address space. This task is accomplished through a virtual-to-physical address translation aided by a memory management unit (MMU). Obviously, not very many systems can physically support providing 4GB of memory to every running process. Instead, virtual memory space is built on the concept of paging. A *page* is a contiguous block of memory with a typical size of 4,096 (0x1000) bytes in Windows. Pages of virtual memory that are currently in use are stored in RAM (primary storage). Unused pages of memory can be swapped to disk (secondary storage) and later restored to RAM when needed again.

Another important concept in Windows memory management is that of memory protections. Memory protection attributes are applied at the finest granularity on memory pages; it is not possible to assign protection attributes to only a portion of page. Some of the available protection attributes that might concern us include:[2]

- *PAGE_EXECUTE.* Memory page is executable, attempts to read from or write to the page results in an access violation.
- *PAGE_EXECUTE_READ.* Memory page is executable and readable, attempts to write to the page result in an access violation.
- *PAGE_EXECUTE_READWRITE.* Memory page is fully accessible. It is executable, can be read from and written to.

---

[1] http://support.microsoft.com/kb/q291988/

[2] http://msdn2.microsoft.com/en-us/library/aa366786.aspx

- *PAGE_NOACCESS.* Memory page is not accessible. Any attempt to execute from, read from, or write to the memory page results in an access violation.

- *PAGE_READONLY.* Memory page is readable only. Any attempt to write to the memory page results in an access violation. If the underlying architecture supports differentiating between reading and executing (not always the case), then any attempt to execute from the memory page also results in an access violation.

- *PAGE_READWRITE.* Memory page is readable and writable. As with PAGE_READ-ONLY, if the underlying architecture supports differentiating between reading and executing, then any attempt to execute from the memory page results in an access violation.

For our purposes we might only be interested in the PAGE_GUARD modifier, which according to MSDN [3] raises a STATUS_GUARD_PAGE_VIOLATION on any attempt to access the guarded page and then subsequently removes the guard protection. Essentially, PAGE_GUARD acts as a one-time access alarm. This is a feature we might want to use to monitor for access to certain regions of memory. Alternatively we could also use the PAGE_NOACCESS attribute.

Familiarity with memory pages, layout, and protection attributes are important for purposes of in-memory fuzzing, as we will see in the next chapter. Memory management is a complex subject that is heavily discussed in many other publications.[4] We encourage you to reference these other works. For our purposes however all you need to know is the following:

- Every Windows process "sees" its own 4GB virtual address space.

- Only the bottom 2GB from 0x00000000 through 0x7FFFFFFF are available for user space, the upper 2GB are reserved as kernel space.

- The virtual address space of a process is implicitly protected from access by other processes.

- The 4GB address space is broken into individual pages with a typical size of 4,096 bytes (0x1000).

- At the finest granularity, memory protection attributes are applied to individual memory pages.

---

[3]   http://msdn2.microsoft.com/en-us/library/aa366786.aspx

[4]   *Microsoft Windows Internals, Fourth Edition,* Mark E. Russinovich, David A. Solomon; *Undocumented Windows 2000 Secrets: A Programmer's Cookbook,* Sven Schreiber; *Undocumented Windows NT,* Prasad Dabak, Sandeep Phadke, Milind Borate.

- The PAGE_GUARD memory protection modifier can be used as a one-time page access alarm.

Study Figure 19.1 to gain a better understanding of where specific elements can be found in the virtual address space of the typical Windows process. Figure 19.1 serves as a useful reference in the next chapter as well, when we discuss the specific development details of an in-memory fuzzing automation tool. Following the figure is a brief description of the various listed elements, in case you are not familiar with them.

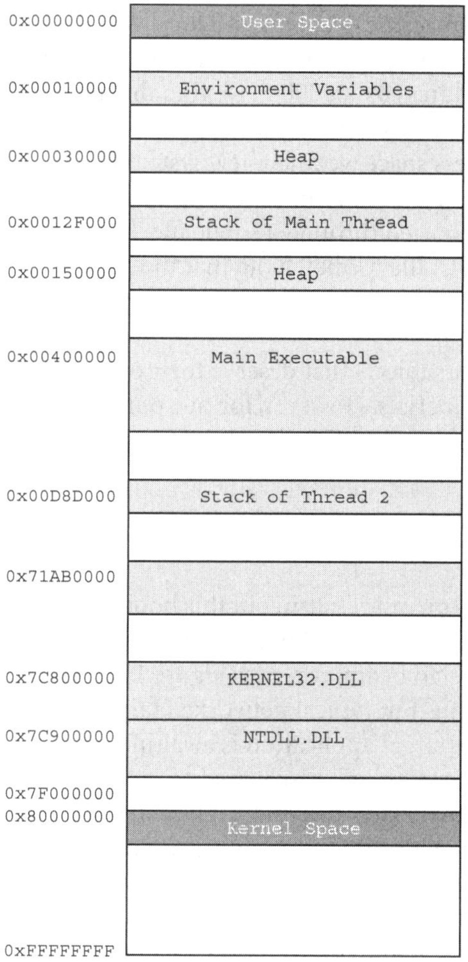

| | |
|---|---|
| 0x00000000 | User Space |
| 0x00010000 | Environment Variables |
| 0x00030000 | Heap |
| 0x0012F000 | Stack of Main Thread |
| 0x00150000 | Heap |
| 0x00400000 | Main Executable |
| 0x00D8D000 | Stack of Thread 2 |
| 0x71AB0000 | |
| 0x7C800000 | KERNEL32.DLL |
| 0x7C900000 | NTDLL.DLL |
| 0x7F000000 | |
| 0x80000000 | Kernel Space |
| 0xFFFFFFFF | |

**Figure 19.1**    Typical Windows memory layout (not drawn to scale)

Let's briefly describe the various elements shown in Figure 19.1 for the benefit of those who are not familiar with them. Starting at the lowest address range, we find the process environment variables at 0x00010000. Recall from Chapter 7, "Environment Variable and Argument Fuzzing," that environment variables are systemwide global variables that are used to define certain behaviors of applications. Higher up in the address range we find two ranges of memory dedicated to the heap at 0x00030000 and 0x00150000. The heap is a pool of memory from which dynamic memory allocations occur through calls such as `malloc()` and `HeapAlloc()`. Note that there can be more then one heap for any given process, just as the diagram shows. Between the two heap ranges we find the stack of the main thread at address 0x0012F000. The stack is a last-in, first-out data structure that is used to keep track of function call chains and local variables. Note that each thread within a process has its own stack. In our example diagram, the stack of thread 2 is located at 0x00D8D000. At address 0x00400000 we find the memory region for our main executable, the .exe file that we executed to get the process loaded in memory. Toward the upper end of the user address space we find a few system DLLs, kernel32.dll and ntdll.dll. DLLs are Microsoft's implementation of shared libraries, common code that is used across applications and exported through a single file. Executables and DLLs both utilize the Portable Executable (PE) file format. Note that the addresses shown in Figure 19.1 will not be the same from process to process and were chosen here simply for example purposes.

Again, we've touched on a number of complex subjects that deserve their own books. We encourage you to reference more in-depth materials. However, for our purposes, we should have armed ourselves with enough information to dive into the subject at hand.

## NO REALLY, WHAT IS IN-MEMORY FUZZING?

We outline and implement two approaches to in-memory fuzzing in this book. In both cases, we are moving our fuzzer from outside the target to within the target itself. The process is best explained and understood visually. To begin, consider Figure 19.2, which depicts a simple control flow diagram of a fictitious but typical networked target.

A loop within the main thread of our example target application is awaiting new client connections. On receiving a connection, a new thread is spawned to process the client request, which is received through one or more calls to `recv()`. The collected data is then passed through some form of unmarshaling or processing routine. The `unmarshal()` routine might be responsible for protocol decompression or decryption but does not actually parse individual fields within the data stream. The processed data is in turn passed to the main parsing routine `parse()`, which is built on top of a number of other routines and library calls. The `parse()` routine processes the various individual fields

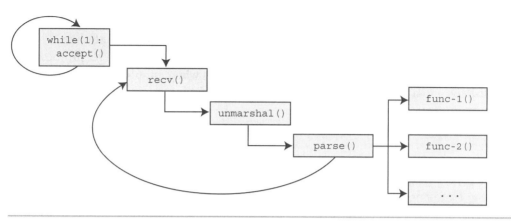

**Figure 19.2**  Example control flow diagram

within the data stream, taking the appropriate requested actions before finally looping back to receive further instructions from the client.

Given this situation, what if instead of transmitting our fuzz data across the wire, we could skip the networking steps entirely? Such code isolation allows us to work directly with the routines which we are most likely going to find bugs, such as the parsing routine. We can then inject faults into the routine and monitor the outcome of those changes while drastically increasing the efficiency of the fuzzing process as everything is done within memory. Through the use of some form of process instrumentation we want to "hook" into our target just before the parsing routines, modify the various inputs the routines accept, and let the routines run their course. Obviously as the subject of this book is fuzzing, we of course want the ability to loop through these steps, automatically modifying the inputs with each iteration and monitoring the results.

## TARGETS

Arguably the most time-consuming requirement for building a network protocol or file format fuzzer is the dissection of the protocol and file format themselves. There have been attempts at automatic protocol dissection that borrow from the field of bioinformatics, a subject that we touch on in Chapter 22, "Automated Protocol Dissection." However, for the most part, protocol dissection is a manual and tedious process.

When dealing with the standard documented protocols such as SMTP, POP, and HTTP, for example, you have the benefit of referencing numerous sources such as RFCs, open source clients, and perhaps even previously written fuzzers. Furthermore, considering the widespread use of these protocols by various applications, it might be worthwhile to implement the protocol in your fuzzer, as it will see a lot of reuse. However, you will frequently find yourself in the situation where the target protocol is undocumented, complex, or proprietary. In such cases where protocol dissection might require considerable time and resources, in-memory fuzzing might serve as a viable time-saving alternative.

What if a target communicates over a trivial protocol that is encapsulated within an open encryption standard? Even worse, what if the protocol is encapsulated within a proprietary encryption or obfuscation scheme? The ever so popular Skype[5] communication suite is a perfect example of a difficult target to audit. The EADS/CRC security team went to great lengths[6] to break beyond the layers of obfuscation and uncover a critical Skype security flaw (SKYPE-SB/2005-003).[7] You might be able to sidestep the problem if the target exposes a nonencrypted interface, but what if it does not? Encrypted protocols are one of the major fuzzing show stoppers. In-memory fuzzing might also allow you to avoid the painstaking process of reverse engineering the encryption routine.

You must consider many factors before committing to this approach when fuzzing your target, the first and most significant being that in-memory fuzzing requires reverse engineering of the target to locate the optimal "hook" points, so the cost of entry could be stifling. In general, in-memory fuzzing is best targeted against closed source targets running on a platform supported by your in-memory fuzzing tools.

## METHOD: MUTATION LOOP INSERTION

The first method of in-memory fuzzing we refer to is mutation loop insertion (MLI). MLI requires that we first manually, through reverse engineering, locate the start and end of the `parse()` routine. Once located, our MLI client can insert a `mutate()` routine into the memory space of the target. The mutation routine is responsible for transforming the data being handled by the parsing routine and can be implemented in a number of ways that we'll cover specifically in the next chapter. Next, our MLI client will insert unconditional jumps from the end of the parsing routine to the start of the mutation routine and the end of the mutation routine to the start of the parsing routine. After this is all said and done, the control flow diagram of our target would look like what's shown in Figure 19.3.

---

[5]   http://www.skype.com

[6]   http://www.ossir.org/windows/supports/2005/2005-11-07/EADS-CCR_Fabrice_Skype.pdf

[7]   http://www.skype.com/security/skype-sb-2005-03.html

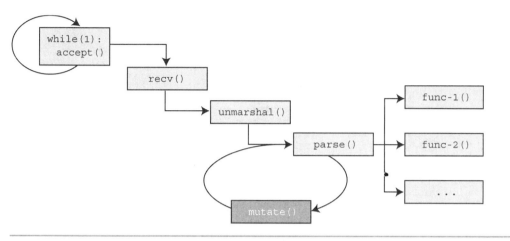

**Figure 19.3** Visual representation of mutation loop insertion

So what happens now? We've created a self-sufficient data mutation loop around the parsing code of our target. There's no longer a need to remotely connect to our target and send data packets. Naturally, this is a significant time saver. Each iteration of the loop will pass different, potentially fault inducing, data to the parsing routines as dictated by `mutate()`.

It goes without saying that our contrived example is overly simplified. Although this was done purposefully to serve as a digestible introduction, it is important to note that in-memory fuzzing is highly experimental. We'll get into these details in Chapter 20, "In-Memory Fuzzing: Automation," as we construct a functional fuzzer.

## METHOD: SNAPSHOT RESTORATION MUTATION

The second method of in-memory fuzzing we refer to as *snapshot restoration mutation* (SRM). Like MLI, we want to bypass the network-centric portions of our target and attack the focal point, in this case the `parse()` routine. Also like MLI, SRM requires locating the start and end of the parsing code. With these locations marked, our SRM client will take a snapshot of the target process when the start of the parsing code is reached. Once parsing is complete, our SRM client will restore the process snapshot, mutate the original data, and reexecute the parsing code. The modified control flow diagram of our target will look like what's shown in Figure 19.4.

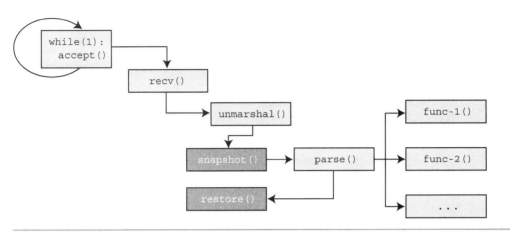

**Figure 19.4**   Visual representation of snapshot restoration mutation.

Again, we've created a self-sufficient data mutation loop around the parsing code of our target. In Chapter 20, we cover the implementation of a functional proof of concept tool to apply both of these described methods in practice. The prototype-quality fuzzer that we construct will help us empirically determine the specific pros and cons of each approach. First, however, let's discuss in more detail one of the major benefits of in-memory fuzzing.

## TESTING SPEED AND PROCESS DEPTH

There is an unavoidable lag associated with network protocol testing in the traditional client–target model. Test cases must individually be transmitted over the wire and depending on the complexity of the fuzzer, the response from the target must be read back and processed. This lag is further exacerbated when fuzzing deep protocol states. Consider, for example, the POP mail protocol that typically provides service over TCP port 110. A valid exchange to retrieve mail might look like (user inputs highlighted in bold) this:

```
$ nc mail.example.com 110
+OK Hello there.
user pedram@openrce.org
+OK Password required.
pass xxxxxxxxxxxx
+OK logged in.
list
```

```
+OK
1 1673
2 19194
3 10187
... [output truncated]...
.
retr 1
+OK 1673 octets follow.
Return-Path: <ralph@openrce.org>
Delivered-To: pedram@openrce.org
… [output truncated]…
retr AAAAAAAAAAAAAAAAAAAAAAAA
-ERR Invalid message number. Exiting.
```

For our network fuzzer to target the argument of the RETR verb, it will have to step through the required process states by reconnecting and reauthenticating with the mail server for each test case. Instead, we could focus solely on the parsing of the RETR argument by testing only at the desired process depth through one of the previously described in-memory fuzzing methods. Recall that process depth and process state were explained in Chapter 4, "Data Representation and Analysis."

## Fault Detection

One of the benefits of in-memory fuzzing is detection of fuzzer-induced faults. Since we are already operating on our target at such a low level, this is an easy addition for the most part. With both the MLI and SRM approaches, our fuzzer, if implemented as a debugger (which it will be), can monitor for exceptional conditions during each mutated iteration. The location of the fault can be saved in conjunction with runtime context information that a researcher can later examine to determine the precise location of the bug. You should note that targets that utilize anti-debugging methodologies, such as Skype previously mentioned, will get in the way of this chosen implementation method.

Our biggest difficulty with fault detection will be filtering out the false positives. Much in the same regard as the Heisenberg uncertainty principle,[8] the sheer act of observing our target process under the microscope of in-memory fuzzing causes it to behave differently. As we are directly modifying the process state of the target in ways that were definitely not originally intended, there is a lot of room for irrelevant faults to occur. Consider Figure 19.5.

---

[8] http://en.wikipedia.org/wiki/Heisenberg_principle

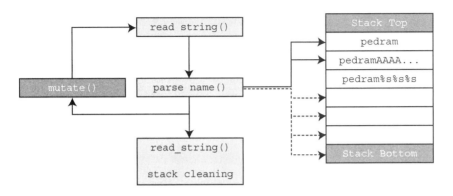

**Figure 19.5**   Stack exhaustion during mutation loop insertion

We applied MLI to wrap around `parse_name()` and `read_string()`. With each iteration the input to `parse_name()` is mutated in an attempt to induce fault. However, because we hook after stack allocations are made and just prior to the stack correction, we are continuously losing stack space with each loop iteration. Eventually, we will exhaust the available stack space and thereby cause an unrecoverable fault that was entirely induced by our fuzzing process and not an existing fault within the target.

## SUMMARY

In-memory fuzzing is not an endeavor for the faint of heart. Before any testing can take place, a skilled researcher must reverse engineer the target to pinpoint the insertion and instrumentation points. Researchers are also required to determine if issues discovered through in-memory fuzzing are indeed accessible with user inputs under normal circumstances. In most cases there will be no such thing as an "immediate" find, but rather a potential input to consider. These setbacks are outweighed by the many benefits provided by the technique.

To our knowledge, the notion of in-memory fuzzing was first introduced to the public by Greg Hoglund of HBGary LLC at the BlackHat Federal[9] and Blackhat USA[10] Security conferences in 2003. HBGary offers a commercial in-memory fuzzing solution called Inspector[11]. In his presentation, Hoglund hints at some of his proprietary technology

---

[9]   http://www.blackhat.com/presentations/bh-federal-03/bh-fed-03-hoglund.pdf

[10]   http://www.blackhat.com/presentations/bh-usa-03/bh-us-03-hoglund.pdf

[11]   http://hbgary.com/technology.shtml

when mentioning process memory snapshots. Memory snapshots are one of the techniques that we discuss in detail during the creation of an automation tool.

In the next chapter we also step through the implementation and usage of a custom in-memory fuzzing framework. To our knowledge, this is the first open source proof of concept code to tackle the task. As advancements are made to the framework they will be posted on the book's Web site at http://www.fuzzing.org.

i

# In-Memory Fuzzing: Automation

*"I hear there's rumors on the Internets that we're going to have a draft."*

—George W. Bush, second presidential debate, St. Louis, MO, October 8, 2004

In the previous chapter, we introduced the concept of in-memory fuzzing. Although we have previously attempted to keep a balance between Windows and UNIX platform coverage, due to the complexity of the topic at hand we decided to focus solely on the Windows platform for this fuzzing approach. More specifically, we cover the 32-bit x86 Windows platform. In this chapter we discuss, in detail, the step by step instruction for creating a proof of concept in-memory fuzzer. We enumerate our desired feature set, cover our approach, and justify our language selection. Finally, after reviewing a case study, we conclude with an overview of the benefits we have introduced and areas of improvement. All of the code we discuss in this chapter will be open source and publicly available at http://www.fuzzing.org. We welcome both feature contributions and bug reports from readers.

As a preliminary warning, please note that although we touch on and explain various low-level aspects of x86 architecture and the Windows platform, we do not cover them in depth. Doing so goes well beyond the scope of this writing. On a positive note, the various concepts we describe in this chapter and the code we develop comes into play in future chapters, such as Chapter 24, "Intelligent Fault Detection."

## REQUIRED FEATURE SET

Recall from Chapter 19, "In-Memory Fuzzing," that we introduced two approaches to in-memory fuzzing, both of which we wish to include in our proof of concept implementation: MLI and SRM. For MLI, we need the ability to modify an instruction for the purpose of creating our loop, "hook" into the target at the start of the loop, and mutate the target buffer at that hook. For SRM we'll need the ability to hook our target process at two specific points, make a copy of the memory space of the target at one hook point, and then restore the memory space of the target at the other hook point. For future reference, Figures 20.1 and 20.2 depict our requirements visually, where the bold text outlines the modifications we need to make to our target process and the dark boxes outline the functionality our in-memory fuzzer must add.

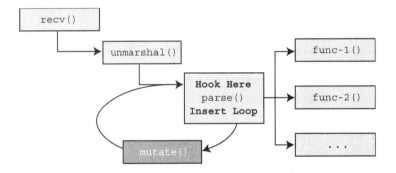

**Figure 20.1**   Modification requirements of mutation loop insertion

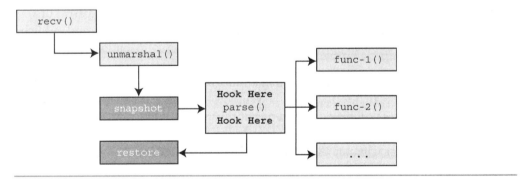

**Figure 20.2**   Modification requirements of snapshot restoration mutation

To implement the listed process *instrumentation* requirements, we are going to write a custom Windows debugger. Creating our in-memory fuzzer as a debugger will thankfully meet all of our requirements. We define the term *instrument* loosely, to cover a number of capabilities. We need to be able to arbitrarily read from and write to the memory space of the target process. We also need to be able to modify the context of any thread within the target process. A thread context[1] contains various processor-specific register data such as the current instruction pointer (EIP), stack pointer (ESP), and frame pointer (EBP) among the rest of the general-purpose registers (EAX, EBX, ECX, EDX, ESI, and EDI). Control over the thread context will allow us to change execution state, something we'll need to do during the restore process of SRM. Thankfully, as we'll see later, the Windows operating system exposes a powerful API that will accommodate all of our needs.

> **NOTE**
>
> As both methods are similar in nature, we decided to focus specifically on SRM for development and automation. We encourage readers to build on the examples within this chapter to implement the MLI approach as an exercise.
>
> SRM has some distinct advantages over MLI. For example, global variable state is restored in SRM but not in MLI. Also, with MLI you must be very careful with your choice of instrumentation points. A careless decision on this front can introduce a memory leak preventing successful fuzzing.

## LANGUAGE CHOICE

Before jumping into the background information on the specific Windows debugging API functions and structures that we will be using, let's determine the language in which we will be developing so that we can represent referential code snippets in that same language. Although the most natural choice of language given our requirements might immediately pop out as C or C++, we decided it would be ideal if we could write the tool in an interpreted language. There are a number of benefits to developing in an interpreted language such as Perl, Python, or Ruby. For our purposes, the greatest advantage is development speed, and for you the reader, it will enhance code readability. We ended up choosing Python for the task after discovering the Python ctypes[2] module, developed

---

[1] http://msdn.microsoft.com/library/default.asp?url=/library/en-us/debug/base/context_str.asp

[2] http://starship.python.net/crew/theller/ctypes/

by Thomas Heller. The ctypes module provides us with an interface to the Windows API as well as the ability to easily create and manipulate complicated C data types directly within Python. The following snippet, for example, demonstrates how easy it is to call the GetCurrentProcessId() function exported by kernel32.dll:

```
from ctypes import *

# create a convenience shortcut to kernel32.
kernel32 = windll.kernel32

# determine the current process ID.
current_pid = kernel32.GetCurrentProcessId()

print "The current process ID is %d" % current_pid
```

Creating and passing C data types is equally as easy. The ctypes module exposes all the basic primitives you will need as native Python classes, as shown in Table 20.1.

**Table 20.1**   ctypes C-Compatible Data Types

| ctypes Type | C Type | Python Type |
| --- | --- | --- |
| c_char | Char | character |
| c_int | Int | Integer |
| c_long | Long | Integer |
| c_ulong | unsigned long | Long |
| c_char_p | Char * | string or None |
| c_void_p | Void * | integer or None |

\* The full list of available primitives can be found at http://starship.python.net/crew/theller/ctypes/tutorial.html

All of the available types can be passed an optional initial value on instantiation. Alternatively, the value can be set by assigning the value attribute. Passing a value by reference is accomplished with ease through the use of the byref() helper function. A key point to remember is that the pointer types such as c_char_p and c_void_p are immutable. To create a block of mutable memory, use the create_string_buffer() helper function. To access or modify the mutable block, use the raw attribute. The following snippet demonstrates these points in a call to ReadProcessMemory():

```
read_buf = create_string_buffer(512)
count    = c_ulong(0)

kernel32.ReadProcessMemory(h_process, \
    0xDEADBEEF, \
    read_buf,   \
    512,        \
    byref(count))

print "Successfully read %d bytes: " % count.value
print read_buf.raw
```

The ReadProcessMemory() API takes a handle to the process whose memory space we want to read from, the address to read from, a pointer to a buffer where the read data is stored, the number of bytes we want to read, and finally a pointer to an integer to store the number of actual bytes we were able to read. While we are on the subject of process memory reading, we should also discuss process memory writing, as demonstrated in the following code excerpt:

```
c_data = c_char_p(data)
length = len(data)
count  = c_ulong(0)

kernel32. WriteProcessMemory(h_process, \
    0xC0CAC01A, \
    c_data,     \
    length,     \
    by_ref(count))

print "Sucessfully wrote %d bytes: " % count.value
```

The WriteProcessMemory() function has a similar format to its sister function ReadProcessMemory(). It requires a handle to the process whose memory space we want to write to, the address to write to, a pointer to a buffer containing the data we want to write, the number of bytes we want to write, and finally a pointer to an integer to store the number of actual bytes we were able to write. As we need the ability to read and write process memory to fulfill a number of our requirements, you will see these routines come into play later in the chapter.

We now have the building blocks necessary for diving into development, so let's briefly cover what we need to know on the API front to create a debugger.

## Windows Debugging API

In Chapter 19, we briefly discussed the memory layout and components of the typical Windows process. Before we continue any further, let's go over some background information on the Windows debugging API that we will be using or abusing, depending on your point of view.

Since Windows NT, the operating system has exposed a powerful set of API functions and structures allowing developers to build an event-driven debugger with relative ease. The basic components of the debugging API can be broken down into the following three categories: functions,[3] events,[4] and structures.[5] As we cover the implementation specifics of our various requirements, we touch on all three of these elements. The first task we have to accomplish is getting our target to run under the control of our debugger. There are two ways of going about this. We can either load the target process under the control of our debugger or alternatively, let the target process start on its own and then attach our debugger to it. To load the process under debugger control, the following code snippet can be used:

```
pi = PROCESS_INFORMATION()
si = STARTUPINFO()

si.cb = sizeof(si);

kernel32.CreateProcessA(path_to_file,
    command_line,   \
    0,              \
    0,              \
    0,              \
    DEBUG_PROCESS,  \
    0,              \
    0,              \
    byref(si),      \
    byref(pi))

print "Started process with pid %d" pi.dwProcessId
```

---

[3]  http://msdn.microsoft.com/library/default.asp?url=/library/en-us/debug/base/debugging_functions.asp

[4]  http://msdn.microsoft.com/library/default.asp?url=/library/en-us/debug/base/debugging_events.asp

[5]  http://msdn.microsoft.com/library/default.asp?url=/library/en-us/debug/base/debugging_structures.asp

Notice the appended A to CreateProcess, Windows APIs are often exported in both Unicode and ANSI versions. The nonappended version of the API serves as a simple wrapper in these cases. For our purposes through ctypes, however, we must call the appended version. Determining if a certain API is exported as both ANSI and Unicode is a simple matter of checking the MSDN page. The MSDN page on CreateProcess,[6] for example, states the following near the bottom: "Implemented as CreateProcessW (Unicode) and CreateProcessA (ANSI)." The PROCESS_INFORMATION and STARTUP_INFO structures are passed by reference to the CreateProcess API and in turn are filled with information we will need later, such as the created process identifier (pi.dwProcessId) and a handle to the created process (pi.hProcess). Alternatively, if we wanted to attach to an already running process, we would call DebugActiveProcess():

```
# attach to the specified process ID.
kernel32. DebugActiveProcess(pid)

# allow detaching on systems that support it.
try:
    kernel32.DebugSetProcessKillOnExit(True)
except:
    pass
```

Notice that neither of the API calls we make in this snippet requires an appended A or W. The DebugActiveProcess() routine attaches our debugger to the specified process identifier. Prior to calling DebugActiveProcess(), we might have to increase our privilege level, but let's worry about that later. The DebugSetProcessKillOnExit()[7] routine has been available since Windows XP and allows us to exit the debugger without killing the debuggee (the process to which we are attached). We wrap the call with a try/except clause to prevent our debugger from exiting with an error if we are running it on a platform that does not support the requested API, such as Windows 2000. Once we have the target process under the control of our debugger, we need to implement the debug event-handling loop. The debug event loop can be thought of as the stereotypical nosy (and old) neighbor in town, Agnes. Agnes sits in front of her window and watches everything that goes on in the neighborhood. Although Agnes sees everything, most of what happens is not interesting enough to motivate her to phone her friends. Occasionally, however, something interesting will happen. The neighbors' kid will chase a cat into a

---

[6] http://msdn.microsoft.com/library/default.asp?url=/library/en-us/dllproc/base/createprocess.asp

[7] http://msdn.microsoft.com/library/default.asp?url=/library/en-us/debug/base/debugsetprocesskillonexit.asp

tree, fall out, and break his arm. Immediately, Agnes will be on the phone with the police. Much like Agnes, our debug event loop will see a lot of events. It is our job to specify which events we are interested in and wish to do something more about. Here is the skeleton of a typical debug event loop:

```
debugger_active = True
dbg             = DEBUG_EVENT()
continue_status = DBG_CONTINUE

while debugger_active:
    ret = kernel32.WaitForDebugEvent(byref(dbg), 100)

  # if no debug event occurred, continue.
  if not ret:
      continue

  event_code = dbg.dwDebugEventCode

  if event_code == CREATE_PROCESS_DEBUG_EVENT:
      # new process created

  if event_code == CREATE_THREAD_DEBUG_EVENT:
      # new thread created

  if event_code == EXIT_PROCESS_DEBUG_EVENT:
      # process exited

  if event_code == EXIT_THREAD_DEBUG_EVENT:
      # thread exited

  if event_code == LOAD_DLL_DEBUG_EVENT:
      # new DLL loaded

  if event_code == UNLOAD_DLL_DEBUG_EVENT:
      # DLL unloaded

  if event_code == EXCEPTION_DEBUG_EVENT:
      # an exception was caught

  # continue processing
  kernel32.ContinueDebugEvent(dbg.dwProcessId, \
      dbg.dwThreadId, \
      continue_status)
```

The debug event handling loop is based primarily on the call to `WaitForDebugEvent()`,[8] which takes a pointer to a DEBUG_EVENT structure as the first argument and the number of milliseconds to wait for a debug event to occur in the debuggee as the second argument. If a debug event occurs, the DEBUG_EVENT structure will contain the debug event type in the attribute `dwDebugEventCode`. We examine that variable to determine if the debug event was triggered due to the creation or exit of a process, creation or exit of a thread, load or unload of a DLL, or a debug exception event. In the case that a debug exception event occurs we can determine specifically what the cause of the exception was by examining the `u.Exception.ExceptionRecord.ExceptionCode` DEBUG_EVENT structure attribute. There are a number of possible exception codes listed on MSDN,[9] but for our purposes we are interested primarily in:

- *EXCEPTION_ACCESS_VIOLATION.* An access violation occurred due to a read or write attempt from an invalid memory address.
- *EXCEPTION_BREAKPOINT.* An exception was triggered due to a breakpoint encounter.
- *EXCEPTION_SINGLE_STEP.* The single step trap is enabled and a single instruction has executed.
- *EXCEPTION_STACK_OVERFLOW.* The offending thread exhausted its stack space. This is typically an indicator of runaway recursion and is usually limited to purely a DoS.

We can interlace whatever logic we wish for handling the various debug events and exceptions. Once we are done processing the reported event, we allow the offending thread to continue with a call to `ContinueDebugEvent()`.

## PUTTING IT ALL TOGETHER

At this stage we have discussed the basics of Windows memory layout, made our list of requirements, chosen our development language, covered the basics of the ctypes module, and dabbled with the fundamentals of the Windows debugging API. A couple of outstanding issues remain:

---

8  http://msdn.microsoft.com/library/default.asp?url=/library/en-us/debug/base/waitfordebugevent.asp

9  http://msdn.microsoft.com/library/default.asp?url=/library/en-us/debug/base/exception_record_str.asp

- How do we implement our need to "hook" into the target process at specific points?
- How do we handle process snapshots and restores?
- How do we locate and mutate target memory space?
- How do we choose our hook points?

## HOW DO WE IMPLEMENT OUR NEED TO "HOOK" INTO THE TARGET PROCESS AT SPECIFIC POINTS?

As we previously touched on in this chapter, process hooking can be achieved in our chosen approach through the use of debugger breakpoints. There are two types of supported breakpoints on our given platform, hardware and software breakpoints. The 80x86 compatible processors support up to four hardware breakpoints. These breakpoints can each be set to trigger on the read, write, or execution of any one-, two-, or four-byte range. To set hardware breakpoints we have to modify the target process context, tinkering with the debug registers DR0 through DR3 and DR7. The first four registers contain the address of the hardware breakpoint. The DR7 register contains the flags specifying which breakpoints are active, over what range, and over what type of access (read, write, or execute). Hardware breakpoints are nonintrusive and do not alter your code. Software breakpoints, on the other hand, must modify the target process and are implemented with the single byte instruction INT3, represented in hexadecimal as 0xCC.

We could use either hardware or software breakpoints to accomplish our given task. In the event that we might at some point require more then four hook points, we decide to utilize software breakpoints. To get a good feel for the process, let's walk through the required steps of setting a software breakpoint in a fictitious program at address 0xDEADBEEF. First, our debugger must read and save the original byte stored at the target address using the ReadProcessMemory API call as mentioned previously and as shown in Figure 20.3.

Notice that the first instruction at the target address is actually two bytes. The next step is to write the INT3 instruction at the target address using the WriteProcessMemory API, also mentioned previously and as shown in Figure 20.4.

But what happened to our previous instructions? Well, the inserted 0xCC is disassembled as the single byte INT3 instruction. The second byte from the mov edi, edi instruction (0xFF), combined with the byte previously representing push ebp (0x55) and the first byte of the mov ebp, esp (0x8B) instruction are disassembled as the call [ebp-75] instruction. The remaining byte 0xEC, is disassembled as the single byte instruction in al, dx. Now when execution reaches the address 0xDEADBEEF, the INT3 instruction will trigger an EXCEPTION_DEBUG_EVENT debug event with an EXCEPTION_BREAK-

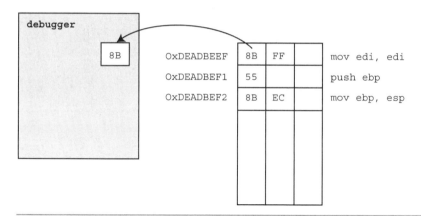

**Figure 20.3** Saving the original byte at a breakpoint address

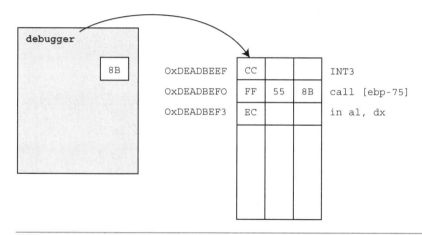

**Figure 20.4** Writing the INT3 opcode

POINT exception code, which our debugger will catch during the debug event loop (remember Agnes?). The process state at this point is shown in Figure 20.5.

So now we have successfully inserted and caught a software breakpoint, but that's only half the battle. Notice that our original instructions are still missing in action. Furthermore, the instruction pointer (EIP, which lets the CPU know where to fetch, decode, and execute the next instruction from) is at 0xDEADBEF0 as opposed to 0xDEADBEEF. This is because the single INT 3 instruction we inserted at 0xDEADBEEF was successfully executed, causing EIP to update to 0xDEADBEEF+1. Before we can con-

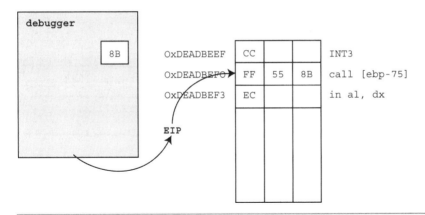

**Figure 20.5**   EXCEPTION_BREAKPOINT caught

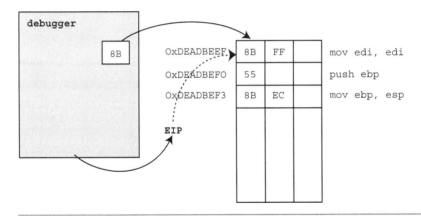

**Figure 20.6**   Adjusting EIP

tinue, we are going to have to correct the value of EIP and restore the original byte at
0xDEADBEEF, as shown in Figure 20.6.

Restoring the byte at 0xDEADBEEF is a task we are already familiar with. However,
changing the value of the instruction pointer, the register EIP, is a different story. We
mentioned earlier in the chapter that the thread context contains the various processor-
specific register data, such as the instruction pointer (EIP) in which we are currently
interested. We can retrieve the context for any given thread by calling the

GetThreadContext()[10] API, passing it the handle for the current thread and a pointer to a CONTEXT structure. We can then modify the contents of the CONTEXT structure and then call the SetThreadContext()[11] API, again passing in the current thread handle to modify the context:

```
context = CONTEXT()
context.ContextFlags = CONTEXT_FULL

kernel32.GetThreadContext(h_thread, byref(context))

context.Eip -= 1

kernel32.SetThreadContext(h_thread, byref(context))
```

At this point, the original execution context is restored and we are ready to let the process continue.

## How Do We Handle Process Snapshots and Restores?

To answer this question we must first consider another question: What changes as a process is running? Well, lots of things. New threads are created and killed. Handles to files, sockets, windows, and other elements are opened and closed. Memory is allocated and released, read from, and written to. The various registers within individual thread contexts are highly volatile and constantly changing. We could accomplish our task using a virtual machine technology, such as VMWare,[12] that allows us to take and restore complete system snapshots. However, the process is painstakingly slow and requires communication between the virtual machine guest and some form of arbiter on the virtual machine host. Instead, we borrow from a previously discussed technique[13] and "cheat" by concerning ourselves with only the thread contexts and changes to memory. Our snapshot process will entail two steps.

In the first step, we save the context of each thread within our target process. We have already seen how easy it is to get and set individual thread contexts. Now we need to wrap that code with the logic responsible for enumerating the system threads that

---

[10] http://msdn.microsoft.com/library/default.asp?url=/library/en-us/debug/base/getthreadcontext.asp

[11] http://msdn.microsoft.com/library/default.asp?url=/library/en-us/debug/base/setthreadcontext.asp

[12] http://www.vmware.com

[13] Greg Hoglund, Runtime Decompilation, BlackHat Proceedings

belong to our target process. To do so, we rely on the Tool Help Functions.[14] First, we obtain a listing of all system threads by specifying the TH32CS_SNAPTHREAD flag:

```
thread_entry = THREADENTRY32()
contexts     = []

snapshot = kernel32.CreateToolhelp32Snapshot( \
    TH32CS_SNAPTHREAD,                         \
    0)
```

Next, we retrieve the first thread entry from the list. Before doing so, however, it is a mandatory requirement of the Thread32First() API that we initialize the dwSize variable within the thread entry structure. We pass the Thread32First() API, our previously taken snapshot, and a pointer to our thread entry structure:

```
thread_entry.dwSize = sizeof(thread_entry)

success = kernel32.Thread32First( \
    snapshot,                      \
    byref(thread_entry))
```

Finally, we loop through the threads looking for ones that belong to the process ID (pid) of our target process. If there are some, we retrieve a thread handle using the OpenThread() API, retrieve the context as before, and append it to a list:

```
while success:
    if thread_entry.th32OwnerProcessID == pid:
        context = CONTEXT()
        context.ContextFlags = CONTEXT_FULL

        h_thread = kernel32.OpenThread( \
            THREAD_ALL_ACCESS,           \
            None,                        \
            thread_id)

        kernel32.GetThreadContext( \
            h_thread,               \
            byref(context))
```

---

[14] http://msdn2.microsoft.com/en-us/library/ms686832.aspx

```
    contexts.append(context)

    kernel32.CloseHandle(h_thread)

  success = kernel32.Thread32Next( \
    snapshot,                      \
    byref(thread_entry))
```

Having saved the context of each of the threads belonging to our process, we can later restore our process snapshot by again looping through all system threads and restoring the saved context for any threads previously seen.

In the second step, we save the contents of each volatile block of memory. Recall from the previous chapter that each process on the 32-bit x86 Windows platform "sees" its own 4GB memory space. Of these 4GB, typically the bottom half is reserved for use by our process (0x0000000–0x7FFFFFFF). This memory space is further segmented into individual pages, typically 4,096 bytes in size. Finally, memory permissions are applied at the finest granularity to each of these individual pages. Instead of storing the contents of each individually used page of memory, we save both time and resources by limiting our snapshot to pages of memory that we deem as volatile. We ignore all pages that have restrictive permissions preventing writing. This includes pages marked as:

- PAGE_READONLY
- PAGE_EXECUTE_READ
- PAGE_GUARD
- PAGE_NOACCESS

We also want to ignore pages that belong to executable images, as they are unlikely to change. Stepping through all available pages of memory requires a simple loop around the VirtualQueryEx()[15] API routine, which provides information about the pages within the specified virtual address range:

```
cursor        = 0
memory_blocks = []
read_buf      = create_string_buffer(length)
count         = c_ulong(0)
mbi           = MEMORY_BASIC_INFORMATION()
```

---

[15] http://msdn2.microsoft.com/en-us/library/aa366907.aspx

```
while cursor < 0xFFFFFFFF:
    save_block = True

    bytes_read = kernel32.VirtualQueryEx( \
        h_process,                       \
        cursor,                          \
        byref(mbi),                      \
        sizeof(mbi))

    if bytes_read < sizeof(mbi):
        break
```

If our call to VirtualQueryEx() fails, we assume that we have exhausted the available
user space and break out of the read loop. For each discovered block of memory in our
loop, we check for favorable page permissions:

```
    if mbi.State != MEM_COMMIT or \
        mbi.Type  == MEM_IMAGE:
        save_block = False

    if mbi.Protect & PAGE_READONLY:
        save_block = False

    if mbi.Protect & PAGE_EXECUTE_READ:
        save_block = False

    if mbi.Protect & PAGE_GUARD:
        save_block = False

    if mbi.Protect & PAGE_NOACCESS:
        save_block = False
```

If we come across a memory block that we wish to include in our snapshot, we read
the contents of the block using the ReadProcessMemory()[16] API and store the raw data as
well as the memory information in our snapshot list. Finally, we increment the memory-
scanning cursor and continue:

```
    if save_block:
        kernel32.ReadProcessMemory( \
            h_process,               \
```

---

[16] http://msdn2.microsoft.com/en-us/library/ms680553.aspx

```
        mbi.BaseAddress,        \
        read_buf,               \
        mbi.RegionSize,         \
        byref(count))

    memory_blocks.append((mbi, read_buf.raw))

  cursor += mbi.RegionSize
```

You might immediately notice that our methodology is flawed. What if a given page at the time of our snapshot is marked as PAGE_READONLY but later updated to be write-able and modified? Good point; the answer is that we miss those cases. We never promised that the approach would be perfect! In fact, let's take this opportunity to again stress the experimental nature of this subject. For the curious readers out there, one potential solution to this shortcoming is to "hook" the various functions that adjust memory per-missions and modify our monitoring based on observed modifications.

Our two steps combined provide the necessary elements for taking and restoring process-specific snapshots.

## How Do We Choose Our Hook Points?

This is the point where we switch gears from science to art, as there is no definitive approach to choosing our hook points. The decision will require the experience of a sea-soned reverse engineer. In essence, we are looking for the start and end of code responsi-ble for parsing user-controlled data. Provided that you have no prior knowledge of the target software, tracing with a debugger is a good start for narrowing down the decision range. Debugger tracing is covered in greater detail in Chapter 23, "Fuzzer Tracking."

To get a good feel for this, we will later walk through an example.

## How Do We Locate and Mutate Target Memory Space?

The final step on our long checklist of prerequisites is choosing the memory locations to mutate. Again, this process can be more of an art than a science and tracing with a debugger can assist in our search. In general, however, we should have chosen an initial hook point such that a pointer to our target data or memory space exists in the near vicinity.

## PyDbg, Your New Best Friend

As you no doubt have gathered by now, writing a debugger takes a good amount of work. Luckily, everything we have covered up to this point (and more) has already been written for you by the authors in a convenient Python class called PyDbg.[17] Why didn't we mention this earlier, you might be asking yourself in annoyance? Well, we lied to you. The fundamentals are important to understand and chances are you would not have paid attention if we had informed you of the shortcut from the start.

Process instrumentation via the Windows debugging API is a breeze with PyDbg. With PyDbg you can easily do the following:

- Read, write, and query memory.
- Enumerate, attach, detach, and terminate processes.
- Enumerate, pause, and resume threads.
- Set, remove, and handle breakpoints.
- Snapshot and restore process state (the SR in SRM).
- Resolve function addresses.
- More...

Consider the following simple example, where we instantiate a PyDbg object, attach to the target process on PID 123, and enter the debug loop:

```
from pydbg import *
from pydbg.defines import *

dbg = new pydbg()
dbg.attach(123)
dbg.debug_event_loop()
```

That's not all that exciting, so let's add some more functionality. Building on the previous example, in the next snippet we set a breakpoint on the Winsock recv() API call and register a callback handler to be called whenever a breakpoint is hit:

```
from pydbg import *
from pydbg.defines import *

ws2_recv = None
```

---

[17] http://openrce.org/downloads/details/208/PaiMei

```
def handler_bp (pydbg, dbg, context):
    global ws2_recv

    exception_address = \
      dbg.u.Exception.ExceptionRecord.ExceptionAddress

    if exception_address == ws2_recv:
        print "ws2.recv() called!"

    return DBG_CONTINUE

dbg = new pydbg()
dbg.set_callback(EXCEPTION_BREAKPOINT, handler_bp)
dbg.attach(123)

ws2_recv = dbg.func_resolve("ws2_32", "recv")
dbg.bp_set(ws2_recv)

dbg.debug_event_loop()
```

The bold text in the preceding snippet highlights our additions. The first addition you see is our defining of a function, handler_bp(), which takes three arguments. The first argument receives our instance of PyDbg. The second argument receives the DEBUG_EVENT[18] structure from the debug event loop and contains a variety of information about the debugging event that just occurred. The third argument receives the context of the thread within which the debugging event occurred. Our breakpoint handler simply checks if the address at which the exception occurred is the same address of the Winsock recv() API. If so, a message is printed. The breakpoint handler returns DBG_CONTINUE to signal to PyDbg that we are done processing the exception and PyDbg should let the target process continue execution. Looking back at the main body of our debugger script, you will see the addition of a call to the PyDbg routine set_callback(). This routine is used for registering a callback function for PyDbg to handle a specified debug event or exception. In this case we were interested in calling handler_bp() whenever a breakpoint is hit. Finally, we see the addition of calls to func_resolve() and bp_set(). The former call is made to resolve the address of the recv() API within the Windows module ws2_32.dll and store it in a global variable. The latter call is made to set a breakpoint at the resolved address. When attached to a target process, any calls to the Winsock recv() API will result in the debugger displaying the message "ws2.recv()

---

[18] http://msdn2.microsoft.com/en-us/library/ms686832.aspx

called" and continue execution as normal. Again, this is not terribly exciting, but now we can take another leap forward and create our first proof of concept in-memory fuzzer.

## A Contrived Example

Having covered a lot of background and prerequisite information, it's about time we produced an initial proof of concept to show you that all of this theoretical nonsense might actually be doable. On the fuzzing.org Web site, you will find fuzz_client.exe and fuzz_server.exe, including the source code for both. Don't study the source code just yet. To reproduce a more real-world scenario, let's assume that reverse engineering is required. This client–server pair is a very simple target. The server, when launched, binds to TCP port 11427 and waits for a client connection. The client connects and sends data to the server, which is later parsed. How is it parsed? We don't really know, and we don't really care at this point, as our goal is to fuzz the target, not review source or binary code. Let's begin by first launching the server:

```
$ ./fuzz_server.exe
Listening and waiting for client to connect...
```

Next, we launch the client, which takes two arguments. The first argument is the IP address of the server. The second argument is the data to transmit to the server for parsing:

```
$ ./fuzz_client.exe 192.168.197.1 'sending some data'
connecting....
sending...
sent...
```

The client successfully connected to the server on 192.168.197.1 and transmitted the string "sending some data." On the server side we see the following additional messages:

```
client connected.
received 17 bytes.
parsing: sending some data
exiting...
```

The server successfully received our transmitted 17 bytes, parsed it, and then exited. When examining the packets that traverse across the network, however, we are unable to locate our data. The packet that should contain our data appears right after the TCP three-way handshake, but instead contains the following bytes as highlighted in the screen shot from Ethereal[19] in Figure 20.7.

The client must have mangled, encrypted, compressed, or otherwise obfuscated the packet data prior to writing it onto the wire. On the server side, it must have deobfuscated the packet data prior to parsing it because we can see the correct string in the output message log. Fuzzing our example server in the traditional manner requires that we reverse engineer the obfuscation routine. Once the secrets of the obfuscation method are revealed we can generate and send arbitrary data. When you see the solution later, you will realize that doing so would have been quite trivial in this case. However, for the sake of sticking with our example, we assume that the obfuscation method will take considerable resources to reverse engineer. This is a perfect example of when in-memory fuzzing can be valuable (surprise, surprise; this was, after all, a contrived example). We will avoid the need for deciphering the obfuscation routine by instead "hooking" into fuzz_server.exe after it has already deobfuscated our transmitted data.

We need to pinpoint two locations within fuzz_server.exe to accomplish our task. The first is the snapshot point. At what point of execution do we want to save the state of the target process? The second is the restore point. At what point of execution do we want to rewind the state of the process, mutate our input, and continue our instrumented execution loop? The answer to both questions requires a little input tracking with a debugger. We'll use OllyDbg,[20] a freely available powerful Windows user-mode debugger.

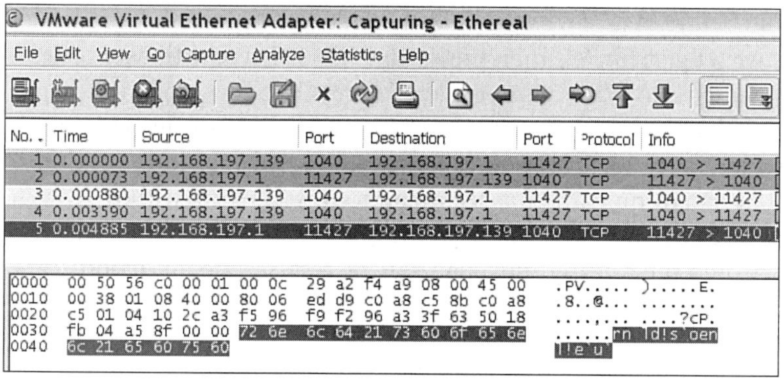

**Figure 20.7**   Ethereal client–server data capture
The Ethereal network sniffer project has moved to Wireshark and is available for download from http://www.wireshark.org

[19] http://www.ethereal.com/, Ethereal: A Network Protocol Analyzer.

[20] http://www.ollydbg.de

Describing the usage and functionality of OllyDbg almost warrants a book of its own, so we'll assume you are already familiar with it. The first thing we need to do is determine where fuzz_server.exe receives data. We know it does so over TCP so let's load fuzz_server.exe into OllyDbg and set a breakpoint on the WS2_32.dll recv() API. We do so by bringing up the module list, selecting WS2_32.dll, and pressing Ctrl + N to bring up the list of names within this module as shown in Figure 20.8. We then scroll down to recv() and press F2 to enable the breakpoint.

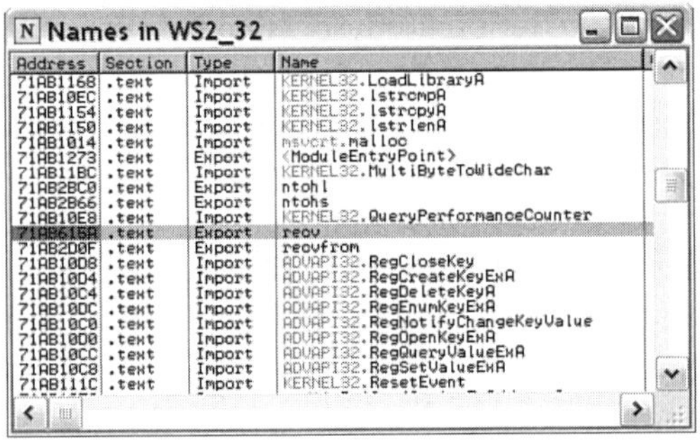

**Figure 20.8**    OllyDbg breakpoint on WS2_32.recv()

With our breakpoint set, we press F9 to continue execution and then run our fuzz_client, just as we did before. As soon as the data is sent, OllyDbg pauses fuzz_server because the breakpoint we set gets hit. We then press Alt + F9 to "Execute til user code." Now the call from fuzz_server into WS2_32 is visible. We press F8 a few times and step over the call to printf(), which displays the server message stating how many bytes were received. Next, as shown in Figure 20.9, we see a call to an unnamed subroutine within fuzz_server at 0x0040100F. Examining the first argument to this function within the OllyDbg dump window reveals that it is a pointer to the obfuscated form of our data that we saw in Ethereal. Could the routine at 0x0040100F be responsible for deobfuscating the packet data?

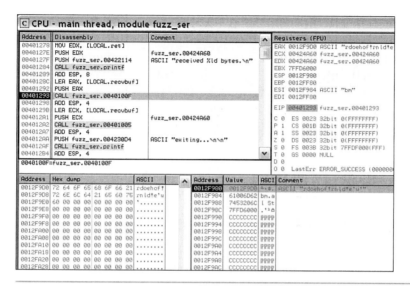

**Figure 20.9**   OllyDbg just before demangle

There is one easy way to find out: Let it execute and see what happens. We press F8 again to step over the call. We can immediately see, as in Figure 20.10, that our obfuscated data in the dump window has been transformed.

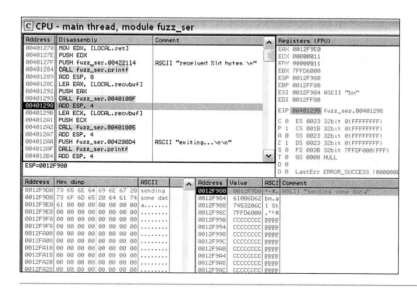

**Figure 20.10**   OllyDbg just after demangle

Great! So we know that our snapshot point has to occur at some point after this routine. Looking further down we see a call to an unnamed routine at 0x00401005 and then a call to printf(). We can see that the string "exiting. . ." is passed as an argument to printf() and recalling from the previously observed behavior of fuzz_server we know that it will soon exit. The routine at 0x00401005 must be our parse routine. Stepping into it with the F7 key reveals an unconditional jump to 0x00401450, the true top of our suspected parse routine shown in Figure 20.11.

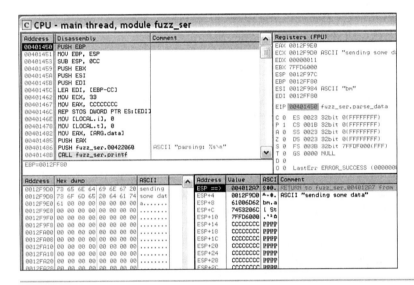

**Figure 20.11**    OllyDbg top of parse routine

Notice that our deobfuscated string "sending some data" appears as the first argument to the parse routine at ESP+4. This looks like a good point for our snapshot hook. We can save the entire state of the process at the top of the parse routine and then at some point after the parse routine is complete restore the process state back. Once we have restored the process, we can modify the contents of the data to be parsed, continue execution, and repeat the process indefinitely. But first, we'll need to locate the restore point. We press Ctrl + F9 to "Execute til return" then press F7 or F8 to get to our return address where, just as in Figure 20.12, we see the call to printf() with the string "exiting[el]" again. Let's choose a restore point after the call to printf(), at 0x004012b7, so we can see fuzz_server print "exiting[el]" prior to the restore. We do this because it makes us feel good that fuzz_server wants to exit but we don't let it.

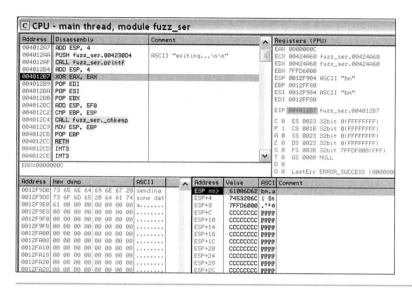

**Figure 20.12** OllyDbg restore point

We know that the routine at 0x0040100F is responsible for decoding. We know that the routine at 0x00401450 is responsible for parsing the decoded data. We've chosen the start of the parser as our snapshot and mutation point. We somewhat arbitrarily chose 0x004012b7 as the restore point, after the call to `printf("exiting[el]")`. We have all the necessary pieces to start coding now and Figure 20.13 presents a conceptual diagram of what we're going to be doing.

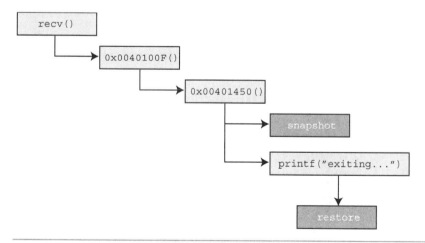

**Figure 20.13** Conceptual diagram

Implementing the in-memory fuzzer with PyDbg does not require much more work than what we have already seen. We begin with our required imports and by defining global variables to store information such as our chosen snapshot and restore points. We then get into the standard PyDbg skeleton code, instantiating a PyDbg object, registering callbacks (the meat and potatoes of this, which we define later), locating our target process, attaching to the target process, setting breakpoints on the snapshot and restore points, and finally entering the debug event loop:

```
from pydbg import *
from pydbg.defines import *

import time
import random

snapshot_hook   = 0x00401450
restore_hook    = 0x004012B7
snapshot_taken = False
hit_count       = 0
address         = 0

dbg = pydbg()
dbg.set_callback(EXCEPTION_BREAKPOINT,handle_bp)
dbg.set_callback(EXCEPTION_ACCESS_VIOLATION,handle_av)

found_target = False
for (pid, proc_name) in dbg.enumerate_processes():
    if proc_name.lower() == "fuzz_server.exe":
        found_target = True
        break

if found_target:
    dbg.attach(pid)
    dbg.bp_set(snapshot_hook)
    dbg.bp_set(restore_hook)
    print "entering debug event loop"
    dbg.debug_event_loop()
else:
    print "target not found."
```

Of the two defined callbacks, the access violation handler is easier to digest, so let's cover that first. We registered this callback in the first place, to detect when a potentially exploitable situation has occurred. It's a fairly simple block of code to understand and it can be easily repurposed in other PyDbg applications. The routine begins by grabbing some useful information from the exception record, such as the address of the instruction that triggered the exception, a flag letting us know whether the violation was due to a read or write, and the memory address that caused the exception. An attempt is made to retrieve the disassembly of the offending instruction and print a message instructing you of the nature of the exception. Finally, prior to terminating the debuggee, an attempt is made to print the current execution context of the target at the time of the exception. The execution context contains the various register values, the contents of the data to which they point (if it is a pointer), and a variable number of stack dereferences (in this case we specified five). For more details regarding the specifics of the PyDbg API, refer to the in-depth documentation at http://pedram.redhive.com/PaiMei/docs/PyDbg/.

```python
def handle_av (pydbg, dbg, context):
    exception_record  = dbg.u.Exception.ExceptionRecord
    exception_address = exception_record.ExceptionAddress
    write_violation   = exception_record.ExceptionInformation[0]
    violation_address = exception_record.ExceptionInformation[1]

    try:
        disasm = pydbg.disasm(exception_address)
    except:
        disasm = "[UNRESOLVED]"
        pass

    print "*** ACCESS VIOLATION @%08x %s ***" % \
      (exception_address, disasm)

    if write_violation:
        print "write violation on",
    else:
        print "read violation on",

    print "%08x" % violation_address

    try:
        print pydbg.dump_context(context, 5, False)
    except:
        pass

    print "terminating debuggee"
    pydbg.terminate_process()
```

Alternatively, we can catch access violations in another debugger such as OllyDbg. To do so, your debugger of choice must be configured with the operating systems as the just-in-time (JIT)[21] debugger. Then the body of the access violation handler can be replaced with:

```
def handle_av (pydbg, dbg, context):
    pydbg.detach()
    return DBG_CONTINUE
```

When an access violation does occur, the familiar dialog box shown in Figure 20.14 will appear.

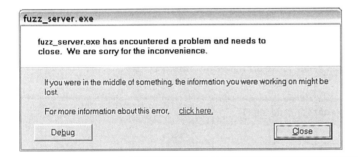

**Figure 20.14**   Fuzz server dies

Selecting the Debug button will pop up your registered JIT debugger for a closer view of what exactly went wrong within the target. The last component to our in-memory fuzzer is the heart of the application, the breakpoint handler. The breakpoint handler will be called whenever execution of fuzz_server reaches the snapshot and restore points on which we previously set breakpoints. This will be the hairiest block of PyDbg code we have seen, so let's dissect it piece by piece. At the top of the function we define the global variables that we will be accessing and grab the address where the breakpoint occurred as the exception_address.

```
def handle_bp (pydbg, dbg, context):
    global snapshot_hook, restore_hook
    global snapshot_taken, hit_count, address
```

---

[21] http://msdn.microsoft.com/library/default.asp?url=/library/en-us/debug/base/debugging_terminology.asp

```
exception_address = \
  dbg.u.Exception.ExceptionRecord.ExceptionAddress
```

We then check to see if we are at the snapshot hook point. If so, we increment the
hit_count variable and print a message regarding our current location.

```
if exception_address == snapshot_hook:
    hit_count += 1
    print "snapshot hook hit #%d\n" % hit_count
```

Next, we check the boolean flag snapshot_taken. If a snapshot of fuzz_server has not
previously been taken, we do so now by calling the PyDbg process_snapshot() routine.
We wrap the operation with a timer for informational purposes and update the flag to
True.

```
# if a process snapshot has not yet been
# taken, take one now.
if not snapshot_taken:
    start = time.time()
    print "taking process snapshot...",
    pydbg.process_snapshot()
    end = time.time() - start
    print "done. took %.03f seconds\n" % end
    snapshot_taken = True
```

Keep in mind that we are still within the if-block where the exception address is
equivalent to the hook point. The next block of code takes care of data mutation. The
conditional check on hit_count ensures that we do not mutate the argument until after
the first iteration through the parse routine with the original data. This is not a necessary
requirement. If a previously allocated address was found (it will become clear where this
address comes from in a moment), we free it using the PyDbg convenience wrapper
virtual_free().

```
if hit_count >= 1:
    if address:
        print "freeing last chunk at",
        print "%08x" % address
        pydbg.virtual_free( \
            address,          \
            1000,             \
            MEM_DECOMMIT)
```

While we are still in the `hit_count >= 1` if-block, we allocate a chunk of memory in the process space of fuzz_server using the PyDbg convenience wrapper `virtual_alloc()`. This is the allocation that we just saw a free for. Why do we allocate memory in the first place? Because instead of modifying the original data passed to the parse routine in place, it is easier for us to place our mutated data elsewhere in the process space of fuzz_server and then simply modify the pointer from the original data to our mutant block. One caveat to note here is that potential stack corruptions might appear as heap corruptions as the vulnerable buffer is being potentially moved off of the stack.

```
print "allocating memory for mutation"
address = pydbg.virtual_alloc( \
    None,                       \
    1000,                       \
    MEM_COMMIT,                 \
    PAGE_READWRITE)
print "allocation at %08x\n" % address
```

We assume that the server might only be able to parse ASCII data and use a simple data generation "algorithm" to fill the allocated mutant block with fuzz data. Starting with a long string of A characters, we choose a random index into the string and insert a random ASCII character. This is simple enough:

```
print "generating mutant...",
fuzz = "A" * 750
random_index = random.randint(0, 750)
mutant   = fuzz[0:random_index]
mutant += chr(random.randint(32,126))
mutant += fuzz[random_index:]
mutant += "\x00"
print "done.\n"
```

Next, we write the fuzz data into the previously allocated memory chunk using the PyDbg convenience routine `write_process_memory()`:

```
print "writing mutant to target memory"
pydbg.write_process_memory(address, mutant)
print
```

Finally, we modify the function argument pointer to point to our newly allocated memory block. Recall from Figure 20.11 that the pointer to the buffer containing our original deobfuscated data lies at positive offset four from our current stack pointer. We then continue execution.

```
print "modifying function argument"
pydbg.write_process_memory( \
    context.Esp + 4,          \
    pydbg.flip_endian(address))
print

print "continuing execution...\n"
```

Looking back at the remainder of the breakpoint callback handler definition we have a final if-block that handles snapshot restores when the restore hook point is reached. This is done by simply calling the PyDbg `process_restore()` API routine. Again, we wrap the block with a timer for informational purposes:

```
if exception_address == restore_hook:
    start = time.time()
    print "restoring process snapshot...",
    pydbg.process_restore()
    end = time.time() - start
    print "done. took %.03f seconds\n" % end
    pydbg.bp_set(restore_hook)

return DBG_CONTINUE
```

That's it ... we're ready to put this bad boy to the test, so we launch the server:

```
$ ./fuzz_server.exe
Listening and waiting for client to connect...
```

We launch the in-memory fuzzer:

```
$ ./chapter_20_srm_poc.py
entering debug event loop
```

And we launch the client:

```
$ ./fuzz_client.exe 192.168.197.1 'sending some data'
connecting....
sending...
sent...
```

As soon as the client transmits its payload, the snapshot hook point is reached and our in-memory fuzzer kicks into action:

```
snapshot / mutate hook point hit #1
taking process snapshot... done. took 0.015 seconds
```

A snapshot is taken and execution continues. Parsing is completed, and fuzz_server prints its output messages and then wants to exit:

```
received 17 bytes.
parsing: sending some data
exiting...
```

Before it has a chance to exit, however, the restore hook point is reached and our in-memory fuzzer kicks into action again:

```
restoring process snapshot... done. took 0.000 seconds
```

The process state of fuzz_server has been successfully rewound to our snapshot point and execution continues. This time, because hit_count is now greater than 1, the mutation block within the breakpoint handler is executed:

```
snapshot / mutate hook point hit #2

allocating chunk of memory to hold mutation
memory allocated at 003c0000

generating mutant... done.
writing mutant into target memory space

modifying function argument to point to mutant

continuing execution...
```

Memory was allocated, a fuzz mutant was generated and written into fuzz_server, and the argument pointer was modified. When execution continues, fuzz_server's output messaging confirms the success of our first snapshot restore mutation:

```
parsing:
AAAAAAAAAAAAAAAAAAAAAAAAAAAAAAAAAAAAAAAAAAAAAAAAAAAAAAAAAAAAAAAAAAAAAAAAAAAAAAAAAAAAAA
AAAAAAAAAAAAAAAAAAAAAAAAAAAAAAAAAAAAAAAAAAAAAAAAAAAAAAAAAAAAAAAAAAAAAAAAAAAAAAAAAAA)AAAAA
AAAAAAAAAAAAAAAAAAAAAAAAAAAAAAAAAAAAAAAAAAAAAAAAAAAAAAAAAAAAAAAAAAAAAAAAAAAAAAAAAAAAAA
AAAAAAAAAAAAAAAAAAAAAAAAAAAAAAAAAAAAAAAAAAAAAAAAAAAAAAAAAAAAAAAAAAAAAAAAAAAAAAAAAAAAAA
AAAAAAAAAAAAAAAAAAAAAAAAAAAAAAAAAAAAAAAAAAAAAAAAAAAAAAAAAAAAAAAAAAAAAAAAAAAAAAAAAAAAAA
AAAAAAAAAAAAAAAAAAAAAAAAAAAAAAAAAAAAAAAAAAAAAAAAAAAAAAAAAAAAAAAAAAAAAAAAAAAAAAAAAAAAAA
AAAAAAAAAAAAAAAAAAAAAAAAAAAAAAAAAAAAAAAAAAAAAAAAAAAAAAAAAAAAAAAAAAAAAAAAAAAAAAAAAAAAAA
AAAAAAAAAAAAAAAAAAAAAAAAAAAAAAAAAAAAAAAAAAAAAAAAAAAAAAAAAAAAAAAAAAAAAAAAAAAAAAAAAAAAAA
AAAAAAAAAAAAAAAAAAAAAAAAAAAAAAAAAAAAAAAAAAAAAAAAAAAAAAAAAAA
exiting...
```

Notice the spliced in ) character, highlighted in bold. Again, fuzz_server wants to exit but never gets the chance because the process state is rewound at our restore point. At the next iteration the previously allocated memory chunk is freed, a new one is created and assigned, and the process continues. Although running this example on your own will yield differing results, when we ran it for the purposes of including the output in the book we received the following:

```
continuing execution...

restoring process snapshot... done. took 0.016 seconds

snapshot / mutate hook point hit #265

freeing last chunk at 01930000
allocating chunk of memory to hold mutation
memory allocated at 01940000

generating mutant... done.

writing mutant into target memory space

modifying function argument to point to mutant

continuing execution...

*** ACCESS VIOLATION @41414141 [UNRESOLVED] ***
read violation on 41414141
terminating debuggee
```

On the 265th iteration of our SRM proof of concept fuzzer a clearly exploitable vulnerability was found in our example target. The access violation @41414141 means that the process was attempting to read and execute an instruction from virtual address 0x41414141 and failed to do so, as that memory location is unreadable. 0x41, if you haven't guessed by now, is the hexadecimal representation for the ASCII character A. Data from our fuzzer caused an overflow and overwrote a return address on the stack. When the function where the overflow occurred returned execution to the caller, the access violation occurred and was picked up by our fuzzer. Attackers can easily exploit this vulnerability, but don't forget, the obfuscation routine will have to be deciphered to attack the server (in the real world you likely can't easily instruct the client to send arbitrary data). Analyzing the source code or binary to reveal the exact nature and cause of this vulnerability is left as an exercise for the reader.

## SUMMARY

We have gone a long way in discussing a mostly theoretical and novel approach to fuzzing. The theory is interesting and reading through the breakdown of the application of the theory is worthwhile. However, we encourage readers to download the example files and run the example test for themselves. The noninteractive medium provided by a book does not do the example justice.

Hopefully the contents of the last two chapters were thought provoking and perhaps even applicable at some point for a specific problem that you might face. The PyDbg platform and example applications are all open source and free to tinker with. Simply download them from http://www.fuzzing.org and enjoy. As with all of our projects, it is our hope that improvements, bug reports, patches, and example uses are communicated back to us in an effort to keep the tools fresh and dynamic.

Although we strayed from the main focus of the book a bit in this chapter, the debugging knowledge gained within this chapter will assist you in general when attempting to automate exception detection. We revisit this topic in more detail in Chapter 24, where we discuss advanced exception detection.

# PART III

# ADVANCED FUZZING TECHNOLOGIES

# Fuzzing Frameworks

*"There's an old saying in Tennessee—I know it's in Texas, probably in Tennessee—that says, fool me once, shame on—shame on you. Fool me—you can't get fooled again."*

—George W. Bush, Nashville, TN, September 17, 2002

There are a number of available specialized fuzzing utilities which target many common and documented network protocols and file formats. These fuzzers exhaustively iterate through a designated protocol and can be used across the board to stress test a variety of applications that support that protocol. For instance, the same specialized SMTP fuzzer could be used against a variety of e-mail transfer programs such as Microsoft Exchange, Sendmail, qmail, etc. Other "dumb" fuzzers take a more generic approach to allow for fuzzing of arbitrary protocols and file formats and perform simple, non-protocol-aware mutations such as bit flipping and byte transposing.

Although these fuzzers are effective against a wide range of common applications, we often have a need for more customization and thorough fuzzing for proprietary and previously untested protocols. This is where fuzzing frameworks become extremely useful.

In this chapter, we explore a number of open source fuzzing frameworks available today, including SPIKE, the ever popular framework which has become a household name (depending on how geeky your household is). We also look at some exciting newcomers in the field such as Autodafé and GPF. Following the dissection of the existing technologies we then see how, despite the power supplied by many general-purpose fuzzing frameworks, we will still need to create a fuzzer from scratch once in a while.

We'll illustrate this point later with a real-world example fuzzing problem and the development of a solution. Finally, we introduce a new framework developed by the authors and explore the advances made by the effort.

## WHAT IS A FUZZING FRAMEWORK?

Some of the fuzzing frameworks available today are developed in C, while others in Python or Ruby. Some offer functionality in their native language, whereas others leverage a custom language. For instance, the Peach fuzzing framework exposes constructs in Python, while dfuz implements its own set of fuzzing objects (both of these frameworks are discussed in more detail later in the chapter). Some abstract data generation and others don't. Some are object oriented and well documented; others are usable for the most part only by the creator. However, the common goal of all fuzzing frameworks is the same; to provide a quick, flexible, reusable, and homogenous development environment to fuzzer developers.

A good fuzzing framework should abstract and minimize a number of tedious tasks. To assist with the first stages of protocol modeling, some frameworks include utilities for converting captured network traffic into a format understandable by the framework. Doing so allows a researcher to import large chunks of empirical data and focus his efforts on a more human-suitable task such as determining protocol field boundaries.

Automatic length calculation is an absolute necessity for a well-rounded framework. Many protocols are implemented using a TLV (Type, Length, Value) style syntax, similar to the ASN.1[1] standard. Consider an example where the first byte of data communication defines the *type* of data to follow: 0x01 for plain text and 0x02 for raw binary. The next two bytes define the *length* of the data to follow. Finally, the remaining bytes define the *value*, or the data, specific to the communication as shown here:

| 01 | 00  07 | F  U  Z  Z  I  N  G |
|----|--------|---------------------|
| Type | Length | Value |

When fuzzing the Value field of this protocol, we must calculate and update the two-byte length field in every test case. Otherwise, we risk our test cases getting immediately dropped if the communication is detected as breaching protocol specifications. Calculating Cyclic Redundancy Check (CRC)[2] calculations and other checksum

---

[1] http://en.wikipedia.org/wiki/Asn.1

[2] http://en.wikipedia.org/wiki/Cyclic_redundancy_check

algorithms are other tasks a useful framework should include. CRC values are commonly found embedded in both file and protocol specifications to identify potentially corrupted data. PNG image files, for example, employ CRC values that allow programs to avoid processing an image if the received CRC does not match the calculated value. Although this is an important feature for security and functionality, it will prohibit fuzzing efforts if the CRC is not correctly updated as a protocol is mutated. As a more extreme example, consider the Distributed Network Protocol (DNP3)[3] specification, which is utilized in Supervisory Control and Data Acquisition (SCADA) communications. Data streams are individually sliced into 250-byte chunks and each chunk is prefixed with a CRC-16 checksum! Finally, consider that the IP addresses of the client, server, or both are frequently seen within transmitted data and that both addresses might change frequently during the course of a fuzz test. It would be convenient for a framework to offer a method of automatically determining and including these values in your generated fuzz test cases.

Most, if not all, frameworks provide methods for generating pseudo-random data. A good framework will take a further step by including a strong list of attack heuristics. An attack heuristic is nothing more than a stored sequence of data that has previously been known to cause a software fault. Format string (%n%n%n%n) and directory traversal (../../../) sequences are common examples of simple attack heuristics. Cycling through a finite list of such test cases prior to falling back on random data generation will save time in many scenarios and is a worthwhile investment.

Fault detection plays an important role in fuzzing and is discussed in detail in Chapter 24, "Intelligent Fault Detection." A fuzzer can detect that its target might have failed at the most simple level if the target is unable to accept a new connection. More advanced fault detection is generally implemented with the assistance of a debugger. An advanced fuzzing framework should allow the fuzzer to directly communicate with a debugger attached to the target application or even bundle a custom debugger technology altogether.

Depending on your personal preference, there may be a long laundry list of minor features that can significantly improve your fuzzer development experience. For example, some frameworks include support for parsing a wide range of formatted data. When copying and pasting raw bytes into a fuzzing script, for example, it would be convenient to be able to paste hex bytes in any of the following formats: 0x41 0x42, \x41 \x42, 4142, and so on.

Fuzzing metrics (see Chapter 23, "Fuzzer Tracking") have also received little attention to date. An advanced fuzzing framework may include an interface for communicating with a metric gathering tool, such as a code coverage monitor.

---

[3] http://www.dnp.org/

Finally, the ideal fuzzing framework will provide facilities that maximize code reuse by making developed components readily available for future projects. If implemented correctly, this concept allows a fuzzer to evolve and get "smarter" the more it is used. Keep these concepts in mind as we explore a number of fuzzing frameworks prior to delving into the design and creation of both a task-specific and general-purpose custom framework.

## EXISTING FRAMEWORKS

In this section, we dissect a number of fuzzing frameworks to gain an understanding of what already exists. We do not cover every available fuzzing framework, but instead, we examine a sampling of frameworks that represent a range of different methodologies. The following frameworks are listed in a general order of maturity and feature richness, starting with the most primitive.

### ANTIPARSER[4]

Written in Python, antiparser is an API designed to assist in the creation of random data specifically for the construction of fuzzers. This framework can be used to develop fuzzers that will run across multiple platforms as the framework depends solely on the availability of a Python interpreter. Use of the framework is pretty straightforward. An instance of the antiparser class must first be created; this class serves as a container. Next, antiparser exposes a number of fuzz types that can be instantiated and appended to the container. Available fuzz types include the following:

- apChar(): An eight-bit C character.
- apCString(): A C-style string; that is, an array of characters terminated by a null byte.
- apKeywords(): A list of values each coupled with a separator, data block, and terminator.
- apLong(): A 32-bit C integer.
- apShort(): A 16-bit C integer.
- apString(): A free form string.

---

[4]  http://antiparser.sourceforge.net/

Of the available data types, `apKeywords()` is the most interesting. With this class, you define a list of keywords, a block of data, a separator between keywords and the data, and finally an optional data block terminator. The class will generate data in the format [keyword] [separator] [data block] [terminator].

antiparser distributes an example script, evilftpclient.py, that leverages the `apKeywords()` data type. Let's examine portions of the script to gain a better understanding of what development on this framework looks like. The following Python code excerpt shows the relevant portions of evilftpclient.py responsible for testing an FTP daemon for format string vulnerabilities in the parsing of FTP verb arguments. This excerpt does not display the functionality for authenticating with the target FTP daemon, for example. For a complete listing, refer to the source.

```python
from antiparser import *

CMDLIST = ['ABOR', 'ALLO', 'APPE', 'CDUP', 'XCUP', 'CWD',
           'XCWD', 'DELE', 'HELP', 'LIST', 'MKD',  'XMKD',
           'MACB', 'MODE', 'MTMD', 'NLST', 'NOOP', 'PASS',
           'PASV', 'PORT', 'PWD',  'XPWD', 'QUIT', 'REIN',
           'RETR', 'RMD',  'XRMD', 'REST', 'RNFR', 'RNTO',
           'SITE', 'SIZE', 'STAT', 'STOR', 'STRU', 'STOU',
           'SYST', 'TYPE', 'USER']

SEPARATOR  = " "
TERMINATOR = "\r\n"

for cmd in CMDLIST:
    ap = antiparser()
    cmdkw = apKeywords()
    cmdkw.setKeywords([cmd])
    cmdkw.setSeparator(SEPARATOR)
    cmdkw.setTerminator(TERMINATOR)

    cmdkw.setContent(r"%n%n%n%n%n%n%n%n%n%n%n%n%n%n%n%n")
    cmdkw.setMode('incremental')
    cmdkw.setMaxSize(65536)
    ap.append(cmdkw)

    sock = apSocket()
    sock.connect(HOST, PORT)

    # print FTP daemon banner
    print sock.recv(1024)
```

```
# send fuzz test
sock.sendTCP(ap.getPayload())

# print FTP daemon response
print sock.recv(1024)
sock.close()
```

The code begins by importing all the available data types and classes from the antiparser framework, defining a list of FTP verbs, the verb argument separator character (space), and the command termination sequence (carriage return followed by newline). Each listed FTP verb is then iterated and tested separately, beginning with the instantiation of a new antiparser container class. Next, the apKeywords() data type comes into play. A list defining a single item, the current verb being tested, is specified as the keywords (keyword in this case). The appropriate verb–argument separation and command termination characters are then defined. The data content for the created apKeyword() object is set to a sequence of format string tokens. If the target FTP server exposes a format string vulnerability in the parsing of verb arguments, this data content will surely trigger it.

The next two calls, setMode('incremental') and setMaxSize(65536), specify that on permutation the data block should grow sequentially to the maximum value of 65,336. However, in this specific case, those two calls are irrelevant, as the fuzzer does not loop through a number of test cases or permutations by calling ap.permute(). Instead, each verb is tested with a single data block.

The remaining lines of code are mostly self-explanatory. The single data type, apKeywords(), is appended to the antiparser container and a socket is created. Once a connection has been established, the test case is generated in the call to ap.getPayload() and transmitted via sock.sendTCP().

It is obvious that antiparser has a number of limitations. The example FTP fuzzer can be easily reproduced in raw Python without assistance from the framework. The ratio of framework-specific code versus generic code when developing fuzzers on antiparser is significantly low in comparison to other frameworks. The framework also lacks many of the desired automations listed in the previous section, such as the ability to automatically calculate and represent the common TLV protocol format. On a final note, the documentation for this framework is slim and, unfortunately, only a single example is available as of version 2.0, which was released in August 2005. Although this framework is simple and provides some benefits for generating simple fuzzers, it is inadequate for handling complex tasks.

## DFUZ[5]

Written in C by Diego Bauche, Dfuz is an actively maintained and frequently updated fuzzing framework. This framework has been used to uncover a variety of vulnerabilities affecting vendors such as Microsoft, Ipswitch, and RealNetworks. The source code is open and available for download but a restrictive license prevents any duplication or modification without express permission of the author. Depending on your needs, this limited license may dissuade you from utilizing the framework. The motivating factor behind this rigid licensing appears to be that the author is unhappy with the quality of his own code (according to the README file). It might be worth a shot to contact him directly if you wish to reuse portions of his code. Dfuz was designed to run on UNIX/Linux and exposes a custom language for developing new fuzzers. This framework is not the most advanced fuzzing framework dissected in this chapter. However, its simple and intuitive design makes it a good framework design case study, so let's examine it in detail.

The basic components that comprise Dfuz include data, functions, lists, options, protocols, and variables. These various components are used to define a set of rules that the fuzzing engine can later parse to generate and transmit data. The following familiar and simple syntax is used to define variables within rule files:

```
var my_variable = my_data
var ref_other   = "1234",$my_variable,0x00
```

Variables are defined with the simple prefix *var* and can be referenced from other locations by prefixing the variable name with a dollar sign ($, like in Perl or PHP). Fuzzer creation is entirely self-contained. This means that unlike antiparser, for example, building a fuzzer on top of this framework is done entirely in its custom scripting language.

Dfuz defines various functions to accomplish frequently needed tasks. Functions are easily recognizable as their names are prefixed with the percent character (%). Defined functions include the following:

- %attach(): Wait until the Enter or Return key is pressed. This is useful for pausing the fuzzer to accomplish another task. For example, if your fuzzing target spawns a new thread to handle incoming connections and you wish to attach a debugger to this new thread, insert a call to %attach() after the initial connection is established, then locate and attach to the target thread.

---

[5]  http://www.genexx.org/dfuz/

- `%length()` or `%calc()`: Calculate and insert the size of the supplied argument in binary format. For example, `%length("AAAA")` will insert the binary value 0x04 into the binary stream. The default output size for these functions is 32 bits, but this can be modified to 8 bits by calling `%length:uint8()` or to 16 bits by calling `%length:uint16()`.

- `%put:<size>(number)`: Insert the specified number into the binary stream. The size can be specified as one of byte, word, or dword, which are aliases of uint8, uint16, and uint32, respectively.

- `%random:<size>()`: Will generate and insert a random binary value of the specified size. Similar to `%put()`, size can be specified as one of byte, word, or dword, which are aliases of uint8, uint16, and uint32, respectively.

- `%random:data(<length>,<type>)`: Generate and insert random data. Length specifies the number of bytes to generate. Type specifies the kind of random data to generate and can be specified as one of ascii, alphanum, plain, or graph.

- `%dec2str(num)`: Convert a decimal number to a string and insert it into the binary stream. For example, `%dec2str(123)` generates 123.

- `%fry()`: Randomly modify the previously defined data. The rule "AAAA",`%fry()`, for example, will cause a random number of the characters in the string "AAAA" to be replaced with a random byte value.

- `%str2bin()`: Parses a variety of hexadecimal string representations into their raw value. For example: 4141, 41 41, and 41-41 would all translate to AA.

Data can be represented in a number of ways. The custom scripting language supports syntax for specifying strings, raw bytes, addresses, data repetitions, and basic data looping. Multiple data definitions can be strung together to form a simple list by using the comma separator. The following examples demonstrate a variety of ways that data can be defined (refer to the documentation for further details):

```
var my_variable1 = "a string"
var my_variable2 = 0x41,|0xdeadbeef|,[Px50],[\x41*200],100
```

Lists are declared with the keyword *list* followed by the list name, the keyword *begin*, a list of data values separated by newlines, and are finally terminated with the keyword *end*. A list can be used to define and index a sequence of data. For example:

```
list my_list:
begin
    some_data
    more_data
    even_more_data
end
```

Like variables, lists can be referenced from other locations by prefixing the list name with a dollar sign ($). With similar syntax to other scripting languages, such as Perl and PHP, a list member can be indexed through square brackets: `$my_list[1]`. Random indexes within a list are also supported through the *rand* keyword: `$my_list[rand]`.

A number of options for controlling the behavior of the overall engine exist, including the following:

- *keep_connecting*: Continue fuzzing the target even if a connection cannot be established.
- *big_endian*: Changes the byte order of data generation to big endian (little endian is the default).
- *little_endian*: Changes the byte order of data generation to little endian (the default).
- *tcp*: Specifies that socket connections should be established over TCP.
- *udp*. Specifies that socket connections should be established over UDP.
- *client_side*: Specifies that the engine will be fuzzing a server and thereby acting as a client.
- *server_side*: Specifies that the engine will be fuzzing a client and thereby acting as a server waiting for a connection.
- *use_stdout*: Generate data to standard output (console) as opposed to a socket-connected peer. This option must be coupled with a host value of "stdout."

To ease the burden of reproducing frequently fuzzed protocols, Dfuz can emulate the FTP, POP3, Telnet, and Server Message Block (SMB) protocols. This functionality is exposed through functions such as `ftp:user()`, `ftp:pass()`, `ftp:mkd()`, `pop3:user()`, `pop3:pass()`, `pop3:dele()`, `telnet:user()`, `telnet:pass()`, `smb:setup()`, and so on. Refer to the Dfuz documentation for a complete listing.

These basic components must be combined with some additional directives to create rule files. As a simple, yet complete example, consider the following rule file (bundled with the framework) for fuzzing an FTP server:

```
port=21/tcp

peer write: @ftp:user("user")
peer read
peer write: @ftp:pass("pass")
peer read
peer write: "CWD /", %random:data(1024,alphanum), 0x0a
peer read
peer write: @ftp:quit()
peer read

repeat=1024
wait=1
# No Options
```

The first directive specifies that the engine must connect over TCP port 21. As no options are specified, it defaults to behaving as a client. The `peer read` and `peer write` directives indicate to the engine when data should be read from and written to the fuzz target, respectively. In this specific rule file, the FTP protocol functionality is used to authenticate with the target FTP server. Next, the Change Working Directory (CWD) command is manually constructed and transmitted to the server. The CWD command is fed 1,024 random bytes of alphanumeric data followed by a terminating newline (0x0a). Finally the connection is closed. The final `repeat` directive specifies that the peer read and write block should be executed 1,024 times. With every test case, Dfuz will establish an authenticated connection with the FTP server, issue a CWD command with a random 1,024-byte alphanumeric string as the argument, and tear down the connection.

Dfuz is a simple and powerful fuzzing framework that can be used to replicate and fuzz many protocols and file formats. The combination of stdout (standard output) support with some basic command-line scripting can transform this framework into a file format, environment variable, or command-line argument fuzzer as well. Dfuz has a relatively quick learning curve and fast development time. The fact that fuzzer development is accomplished entirely in its own scripting language is a double-edged sword. It is a positive in that nonprogrammers can describe and fuzz protocols on this framework and it is a negative in that experienced programmers cannot leverage the innate powers and features exposed by a mature programming language. Dfuz promotes some code reuse, but not nearly as much as other frameworks, such as Peach. A key feature currently lacking is the availability of an intelligent set of attack heuristics. Overall, Dfuz is an interesting case study for a well-designed fuzzing framework and a good tool to keep in the back pocket.

# SPIKE[6]

SPIKE, written by Dave Aitel, is probably the most widely used and recognized fuzzing framework. SPIKE is written in C and exposes an API for quickly and efficiently developing network protocol fuzzers. SPIKE is open source and released under the flexible GNU General Public License (GPL).[7] This favorable licensing has allowed for the creation of SPIKEfile, a repurposed version of the framework designed specifically for file format fuzzing (see Chapter 12, "File Format Fuzzing: Automation on UNIX"). SPIKE utilizes a novel technique for representing and thereafter fuzzing network protocols. Protocol data structures are broken down and represented as blocks, also referred to as a SPIKE, which contains both binary data and the block size. Block-based protocol representation allows for abstracted construction of various protocol layers with automatic size calculations. To better understand the block-based concept, consider the following simple example from the whitepaper "The Advantages of Block-Based Protocol Analysis for Security Testing":[8]

```
s_block_size_binary_bigendian_word("somepacketdata");
s_block_start("somepacketdata")
s_binary("01020304");
s_block_end("somepacketdata");
```

This basic SPIKE script (SPIKE scripts are written in C) defines a block named somepacketdata, pushes the four bytes 0x01020304 into the block and prefixes the block with the block length. In this case the block length would be calculated as 4 and stored as a big endian word. Note that most of the SPIKE API is prefixed with either s_ or spike_. The s_binary() API is used to add binary data to a block and is quite liberal with its argument format, allowing it to handle a wide variety of copied and pasted inputs such as the string 4141 \x41 0x41 41 00 41 00. Although simple, this example demonstrates the basics and overall approach of constructing a SPIKE. As SPIKE allows blocks to be embedded within other blocks, arbitrarily complex protocols can be easily broken down into their smallest atoms. Expanding on the previous example:

---

[6]  http://www.immunitysec.com/resources-freesoftware.shtml

[7]  http://www.gnu.org/copyleft/gpl.html

[8]  http://www.immunitysec.com/downloads/advantages_of_block_based_analysis.pdf

```
s_block_size_binary_bigendian_word("somepacketdata");
s_block_start("somepacketdata")
s_binary("01020304");
s_blocksize_halfword_bigendian("innerdata");
s_block_start("innerdata");
s_binary("00 01");
s_binary_bigendian_word_variable(0x02);
s_string_variable("SELECT");
s_block_end("innerdata");
s_block_end("somepacketdata");
```

In this example, two blocks are defined, somepacketdata and innerdata. The latter block is contained within the former block and each individual block is prefixed with a size value. The newly defined innerdata block begins with a static two-byte value (0x0001), followed by a four-byte variable integer with a default value of 0x02, and finally a string variable with a default value of SELECT. The s_binary_bigendian_word_variable() and s_string_variable() APIs will loop through a predefined set of integer and string variables (attack heuristics), respectively, that have been known in the past to uncover security vulnerabilities. SPIKE will begin by looping through the possible word variable mutations and then move on to mutating the string variable. The true power of this framework is that SPIKE will automatically update the values for each of the size fields as the various mutations are made. To examine or expand the current list of fuzz variables, look at SPIKE/src/spike.c. Version 2.9 of the framework contains a list of almost 700 error-inducing heuristics.

Using the basic concepts demonstrated in the previous example, you can begin to see how arbitrarily complex protocols can be modeled in this framework. A number of additional APIs and examples exist. Refer to the SPIKE documentation for further information. Sticking to the running example, the following code excerpt is from an FTP fuzzer distributed with SPIKE. This is not the best showcase of SPIKE's capabilities, as no blocks are actually defined, but it helps to compare apples with apples.

```
s_string("HOST ");
s_string_variable("10.20.30.40");
s_string("\r\n");

s_string_variable("USER");
s_string(" v);
s_string_variable("bob");
s_string("\r\n");
s_string("PASS ");
s_string_variable("bob");
s_string("\r\n");
```

```
s_string("SITE ");
s_string_variable("SEDV");
s_string("\r\n");

s_string("ACCT ");
s_string_variable("bob");
s_string("\r\n");

s_string("CWD ");
s_string_variable(".");
s_string("\r\n");

s_string("SMNT ");
s_string_variable(".");
s_string("\r\n");

s_string("PORT ");
s_string_variable("1");
s_string(",");
s_string_variable("2");
s_string(",");
s_string_variable("3");
s_string(",");
s_string_variable("4");
s_string(",");
s_string_variable("5");
s_string(",");
s_string_variable("6");
s_string("\r\n");
```

SPIKE is sporadically documented and the distributed package contains many deprecated components that can lead to confusion. However, a number of working examples are available and serve as excellent references for familiarizing with this powerful fuzzing framework. The lack of complete documentation and disorganization of the distribution package has led some researchers to speculate that SPIKE is purposefully broken in a number of areas to prevent others from uncovering vulnerabilities privately discovered by the author. The veracity of this claim remains unverified.

Depending on your individual needs, one major pitfall of the SPIKE framework is the lack of support for Microsoft Windows, as SPIKE was designed to run in a UNIX environment, although there are mixed reports of getting SPIKE to function on the Windows platform through Cygwin.[9] Another factor to consider is that even minor changes to the framework, such as the addition of new fuzz strings, require a recompilation. On a final

---

[9] http://www.cygwin.com/

negative note, code reuse between developed fuzzers is a manual copy-and-paste effort. New elements such as a fuzzer for e-mail addresses cannot simply be defined and later referenced globally across the framework.

Overall, SPIKE has proven to be effective and has been used by both its author and others to uncover a variety of high-profile vulnerabilities. SPIKE also includes utilities such as a proxy, allowing a researcher to monitor and fuzz communications between a browser and a Web application. SPIKE's fault-inducing capabilities have gone a long way in establishing the value of fuzzing on a whole. The block-based approach to fuzzing has gained popularity evident in that since the initial public release of SPIKE, a number of fuzzing frameworks have adopted the technique.

## PEACH[10]

Peach, released by IOACTIVE, is a cross-platform fuzzing framework written in Python and originally released in 2004. Peach is open source and openly licensed. Compared with the other available fuzzing frameworks, Peach's architecture is arguably the most flexible and promotes the most code reuse. Furthermore, in the author's opinion, it has the most interesting name (peach, fuzz—get it?). The framework exposes a number of basic components for constructing new fuzzers, including generators, transformers, protocols, publishers, and groups.

Generators are responsible for generating data ranging from simple strings to complex layered binary messages. Generators can be chained together to simplify the generation of complex data types. Abstraction of data generation into its own object allows for easy code reuse across implemented fuzzers. Consider, for example, that an e-mail address generator was developed during an SMTP server audit. That generator can be transparently reused in another fuzzer that requires generation of e-mail addresses.

Transformers change data in a specific way. Example transformers might include a base64 encoder, gzip, and HTML encoding. Transformers can also be chained together and can be bound to a generator. For example, a generated e-mail address can be passed through a URL-encoding transformer and then again through a gzip transformer. Abstraction of data transformation into its own object allows for easy code reuse across implemented fuzzers. Once a given transformation is implemented, it can be transparently reused by all future developed fuzzers.

Publishers implement a form of transport for generated data through a protocol. Example publishers include file publishers and TCP publishers. Again, the abstraction of this concept into its own object promotes code reuse. Although not possible in the

---

[10] http://peachfuzz.sourceforge.net

current version of Peach, the eventual goal for publishers is to allow transparent interfacing with any publisher. Consider, for example, that you create a GIF image generator. That generator should be able to publish to a file or post to a Web form by simply swapping the specified publisher.

Groups contain one or more generators and are the mechanism for stepping through the values that a generator is capable of producing. Several stock group implementations are included with Peach. An additional component, the Script object, is a simple abstraction for reducing the amount of redundant code required for implementing looping through data through calls to group.next() and protocol.step().

As a complete, but simple example, consider the following Peach fuzzer designed to brute force the password of an FTP user from a dictionary file:

```
from Peach              import *
from Peach.Transformers import *
from Peach.Generators   import *
from Peach.Protocols    import *
from Peach.Publishers   import *

loginGroup = group.Group()
loginBlock = block.Block()
loginBlock.setGenerators((
    static.Static("USER username\r\nPASS "),
    dictionary.Dictionary(loginGroup, "dict.txt"),
    static.Static("\r\nQUIT\r\n")
    ))

loginProt = null.NullStdout(ftp.BasicFtp('127.0.0.1', 21), loginBlock)


script.Script(loginProt, loginGroup, 0.25).go()
```

The fuzzer begins by importing the various components of the Peach framework. Next, a new block and group is instantiated. The block is defined to pass a username and then the verb of the password command. The next element of the block imports a dictionary of potential passwords. This is the block element that will be iterated during fuzzing. The final element of the block terminates the password command and issues the FTP quit command to disconnect from the server. A new protocol is defined, extending from the already available FTP protocol. Finally, a script object is created to orchestrate the looping of connections and iterations through the dictionary. The first thought that might come to mind after looking over this script is that interfacing with the framework is not very intuitive. This is a valid criticism and probably the biggest pitfall of the Peach framework. Developing your first fuzzer in Peach will definitely take you longer than developing your first fuzzer in Autodafé or Dfuz.

The Peach architecture allows a researcher to focus on the individual subcomponents of a given protocol, later tying them together to create a complete fuzzer. This approach to fuzzer development, although arguably not as fast as the block-based approach, certainly promotes the most code reuse of any other fuzzing framework. For example, if a gzip transformer must be developed to test an antivirus solution, then it becomes available in the library for transparent use later on to test an HTTP server's capability of handling compressed data. This is a beautiful facet of Peach. The more you use it, the smarter it gets. Thanks to its pure Python implementation, a Peach fuzzer can be run from any environment with a suitable Python installation. Furthermore, by leveraging existing interfaces such as Python's, Microsoft's COM,[11] or Microsoft .NET packages, Peach allows for direct fuzzing of ActiveX controls and managed code. Examples are also provided for directly fuzzing Microsoft Windows DLLs as well as embedding Peach into C/C++ code for creating instrumented clients and servers.

Peach is under active development and as of the time of publication the latest available version is 0.5 (released in April 2006). Although Peach is highly advanced in theory, it is unfortunately not thoroughly documented, nor is it widely used. This lack of reference material results in a substantial learning curve that might dissuade you from considering this framework. The author of Peach has introduced some novel ideas and created a strong foundation for expansion. On a final note, a Ruby port of the Peach framework has been announced, although no further details were available at of the time of writing.

## GENERAL PURPOSE FUZZER[12]

General Purpose Fuzzer (GPF), released by Jared DeMott of Applied Security, is named as a play on words on the commonly recognized term general protection fault. GPF is actively maintained, available as open source under the GPL license, and is developed to run on a UNIX platform. As the name implies, GPF is designed as a generic fuzzer; unlike SPIKE, it can generate an infinite number of mutations. This is not to say that generation fuzzers are superior to heuristic fuzzers, as both methodologies have pros and cons. The major advantage of GPF over the other frameworks listed in this section is the low cost of entry in getting a fuzzer up and running. GPF exposes functionality through a number of modes, including PureFuzz, Convert, GPF (main mode), Pattern Fuzz, and SuperGPF.

---

[11] http://en.wikipedia.org/wiki/Component_Object_Model

[12] http://www.appliedsec.com/resources.html

PureFuzz is an easy-to-use purely random fuzzer, similar to attaching /dev/urandom to a socket. Although the generated input space is unintelligent and infinite, this technique has discovered vulnerabilities in the past, even in common enterprise software. The main advantage of PureFuzz over the netcat and /dev/urandom combination is that PureFuzz exposes a seed option allowing for pseudo-random stream replay. Furthermore, in the event that PureFuzz is successful, the specific packets responsible for causing an exception can be pinpointed through the use of a range option.

## RANDOM CAN BE EFFECTIVE, TOO!

Many assume that fuzzers such as GPF's PureFuzz that generate purely random data are too simplistic to ever be of use. To dispel this common misconception, consider the following real-world example concerning Computer Associates' BrightStor ARCserve Backup solution. In August 2005, a trivially exploitable stack-based buffer overflow vulnerability was discovered in the agent responsible for handling Microsoft SQL Server backup.[13] All that is required to trigger the vulnerability is to transmit more than 3,168 bytes to the affected daemon listening on TCP port 6070.

This vulnerability can be easily discovered by random fuzzing with minimal setup and no protocol analysis. Take this example as proof that it can definitely be worthwhile to run a fuzzer such as PureFuzz while manual efforts to construct an intelligent fuzzer are underway.

Convert is a GPF utility that can translate libpcap files, such as those generated by Ethereal[14] and Wireshark,[15] into a GPF file. This utility alleviates some tedium from the initial stages of protocol modeling by converting the binary pcap (packet capture) format into a human-readable and ready-to-modify text-based format.

In GPF's main mode, a GPF file and various command-line options are supplied to control a variety of basic protocol attacks. Captured traffic is replayed, portions of which are mutated in various ways. Mutations include insertion of progressively larger string sequences and format string tokens, byte cycling, and random mutations, among others.

[13] http://labs.idefense.com/intelligence/vulnerabilities/display.php?id=287

[14] http://www.ethereal.com

[15] http://www.wireshark.org

This fuzzing mode is manually intensive as the bulk of its logic is built on the analyst's instinct.

Pattern Fuzz (PF) is the most notable GPF mode due to its ability to automatically tokenize and fuzz detected plain text portions of protocols. PF examines target protocols for common ASCII boundaries and field terminators and automatically fuzzes them according to set of internal rules. The internal rules are defined in C code named tokAids. The ASCII mutation engine is defined as a tokAid (normal_ascii) and there are a few others (e.g., DNS). To accurately and intelligently model and fuzz a custom binary protocol, a tokAid must be written and compiled.

SuperGPF is a Perl script GPF wrapper written to address situations where a specific socket endpoint has been targeted for fuzzing but the researcher has no idea where to begin. SuperGPF combines a GPF capture with a text file containing valid protocol commands and generates thousands of new capture files. The script then starts multiple instances of GPF in varying fuzz modes to bombard the target with a wide variety of generated data. SuperGPF is limited to the fuzzing of ASCII protocols only.

Again, we provide an example GPF script to compare and contrast with previously shown FTP fuzzers:

```
Source:S Size:20 Data:220 (vsFTPd 1.1.3)
Source:C Size:12 Data:USER fuzzy
Source:S Size:34 Data:331 Please specify the password.
Source:C Size:12 Data:PASS wuzzy
Source:S Size:33 Data:230 Login successful. Have fun.
Source:C Size:6 Data:QUIT
Source:S Size:14 Data:221 Goodbye.
```

The biggest setback to working with GPF is its complexity. The learning curve required to get started with GPF is significant. Modeling proprietary binary protocols with tokAids is not as simple as other alternatives, such as SPIKE's block-based approach, and furthermore requires compilation to use. Finally, a heavy dependence on command-line options results in unwieldy commands such as the following:

```
GPF ftp.gpf client localhost 21 ? TCP 8973987234 100000 0 + 6 6 100 100 5000 43 finish
0 3 auto none -G b
```

Overall, GPF is a valuable tool due to both its flexibility and extensibility. The varying modes allow a researcher to start fuzzing quickly while working on setting up a second and more intelligent wave of attacks. The capability to automatically process and fuzz ASCII protocols is powerful and stands out among other frameworks. As of the time of writing, the author of GPF is currently developing a new fuzzing mode that leverages the fundamentals of evolutionary computing to automatically dissect and intelligently fuzz unknown protocols. This advanced approach to fuzzing is discussed in more detail in Chapter 22, "Automated Protocol Dissection."

## AUTODAFÉ[16]

Quite simply, Autodafé can be described as the next generation of SPIKE and can be used to fuzz both network protocols and file formats. Autodafé is released under the flexible GNU GPL by Martin Vuagnoux and is designed to run on UNIX platforms. Similar to SPIKE, Autodafé's core fuzzing engine takes a block-based approach for protocol modeling. The following excerpt from the whitepaper "Autodafé, an Act of Software Torture"[17] demonstrates the block-based language used by Autodafé and will look familiar to SPIKE users:

```
string("dummy");            /* define a constant string */
string_uni("dummy");        /* define a constant unicode string */
hex(0x0a 0a \x0a);          /* define a hexadecimal constant value */
block_begin("block");       /* define the beginning of a block */
block_end("block");         /* define the end of a block */
block_size_b32("block");    /* 32 bits big-endian size of a block */
block_size_l32("block");    /* 32 bits little-endian size of a block */
block_size_b16("block");    /* 16 bits big-endian size of a block */
block_size_l16("block");    /* 16 bits little-endian size of a block */
block_size_8("block");      /* 8 bits size of a block */
block_size_8("block");      /* 8 bits size of a block */
block_size_hex_string("a"); /* hexadecimal string size of a block
block_size_dec_string("b"); /* decimal string size of a block */
block_crc32_b("block");     /* crc32 of a block in big-endian */
block_crc32_l("block");     /* crc32 of a block in little-endian */
send("block");              /* send the block */
recv("block");              /* receive the block */
fuzz_string("dummy");       /* fuzz the string "dummy" */
fuzz_string_uni("dummy");   /* fuzz the unicode string "dummy" */
fuzz_hex(0xff ff \xff);     /* fuzz the hexadecimal value */
```

This functionality is deceivingly simple as with it, it is possible to represent the majority of binary and plain text protocol formats.

---

[16] http://autodafe.sourceforge.net

[17] http://autodafe.sourceforge.net/docs/autodafe.pdf

The main goal of the Autodafé framework is to reduce the size and complexity of the total fuzzing input space to more efficiently focus on areas of the protocol that are likely to result in the discovery of security vulnerabilities. Calculating the input space, or complexity, for a complete fuzz audit is simple. Consider the following simple Autodafé script:

```
fuzz_string("GET");
string(" /");
fuzz_string("index.html");
string(" HTTP/1.1");
hex(0d 0a);
```

Once launched against a target Web server, this script will first iterate through a number of HTTP verb mutations followed by a number of verb argument mutations. Assume that Autodafé contains a fuzz string substitution library with 500 entries. The total number of test cases required to complete this audit is 500 times the number of variables to fuzz, for a total of 1,000 test cases. In most real-world cases, the substitution library will be at least double that size and there could be hundreds of variables to fuzz. Autodafé applies an interesting technique named Markers Technique to provide a weight to each fuzz variable. Autodafé defines a marker as data, string or numeric, that is controllable by the user (or fuzzer). The applied weights are used to determine the order in which to process the fuzz variables, focusing on those that are more likely to result in the discovery of security vulnerabilities.

To accomplish this task, Autodafé includes a debugger component named adbg. Debugging technologies have traditionally been used along side fuzzers and even included with specific fuzzing tools such as FileFuzz (see Chapter 13, "File Format Fuzzing: Automation on Windows"), but Autodafé is the first fuzzing framework to explicitly include a debugger. The debugger component is used by Autodafé to set breakpoints on common dangerous APIs such as `strcpy()`, which is known as a source of buffer overflows, and `fprintf()`, which is known as a source of format string vulnerabilities. The fuzzer transmits test cases to both the target and the debugger simultaneously. The debugger then monitors dangerous API calls looking for strings originating from the fuzzer.

Every fuzz variable is considered a marker. The weight for an individual marker detected to pass through a dangerous API is increased. Markers that do not touch dangerous APIs are not fuzzed during the first pass. Markers with heavier weights are given priority and fuzzed first. In the event that the debugger detects an access violation, the fuzzer is automatically informed and the responsible test case is recorded. By prioritizing the fuzz variables and ignoring those that never cross a dangerous API, the total input space can be drastically reduced.

Autodafé includes a couple of additional tools to help quick and efficient fuzzer development. The first tool, PDML2AD, can parse pack data XML (PDML) files exported by Ethereal and Wireshark into the block-based Autodafé language. If your target protocol is among the more than 750 protocols that these popular network sniffers recognize, then the majority of the tedious block-based modeling can be handled automatically. Even in the event that your target protocol is unrecognized, PDML2AD can still provide a few shortcuts, as it will automatically detect plain text fields and generate the appropriate calls to hex(), string(), and so on. The second tool, TXT2AD, is a simple shell script that will convert a text file into an Autodafé script. The third and final tool, ADC, is the Autodafé compiler. ADC is useful when developing complex Autodafé scripts as it can detect common errors such as incorrect function names and unclosed blocks.

Autodafé is a well-thought-out advanced fuzzing framework that expands on the groundwork laid out by SPIKE. Autodafé shares many of the same pros and cons as SPIKE. The most impressive feature of this framework is the debugging component, which stands out among the other frameworks. Again, depending on individual needs, the lack of Microsoft Windows support might immediately disqualify this framework from consideration. Modifications to the framework require recompilation and once again code reuse between fuzz scripts is not as transparent and effortless as it could be.

## CUSTOM FUZZER CASE STUDY: SHOCKWAVE FLASH

A good representation of the currently available fuzzing frameworks was discussed in the previous section. For a more complete listing, refer to this book's companion Web site at http://www.fuzzing.org. We encourage you to download the individual framework packages and explore the complete documentation and various examples. No single framework stands out as the best of breed, able to handle any job thrown at it better than the others. Instead, one framework might be more applicable depending on the specific target, goals, timeline, budget, and other factors. Familiarity with a few frameworks will provide a testing team with the flexibility to apply the best tool for any given job.

Although most protocols and file formats can be easily described in at least one of the publicly available fuzzing frameworks, there will be instances where none of them are applicable. When dealing with specialized software or protocol auditing, the decision to build a new, target-specific fuzzer can yield greater results and save time over the life of the audit. In this section we discuss Adobe's Macromedia Shockwave Flash[18] (SWF) file

---

[18] http://www.macromedia.com/software/flash/about/

format as a real-world fuzzing target and provide portions of a custom-built testing solution. Security vulnerabilities in Shockwave Flash are typically high impact as some version of Flash Player is installed on almost every desktop on the planet. In fact, modern Microsoft Windows operating systems ship with a functional version of Flash Player by default. Dissecting every detail of a full-blown SWF audit is well beyond the scope of this chapter, so only the most relevant and interesting portions are discussed. For further information, up-to-date results, and code listings,[19] visit the official book Web site at http://www.fuzzing.org.

A couple of factors make SWF a great candidate for a custom fuzzing solution. First, the structure of the SWF file format is completely documented in an Adobe developer reference titled "Macromedia Flash (SWF) and Flash Video (FLV) File Format Specification."[20] The version of the document referenced for this writing was version 8. Unless you are auditing an open source or in-house developed file format, such thorough documentation is not usually available and might limit your testing to more generic approaches. With this specific case, we will most definitely leverage every detail provided by Adobe and Macromedia. Examining the specification reveals that the SWF file format is largely parsed as a bit stream versus the typical byte-level granularity by which most files and protocols are parsed. As SWFs are typically delivered over the Web, streamlined size is likely the motivation behind the choice to parse at the bit level. This adds a level of complexity for our fuzzer and provides further reason to create a custom solution, as none of the fuzzing frameworks we explored in this chapter support bit types.

## MODELING SWF FILES

The first milestone that must be met to successfully fuzz the SWF file format is for our fuzzer to be able to both mutate and generate test cases. SWF consists of a header followed by a series of tags that resemble the following high-level structure:

```
[Header]
  <magic>
  <version>
  <length>
  <rect>
    [nbits]
    [xmin]
```

---

[19] This research is largely and actively conducted by Aaron Portnoy of TippingPoint.

[20] http://www.adobe.com/licensing/developer/

```
    [xmax]
    [ymin]
    [ymax]
  <framerate>
  <framecount>

[FileAttributes Tag]
[Tag]
  <header>
  <data>
    <datatypes>
    <structs>
    ...
[Tag]
  <header>
  <data>
    <datatypes>
    <structs>
    ...
...
[ShowFrame Tag]
[End Tag]
```

This is how the various fields break down:

- magic. Consists of three bytes and for any valid SWF file must be "FWS."

- version. Consists of a single byte representing the numerical version of Flash that generated the file.

- length. A four-byte value indicating the size of the entire SWF file.

- rect. This field is divided into five components:

  - nbits. This is five bits wide and indicates the length, in bits, of each of the next four fields.

  - xmin, xmax, ymin, and ymax. These fields represent the screen coordinates to which to render the Flash content. Note that these fields do not represent pixels but rather *twips,* a Flash unit of measurement that represents 1/20th of a "logical pixel."

The rect field is where we can start to see the complexity of this file format. If the value of the nbits field is 3, then the total length of the rect portion of the header is 5 + 3 + 3 + 3 + 3 = 17 bits. If the value of the nbits field is 4 then the total length of the rect portion of the header is 5 + 4 + 4 + 4 + 4 = 21 bits. Representing this structure with one of the available fuzzing frameworks is not a simple task. The final two fields in the header represent the speed at which to play back frames and the number of total frames in the SWF file.

Following the header is a series of tags that define the content and behavior of the Flash file. The first tag, FileAttributes, was introduced in Flash version 8 and is a mandatory tag that serves two purposes. First, the tag specifies whether or not the SWF file contains various properties such as a title and description. This information is not used internally but is instead made available for reference by external processes such as search engines. Second, the tag specifies whether the Flash Player should grant the SWF file either local or network file access. Each SWF file has a variable number of remaining tags that fall into one of two categories: definition and control tags. Definition tags define content such as shapes, buttons, and sound. Control tags define concepts such as placement and motion. The Flash Player processes the tags until it hits a ShowFrame tag, at which point content is rendered to screen. The SWF file is terminated with the mandatory End tag.

There are a number of available tags to choose from, each consisting of a two-byte tag header followed by data. Depending on the length of the data, the tag can be defined as long or short. If the length of the data is less than 63 bits, then the tag is considered short and is defined as: [ten-bit tag id] [six-bit data length] [data]. If the data block is larger, then the tag is considered long and is defined with an additional four-byte field in the header that specifies the length of the data: [ten-bit tag id] [111111] [four-byte data length] [data]. Again, we can see that the complexity of the SWF format does not lend itself well to being modeled within any of the aforementioned fuzzing frameworks.

Things only get worse from here. Each tag has its own set of fields. Some contain raw data, whereas others consist of SWF basic types named structures (struct or structs). Each struct consists of a set of defined fields that can include both raw data and even other structs! It still only gets worse. Groups of fields within both tags and structs may or may not be defined depending on the value of another field within that same tag or struct. Even the explanation can get confusing, so let's start building from the ground up and then show some examples to better explain everything.

To begin, we define a bit field class in Python for representing arbitrary numeric fields of variable bit lengths. We extend this bit field class to define bytes (chars), words (shorts), dwords (longs), and qwords (doubles) as they can be easily defined as 8-bit, 16-bit, 32-bit, and 64-bit instantiations of the bit field class. These basic data structures are accessible under the package Sulley (not to be confused with the Sulley fuzzing framework discussed in the next section):

```
BIG_ENDIAN    = ">"
LITTLE_ENDIAN = "<"
```

```python
class bit_field (object):
    def __init__ (self, width, value=0, max_num=None):
        assert(type(value) is int or long)

        self.width    = width
        self.max_num  = max_num
        self.value    = value
        self.endian   = LITTLE_ENDIAN
        self.static   = False
        self.s_index  = 0

        if self.max_num == None:
            self.max_num = self.to_decimal("1" * width)

    def flatten (self):
        '''
        @rtype:  Raw Bytes
        @return: Raw byte representation
        '''

        # pad the bit stream to the next byte boundary.
        bit_stream = ""

        if self.width % 8 == 0:
            bit_stream += self.to_binary()
        else:
            bit_stream  = "0" * (8 - (self.width % 8))
            bit_stream += self.to_binary()


        flattened = ""

        # convert the bit stream from a string of bits into raw bytes.
        for i in xrange(len(bit_stream) / 8):
            chunk = bit_stream[8*i:8*i+8]
            flattened += struct.pack("B", self.to_decimal(chunk))

        # if necessary, convert the endianess of the raw bytes.
        if self.endian == LITTLE_ENDIAN:
            flattened = list(flattened)
            flattened.reverse()
            flattened = "".join(flattened)

        return flattened

    def to_binary (self, number=None, bit_count=None):
        '''
```

```
        @type number:      Integer
        @param number:     (Opt., def=self.value) Number to convert
        @type bit_count:   Integer
        @param bit_count:  (Opt., def=self.width) Width of bit string

        @rtype:  String
        @return: Bit string
        '''

        if number == None:
            number = self.value

        if bit_count == None:
            bit_count = self.width

        return "".join(map(lambda x:str((number >> x) & 1), \
                range(bit_count -1, -1, -1)))

    def to_decimal (self, binary):
        '''
        Convert a binary string into a decimal number and return.
        '''

        return int(binary, 2)

    def randomize (self):
        '''
        Randomize the value of this bitfield.
        '''

        self.value = random.randint(0, self.max_num)

    def smart (self):
        '''
        Step the value of this bitfield through a list of smart values.
        '''

        smart_cases = \
        [
            0,
            self.max_num,
            self.max_num / 2,
            self.max_num / 4,
            # etc...
        ]
```

```
        self.value    = smart_cases[self.s_index]
        self.s_index += 1


class byte (bit_field):
    def __init__ (self, value=0, max_num=None):
        if type(value) not in [int, long]:
            value = struct.unpack(endian + "B", value)[0]

        bit_field.__init__(self, 8, value, max_num)


class word (bit_field):
    def __init__ (self, value=0, max_num=None:
        if type(value) not in [int, long]:
            value = struct.unpack(endian + "H", value)[0]

        bit_field.__init__(self, 16, value, max_num)


class dword (bit_field):
    def __init__ (self, value=0, max_num=None):
        if type(value) not in [int, long]:
            value = struct.unpack(endian + "L", value)[0]

        bit_field.__init__(self, 32, value, max_num)


class qword (bit_field):
    def __init__ (self, value=0, max_num=None):
        if type(value) not in [int, long]:
            value = struct.unpack(endian + "Q", value)[0]

        bit_field.__init__(self, 64, value, max_num)


# class aliases
bits   = bit_field
char   = byte
short  = word
long   = dword
double = qword
```

The bit_field base class defines the width of the field (width), the maximum number the field is capable of representing (max_num), the value of the field (value), the bit order of the field (endian), a flag specifying whether or not the field's value can be modi-fied (static), and finally an internally used index (s_index). The bit_field class further defines a number of useful functions:

- The flatten() routine converts and returns a byte-bounded sequence of raw bytes from the field.
- The to_binary() routine can convert a numeric value into a string of bits.
- The to_decimal() routine does the opposite by converting a string of bits into a numeric value.
- The randomize() routine updates the field value to a random value within the fields valid range.
- The smart() routine updates the field value through a sequence of "smart" bound-aries, and only an excerpt of these numbers is shown.

When constructing a complex type from the bit_field building block, these last two routines can be called to mutate the generated data structure. The data structure can then be traversed and written to a file by recursively calling the flatten() routines of each individual component.

Using these basic types, we can now begin to define the more simple SWF structs, such as RECT and RGB. The following code excerpts show the definitions of these classes, which inherit from a base class not shown (refer to http://www.fuzzing.org for the defi-nition of the base class):

```
class RECT (base):
    def __init__ (self, *args, **kwargs):
        base.__init__(self, *args, **kwargs)

        self.fields = \
        [
          ("Nbits", sulley.numbers.bits(5, value=31, static=True)),
          ("Xmin" , sulley.numbers.bits(31)),
          ("Xmax" , sulley.numbers.bits(31)),
          ("Ymin" , sulley.numbers.bits(31)),
          ("Ymax" , sulley.numbers.bits(31)),
        ]

class RGB (base):
    def __init__ (self, *args, **kwargs):
        base.__init__(self, *args, **kwargs)

        self.fields = \
        [
```

```
      ("Red"   , sulley.numbers.byte()),
      ("Green", sulley.numbers.byte()),
      ("Blue"  , sulley.numbers.byte()),
    ]
```

This excerpt also shows a simple shortcut that was discovered and agreed on during development. To simplify fuzzing, variable width fields are all defined at their maximum length. To represent structs with dependent fields a new primitive, dependent_bit_field, was derived from the bit_field class as shown here:

```
class dependent_bit_field (sulley.numbers.bit_field):
    def __init__ (self, width, value=0, max_num=None, static=False, \
                  parent=None, dep=None, vals=[]):
        self.parent = parent
        self.dep    = dep
        self.vals   = vals

        sulley.numbers.bit_field.__init__(self, width, value, \
                                          max_num, static)

    def flatten (self):
        # if there is a dependency for flattening (including) this
        # structure, then check it.
        if self.parent:
            #                              VVV - object value
            if self.parent.fields[self.dep][1].value not in self.vals:
                # dependency not met, don't include this object.
                return ""

        return sulley.numbers.bit_field.flatten(self)
```

This extended class specifies a field index and value to examine prior to generating and returning data. If the appropriate field referenced by dep does not contain a value from the list vals then no data is returned. The MATRIX struct demonstrates the usage of this newly defined primitive:

```
class MATRIX (base):
    def __init__ (self, *args, **kwargs):
        base.__init__(self, *args, **kwargs)

        self.fields = \
        [
          ("HasScale"       , sulley.numbers.bits(1)),
```

```
    ("NScaleBits"    , dependent_bits(5, 31, parent=self, \
                        dep=0, vals=[1])),
    ("ScaleX"        , dependent_bits(31, parent=self, \
                        dep=0, vals=[1])),
    ("ScaleY"        , dependent_bits(31, parent=self, \
                        dep=0, vals=[1])),

    ("HasRotate"     , sulley.numbers.bits(1)),

    ("NRotateBits"   , dependent_bits(5, 31, parent=self, \
                        dep=4, vals=[1])),
    ("skew1"         , dependent_bits(31, parent=self, \
                        dep=0, vals=[1])),
    ("skew2"         , dependent_bits(31, parent=self, \
                        dep=0, vals=[1])),

    ("NTranslateBits" , sulley.numbers.bits(5, value=31)),
    ("TranslateX"     , sulley.numbers.bits(31)),
    ("TranslateY"     , sulley.numbers.bits(31)),
]
```

From this excerpt, the NScaleBits field within the MATRIX struct is defined as a five-bit-wide field with a default value of 31 that is included in the struct only if the value of the field at index 0 (HasScale) is equal to 1. The ScaleX, ScaleY, skew1, and skew2 fields also depend on the HasScale field. In other words, if HasScale is 1, then those fields are valid. Otherwise, those fields should not be defined. Similarly, the NRotateBits field is dependent on the value of the field at index 4 (HasRotate). At the time of writing, more than 200 SWF structs have been accurately defined in this notation.[21]

With all the necessary primitives and structs, we can now begin to define whole tags. First, a base class is defined from which all tags are derived:

```
class base (structs.base):
    def __init__ (self, parent=None, dep=None, vals=[]):
        self.tag_id = None
        (structs.base).__init__(self, parent, dep, vals)

    def flatten (self):
        bit_stream = structs.base.flatten(self)

        # pad the bit stream to the next byte boundary.
```

---

[21] Again, visit http://www.fuzzing.org for the code.

```
    if len(bit_stream) % 8 != 0:
        bit_stream  = "0" * (8-(len(bit_stream)%8)) + bit_stream

    raw = ""

    # convert the bit stream from a string of bits into raw bytes.
    for i in xrange(len(bit_stream) / 8):
        chunk = bit_stream[8*i:8*i+8]
        raw += pack("B", self.to_decimal(chunk))

    raw_length = len(raw)

    if raw_length >= 63:
        # long (record header is a word + dword)
        record_header = self.tag_id
        record_header <<= 6
        record_header |= 0x3f
        flattened = pack('H', record_header)

        record_header <<= 32
        record_header |= raw_length
        flattened += pack('Q', record_header)
        flattened += raw

    else:
        # short (record_header is a word)
        record_header = self.tag_id
        record_header <<= 6
        record_header |= raw_length
        flattened = pack('H', record_header)
        flattened += raw

    return flattened
```

The flatten() routine for the base tag class automatically calculates the length of the data portion and generates the correct short or long header. At the time of writing more than 50 SWF tags have been accurately defined on this framework. Here are a few examples of simple and medium complexity:

```
class PlaceObject (base):
    def __init__ (self, *args, **kwargs):
        base.__init__(self, *args, **kwargs)

        self.tag_id = 4
```

```
        self.fields = \
        [
          ("CharacterId"     , sulley.numbers.word(value=0x01)),
          ("Depth"           , sulley.numbers.word()),
          ("Matrix"          , structs.MATRIX()),
          ("ColorTransform"  , structs.CXFORM()),
        ]


class DefineBitsLossless (base):
    def __init__ (self, *args, **kwargs):
        base.__init__(self, *args, **kwargs)

        self.tag_id = 20
        self.fields = \
        [
          ("CharacterId"          , sulley.numbers.word()),
          ("BitmapFormat"         , sulley.numbers.byte()),
          ("BitmapWidth"          , sulley.numbers.word()),
          ("BitmapHeight"         , sulley.numbers.word()),
          ("BitmapColorTableSize" , structs.dependent_byte( \
                                     parent=self, dep=1, vals=[3])),
          ("ZlibBitmapData"       , structs.COLORMAPDATA( \
                                     parent=self, dep=1, vals=[3])),
          ("ZlibBitMapData_a"     , structs.BITMAPDATA( \
                                     parent=self, dep=1, vals=[4, 5])),
        ]


class DefineMorphShape (base):
    def __init__ (self, *args, **kwargs):
        base.__init__(self, *args, **kwargs)

        self.tag_id = 46
        self.fields = \
        [
          ("CharacterId"     , sulley.numbers.word()),
          ("StartBounds"     , structs.RECT()),
          ("EndBounds"       , structs.RECT()),
          ("Offset"          , sulley.numbers.word()),
          ("MorphFillStyles" , structs.MORPHFILLSTYLE()),
          ("MorphLineStyles" , structs.MORPHLINESTYLES()),
          ("StartEdges"      , structs.SHAPE()),
          ("EndEdges"        , structs.SHAPE()),
        ]
```

A lot of information has been presented, so let's review. To properly model an arbitrary SWF, we began with the most basic primitive `bit_field`. From there, we derived primitives for bytes, words, dwords, and qwords. Also from `bit_field`, we derived `dependent_bit_field`, from which we further derived dependent bytes, words, dwords, and qwords. These types, in conjunction with a new base class, form the basis for SWF structs. A base class for tags is derived from the structs base class that in conjunction with structs and primitives form SWF tags. The relationship depicted in Figure 21.1 can further clarify.

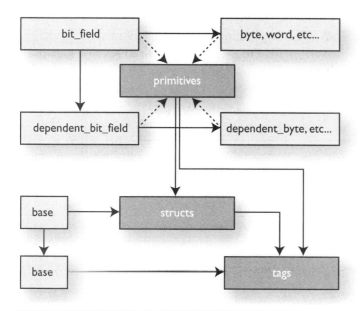

**Figure 21.1**   SWF fuzzer component relationship

Some other building blocks, such as string primitives, are also necessary for complete SWF modeling. Refer to the source for their definitions. With all these classes in place, we construct a global SWF container and begin instantiating and appending tags to it. The resulting data structure can then be easily traversed and modified either manually or automatically with each individual component's `randomize()` or `smart()` routines. Finally, the structure can be written to a file by once again traversing the complex data structure and concatenating the results of the `flatten()` routine. This design allows for special cases to be transparently handled within individual tags or structs.

## GENERATING VALID DATA

Not long after conquering our first challenge of successfully representing basic SWF structures, we come across another. The SWF specification states that tags can only depend on previously defined tags. When fuzzing a tag with multiple dependencies, all of the dependencies must first be successfully parsed; otherwise, the target tag is never reached. Guessing valid field values is a painstaking process, but there is a clever alternative. Utilizing the Google SOAP API,[22] we can search the Web for SWF files with the keyword filetype:swf. A simple script is written to incrementally search for a filetype:swf, b filetype:swf, and through to z filetype:swf. The script parses the returned results looking for and downloading discovered SWF files. Files are named by the MD5 hash to prevent storage of duplicates.

Approximately 10,000 unique SWF files consuming more than 3GB of space have been spidered. Examination of the version field in the SWF header can reveal a statistical sample of the distribution, which is shown in Table 21.1.

**Table 21.1**    Spidered Flash SWF Version Distribution

| SWF Version | % of Total |
| --- | --- |
| Flash 8 | < 1% |
| Flash 7 | ~ 2% |
| Flash 6 | ~ 11% |
| Flash 5 | ~ 55% |
| Flash 4 | ~ 28% |
| Flash 1 - Flash 3 | ~ 3% |

These results are interesting. Unfortunately, no conclusions can be drawn as to the distribution of active Flash Players from these statistics. Another script is then written that parses each file, extracting and storing individual tags. This repository of valid tags can now be used to assist in the creation of SWF test cases.

---

[22] http://www.google.com/apis/index.html

## FUZZING ENVIRONMENT

The PaiMei[23] reverse engineering framework is used to facilitate the instantiation and monitoring of individual test cases. PaiMei is a set of pure Python classes designed to assist in the development of reverse engineering automation tools. Use of the framework is described in more detail in Chapter 23. The actual testing process is similar to that used by the generic PaiMei FileFuzz as follows:

1. Load an SWF test case within a Flash Player under the PaiMei PyDbg scripted debugger.

2. Start the player and monitor execution for five seconds. The delay of five seconds is arbitrarily chosen and assumes that if an error is going to occur during the parsing of the SWF file it will occur within this time frame.

3. If, within that time, an error is detected, store the test case and relevant debug information.

4. If, within that time, no error is detected, close the Flash Player instance.

5. Continue to the next test case.

For more efficient testing, we can modify the frame rate in the SWF header from the default value of 0x000C to the maximum value of 0xFFFF. By doing so, we allow for larger portions of the SWF file to be processed during the five seconds allotted to each test case. The default method of viewing SWF files is to load them in a Web browser such as Microsoft Internet Explorer or Mozilla Firefox. Although this approach is acceptable for this specific case, an alternative method that comes in handy, especially for fuzzing ActionScript,[24] is to use SAFlashPlayer.exe. This small stand-alone player is distributed with Macromedia Studio.[25]

## TESTING METHODOLOGIES

The most generic approach to fuzzing SWF files is to use bit flipping. This rudimentary testing technique has been seen in previous chapters at the byte level. Applying this technique at the more granular bit level for SWF is prudent as a single byte might span more than one field. Moving a step beyond bit flipping, a custom-written SWF tag parsing script can be used to change the order of tags within an individual SWF file and swap

---

[23] http://openrce.org/downloads/details/208/PaiMei

[24] http://en.wikipedia.org/wiki/ActionScript

[25] http://www.adobe.com/products/studio/

tags between two different SWFs. Finally, the most thorough approach for SWF fuzzing is to individually stress test every field within every struct and tag. The previously generated tag and struct repository can be referenced to piecemeal a base SWF for mutation.

With all three approaches, the generated files are fed through the fuzzing environment in the same way. In the next section, we explore a new fuzzing framework introduced and released by the authors in conjunction with this book.

## SULLEY: FUZZING FRAMEWORK

Sulley is a fuzzer development and fuzz testing framework consisting of multiple extensible components. Sulley (in our humble opinion) exceeds the capabilities of most previously published fuzzing technologies, both commercial and those in the public domain. The goal of the framework is to simplify not only data representation, but data transmission and target monitoring as well. Sulley is affectionately named after the creature from Monsters, Inc.[26] because, well, he is fuzzy. You can download the latest version of Sulley from http://www.fuzzing.org/sulley.

Modern-day fuzzers are, for the most part, solely focused on data generation. Sulley not only has impressive data generation, but has taken this a step further and includes many other important aspects a modern fuzzer should provide. Sulley watches the network and methodically maintains records. Sulley instruments and monitors the health of the target, and is capable of reverting to a good state using multiple methods. Sulley detects, tracks, and categorizes detected faults. Sulley can fuzz in parallel, significantly increasing test speed. Sulley can automatically determine what unique sequence of test cases triggers faults. Sulley does all this and more, automatically, and without attendance. Overall usage of Sulley breaks down to the following:

1. *Data representation*: This is the first step in using any fuzzer. Run your target and tickle some interfaces while snagging the packets. Break down the protocol into individual requests and represent them as blocks in Sulley.

2. *Session*: Link your developed requests together to form a session, attach the various available Sulley monitoring agents (socket, debugger, etc.), and commence fuzzing.

3. *Postmortem*: Review the generated data and monitored results. Replay individual test cases.

---

[26] http://www.pixar.com/featurefilms/inc/chars_pop1.html

Once you have downloaded the latest Sulley package from http://www.fuzzing.org, unpack it to a directory of your choosing. The directory structure is relatively complex, so let's take a look at how everything is organized.

## SULLEY DIRECTORY STRUCTURE

There is some rhyme and reason to the Sulley directory structure. Maintaining the directory structure will ensure that everything remains organized while you expand the fuzzer with Legos, requests, and utilities. The following hierarchy outlines what you will need to know about the directory structure:

- *archived_fuzzies*: This is a free-form directory, organized by fuzz target name, to store archived fuzzers and data generated from fuzz sessions.
  - *trend_server_protect_5168*: This retired fuzz is referenced during the step-by-step walk-through later in this document.
  - *trillian_jabber*: Another retired fuzz referenced from the documentation.
- *audits*: Recorded PCAPs, crash bins, code coverage, and analysis graphs for active fuzz sessions should be saved to this directory. Once retired, recorded data should be moved to archived_fuzzies.
- *docs*: This is documentation and generated Epydoc API references.
- *requests*: Library of Sulley requests. Each target should get its own file, which can be used to store multiple requests.
  - *__REQUESTS__.html*: This file contains the descriptions for stored request categories and lists individual types. Maintain alphabetical order.
  - *http.py*: Various Web server fuzzing requests.
  - *trend.py*: Contains the requests associated with the complete fuzz walkthrough discussed later in this document.
- *sulley*: The fuzzer framework. Unless you want to extend the framework, you shouldn't need to touch these files.
  - *legos*: User-defined complex primitives.
    - *ber.py*: *ASN.1/BER primitives.*
    - *dcerpc.py*: *Microsoft RPC NDR primitives.*
    - *misc.py*: *Various uncategorized complex primitives such as e-mail addresses and hostnames.*
    - *xdr.py*: *XDR types.*
  - *pgraph*: Python graph abstraction library. Utilized in building sessions.

- *utils*: Various helper routines.
  - *dcerpc.py*: *Microsoft RPC helper routines such as for binding to an interface and generating a request.*
  - *misc.py*: *Various uncategorized routines such as CRC-16 and UUID manipulation routines.*
  - *scada.py*: *SCADA-specific helper routines including a DNP3 block encoder.*
- *__init__.py*: The various s_ aliases that are used in creating requests are defined here.
- *blocks.py*: Blocks and block helpers are defined here.
- *pedrpc.py*: This file defines client and server classes that are used by Sulley for communications between the various agents and the main fuzzer.
- *primitives.py*: The various fuzzer primitives including static, random, strings, and integers are defined here.
- *sessions.py*: Functionality for building and executing a session.
- *sex.py*: Sulley's custom exception handling class.
- *unit_tests*: Sulley's unit testing harness.
- *utils*: Various stand-alone utilities.
  - *crashbin_explorer.py*: Command-line utility for exploring the results stored in serialized crash bin files.
  - *pcap_cleaner.py*: Command-line utility for cleaning out a PCAP directory of all entries not associated with a fault.
  - *network_monitor.py*: PedRPC-driven network monitoring agent.
  - *process_monitor.py*: PedRPC-driven debugger-based target monitoring agent.
  - *unit_test.py*: Sulley's unit testing harness.
  - *vmcontrol.py*: PedRPC-driven VMWare controlling agent.

Now that the directory structure is a bit more familiar, let's take a look at how Sulley handles data representation. This is the first step in constructing a fuzzer.

## DATA REPRESENTATION

Aitel had it right with SPIKE: We've taken a good look at every fuzzer we can get our hands on and the block-based approach to protocol representation stands above the others, combining both simplicity and the flexibility to represent most protocols. Sulley utilizes a block-based approach to generate individual requests, which are then later tied together to form a session. To begin, initialize with a new name for your request:

```
s_initialize("new request")
```

Now you start adding primitives, blocks, and nested blocks to the request. Each primitive can be individually rendered and mutated. Rendering a primitive returns its contents in raw data format. Mutating a primitive transforms its internal contents. The concepts of rendering and mutating are abstracted from fuzzer developers for the most part, so don't worry about it. Know, however, that each mutatable primitive accepts a default value that is restored when the fuzzable values are exhausted.

### Static and Random Primitives

Let's begin with the simplest primitive, s_static(), which adds a static unmutating value of arbitrary length to the request. There are various aliases sprinkled throughout Sulley for your convenience, s_dunno(), s_raw(), and s_unknown() are aliases of s_static():

```
# these are all equivalent:
s_static("pedram\x00was\x01here\x02")
s_raw("pedram\x00was\x01here\x02")
s_dunno("pedram\x00was\x01here\x02")
s_unknown("pedram\x00was\x01here\x02")
```

Primitives, blocks, and so on all take an optional name keyword argument. Specifying a name allows you to access the named item directly from the request via request.names["name"] instead of having to walk the block structure to reach the desired element. Related to the previous, but not equivalent, is the s_binary() primitive, which accepts binary data represented in multiple formats. SPIKE users will recognize this API, as its functionality is (or rather should be) equivalent to what you are already familiar with:

```
# yeah, it can handle all these formats.
s_binary("0xde 0xad be ef \xca fe 00 01 02 0xba0xdd f0 0d")
```

Most of Sulley's primitives are driven by fuzz heuristics and therefore have a limited number of mutations. An exception to this is the s_random() primitive, which can be utilized to generate random data of varying lengths. This primitive takes two mandatory arguments, 'min_length' and 'max_length', specifying the minimum and maximum length of random data to generate on each iteration, respectively. This primitive also accepts the following optional keyword arguments:

- *num_mutations (integer, default=25)*: Number of mutations to make before reverting to default.

- *fuzzable (boolean, default=True)*: Enable or disable fuzzing of this primitive.
- *name (string, default=None)*: As with all Sulley objects, specifying a name gives you direct access to this primitive throughout the request.

The `num_mutations` keyword argument specifies how many times this primitive should be rerendered before it is considered exhausted. To fill a static sized field with random data, set the values for '`min_length`' and '`max_length`' to be the same.

### Integers

Binary and ASCII protocols alike have various-sized integers sprinkled all throughout them, for instance the Content-Length field in HTTP. Like most fuzzing frameworks, a portion of Sulley is dedicated to representing these types:

- one byte: s_byte(), s_char()
- two bytes: s_word(), s_short()
- four bytes: s_dword(), s_long(), s_int()
- eight bytes: s_qword(), s_double()

The integer types each accept at least a single parameter, the default integer value. Additionally the following optional keyword arguments can be specified:

- *endian (character, default='<')*: Endianess of the bit field. Specify < for little endian and > for big endian.
- *format (string, default="binary")*: Output format, "binary" or "ascii," controls the format in which the integer primitives render. For example, the value 100 is rendered as "100" in ASCII and "\x64" in binary.
- *signed (boolean, default=False)*: Make size signed versus unsigned, applicable only when format="ascii".
- *full_range (boolean, default=False)*: If enabled, this primitive mutates through all possible values (more on this later).
- *fuzzable (boolean, default=True)*: Enable or disable fuzzing of this primitive.
- *name (string, default=None)*: As with all Sulley objects specifying a name gives you direct access to this primitive throughout the request.

The *full_range* modifier is of particular interest among these. Consider you want to fuzz a DWORD value; that's 4,294,967,295 total possible values. At a rate of 10 test cases per second, it would take 13 years to finish fuzzing this single primitive! To reduce this vast input space, Sulley defaults to trying only "smart" values. This includes the plus and minus 10 border cases around 0, the maximum integer value (MAX_VAL), MAX_VAL divided by 2, MAX_VAL divided by 3, MAX_VAL divided by 4, MAX_VAL divided by 8, MAX_VAL divided by 16, and MAX_VAL divided by 32. Exhausting this reduced input space of 141 test cases requires only seconds.

### Strings and Delimiters

Strings can be found everywhere. E-mail addresses, hostnames, usernames, passwords, and more are all examples of string components you will no doubt come across when fuzzing. Sulley provides the `s_string()` primitive for representing these fields. The primitive takes a single mandatory argument specifying the default, valid value for the primitive. The following additional keyword arguments can be specified:

- *size (integer, default=-1).* Static size for this string. For dynamic sizing, leave this as -1.
- *padding (character, default='\x00').* If an explicit size is specified and the generated string is smaller than that size, use this value to pad the field up to size.
- *encoding (string, default="ascii").* Encoding to use for string. Valid options include whatever the Python `str.encode()` routine can accept. For Microsoft Unicode strings, specify "utf_16_le".
- *fuzzable (boolean, default=True).* Enable or disable fuzzing of this primitive.
- *name (string, default=None).* As with all Sulley objects, specifying a name gives you direct access to this primitive throughout the request.

Strings are frequently parsed into subfields through the use of delimiters. The space character, for example, is used as a delimiter in the HTTP request GET `/index.html` HTTP/1.0. The front slash (/) and dot (.) characters in that same request are also delimiters. When defining a protocol in Sulley, be sure to represent delimiters using the `s_delim()` primitive. As with other primitives, the first argument is mandatory and used to specify the default value. Also as with other primitives, `s_delim()` accepts the optional 'fuzzable' and 'name' keyword arguments. Delimiter mutations include repetition, substitution, and exclusion. As a complete example, consider the following sequence of primitives for fuzzing the HTML body tag.

```
# fuzzes the string: <BODY bgcolor="black">
s_delim("<")
s_string("BODY")
s_delim(" ")
s_string("bgcolor")
s_delim("=")
```

```
s_delim("\"")
s_string("black")
s_delim("\"")
s_delim(">")
```

## Blocks

Having mastered primitives, let's next take a look at how they can be organized and nested within blocks. New blocks are defined and opened with s_block_start() and closed with s_block_end(). Each block must be given a name, specified as the first argument to s_block_start(). This routine also accepts the following optional keyword arguments:

- *group (string, default=None).* Name of group to associate this block with (more on this later).
- *encoder (function pointer, default=None).* Pointer to a function to pass rendered data to prior to returning it.
- *dep (string, default=None).* Optional primitive whose specific value on which this block is dependent.
- *dep_value (mixed, default=None).* Value that field dep must contain for block to be rendered.
- *dep_values (list of mixed types, default=[]).* Values that field dep can contain for block to be rendered.
- *dep_compare (string, default="==").* Comparison method to apply to dependency. Valid options include: ==, !=, >, >=, <, and <=.

Grouping, encoding, and dependencies are powerful features not seen in most other frameworks and they deserve further dissection.

### Groups

Grouping allows you to tie a block to a group primitive to specify that the block should cycle through all possible mutations for each value within the group. The group primitive is useful, for example, for representing a list of valid opcodes or verbs with similar argument structures. The primitive s_group() defines a group and accepts two mandatory arguments. The first specifies the name of the group and the second specifies the list of possible raw values to iterate through. As a simple example, consider the following complete Sulley request designed to fuzz a Web server:

```
# import all of Sulley's functionality.
from sulley import *

# this request is for fuzzing: {GET,HEAD,POST,TRACE} /index.html HTTP/1.1

# define a new block named "HTTP BASIC".
s_initialize("HTTP BASIC")

# define a group primitive listing the various HTTP verbs we wish to fuzz.
s_group("verbs", values=["GET", "HEAD", "POST", "TRACE"])

# define a new block named "body" and associate with the above group.
if s_block_start("body", group="verbs"):
    # break the remainder of the HTTP request into individual primitives.
    s_delim(" ")
    s_delim("/")
    s_string("index.html")
    s_delim(" ")
    s_string("HTTP")
    s_delim("/")
    s_string("1")
    s_delim(".")
    s_string("1")
    # end the request with the mandatory static sequence.
    s_static("\r\n\r\n")
# close the open block, the name argument is optional here.
s_block_end("body")
```

The script begins by importing all of Sulley's components. Next a new request is initialized and given the name HTTP BASIC. This name can later be referenced for accessing this request directly. Next, a group is defined with the name verbs and the possible string values GET, HEAD, POST, and TRACE. A new block is started with the name body and tied to the previously defined group primitive through the optional group keyword argument. Note that s_block_start() always returns True, which allows you to optionally "tab out" its contained primitives using a simple if clause. Also note that the name argument to s_block_end() is optional. These framework design decisions were made purely for aesthetic purposes. A series of basic delimiter and string primitives are then defined within the confinements of the body block and the block is closed. When this defined request is loaded into a Sulley session, the fuzzer will generate and transmit all possible values for the block body, once for each verb defined in the group.

*Encoders*

Encoders are a simple, yet powerful block modifier. A function can be specified and attached to a block to modify the rendered contents of that block prior to return and transmission over the wire. This is best explained with a real-world example. The DcsProcessor.exe daemon from Trend Micro Control Manager listens on TCP port 20901 and expects to receive data formatted with a proprietary XOR encoding routine. Through reverse engineering of the decoder, the following XOR encoding routine was developed:

```
def trend_xor_encode (str):
    key = 0xA8534344
    ret = ""

    # pad to 4 byte boundary.
    pad = 4 - (len(str) % 4)

    if pad == 4:
        pad = 0

    str += "\x00" * pad

    while str:
        dword  = struct.unpack("<L", str[:4])[0]
        str    = str[4:]
        dword ^= key
        ret   += struct.pack("<L", dword)
        key    = dword

    return ret
```

Sulley encoders take a single parameter, the data to encode, and return the encoded data. This defined encoder can now be attached to a block containing fuzzable primitives, allowing the fuzzer developer to continue as if this little hurdle never existed.

*Dependencies*

Dependencies allow you to apply a conditional to the rendering of an entire block. This is accomplished by first linking a block to a primitive on which it will be dependent using the optional dep keyword parameter. When the time comes for Sulley to render the dependent block, it will check the value of the linked primitive and behave accordingly. A dependent value can be specified with the dep_value keyword parameter. Alternatively, a list of dependent values can be specified with the dep_values keyword parameter.

Finally, the actual conditional comparison can be modified through the `dep_compare` keyword parameter. For example, consider a situation where depending on the value of an integer, different data is expected:

```
s_short("opcode", full_range=True)

# opcode 10 expects an authentication sequence.
if s_block_start("auth", dep="opcode", dep_value=10):
    s_string("USER")
    s_delim(" ")
    s_string("pedram")
    s_static("\r\n")
    s_string("PASS")
    s_delim(" ")
    s_delim("fuzzywuzzy")
s_block_end()

# opcodes 15 and 16 expect a single string hostname.
if s_block_start("hostname", dep="opcode", dep_values=[15, 16]):
    s_string("pedram.openrce.org")
s_block_end()

# the rest of the opcodes take a string prefixed with two underscores.
if s_block_start("something", dep="opcode", dep_values=[10, 15, 16],
dep_compare="!="):
    s_static("__")
    s_string("some string")
s_block_end()
```

Block dependencies can be chained together in any number of ways, allowing for powerful (and unfortunately complex) combinations.

### Block Helpers

An important aspect of data generation that you must become familiar with to effectively utilize Sulley is the block helper. This category includes sizers, checksums, and repeaters.

#### Sizers

SPIKE users will be familiar with the `s_sizer()` (or `s_size()`) block helper. This helper takes the block name to measure the size of as the first parameter and accepts the following additional keyword arguments:

- *length (integer, default=4).* Length of size field.
- *endian (character, default='<').* Endianess of the bit field. Specify '<' for little endian and '>' for big endian.
- *format (string, default="binary").* Output format, "binary" or "ascii", controls the format in which the integer primitives render.
- *inclusive (boolean, default=False).* Should the sizer count its own length?
- *signed (boolean, default=False).* Make size signed versus unsigned, applicable only when format="ascii".
- *fuzzable (boolean, default=False).* Enable or disable fuzzing of this primitive.
- *name (string, default=None).* As with all Sulley objects, specifying a name gives you direct access to this primitive throughout the request.

Sizers are a crucial component in data generation that allow for the representation of complex protocols such as XDR notation, ASN.1, and so on. Sulley will dynamically calculate the length of the associated block when rendering the sizer. By default, Sulley will not fuzz size fields. In many cases this is the desired behavior; in the event it isn't, however, enable the fuzzable flag.

### Checksums
Similar to sizers, the `s_checksum()` helper takes the block name to calculate the checksum of as the first parameter. The following optional keyword arguments can also be specified:

- *algorithm (string or function pointer, default="crc32").* Checksum algorithm to apply to target block (crc32, adler32, md5, sha1).
- *endian (character, default='<').* Endianess of the bit field. Specify '<' for little endian and '>' for big endian.
- *length (integer, default=0).* Length of checksum, leave as 0 to autocalculate.
- *name (string, default=None).* As with all Sulley objects, specifying a name gives you direct access to this primitive throughout the request.

The algorithm argument can be one of crc32, adler32, md5, or sha1. Alternatively, you can specify a function pointer for this parameter to apply a custom checksum algorithm.

### Repeaters
The `s_repeat()` (or `s_repeater()`) helper is used for replicating a block a variable number of times. This is useful, for example, when testing for overflows during the parsing of tables with multiple elements. This helper takes three mandatory arguments: the name

of the block to be repeated, the minimum number of repetitions, and the maximum number of repetitions. Additionally, the following optional keyword arguments are available:

- *step (integer, default=1).* Step count between min and max reps.
- *fuzzable (boolean, default=False).* Enable or disable fuzzing of this primitive.
- *name (string, default=None).* As with all Sulley objects, specifying a name gives you direct access to this primitive throughout the request.

Consider the following example that ties all three of the introduced helpers together. We are fuzzing a portion of a protocol that contains a table of strings. Each entry in the table consists of a two-byte string type field, a two-byte length field, a string field, and finally a CRC-32 checksum field that is calculated over the string field. We don't know what the valid values for the type field are, so we'll fuzz that with random data. Here is what this portion of the protocol might look like in Sulley:

```
# table entry: [type][len][string][checksum]
if s_block_start("table entry"):
    # we don't know what the valid types are, so we'll fill this in with random data.
    s_random("\x00\x00", 2, 2)

    # next, we insert a sizer of length 2 for the string field to follow.
    s_size("string field", length=2)

    # block helpers only apply to blocks, so encapsulate the string primitive in one.
    if s_block_start("string field"):
        # the default string will simply be a short sequence of Cs.
        s_string("C" * 10)
    s_block_end()

    # append the CRC-32 checksum of the string to the table entry.
    s_checksum("string field")
s_block_end()

# repeat the table entry from 100 to 1,000 reps stepping 50 elements on each
iteration.
s_repeat("table entry", min_reps=100, max_reps=1000, step=50)
```

This Sulley script will fuzz not only table entry parsing, but might discover a fault in the processing of overly long tables.

## Legos

Sulley utilizes legos for representing user-defined components such as e-mail addresses, hostnames, and protocol primitives used in Microsoft RPC, XDR, ASN.1, and others. In ASN.1 / BER strings are represented as the sequence [0x04][0x84][dword length][string]. When fuzzing an ASN.1-based protocol, including the length and type prefixes in front of every string can become cumbersome. Instead we can define a lego and reference it:

```
s_lego("ber_string", "anonymous")
```

Every lego follows a similar format with the exception of the optional options keyword argument, which is specific to individual legos. As a simple example, consider the definition of the tag lego, helpful when fuzzing XMLish protocols:

```
class tag (blocks.block):
    def __init__ (self, name, request, value, options={}):
        blocks.block.__init__(self, name, request, None, None, None, None)

        self.value   = value
        self.options = options

        if not self.value:
            raise sex.error("MISSING LEGO.tag DEFAULT VALUE")

        #
        # [delim][string][delim]

        self.push(primitives.delim("<"))
        self.push(primitives.string(self.value))
        self.push(primitives.delim(">"))
```

This example lego simply accepts the desired tag as a string and encapsulates it within the appropriate delimiters. It does so by extending the block class and manually adding the tag delimiters and user-supplied string to the block via self.push().

Here is another example that produces a simple lego for representing ASN.1 / BER[27] integers in Sulley. The lowest common denominator was chosen to represent all integers as four-byte integers that follow the form: [0x02][0x04][dword], where 0x02 specifies integer type, 0x04 specifies the integer is four bytes long, and the dword represents the

---

[27] http://luca.ntop.org/Teaching/Appunti/asn1.html

actual integer we are passing. Here is what the definition looks like from sulley\legos\ber.py:

```
class integer (blocks.block):
    def __init__ (self, name, request, value, options={}):
        blocks.block.__init__(self, name, request, None, None, None, None)

        self.value   = value
        self.options = options

        if not self.value:
            raise sex.error("MISSING LEGO.ber_integer DEFAULT VALUE")

        self.push(primitives.dword(self.value, endian=">"))


    def render (self):
        # let the parent do the initial render.
        blocks.block.render(self)

        self.rendered = "\x02\x04" + self.rendered
        return self.rendered
```

Similar to the previous example, the supplied integer is added to the block stack with self.push(). Unlike the previous example, the render() routine is overloaded to prefix the rendered contents with the static sequence \x02\x04 to satisfy the integer representation requirements previously described. Sulley grows with the creation of every new fuzzer. Developed blocks and requests expand the request library and can be easily referenced and used in the construction of future fuzzers. Now it's time to take a look at building a session.

## SESSION

Once you have defined a number of requests it's time to tie them together in a session. One of the major benefits of Sulley over other fuzzing frameworks is its capability of fuzzing deep within a protocol. This is accomplished by linking requests together in a graph. In the following example, a sequence of requests are tied together and the pgraph library, which the session and request classes extend from, is leveraged to render the graph in uDraw format as shown in Figure 21.2:

```
from sulley import *

s_initialize("helo")
s_static("helo")
```

```
s_initialize("ehlo")
s_static("ehlo")

s_initialize("mail from")
s_static("mail from")

s_initialize("rcpt to")
s_static("rcpt to")

s_initialize("data")
s_static("data")

sess = sessions.session()
sess.connect(s_get("helo"))
sess.connect(s_get("ehlo"))
sess.connect(s_get("helo"),      s_get("mail from"))
sess.connect(s_get("ehlo"),      s_get("mail from"))
sess.connect(s_get("mail from"), s_get("rcpt to"))
sess.connect(s_get("rcpt to"),   s_get("data"))

fh = open("session_test.udg", "w+")
fh.write(sess.render_graph_udraw())
fh.close()
```

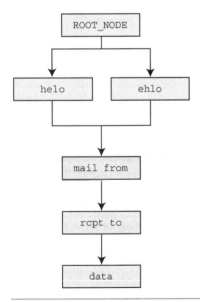

**Figure 21.2**   Example SMTP session graph structure

When it comes time to fuzz, Sulley walks the graph structure, starting with the root node and fuzzing each component along the way. In this example it begins with the `helo` request. Once complete, Sulley will begin fuzzing the `mail from` request. It does so by prefixing each test case with a valid `helo` request. Next, Sulley moves on to fuzzing the `rcpt to` request. Again, this is accomplished by prefixing each test case with a valid `helo` and `mail from` request. The process continues through `data` and then restarts down the `ehlo` path. The ability to break a protocol into individual requests and fuzz all possible paths through the constructed protocol graph is powerful. Consider, for example, an issue disclosed against Ipswitch Collaboration Suite in September 2006.[28] The software fault in this case was a stack overflow during the parsing of long strings contained within the characters @ and :. What makes this case interesting is that this vulnerability is only exposed over the `EHLO` route and not the `HELO` route. If our fuzzer is unable to walk all possible protocol paths, then issues such as this might be missed.

When instantiating a session, the following optional keyword arguments can be specified:

- *session_filename (string, default=None)*. Filename to which to serialize persistent data. Specifying a filename allows you to stop and resume the fuzzer.
- *skip (integer, default=0)*. Number of test cases to skip.
- *sleep_time (float, default=1.0)*. Time to sleep in between transmission of test cases.
- *log_level (integer, default=2)*. Set the log level; a higher number indicates more log messages.
- *proto (string, default="tcp")*. Communication protocol.
- *timeout (float, default=5.0)*. Seconds to wait for a `send()` or `recv()` to return prior to timing out.

Another advanced feature that Sulley introduces is the ability to register callbacks on every edge defined within the protocol graph structure. This allows us to register a function to call between node transmissions to implement functionality such as challenge response systems. The callback method must follow this prototype:

```
def callback(node, edge, last_recv, sock)
```

Here, `node` is the node about to be sent, `edge` is the last edge along the current fuzz path to `node`, `last_recv` contains the data returned from the last socket transmission, and `sock` is the live socket. A callback is also useful in situations where, for example, the size of the next pack is specified in the first packet. As another example, if you need to fill

---

[28] http://www.zerodayinitiative.com/advisories/ZDI-06-028.html

in the dynamic IP address of the target, register a callback that snags the IP from
sock.getpeername()[0]. Edge callbacks can also be registered through the optional keyword argument callback to the session.connect() method.

### Targets and Agents

The next step is to define targets, link them with agents, and add the targets to the session. In the following example, we instantiate a new target that is running inside a
VMWare virtual machine and link it to three agents:

```
target = sessions.target("10.0.0.1", 5168)

target.netmon     = pedrpc.client("10.0.0.1",  26001)
target.procmon    = pedrpc.client("10.0.0.1",  26002)
target.vmcontrol = pedrpc.client("127.0.0.1", 26003)

target.procmon_options = \
{
    "proc_name"      : "SpntSvc.exe",
    "stop_commands"  : ['net stop "trend serverprotect"'],
    "start_commands" : ['net start "trend serverprotect"'],
}

sess.add_target(target)
sess.fuzz()
```

The instantiated target is bound on TCP port 5168 on the host 10.0.0.1. A network
monitor agent is running on the target system, listening by default on port 26001. The
network monitor will record all socket communications to individual PCAP files labeled
by test case number. The process monitor agent is also running on the target system, listening by default on port 26002. This agent accepts additional arguments specifying the
process name to attach to, the command to stop the target process, and the command to
start the target process. Finally the VMWare control agent is running on the local system,
listening by default on port 26003. The target is added to the session and fuzzing begins.
Sulley is capable of fuzzing multiple targets, each with a unique set of linked agents. This
allows you to save time by splitting the total test space across the various targets.

Let's take a closer look at each individual agent's functionality.

### Agent: Network Monitor (network_monitor.py)

The network monitor agent is responsible for monitoring network communications and
logging them to PCAP files on disk. The agent is hard-coded to bind to TCP port 26001
and accepts connections from the Sulley session over the PedRPC custom binary protocol. Prior to transmitting a test case to the target, Sulley contacts this agent and requests

that it begin recording network traffic. Once the test case has been successfully transmitted, Sulley again contacts this agent, requesting it to flush recorded traffic to a PCAP file on disk. The PCAP files are named by test case number for easy retrieval. This agent does not have to be launched on the same system as the target software. It must, however, have visibility into sent and received network traffic. This agent accepts the following command-line arguments:

```
ERR> USAGE: network_monitor.py
    <-d|-device DEVICE #>    device to sniff on (see list below)
    [-f|-filter PCAP FILTER] BPF filter string
    [-p|-log_path PATH]      log directory to store pcaps to
    [-l|-log_level LEVEL]    log level (default 1), increase for more verbosity

Network Device List:
    [0] \Device\NPF_GenericDialupAdapter
    [1] {2D938150-427D-445F-93D6-A913B4EA20C0}  192.168.181.1
    [2] {9AF9AAEC-C362-4642-9A3F-0768CDA60942}  0.0.0.0
    [3] {9ADCDA98-A452-4956-9408-0968ACC1F482}  192.168.81.193
    ...
```

### Agent: Process Monitor (process_monitor.py)

The process monitor agent is responsible for detecting faults that might occur in the target process during fuzz testing. The agent is hard-coded to bind to TCP port 26002 and accepts connections from the Sulley session over the PedRPC custom binary protocol. After successfully transmitting each individual test case to the target, Sulley contacts this agent to determine if a fault was triggered. If so, high-level information regarding the nature of the fault is transmitted back to the Sulley session for display through the internal Web server (more on this later). Triggered faults are also logged in a serialized "crash bin" for postmortem analysis. This functionality is explored in further detail later. This agent accepts the following command-line arguments:

```
ERR> USAGE: process_monitor.py
    <-c|-crash_bin FILENAME> filename to serialize crash bin class to
    [-p|-proc_name NAME]     process name to search for and attach to
    [-i|-ignore_pid PID]     ignore this PID when searching for the target process
    [-l|-log_level LEVEL]    log level (default 1), increase for more verbosity
```

### Agent: VMWare Control (vmcontrol.py)

The VMWare control agent is hard-coded to bind to TCP port 26003 and accepts connections from the Sulley session over the PedRPC custom binary protocol. This agent exposes an API for interacting with a virtual machine image, including the ability to start, stop, suspend, or reset the image as well as take, delete, and restore snapshots. In the event that a fault has been detected or the target cannot be reached, Sulley can contact this agent and revert the virtual machine to a known good state. The test sequence honing tool will rely heavily on this agent to accomplish its task of identifying the exact sequence of test cases that trigger any given complex fault. This agent accepts the following command-line arguments:

```
ERR> USAGE: vmcontrol.py
    <-x|-vmx FILENAME>      path to VMX to control
    <-r|-vmrun FILENAME>    path to vmrun.exe
    [-s|-snapshot NAME>     set the snapshot name
    [-l|-log_level LEVEL]   log level (default 1), increase for more verbosity
```

### Web Monitoring Interface

The Sulley session class has a built-in minimal Web server that is hard-coded to bind to port 26000. Once the `fuzz()` method of the session class is called, the Web server thread spins off and the progress of the fuzzer including intermediary results can be seen. An example screen shot is shown in Figure 21.3.

The fuzzer can be paused and resumed by clicking the appropriate buttons. A synopsis of each detected fault is displayed as a list with the offending test case number listed in the first column. Clicking the test case number loads a detailed crash dump at the time of the fault. This information is of course also available in the crash bin file and accessible programmatically. Once the session is complete, it's time to enter the postmortem phase and analyze the results.

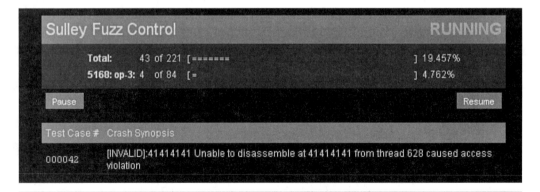

**Figure 21.3**   Sulley Web monitoring interface

## Postmortem

Once a Sulley fuzz session is complete, it is time to review the results and enter the post-mortem phase. The session's built-in Web server will provide you with early indications on potentially uncovered issues, but this is the time you will actually separate out the results. A couple of utilities exist to help you along in this process. The first is the crashbin_explorer.py utility, which accepts the following command-line arguments:

```
$ ./utils/crashbin_explorer.py
    USAGE: crashbin_explorer.py <xxx.crashbin>
        [-t|-test #]     dump the crash synopsis for a specific test case number
        [-g|-graph name] generate a graph of all crash paths, save to 'name'.udg
```

We can use this utility, for example, to view every location at which a fault was detected and furthermore list the individual test case numbers that triggered a fault at that address. The following results are from a real-world audit against the Trillian Jabber protocol parser:

```
$ ./utils/crashbin_explorer.py audits/trillian_jabber.crashbin
    [3] ntdll.dll:7c910f29 mov ecx,[ecx] from thread 664 caused access violation
            1415, 1416, 1417,
    [2] ntdll.dll:7c910e03 mov [edx],eax from thread 664 caused access violation
            3780, 9215,
    [24] rendezvous.dll:4900c4f1 rep movsd from thread 664 caused access violation
            1418, 1419, 1420, 1421, 1422, 1423, 1424, 1425, 3443, 3781, 3782, 3783,
            3784, 3785, 3786, 3787, 9216, 9217, 9218, 9219, 9220, 9221, 9222, 9223,
    [1] ntdll.dll:7c911639 mov cl,[eax+0x5] from thread 664 caused access violation
            3442,
```

None of these listed fault points might stand out as an obviously exploitable issue. We can drill further down into the specifics of an individual fault by specifying a test case number with the -t command-line switch. Let's take a look at test case number 1416:

```
$ ./utils/crashbin_explorer.py audits/trillian_jabber.crashbin -t 1416
    ntdll.dll:7c910f29 mov ecx,[ecx] from thread 664 caused access violation
    when attempting to read from 0x263b7467
    CONTEXT DUMP
      EIP: 7c910f29 mov ecx,[ecx]
      EAX: 039a0318 (  60424984) -> gt;&gt;&gt;...&gt;&gt;&gt;&gt;&gt;(heap)
      EBX: 02f40000 (  49545216) ->    PP@ (heap)
      ECX: 263b7467 ( 641430631) -> N/A
      EDX: 263b7467 ( 641430631) -> N/A
```

```
    EDI: 0399fed0 (  60423888) -> #e<root><message>&gt;&gt;&gt;...&gt;&gt;& (heap)
    ESI: 039a0310 (  60424976) -> gt;&gt;&gt;...&gt;&gt;&gt;&gt;&gt;(heap)
    EBP: 03989c38 (  60333112) -> \|gt;&t]IP"Ix;IXIox@ @x@PP8|p|Hg9I P (stack)
    ESP: 03989c2c (  60333100) -> \|gt;&t]IP"Ix;IXIox@ @x@PP8|p|Hg9I (stack)
    +00: 02f40000 (  49545216) ->    PP@ (heap)
    +04: 0399fed0 (  60423888) -> #e<root><message>&gt;&gt;&gt;...&gt;&gt;& (heap)
    +08: 00000000 (         0) -> N/A
    +0c: 03989d0c (  60333324) -> Hg9I Pt]I@"ImI,IIpHsoIPnIX{ (stack)
    +10: 7c910d5c (2089880924) -> N/A
    +14: 02f40000 (  49545216) ->    PP@ (heap)
 disasm around:
        0x7c910f18 jnz 0x7c910fb0
        0x7c910f1e mov ecx,[esi+0xc]
        0x7c910f21 lea eax,[esi+0x8]
        0x7c910f24 mov edx,[eax]
        0x7c910f26 mov [ebp+0xc],ecx
        0x7c910f29 mov ecx,[ecx]
        0x7c910f2b cmp ecx,[edx+0x4]
        0x7c910f2e mov [ebp+0x14],edx
        0x7c910f31 jnz 0x7c911f21

 stack unwind:
        ntdll.dll:7c910d5c
        rendezvous.dll:49023967
        rendezvous.dll:4900c56d
        kernel32.dll:7c80b50b
 SEH unwind:
        03989d38 -> ntdll.dll:7c90ee18
        0398ffdc -> rendezvous.dll:49025d74
        ffffffff -> kernel32.dll:7c8399f3
```

Again, nothing too obvious might stand out, but we know that we are influencing this specific access violation as the register being invalidly dereferenced, ECX, contains the ASCII string: "&;tg". String expansion issue perhaps? We can view the crash locations graphically, which adds an extra dimension displaying the known execution paths using the -g command-line switch. The following generated graph (Figure 21.4) is again from a real-world audit against the Trillian Jabber parser:

We can see that although we've uncovered four different crash locations, the source of the issue appears to be the same. Further research reveals that this is indeed correct. The specific flaw exists in the Rendezvous/Extensible Messaging and Presence Protocol (XMPP) messaging subsystem. Trillian locates nearby users through the _presence

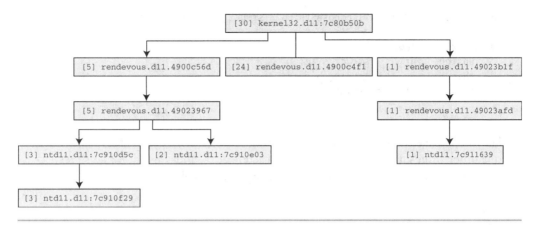

**Figure 21.4**  Sulley crash bin graphical exploration

mDNS (multicast DNS) service on UDP port 5353. Once a user is registered through mDNS, messaging is accomplished via XMPP over TCP port 5298. Within plugins\rendezvous.dll, the following logic is applied to received messages:

```
4900C470 str_len:
4900C470     mov cl, [eax]      ; *eax = message+1
4900C472     inc eax
4900C473     test cl, cl
4900C475     jnz short str_len

4900C477     sub eax, edx
4900C479     add eax, 128       ; strlen(message+1) + 128
4900C47E     push eax
4900C47F     call _malloc
```

The string length of the supplied message is calculated and a heap buffer in the amount of length + 128 is allocated to store a copy of the message, which is then passed through expatxml.xmlComposeString(), a function called with the following prototype:

CHAPTER 21 FUZZING FRAMEWORKS

```
plugin_send(MYGUID, "xmlComposeString", struct xml_string_t *);

struct xml_string_t {
    unsigned int    struct_size;
    char            *string_buffer;
    struct xml_tree_t *xml_tree;
};
```

The xmlComposeString() routine calls through to expatxml.19002420(), which, among other things, HTML encodes the characters &, >, and < as &, >, and <, respectively. This behavior can be seen in the following disassembly snippet:

```
19002492 push 0
19002494 push 0
19002496 push offset str_Amp       ; "&amp;"
1900249B push offset ampersand     ; "&"
190024A0 push eax
190024A1 call sub_190023A0

190024A6 push 0
190024A8 push 0
190024AA push offset str_Lt        ; "&lt;"
190024AF push offset less_than     ; "<"
190024B4 push eax
190024B5 call sub_190023A0

190024BA push
190024BC push
190024BE push offset str_Gt        ; "&gt;"
190024C3 push offset greater_than  ; ">"
190024C8 push eax
190024C9 call sub_190023A0
```

As the originally calculated string length does not account for this string expansion, the following subsequent in-line memory copy operation within rendezvous.dll can trigger an exploitable memory corruption:

```
4900C4EC mov ecx, eax
4900C4EE shr ecx, 2
4900C4F1 rep movsd
4900C4F3 mov ecx, eax
4900C4F5 and ecx, 3
4900C4F8 rep movsb
```

Each of the faults detected by Sulley were in response to this logic error. Tracking fault locations and paths allowed us to quickly postulate that a single source was responsible. A final step we might wish to take is to remove all PCAP files that do not contain information regarding a fault. The pcap_cleaner.py utility was written for exactly this task:

```
$ ./utils/pcap_cleaner.py
    USAGE: pcap_cleaner.py <xxx.crashbin> <path to pcaps>
```

This utility will open the specified crash bin file, read in the list of test case numbers that triggered a fault, and erase all other PCAP files from the specified directory. To better understand how everything ties together, from start to finish, we will walk through a complete real-world example audit.

## A COMPLETE WALKTHROUGH

This example touches on many intermediate to advanced Sulley concepts and should hopefully solidify your understanding of the framework. Many details regarding the specifics of the target are skipped in this walkthrough, as the main purpose of this section is to demonstrate the usage of a number of advanced Sulley features. The chosen target is Trend Micro Server Protect, specifically a Microsoft DCE/RPC endpoint on TCP port 5168 bound to by the service SpntSvc.exe. The RPC endpoint is exposed from TmRpcSrv.dll with the following Interface Definition Language (IDL) stub information:

```
// opcode: 0x00, address: 0x65741030
// uuid: 25288888-bd5b-11d1-9d53-0080c83a5c2c
// version: 1.0

error_status_t rpc_opnum_0 (
[in] handle_t arg_1,                        // not sent on wire
[in] long trend_req_num,
[in][size_is(arg_4)] byte some_string[],
[in] long arg_4,
[out][size_is(arg_6)] byte arg_5[],         // not sent on wire
[in] long arg_6
);
```

Neither of the parameters arg_1 and arg_6 is actually transmitted across the wire. This is an important fact to consider later when we write the actual fuzz requests. Further examination reveals that the parameter trend_req_num has special meaning. The upper and lower halves of this parameter control a pair of jump tables that expose a plethora of reachable subroutines through this single RPC function. Reverse engineering the jump tables reveals the following combinations:

- When the value for the upper half is 0x0001, 1 through 21 are valid lower half values.
- When the value for the upper half is 0x0002, 1 through 18 are valid lower half values.
- When the value for the upper half is 0x0003, 1 through 84 are valid lower half values.
- When the value for the upper half is 0x0005, 1 through 24 are valid lower half values.
- When the value for the upper half is 0x000A, 1 through 48 are valid lower half values.
- When the value for the upper half is 0x001F, 1 through 24 are valid lower half values.

We must next create a custom encoder routine that will be responsible for encapsulating defined blocks as a valid DCE/RPC request. There is only a single function number, so this is simple. We define a basic wrapper around `utils.dcerpc.request()`, which hard-codes the opcode parameter to zero:

```
# dce rpc request encoder used for trend server protect 5168 RPC service.
# opnum is always zero.
def rpc_request_encoder (data):
    return utils.dcerpc.request(0, data)
```

### Building the Requests

Armed with this information and our encoder we can begin to define our Sulley requests. We create a file requests\trend.py to contain all our Trend-related request and helper definitions and begin coding. This is an excellent example of how building a fuzzer request within a language (as opposed to a custom language) is beneficial as we take advantage of some Python looping to automatically generate a separate request for each valid upper value from `trend_req_num`:

```
for op, submax in [(0x1, 22), (0x2, 19), (0x3, 85), (0x5, 25), (0xa, 49), (0x1f, 25)]:
    s_initialize("5168: op-%x" % op)
    if s_block_start("everything", encoder=rpc_request_encoder):
        # [in] long trend_req_num,
        s_group("subs", values=map(chr, range(1, submax)))
        s_static("\x00")                  # subs is actually a little endian word
        s_static(struct.pack("<H", op))   # opcode

        # [in][size_is(arg_4)] byte some_string[],
        s_size("some_string")
```

```
    if s_block_start("some_string", group="subs"):
        s_static("A" * 0x5000, name="arg3")
    s_block_end()

    # [in] long arg_4,
    s_size("some_string")

    # [in] long arg_6
    s_static(struct.pack("<L", 0x5000)) # output buffer size
s_block_end()
```

Within each generated request a new block is initialized and passed to our previously defined custom encoder. Next, the s_group() primitive is used to define a sequence named subs that represents the lower half value of trend_req_num we saw earlier. The upper half word value is next added to the request stream as a static value. We will not be fuzzing the trend_req_num as we have reverse engineered its valid values; had we not, we could enable fuzzing for these fields as well. Next, the NDR size prefix for some_string is added to the request. We could optionally use the Sulley DCE/RPC NDR lego primitives here, but because the RPC request is so simple we decide to represent the NDR format manually. Next, the some_string value is added to the request. The string value is encapsulated in a block so that its length can be measured. In this case we use a static-sized string of the character A (roughly 20k worth). Normally we would insert an s_string() primitive here, but because we know Trend will crash with any long string, we reduce the test set by utilizing a static value. The length of the string is appended to the request again to fulfill the size_is requirement for arg_4. Finally, we specify an arbitrary static size for the output buffer size and close the block. Our requests are now ready and we can move on to creating a session.

### Creating the Session

We create a new file in the top-level Sulley folder named fuzz_trend_server_protect_5168.py for our session. This file has since been moved to the archived_fuzzies folder because it has completed its life. First things first, we import Sulley and the created Trend requests from the request library:

```
from sulley   import *
from requests import trend
```

Next, we are going to define a presend function that is responsible for establishing the DCE/RPC connection prior to the transmission of any individual test case. The presend routine accepts a single parameter, the socket on which to transmit data. This is a simple routine to write thanks to the availability of `utils.dcerpc.bind()`, a Sulley utility routine:

```
def rpc_bind (sock):
    bind = utils.dcerpc.bind("25288888-bd5b-11d1-9d53-0080c83a5c2c", "1.0")
    sock.send(bind)

    utils.dcerpc.bind_ack(sock.recv(1000))
```

Now it's time to initiate the session and define a target. We'll fuzz a single target, an installation of Trend Server Protect housed inside a VMWare virtual machine with the address 10.0.0.1. We'll follow the framework guidelines by saving the serialized session information to the audits directory. Finally, we register a network monitor, process monitor, and virtual machine control agent with the defined target:

```
sess   = sessions.session(session_filename="audits/trend_server_protect_5168.session")
target = sessions.target("10.0.0.1", 5168)

target.netmon    = pedrpc.client("10.0.0.1",  26001)
target.procmon   = pedrpc.client("10.0.0.1",  26002)
target.vmcontrol = pedrpc.client("127.0.0.1", 26003)
```

Because a VMWare control agent is present, Sulley will default to reverting to a known good snapshot whenever a fault is detected or the target is unable to be reached. If a VMWare control agent is not available but a process monitor agent is, then Sulley attempts to restart the target process to resume fuzzing. This is accomplished by specifying the `stop_commands` and `start_commands` options to the process monitor agent:

```
target.procmon_options = \
{
    "proc_name"      : "SpntSvc.exe",
    "stop_commands"  : ['net stop "trend serverprotect"'],
    "start_commands" : ['net start "trend serverprotect"'],
}
```

The `proc_name` parameter is mandatory whenever you use the process monitor agent; it specifies what process name to which the debugger should attach and in which to look for faults. If neither a VMWare control agent nor a process monitor agent is available, then Sulley has no choice but to simply provide the target time to recover in the event a data transmission is unsuccessful.

Next, we instruct the target to start by calling the VMWare control agents `restart_target()` routine. Once running, the target is added to the session, the presend routine is defined, and each of the defined requests is connected to the root fuzzing node. Finally, fuzzing commences with a call to the session classes' `fuzz()` routine.

```
# start up the target.
target.vmcontrol.restart_target()

print "virtual machine up and running"

sess.add_target(target)
sess.pre_send = rpc_bind
sess.connect(s_get("5168: op-1"))
sess.connect(s_get("5168: op-2"))
sess.connect(s_get("5168: op-3"))
sess.connect(s_get("5168: op-5"))
sess.connect(s_get("5168: op-a"))
sess.connect(s_get("5168: op-1f"))
sess.fuzz()
```

### Setting Up the Environment

The final step before launching the fuzz session is to set up the environment. We do so by bringing up the target virtual machine image and launching the network and process monitor agents directly within the test image with the following command-line parameters:

```
network_monitor.py -d 1 \
                   -f "src or dst port 5168" \
                   -p audits\trend_server_protect_5168

process_monitor.py -c audits\trend_server_protect_5168.crashbin \
                   -p SpntSvc.exe
```

Both agents are executed from a mapped share that corresponds with the Sulley top-level directory from which the session script is running. A Berkeley Packet Filter (BPF) filter string is passed to the network monitor to ensure that only the packets we are interested in are recorded. A directory within the audits folder is also chosen where the network monitor will create PCAPs for every test case. With both agents and the target process running, a live snapshot is made as named sulley ready and waiting.

Next, we shut down VMWare and launch the VMWare control agent on the host system (the fuzzing system). This agent requires the path to the vmrun.exe executable, the path to the actual image to control, and finally the name of the snapshot to revert to in the event of a fault discovery of data transmission failure:

```
vmcontrol.py -r "c:\\VMware\vmrun.exe"
              -x "v:\vmfarm\Trend\win_2000_pro.vmx"
              -snapshot "sulley ready and waiting"
```

### Ready, Set, Action! And Postmortem

Finally, we are ready. Simply launch fuzz_trend_server_protect_5168.py, connect a Web browser to http://127.0.0.1:26000 to monitor the fuzzer progress, sit back, watch, and enjoy.

When the fuzzer completes running through its list of 221 test cases, we discover that 19 of them triggered faults. Using the crashbin_explorer.py utility we can explore the faults categorized by exception address:

```
$ ./utils/crashbin_explorer.py audits/trend_server_protect_5168.crashbin
    [6] [INVALID]:41414141 Unable to disassemble at 41414141 from thread 568 caused
access violation
            42, 109, 156, 164, 170, 198,
    [3] LogMaster.dll:63272106 push ebx from thread 568 caused access violation
            53, 56, 151,
    [1] ntdll.dll:77fbb267 push dword [ebp+0xc] from thread 568 caused access
violation
            195,
    [1] Eng50.dll:6118954e rep movsd from thread 568 caused access violation
            181,
    [1] ntdll.dll:77facbbd push edi from thread 568 caused access violation
            118,
    [1] Eng50.dll:61187671 cmp word [eax],0x3b from thread 568 caused access violation
            116,
    [1] [INVALID]:0058002e Unable to disassemble at 0058002e from thread 568 caused
access violation
            70,
    [2] Eng50.dll:611896d1 rep movsd from thread 568 caused access violation
            152, 182,
    [1] StRpcSrv.dll:6567603c push esi from thread 568 caused access violation
            106,
```

```
[1] KERNEL32.dll:7c57993a cmp ax,[edi] from thread 568 caused access violation
     165,
[1] Eng50.dll:61182415 mov edx,[edi+0x20c] from thread 568 caused access violation
     50,
```

Some of these are clearly exploitable issues, for example, the test cases that resulted with an EIP of 0x41414141. Test case 70 seems to have stumbled on a possible code execution issue as well, a Unicode overflow (actually this can be a straight overflow with a bit more research). The crash bin explorer utility can generate a graph view of the detected faults as well, drawing paths based on observed stack backtraces. This can help pinpoint the root cause of certain issues. The utility accepts the following command-line arguments:

```
$ ./utils/crashbin_explorer.py
    USAGE: crashbin_explorer.py <xxx.crashbin>
        [-t|-test #]     dump the crash synopsis for a specific test case number
        [-g|-graph name] generate a graph of all crash paths, save to 'name'.udg
```

We can, for example, further examine the CPU state at the time of the fault detected in response to test case 70:

```
$ ./utils/crashbin_explorer.py audits/trend_server_protect_5168.crashbin -t 70
    [INVALID]:0058002e Unable to disassemble at 0058002e from thread 568 caused access
violation
    when attempting to read from 0x0058002e
    CONTEXT DUMP
      EIP: 0058002e Unable to disassemble at 0058002e
      EAX: 00000001 (        1) -> N/A
      EBX: 0259e118 ( 39444760) -> A.....AAAAA (stack)
      ECX: 00000000 (        0) -> N/A
      EDX: ffffffff (4294967295) -> N/A
      EDI: 00000000 (        0) -> N/A
      ESI: 0259e33e ( 39445310) -> A.....AAAAA (stack)
      EBP: 00000000 (        0) -> N/A
      ESP: 0259d594 ( 39441812) -> LA.XLT.......MPT.MSG.OFT.PPS.RT (stack)
      +00: 0041004c (  4259916) -> N/A
      +04: 0058002e (  5767214) -> N/A
      +08: 0054004c (  5505100) -> N/A
      +0c: 0056002e (  5636142) -> N/A
      +10: 00530042 (  5439554) -> N/A
      +14: 004a002e (  4849710) -> N/A
    disasm around:
          0x0058002e Unable to disassemble
```

```
SEH unwind:
         0259fc58 -> StRpcSrv.dll:656784e3
         0259fd70 -> TmRpcSrv.dll:65741820
         0259fda8 -> TmRpcSrv.dll:65741820
         0259ffdc -> RPCRT4.dll:77d87000
         ffffffff -> KERNEL32.dll:7c5c216c
```

You can see here that the stack has been blown away by what appears to be a Unicode string of file extensions. You can pull up the archived PCAP file for the given test case as well. Figure 21.5 shows an excerpt of a screen shot from Wireshark examining the contents of one of the captured PCAP files.

A final step we might wish to take is to remove all PCAP files that do not contain information regarding a fault. The pcap_cleaner.py utility was written for exactly this task:

```
$ ./utils/pcap_cleaner.py
    USAGE: pcap_cleaner.py <xxx.crashbin> <path to pcaps>
```

This utility will open the specified crash bin file, read in the list of test case numbers that triggered a fault, and erase all other PCAP files from the specified directory. The discovered code execution vulnerabilities in this fuzz were all reported to Trend and have resulted in the following advisories:

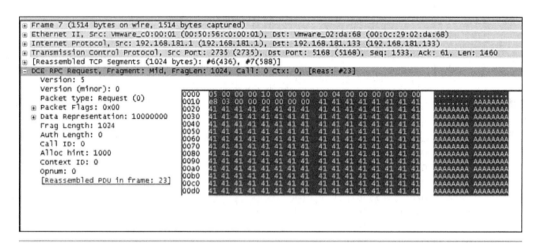

**Figure 21.5**   Wireshark DCE/RPC dissector

- TSRT-07-01: Trend Micro ServerProtect StCommon.dll Stack Overflow Vulnerabilities
- TSRT-07-02: Trend Micro ServerProtect eng50.dll Stack Overflow Vulnerabilities

This is not to say that all possible vulnerabilities have been exhausted in this interface. In fact, this was the most rudimentary fuzzing possible of this interface. A secondary fuzz that actually uses the `s_string()` primitive as opposed to simply a long string can now be beneficial.

## SUMMARY

Fuzzing frameworks provide a flexible, reusable, and homogenous development environment for bug hunters and QA teams.. After going through the list of available fuzzing frameworks in this chapter, it should be fairly obvious that there is not a clear winner. All of them provide a reasonable framework to build on, but your selection of a specific framework will generally be driven by the target to be fuzzed and familiarity, or lack thereof, with the programming language used by a particular framework. The Adobe Macromedia Shockwave Flash's SWF file format case study illustrates that frameworks remain an immature technology and you are still likely to encounter situations where none of the existing frameworks are capable of meeting your needs. As demonstrated, it might on occasion thus be necessary to develop a custom fuzzing solution, leveraging reusable components developed for the task at hand. Hopefully this case study was thought provoking and will provide some guidance when you encounter your own exotic fuzzing tasks.

In the final section of this chapter we introduced and explored a new fuzzing framework, Sulley. Various aspects of this fuzzing framework were dissected to clearly demonstrate the advancements made by this endeavor. Sulley is the latest in an increasingly long line of fuzzing frameworks and is actively maintained by the authors of this book. Check http://www.fuzzing.org for ongoing updates, further documentation, and up-to-date examples.

# Automated Protocol Dissection

*"I know how hard it is for you to put food on your family."*

—George W. Bush, Greater Nashua, NH, January 27, 2000

Previous chapters took a close look at a wide range of fuzzers. From simple byte-mutating generic file fuzzers to the most currently evolved fuzzing frameworks, fuzzing technologies overcome a number of automated software testing hurdles. In this chapter, we introduce the most advanced forms of fuzzing and the attempts to solve a dilemma common among all fuzzing technologies. Specifically, we tackle the indomitable task of breaking down a protocol into its basic building blocks.

The chapter begins with a discussion of primitive techniques targeted at automating protocol dissection and then advances into the application of bioinformatics and genetic algorithms. At the cutting edge of the automated software testing field, these subjects are largely theoretical and are currently being actively researched by a number of individuals.

## WHAT'S THE PROBLEM WITH FUZZING?

The single most painful aspect of fuzz testing is the barrier to entry, especially when dealing with undocumented, complex binary protocols that require a great deal of research to understand. Imagine the task of fuzzing the Microsoft SMB protocol prior to

1992, when the first version of Samba[1] was released. The Samba project has since matured into a full-fledged and Windows-compatible SMB client–server. This is possible thanks to countless volunteer man hours. Do you currently have such a large team and over a decade of time to fuzz a similarly undocumented proprietary protocol?

## SAMBA

SAMBA saw its beginnings on January 10, 1992, when Andrew Tridgell from Australian National University posted a message to the vmsnet.networks.desktop. pathworks newsgroup.[2] In that message he announced the availability of a UNIX file sharing service compatible with Pathworks for DOS. That project became known as nbserver, but the name was changed to Samba in April 1994 when Tridgell received a letter from Syntax Corp. complaining about possible trademark infringement.[3] A decade and a half later, Samba has evolved into one of the most widely used open source projects ever.

Fuzzing your own protocols is easy. You are familiar with the format, the nuances, the complexities and even which areas you might have coded on little sleep and want to give extra attention to. Fuzzing a documented protocol such as HTTP is relatively easy as well. Detailed RFCs[4] and other public documents are available for reference. It's a simple matter of data entry to produce an effective and thorough series of test cases. Beware however, even though a protocol is both common and documented does not guarantee that a software vendor has strictly adhered to the published standards. Consider the real-world example with Ipswitch IMail. In September 2006 a remotely exploitable stack overflow vulnerability was publicly disclosed[5] affecting Ipswitch's SMTP daemon. The flaw exists due to a lack of bounds checking during the parsing of long strings contained within the characters @ and :. When looking at the right area in the binary the issue is trivial to spot. However, as the vulnerable functionality is a proprietary Ipswitch feature

---

[1]  http://www.samba.org

[2]  http://groups.google.com/group/vmsnet.networks.desktop.pathworks/msg/7d939a9e7e419b9c

[3]  http://www.samba.org/samba/docs/10years.html

[4]  http://www.w3.org/Protocols/rfc2616/rfc2616.html

[5]  http://www.zerodayinitiative.com/advisories/ZDI-06-028.html

and not documented in any standard, there is less of a chance that a fuzzer would discover it.

Fuzzing a proprietary third-party protocol, no matter how simple, can be challenging at best. Pure random fuzzing is quickest to implement but yields far from intelligent results. Other generic techniques, such as byte flipping, provide better testing but require an extra step: Valid traffic between the client and server must first be observed. Fortunately, triggering communications between an arbitrary client–server pair is a simple task in most cases. However, there is no way to state with certainty what percentage of the protocol remains unobserved. For example, take HTTP with no assumptions of prior knowledge. Observing traffic for a short period of time will likely reveal the GET and POST actions. However, more obscure actions such as HEAD, OPTIONS, and TRACE are less likely to be observed. How do we uncover the less frequently used portions of an arbitrary protocol? To better dissect the target protocol, a reverse engineer can be unleashed on the client and server binaries. This is an expensive step as experienced reverse engineers are highly skilled and hard to find. In some cases, particularly with plain text protocols, additional functionality may sometimes be guessed. This luxury is less often available with a binary protocol.

Before going to the expensive of hiring or tasking of a skilled reverse engineer, be sure to leverage the work of others. The world is a big place and chances are that if you want details on a proprietary protocol, someone else has faced the same frustration. Before diving too deep be sure to ask your friend Google what he knows about the problem. You might be pleasantly surprised to uncover unofficial documentation produced by another individual that has already taken on the same challenge. Wotsit.org is also a great resource for file formats, both documented and undocumented. For network protocols, the source code to Wireshark and Ethereal also provides a good starting point, as this code includes protocol definitions for many of the better known proprietary protocols that have already been thoroughly dissected.

When the burden of deciphering a proprietary protocol falls solely on your shoulders, a less manually intensive approach is strongly desired. This chapter is dedicated to various methodologies that can assist in automating the process of detecting the signals, or structure, among the noise, or data, within network protocols and file formats.

## HEURISTIC TECHNIQUES

The two techniques presented in this section are not true forms of automated protocol dissection. Rather, these heuristic-based techniques can be applied to improve fuzzing automation and performance. They are presented here to kick the chapter off prior to delving into more complicated methodologies.

## PROXY FUZZING

The first heuristic-based dissection technique we discuss is implemented by a privately developed[6] fuzzing engine aptly named ProxyFuzzer. In the typical network-based client–server model, there is direct communication between the client and the server as shown in Figure 22.1.

As the name implies, a proxy fuzzer must sever the connection between client and server to position itself as a relay. To effectively accomplish this task, both the client and server must be manually configured[7] to look for one another at the address of the proxy. In other words, the client sees the proxy as the server and the server sees the proxy as the client. The new network diagram including the spliced-in fuzzer is shown in Figure 22.2.

The solid connecting lines between the nodes shown in Figure 22.2 represent original unmodified data that at this point has simply been rerouted through the proxy. In its default mode, ProxyFuzzer blindly relays received traffic on both ends while recording the transactions in a format suitable for programmatic modification or replay. This is a

**Figure 22.1**   Typical client–server communication path

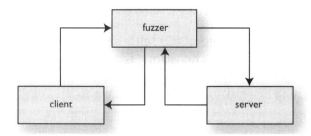

**Figure 22.2**   Transparent inline proxy

---

[6]   Look for the release of this tool by Cody Pierce of TippingPoint.

[7]   This process can actually be automated through some IP trickery, which isn't discussed for the sake of simplicity.

handy feature on its own as it allows researchers to skip the intermediary steps associated with generating and modifying raw packet capture (PCAP) files. As an aside, modifying and replaying recorded transactions is an excellent manual approach for reversing unknown protocols and is a technique well implemented by Matasano's Protocol Debugger (PDB).[8]

Once ProxyFuzzer has been successfully configured and validated to be functioning, its automatic mutation engine can be enabled. In this mode, ProxyFuzzer processes relayed traffic looking for plain text components. It does so by identifying bytes that fall within the valid ASCII range in sequences longer than a specified threshold. Once identified, the discovered strings are either randomly lengthened or modified with invalid characters and format string tokens. Figure 22.3 depicts the mutated streams with dashed lines.

Although simplistic, ProxyFuzzer is extremely easy to use, provides assistance with manual analysis, and has even discovered security vulnerabilities in its current form! Perhaps the greatest benefit to inline (proxy) fuzzing is that the majority of the protocol remains intact while individual fields are mutated. Leaving the bulk of the data transfer untouched allows for successful fuzzing with little analysis. Consider, for example, complex protocols that implement sequence numbers at the data level. An invalid sequence number results in the immediate detection of protocol corruption and the remainder of the data, including the fuzzed field, is not parsed. By sitting inline, a fuzzer can leverage valid transactions and generate mutations valid enough to reach the parser.

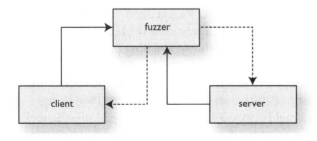

**Figure 22.3**   Autonomous inline mutation

___
8   http://www.matasano.com/log/399/pdb-blackhat-talk-materials-as-promised/

## ProxyFuzzer Results

ProxyFuzzer is rudimentary even in comparison to the most basic fuzzers covered in previous chapters. Nevertheless, it has already been proven effective against popular (and obviously not well coded) enterprise software. With absolutely no setup or assistance, ProxyFuzzer has discovered two remotely exploitable vulnerabilities in Computer Associates' Brightstor backup software.

The first issue manifests during a postauthentication transaction, limiting the severity of the impact. During standard client–server communications over TCP port 6050, a long filename triggers a trivially exploitable stack overflow vulnerability in UnivAgent.exe.

The second issue exists within the igateway.exe HTTP daemon, which communicates over TCP port 5250. This issue only manifests if the debug flag is enabled, limiting the severity of impact. The requested filename is insecurely passed through a call to `fprintf()`, exposing an exploitable format string vulnerability.

Neither of these discovered issues are particularly "sexy" standing among a pool of elegant vulnerabilities. Yet, considering the minimal effort that was required to uncover these bugs, perhaps ProxyFuzzer should always be given the first chance.

## Improved Proxy Fuzzing

Improvements are currently under development to make ProxyFuzzer "smarter." Additional heuristics have been considered to assist in automated field detection and subsequent mutation. The current traffic parser is capable of isolating plain text fields from the remainder of a binary protocol. Identified plain text fields should be further processed, looking for common field delimiters and terminators such as spaces, colons, and so on. Additionally, raw bytes prior to detected strings can be searched for string length and type specifications (i.e., TLV fields). Possible length prefixes can then be verified through cross-examination across a number of packets. Raw bytes after strings can also be studied to detect padding of static fields. IP addresses of both the client and server frequently appear within the data stream (outside of the TCP/IP headers). As this information is known, the analysis engine can scan network data for both raw and ASCII representations.

By assuming that most simple protocols can be described as a sequence of fields that fall into one of the categories shown in Figure 22.4, we can begin to model the hierarchy of an unknown protocol through a series of guesses and validations.

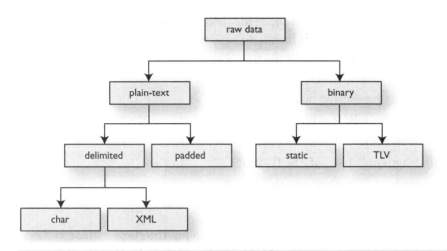

**Figure 22.4**  Hierarchical protocol breakdown

This rudimentary technique will likely provide little value in dissecting complex binary protocols such as SMB. However, the end goal here is not to conduct a full protocol dissection, but rather to extend the range of simple protocols suitable for automatic fuzzing. As an applied example, consider the following contrived network data, shown here as one transaction per line with raw hex bytes bounded by the pipe (|) character:

```
|00 04|user|00 06|pedram|0a 0a 00 01|code rev 254|00 00 00 00 be ef|END
|00 04|user|00 04|cody|0a 0a 00 02|code rev 11|00 00 00 00 00 de ad|END
|00 04|user|00 05|aaron|0a 0a 00 03|code rev 31337|00 00 00 c0 1a|END
```

A human (and perhaps even a dolphin) can easily glance over these three transactions and quickly make educated guesses as to the specifics of the protocol. Let's take a look at what our improved auto-analysis might uncover by examining solely the first transaction. To begin, a four-byte IP address field is quickly detected and anchored on (0a 0a 00 01 = private IP address 10.10.0.1). Next, four ASCII strings are detected: user, pedram, code rev 254, and END. The byte values ahead of each string are scanned for a one-byte valid length value, then a two-byte, three-byte, and finally four-byte value. The analysis routine can now guess that the protocol begins with two variable length strings, prefixed with a two-byte length, followed by the IP address of the connecting client. Scanning the next string for a length prefix yields no results. Assuming that this next ASCII field is of a static size, the engine looks for and finds four trailing null bytes. This next field is guessed to be a 10-byte static-sized ASCII field. The final string, END, contains no length prefix, nor is it followed by padding. This field is assumed to be a three-byte static-sized

ASCII field. No assumption can be made about the field containing the remaining two bytes, 0xbeef. It can be static or variable length, so further analysis is required. Putting it all together, the engine was able to deduce the following protocol structure from the first transaction:

- Two-byte string length followed by string.
- Two-byte string length followed by string.
- Four-byte client IP address.
- 10-byte static-length null-padded ASCII string.
- Unknown binary field of static or variable length.
- Three-byte static-length ASCII string.

   The engine now proceeds to subsequent transactions to put the guesses made in the initial analysis to test. By doing so certain assumptions are confirmed and others are invalidated, all the while continuing to improve the accuracy of the modeled protocol. Unlike other simplified examples, this heuristic-based approach will fail on more complicated protocols. Keep in mind that the purpose was not to completely understand the underlying protocol, but rather improve unassisted fuzzing.

## DISASSEMBLY HEURISTICS

The application of (dis)assembly-level heuristics to assist in fuzzer effectiveness is a concept that has yet to be used by any publicly available fuzzing tools or frameworks. The concept is simple: While fuzzing, monitor code execution on the target through the use of a runtime instrumentation tool such as a debugger. In the debugger, look for static string and integer comparisons. Pass this information back to the fuzzer to be considered for inclusion in future generated test cases. Results will vary from case to case; however, the fuzzer can undoubtedly generate smarter data by properly leveraging this feedback loop. Consider the following code excerpt from real-world production server software:

```
0040206C call ds:__imp__sscanf
00402072 mov eax, [esp+5DA4h+var_5CDC]
00402079 add esp, 0Ch
0040207C cmp eax, 3857106359        ; string prefix check
00402081 jz   short loc_40208D
00402083 push offset `string'       ; "access protocol error"
00402088 jmp loc_401D61
```

Raw network data is converted into an integer with the assistance of the `sscanf()` API. The resulting integer is then compared against the static integer value 3857106359 and if the values do not match then the protocol parser returns due to an "access protocol error." The first time the fuzzer traverses this block of code the debugger component will discover the "magic" value and pass it through the feedback loop. The fuzzer can then include the value in a number of formats in hopes of tickling the target in the correct manner to expose further code coverage. Without the feedback loop, the fuzzer is dead in the water.

A proof of concept implementation of a target monitoring fuzzer feedback debugger was developed in little more than a couple of hours using the PyDbg component of the PaiMei[9] reverse engineering framework. Check http://www.fuzzing.org for the relevant source code.

With the more primitive techniques covered, we next take a look at a more advanced approach toward dissection automation with the introduction of bioinformatics.

## BIOINFORMATICS

Wikipedia defines bioinformatics, or computational biology, as a broad term that generalizes the use of "applied mathematics, informatics, statistics, computer science, artificial intelligence, chemistry and biochemistry to solve biological problems usually on the molecular level."[10] In essence, bioinformatics encompasses various techniques that can be applied to discover patterns in long sequences of complex but structured data, such as gene sequences. Network protocols can also be viewed as long sequences of complex but structured data. Can software testers therefore borrow techniques from biologists to make fuzzing any easier?

The most basic analysis in bioinformatics is the ability to align two sequences, regardless of length, to maximize likeness. Gaps can be inserted into either sequence during alignment to facilitate this goal. Consider the following amino acid sequence alignment:

```
Sequence One: ACAT   TACAGGA
Sequence Two: ACATTCCTACAGGA
```

Three gaps were inserted into the first sequence to force length alignment and maximize similarity. A number of algorithms exist for accomplishing this and other sequence

---

[9]  http://openrce.org/downloads/details/208/PaiMei

[10]  http://en.wikipedia.org/wiki/Bioinformatics

alignment tasks. One such algorithm, the Needleman-Wunsch (NW) algorithm,[11] was originally proposed in 1970 by Saul Needleman[12] and Christian Wunsch.[13] The NW algorithm is commonly applied in the field of bioinformatics to align two sequences of proteins or nucleotides. This algorithm is an example of "dynamic programming," which is a method of solving larger problems by breaking them into a number of smaller problems.

Perhaps the first public demonstration of applying theorems from bioinformatics to the world of network protocol analysis was in late 2004 at the ToorCon[14] hacker conference held in San Diego, California. At the conference, Marshall Beddoe unveiled an experimental Python framework named Protocol Informatics (PI) that made quite a splash, even picking up a *Wired* article.[15] The original Web site has since been taken down and the framework has not been actively maintained. As the author of PI was hired by security analysis company Mu Security,[16] some speculate that the technology is no longer publicly available to make way for a commercial offering. Fortunately, a copy of the beta-quality PI code is still available for download from Packet Storm.[17]

The objective of the PI framework is to automatically deduce the field boundaries of arbitrary protocols through analysis of large quantities of observed data. PI has been demonstrated to successfully identify fields from the HTTP, ICMP, and SMB protocols. It does so with the assistance of the Smith-Waterman[18] (SW) local sequence alignment algorithm, the NW global sequence alignment algorithm, similarity matrices and phylogenetic trees. Although the fine details of the bioinformatics sciences applied by the PI framework goes beyond the scope of this book, the high-level overview and at least the names of the algorithms utilized are presented here.

Network protocols can contain a number of drastically different message types. Attempting a sequence alignment between different message types is fruitless. To address this issue, the SW algorithm for local sequence alignment is first applied to a pair of sequences to locate and match similar subsequences. These locations and matched pairs are later used to assist the NW global sequence alignment. Similarity matrices are used to

---

[11] http://en.wikipedia.org/wiki/Needleman-Wunsch_algorithm

[12] http://en.wikipedia.org/wiki/Saul_Needleman

[13] http://en.wikipedia.org/wiki/Christian_Wunsch

[14] http://www.toorcon.org

[15] http://www.wired.com/news/infostructure/0,1377,65191,00.html

[16] http://www.musecurity.com

[17] http://packetstormsecurity.org/sniffers/PI.tgz

[18] http://en.wikipedia.org/wiki/Smith-Waterman

assist the NW algorithm in optimizing the alignment between sequences. Two commonly used matrices, Percent Accepted Mutation (PAM) and the Blocks Substitution Matrix (BLOSUM), are applied by the PI framework to more appropriately align sequences based on data types. In application, this generalizes to aligning binary data with other binary data and ASCII data with other ASCII data. The distinction allows for more accurate identification of variable length fields within the protocol structure. The PI framework takes this a step further by performing multiple sequence alignment to better understand the target protocol. To dodge the computational infeasibility of applying NW directly, the Unweighted Pairwise Mean by Arithmetic Averages (UPGMA) algorithm is used to generate a phylogenetic tree that is then used as a heuristic guide to perform multiple alignments.

Let's look at the framework in action by examining its ability to dissect a simple fixed length protocol, the ICMP.[19] Here are the basic steps to using the PI framework to dissect ICMP. First, some ICMP packets must be gathered for analysis:

```
# tcpdump -s 42 -c 100 -nl -w icmp.dump icmp
```

Next, the captured traffic can be run through the PI framework:

```
# ./main.py -g -p ./icmp.dump
Protocol Informatics Prototype (v0.01 beta)
Written by Marshall Beddoe <mbeddoe@baselineresearch.net>
Copyright (c) 2004 Baseline Research
Found 100 unique sequences in '../dumps/icmp.out'
Creating distance matrix .. complete
Creating phylogenetic tree .. complete
Discovered 1 clusters using a weight of 1.00
Performing multiple alignment on cluster 1 .. complete
Output of cluster 1
0097 x08 x00 xad x4b x05 xbe x00 x60
0039 x08 x00 x30 x54 x05 xbe x00 x26
0026 x08 x00 xf7 xb2 x05 xbe x00 x19
0015 x08 x00 x01 xdb x05 xbe x00 x0e
0048 x08 x00 x4f xdf x05 xbe x00 x2f
0040 x08 x00 xf8 xa4 x05 xbe x00 x27
0077 x08 x00 xe8 x28 x05 xbe x00 x4c
0017 x08 x00 xe8 x6c x05 xbe x00 x10
0027 x08 x00 xc3 xa9 x05 xbe x00 x1a
0087 x08 x00 xdd xc1 x05 xbe x00 x56
```

---

[19] http://en.wikipedia.org/wiki/Internet_Control_Message_Protocol

```
0081 x08 x00 x88 x42 x05 xbe x00 x50
0058 x08 x00 xb0 x42 x05 xbe x00 x39
0013 x08 x00 x3e x38 x05 xbe x00
0067 x08 x00 x99 x36 x05 xbe x00 x42
0055 x08 x00 x0f x56 x05 xbe x00 x36
0004 x08 x00 xe6 xda x05 xbe x00 x03
0028 x08 x00 x83 xd9 x05 xbe x00 x1b
0095 x08 x00 xc1 xd9 x05 xbe x00 x5e
0093 x08 x00     xb6 x05 xbe x00 x5c
[ output trimmed for sake of brevity ]
0010 x08 x00 xd1 xb6 x05 xbe x00
0024 x08 x00 x11 x8f x05 xbe x00 x17
0063 x08 x00 x11 x04 x05 xbe x00 x3e
0038 x08 x00 x37 x3b x05 xbe x00 x25
DT   BBB ZZZ BBB BBB BBB BBB ZZZ AAA
MT   000 000 081 089 000 000 000 100
Ungapped Consensus:
CONS x08 x00 x3f x18 x05 xbe x00 ???
DT   BBB ZZZ BBB BBB BBB BBB ZZZ AAA
MT   000 000 081 089 000 000 000 100
Step 3: Analyze Consensus Sequence
Pay attention to datatype composition and mutation rate.
Offset 0: Binary data, 0% mutation rate
Offset 1: Zeroed data, 0% mutation rate
Offset 2: Binary data, 81% mutation rate
Offset 3: Binary data, 89% mutation rate
Offset 4: Binary data, 0% mutation rate
Offset 5: Binary data, 0% mutation rate
Offset 6: Zeroed data, 0% mutation rate
Offset 7: ASCII data, 100% mutation rate
```

Although not immediately obvious, the results of the generated analysis translate into the following protocol structure:

```
[ 1 byte ] [ 1 byte ] [ 2 byte ] [ 2 byte ] [ 1 byte ] [ 1 byte ]
```

The results are not far off from the real structure of the protocol:

```
[ 1 byte ] [ 1 byte ] [ 2 byte ] [ 2 byte ] [ 2 byte ]
```

The mistake in identifying the last field is due to the limited number of ICMP packets captured for analysis. The misidentified field is actually a 16-bit sequence number. As only 100 packets were used, the greatest significant byte of the field was never incremented. Had more data been passed to PI, the field size would have been correctly identified.

The application of bioinformatics to automated protocol dissection is a very interesting and advanced approach. Results are currently limited and a number of researchers are skeptical about the overall benefit of applying these techniques.[20] Nevertheless, as the PI framework has provided evidence of success, we can hope to see future developments on this methodology.

## GENETIC ALGORITHMS

A genetic algorithm (GA) is an approximating search technique used by software that mimics evolution. A GA performs mutations on a base population while maintaining favored hereditary traits in future generations. Rules of natural selection are applied to choose generated samples that are more "fit" for their environment. The chosen samples are then mated and mutated and the process continues. Three components are typically required to define a GA:

- A *representation* of what the solution might look like.
- A *fitness function* for evaluating how good an individual solution might be.
- A *reproduction* function responsible for mutation and crossover between two solutions.

To better illustrate these concepts, let's consider a simple problem and its GA solution. The groundbreaking problem we would like to solve is maximizing the number of 1s in a binary string of length 10. The representation and fitness function for this problem are straightforward. Possible solutions are represented as a string of binary digits and the fitness function is defined as the count of the number of ones within the string. For our reproduction or mating function, we arbitrarily choose to swap the two strings at positions 3 and 6 and to randomly flip a bit in the offspring. This mating function might not be the most effective, but it satisfies our needs. The swapping rules allow parents to pass hereditary information and the bit flip accounts for random mutation. The GA evolves as follows:

1. Start with a randomly generated population of solutions.
2. Apply the fitness function to each solution and select the most "fit."

---

[20] http://www.matasano.com/log/294/protocol-informatics/

**3.** Apply the mating function to the selected solutions.

**4.** The resulting offspring replace the original population and the process loops.

To see it in action, let's begin with a population of four randomly generated binary strings (solutions) and calculate each one's fitness:

```
0100100000        2
1000001010        3
1110100111        7
0000001000        1
```

The center pair (highlighted in bold) are calculated as the most "fit" and are therefore chosen to mate (lucky them). Swapping at position 3 generates one pair of offspring and swapping at position 6 generates another:

```
1000001010        3     100 + 0100111 -> 1000100111
1110100111        7     111 + 0001010 -> 1110001010

1000001010        3     100000 + 0111 -> 1000000111
1110100111        7     111010 + 1010 -> 1110101010
```

The generated offspring then go through a random mutation (highlighted in bold) and the fitness function is applied again:

```
1000100111   ->   1010100111        6
1110001010   ->   1110000010        4
1000000111   ->   1000001111        5
1110101010   ->   1110101110        7
```

We can see the success of the GA as the average fitness of the new population has increased. In this specific example, we used a static mutation rate. In a more advanced example, we might choose to automatically raise the rate of mutation if generated offspring are not evolving over some threshold of time. Note that genetic algorithms are considered stochastic global optimizers. In other words, there is a random component to the algorithm so outputs are constantly changing. However, although a GA will continue to find better solutions it might not ever find the best possible solution (a string of all 1s in our example), regardless of runtime.

Applying genetic algorithms to improve fuzz testing is a subject matter that was most recently researched by a team at the University of Central Florida (UCF) and presented at the BlackHat US 2006 USA security conference.[21] The UCF team demonstrated a proof of concept tool, named Sidewinder, capable of automatically crafting inputs to force a designated execution path. The GA solutions in this case are generated fuzz data that are represented as context-free grammars.[22] A nontraditional fuzzing approach was then decided on to define a fitness function. Instead of generating data and monitoring for faults, potentially vulnerable code locations such as insecure API calls (e.g., strcpy) are first statically located. This step in the process is similar to how Autodafé locates points of code to apply increased weight to markers as discussed in the previous chapter. Next, the control-flow graph (CFG; not to be confused with a context-free grammar) for the entire target binary is examined and the subgraphs between the socket data entry points (calls to recv) and potentially vulnerable code locations are extracted. Figure 22.5 depicts an example CFG containing both of these points. For a detailed definition and explanation of CFGs, refer to Chapter 23, "Fuzzer Tracking."

In the next step, the nodes on all paths connecting the entry point and the target vulnerable code must be identified. Figure 22.6 shows the same CFG with the nodes along the connecting path highlighted in black.

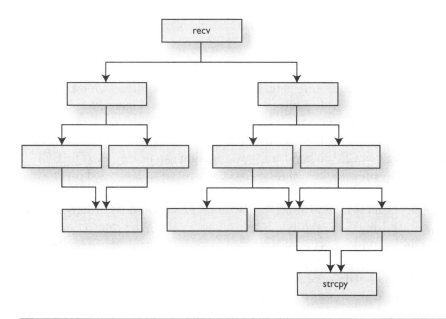

**Figure 22.5**    Control-flow graph containing potential vulnerability

[21] http://www.blackhat.com/html/bh-usa-06/bh-usa-06-speakers.html#Embleton

[22] http://en.wikipedia.org/wiki/Context-free_grammar

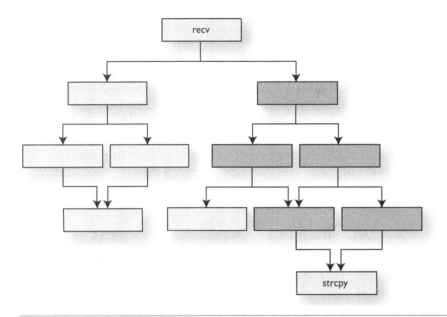

**Figure 22.6**  Control-flow graph with connecting path highlighted

Next, the exit nodes within the same CFG are identified. An exit node is defined as the border node just outside the connecting path. If an exit node is reached then execution has deviated from any of the possible paths to the vulnerable code. Figure 22.7 shows the same CFG as before, with nodes along the connecting path highlighted in black. Additionally, the exit nodes are highlighted in white.

With the final highlighted CFG in hand, a fitness function can be defined. The UCF team applied a Markov process to the resulting CFG to calculate fitness based on the probability of traversing certain paths. In application and simpler terms, the following steps take place. A debugger is used to attach to the target process and set breakpoints on the entry node, the target node, the exit nodes, and all nodes along the connecting path. These breakpoints are monitored as they are reached to evaluate the progress on the run-time execution path for a given input (solution). Execution is tracked until an exit node is reached. Inputs are generated by the fuzzer and fed to the target process. Inputs with the highest "fitness" values are chosen to reproduce and the process continues until the target node, designating a potential vulnerability, is successfully reached.

Sidewinder combines static analysis, graph theory, and debugger instrumented run-time analysis to essentially brute force an input that can reach arbitrary locations within the target process. Although a powerful concept, there are a number of current limitations that make this a far from perfect solution. First, not all CFG structures are suitable

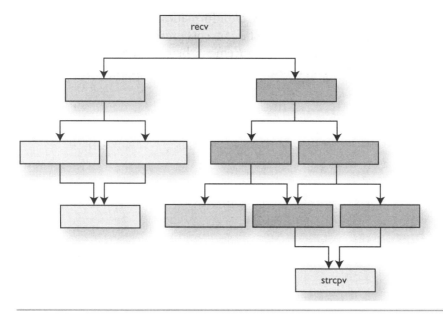

**Figure 22.7**   Control-flow graph with exit nodes highlighted

for genetic algorithms to learn from. Specifically, some dependency must exist between the graph structure and data parsing. Also, extraction of accurate CFGs through static analysis is not always possible. An inaccurately extracted CFG will more than likely cause the entire process to fail. Finally, this approach can take an inordinately long time to generate valid data for protocols that contain TLV style fields. When fuzzing a protocol with a calculated CRC value, for example, our sun will likely supernova before the GA produces any useful results.

All in all, this technique is interesting to study and certainly adds value in some cases. Perhaps the best usage of Sidewinder is to assist a fuzzer in mutating inputs to traverse a small subpath to increase code coverage when necessary, as opposed to discovering an input that can traverse the entire connecting path from entry to target.

## SUMMARY

This chapter began with the statement that the most difficult aspect to fuzzing is overcoming the barrier to entry involved with understanding and modeling the target protocol or file format. Three general methodologies to assist in both manual and automated dissection were presented. Heuristic techniques, bioinformatics, and GAs were each described and reviewed as possible solutions. The concepts presented in this chapter are at the cutting edge of fuzzing research with advancements being made on a daily basis. For more up-to-date information and resources, visit http://www.fuzzing.org.

# Fuzzer Tracking

*"Well, I think if you say you're going to do something and don't do it, that's trust-worthiness."*

—George W. Bush, in a CNN online chat, August 30, 2000

In previous chapters, we have defined fuzzing, exposed fuzzing targets, enumerated various fuzzing classes, and discussed various methods of data generation. However, we have yet to cover the matter of tracking the progress of our various fuzzer technologies. The notion of fuzzer tracking has not yet received a great deal of attention in the security community. To our knowledge, none of the currently available commercial or freely available fuzzers have addressed this topic.

In this chapter we define fuzzer tracking, also known as code coverage. We discuss its benefits, explore various implementation approaches, and, of course, in the spirit of the rest of this book, build a functional prototype that can be united with our previously developed fuzzers to provide a more powerful level of analysis.

## WHAT EXACTLY ARE WE TRACKING?

At the lowest programmatic level, the CPU is executing assembly instructions, or commands that the CPU understands. The available instruction set will differ depending on the underlying architecture of your target. The familiar IA-32 / x86 architecture for example, is a Complex Instruction Set Computer[1] (CISC) architecture that exposes more than 500 instructions, including, of course, the ability to perform basic mathematic operations and manipulate memory. Contrast this architecture with a Reduced Instruction Set Computer (RISC) microprocessor, such as SPARC, which exposes fewer than 200 instructions.[2]

## CISC VERSUS RISC

The term CISC is actually a retroactive definition used to differentiate the design from the RISC concept, which was developed in the late 1970s by researchers at IBM. The main philosophical differences between the designs are that RISC processors are arguably faster and cheaper to produce, whereas CISC processors call main memory less frequently and need fewer lines of code to accomplish the same task. The debate over which architecture is superior has recently reached new heights of obsession with the rise of fanatical Apple Mac users, whose precious deity, until recently, was available solely on the PowerPC RISC processor.

Interestingly, despite the vast availability of complex instructions on the x86 processor, about a dozen instructions are executed more then half the time on average.[3]

Whether you are working on CISC or RISC, the actual individual instructions are less often written by a human programmer but rather *compiled* or translated into this low-level language from a higher level language, such as C or C++. In general, the programs you interact with on a regular basis contain from tens of thousands to millions of instructions. Every interaction with the software causes instruction execution. The simple acts of clicking your mouse, processing of a network request, or opening a file all require numerous instructions to be executed.

If we are able to cause a Voice over IP (VoIP) software phone (softphone) to crash during a fuzz audit, how do we know which set of instructions was responsible for the fault? The typical approach taken by researchers today is to work backward, by examining logs

---

[1]   http://www.intel.com/intelpress/chapter-scientific.pdf

[2]   The exact *number* of instructions exposed by these architectures can be debated, but the general idea stands. CISC architectures implement many more instructions than their RISC counterparts.

[3]   http://www.openrce.org/blog/view/575

and attaching a debugger to pinpoint the location of the fault. An alternative approach is to work forward, by actively monitoring which instructions are executed in response to our generated fuzz requests. Some debuggers, such as OllyDbg, implement tracing functionality that allows users to track all executed instructions. Unfortunately, such tracing functionality is typically very resource intensive and not practical beyond very focused efforts. Following our example, when the VoIP softphone does crash, we can review the executed instructions to determine where along the process the fault occurred.

When writing software, one of the most basic forms of debugging it is to insert print statements throughout code. This way, as the program executes, the developer is made aware of where execution is taking place and the order in which the various logical blocks are executing. We essentially want to accomplish the same task but at a lower level where we don't have the ability to insert arbitrary print statements.

We define this process of monitoring and recording the exact instructions executed during the processing of various requests as "fuzzer tracking." A more generic term for this process with which you might already be familiar is *code coverage,* and this term will be used interchangeably throughout the chapter. Fuzzer tracking is a fairly simple process and as we will soon see, creates a number of opportunities for us to improve our fuzz analysis.

## BINARY VISUALIZATION AND BASIC BLOCKS

An essential concept with regard to our discussion on code coverage is the understanding of binary visualization, which will be utilized in the design and development of our prototype fuzzer tracker. Disassembled binaries can be visualized as graphs known as *call graphs.* This is accomplished by representing each function as a node and the calls between functions as edges between the nodes. This is a useful abstraction for viewing the structure of an overall binary as well as the relationships between the various functions. Consider the contrived example in Figure 23.1.

Most of the nodes in Figure 23.1 contain a label prefixed with sub_ followed by an eight- character hexadecimal number representing the address of the subroutine in memory. This naming convention is used by the DataRescue Interactive Disassembler Pro (IDA Pro)[4] disassembler for automatically generating names for functions without symbolic information. Other disassembling engines use similar naming schemes. When analyzing closed source binary applications, the lack of symbolic information results in the majority of functions being named in this form. Two of the nodes in Figure 23.1 do

---

[4] http://www.datarescue.com

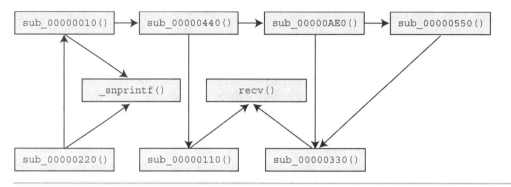

**Figure 23.1** Simple call graph

have symbolic names and were labeled appropriately, snprintf() and recv(). From a quick glance at this call graph, we can immediately determine that the unnamed subroutines sub_00000110() and sub_00000330(), are responsible for processing network data due to their relationship to recv().

## CFGs

Disassembled functions can also be visualized as graphs known as CFGs. This is accomplished by representing each basic block as a node and the branches between the basic blocks as edges between the nodes. This naturally leads to the question of what a basic block is? A basic block is defined as a sequence of instructions where each instruction within the block is guaranteed to be run, in order, once the first instruction of the basic block is reached. To elaborate further, a basic block typically starts at the following conditions:

- The start of a function
- The target of a branch instruction
- The instruction after a branch instruction

Basic blocks typically terminate at the following conditions:

- A branch instruction
- A return instruction

This is a simplified list of basic block start and stop points. A more complete list would take into consideration calls to functions that do not return and exception handling. However, for our purposes, this definition will do just fine.

## CFGs ILLUSTRATED

To drive the point home, consider the following excerpt of instructions from an imaginary subroutine sub_00000010. The [el] sequences in Figure 23.2 represent any number of arbitrary *nonbranching* instructions. This view of a disassembled function is also known as a *dead listing*, an example of which is shown in Figure 23.2.

```
00000010  sub_00000010
00000010  push ebp
00000011  mov ebp, esp
00000013  sub esp, 128h

00000025  jz 00000050
0000002B  mov eax, 0Ah
00000030  mov ebx, 0Ah

00000050  xor eax, eax
00000052  xor ebx, ebx

```

**Figure 23.2**   Disassembled dead listing of sub_00000010

Breaking the dead listing into basic blocks is a simple task following the previously outlined rules. The first basic block starts at the top of the function at 0x00000010 and ends with the first branch instruction at 0x00000025. The next instruction after the branch at 0x0000002B, as well as the target of the branch at 0x00000050, each mark the start of a new basic block. Once broken into its basic blocks, the CFG of the subroutine shown in Figure 23.2 looks like Figure 23.3.

This is a useful abstraction for viewing the various control-flow paths through a function as well as spotting logical loops. The key point to remember with CFGs is that each block of instructions is guaranteed to be executed together. In other words, if the first instruction in the block is executed, then all the instructions in that block will be executed. Later, we will see how this knowledge can help us take necessary shortcuts in the development of our fuzzer tracker.

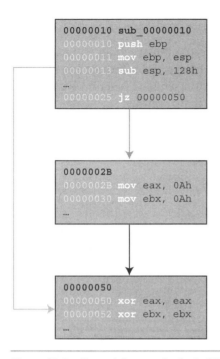

**Figure 23.3**   Control-flow graph of sub_00000010

## ARCHITECTING A FUZZER TRACKER

We can take a number of approaches to implementing a custom code coverage tool. If you have already read prior chapters, perhaps the first approach that comes to mind is to use a debugger with tracing functionality to monitor and log every instruction that is executed. This is the exact approach that OllyDbg utilizes to implement its "debug\trace into" and "debug\trace over" functionality. We could replicate this functionality by building on the same PyDbg library we utilized in Chapter 20, "In-Memory Fuzzing: Automation," with the following logic:

1. Attach to or load the target process we are fuzzing.
2. Register a single step handler and raise the single step flag.
3. Within the single step handler, log the current instruction address and reraise the single step flag.
4. Continue until process exit or crash.

This simplistic approach can be implemented on top of PyDbg in just under 50 lines of Python. However, it is not a favorable approach as instrumentation of each instruction within a process via a debugger adds a great deal of latency that, in many cases, makes the approach unusable. If you don't believe it, try it out for yourself with the relevant code listed in the sidebar, which is also available online at http://www.fuzzing.org. Furthermore, simply determining and logging executed instructions covers only a single aspect of our overall goal. To produce better reports we need more information about our target.

We implement our fuzzer tracker using a three-phase approach:

- First, we will statically profile our target.
- The second step is the actual live tracking and recording of which instructions within our target are executing in response to our fuzzer.
- The third and final step involves cross-referencing the generated live data with the profile data from Step 1 to produce a useful tracking report.

## PROFILING

Assuming we have the capability of determining which instructions were executed within any given application, what other bits of information would we like to know about that application to make more sense of the data set at hand? For example, we minimally would like to know the total number of instructions in our target. That way, we can determine what percentage of the underlying code within a target application is responsible for handling any given task. Ideally, we would like to have a more detailed breakdown of the instruction set:

- How many instructions are in our target?
- How many functions?
- How many basic blocks?
- Which instructions within our target pertain to standard support libraries?
- Which instructions within our target did our developers write?
- What lines of source does any individual instruction translate from?
- What instructions and data are reachable and can be influenced by network or file data?

Various tools and techniques can be utilized to answer these questions. Most development environments have the capability of producing symbolic debugger information that can assist us in more accurately addressing these questions as well. For our purposes, we assume that access to source code is not readily available.

To provide answers to these key questions, we build our profiler on top of IDA Pro's disassembler. We can easily glean statistics on instructions and functions from IDA. By implementing a simple algorithm based on the rules for basic blocks, we can easily extract a list of all the basic blocks contained within each function as well.

## TRACING

Because single stepping through a program can be time consuming and unnecessary, how else can we trace instruction coverage? Recall from our previous definition that a basic block is simply a sequence of instructions where each instruction within the block is guaranteed to be run, in order. If we can track the execution of basic blocks, then we are inherently tracking the execution of instructions. We can accomplish this task with the combination of a debugger and information gleaned from our profiling step. Utilizing the PyDbg library, we can implement this concept with the following logic:

1. Attach to or load the target process we are fuzzing.
2. Register a breakpoint handler.
3. Set a breakpoint at the start of each basic block.
4. Within the breakpoint handler, log the current instruction address and optionally restore the breakpoint.
5. Continue until process exit or crash.

By recording hits on basic blocks as opposed to individual instructions, we can greatly improve performance over traditional tracing functionality, such as the limited approach utilized by OllyDbg mentioned earlier. If we are only interested in which basic blocks are executed, then there is no need to restore breakpoints in Step 4. Once a basic block is hit, we will have recorded this fact within the handler and we are no longer interested in knowing if and when the basic block is ever reached again in the future. However, if we are also interested in the sequence in which basic blocks are executed, we must restore breakpoints in Step 4. If the same basic block is hit again and again, perhaps within a loop, then we will have recorded each iterative hit. Restoring breakpoints provides us with more contextual information. Letting breakpoints expire gives us a boost in speed. The decision to take one approach versus the other will likely depend on the task at hand and as such should be configurable as an option in our tool.

In situations where we are tracking a large number of basic blocks, the tracking speed might not be where we want it to be. In such situations, we can further abstract from the instruction level by tracking executed functions versus executed basic blocks. This requires minimal changes to our logic. Simply set breakpoints on the basic blocks that start a function instead of on all basic blocks. Again, the decision to take one approach versus the other might change from run to run and as such should be a configurable option in our tool.

## SIMPLISTIC PYDBG SINGLE-STEP CODE COVERAGE TOOL

For the curious reader, the following PyDbg script demonstrates the implementation of a single stepper. On initial attach and breakpoint the script places every existing thread into single-step mode. A handler is registered for the creation of new threads to place those in single-step mode as well.

The only "tricky" factor to developing the PyDbg single stepper is handling context switches into the kernel. On every single step the script checks if the current instruction is sysenter. This instruction is the gateway to the kernel used by modern Microsoft Windows operating systems. When the sysenter instruction is encountered, a breakpoint is set on the address that the kernel will return to and the thread is allowed to execute normally (i.e., not in single-step mode).

Once the thread comes back from the kernel, the single stepping is reengaged. The code for curious readers is shown next.

```
from pydbg import *
from pydbg.defines import *

# breakpoint handler.
def on_bp (dbg):
    ea    = dbg.exception_address
    disasm = dbg.disasm(ea)

    # put every thread in single step mode.
    if dbg.first_breakpoint:
        for tid in dbg.enumerate_threads():
            handle = dbg.open_thread(tid)
            dbg.single_step(True, handle)
            dbg.close_handle(handle)

    print "%08x: %s" % (ea, disasm)
    dbg.single_step(True)
```

```
    return DBG_CONTINUE

# single step handler.
def on_ss (dbg):
    ea     = dbg.exception_address
    disasm = dbg.disasm(ea)

    print "%08x: %s" % (ea, disasm)

    # we can't single step into kernel space
    # so set a breakpoint on the return and continue
    if disasm == "sysenter":
        ret_addr = dbg.get_arg(0)
        dbg.bp_set(ret_addr)
    else:
        dbg.single_step(True)

    return DBG_CONTINUE

# create thread handler.
def on_ct (dbg):
    # put newly created threads in single step mode.
    dbg.single_step(True)
    return DBG_CONTINUE

dbg = pydbg()
dbg.set_callback(EXCEPTION_BREAKPOINT,      on_bp)
dbg.set_callback(EXCEPTION_SINGLE_STEP,     on_ss)
dbg.set_callback(CREATE_THREAD_DEBUG_EVENT, on_ct)

try:
    dbg.attach(123)
    dbg.debug_event_loop()
except pdx, x:
    dbg.cleanup().detach()
    print x._str_()
```

Another convenient feature to implement in our fuzzer tracking tool is the ability to filter prerecorded code coverage from new recordings. This feature can be leveraged to easily filter out the functions, basic blocks, and instructions that are responsible for processing tasks in which we are not interested. An example of such uninteresting code is that which is responsible for processing GUI events (mouse clicks, menu selection, etc.).

We'll see how this can come into play later in a sidebar on code coverage for vulnerability discovery.

## CROSS-REFERENCING

In the third and final step, we combine the information from static profiling with the outputs from our runtime tracker to produce accurate and useful reports addressing points such as these:

- What areas of code are responsible for processing our inputs?
- What percentage of our target have we covered?
- What was the execution path that resulted in a particular fault?
- Which logical decisions within our target were not exercised?
- Which logical decisions within our target are dependent directly on supplied data?

The last two bullet points in this list pertain to making educated decisions on ways to improve our fuzzer, rather than pinpointing any specific flaw in that actual target application. We cover these points further later in the chapter when discussing the various benefits that fuzzer tracking can provide us.

### CODE COVERAGE FOR VULNERABILITY DISCOVERY

A remotely exploitable buffer overflow affecting Microsoft Outlook Express during the parsing of Network News Transfer Protocol (NNTP) responses[5] was published on June 14, 2005. Let's examine the benefits of code coverage analysis on this issue as it applies to a vulnerability researcher. The crux of the Microsoft advisory reads as follows:

*A remote code execution vulnerability exists in Outlook Express when it is used as a newsgroup reader. An attacker could exploit the vulnerability by constructing a malicious newsgroup server that could that potentially allow remote code execution if a user queried the server for news. An attacker who successfully exploited this vulnerability could take complete control of an affected system. However, user interaction is required to exploit this vulnerability.*

[5] http://www.microsoft.com/technet/security/bulletin/MS05-030.mspx

Not much information to go on there, and certainly not enough to be of any use to IDS or IPS signature developers, for example. All we know is that the bug manifests itself when connecting Outlook Express to a malicious NNTP server. Utilizing a previously available and open source code coverage tool, Process Stalker,[6] let's try and see if we can narrow down the issue some. The specific command-line options and usage of Process Stalker are outside the scope of this book. To see the specific details behind this example, please see the original OpenRCE article.[7]

By installing the available patch and monitoring which files within the Outlook Express installation directory were modified, we are able to determine that MSOE.DLL must contain the vulnerable code. Analyzing this module with the Process Stalker IDA Pro plug-in reveals a total of approximately 4,800 functions and 58,000 basic blocks. It would be quite a daunting task to manually sift through this data. To narrow our field of interest, we can utilize Process Stalker to locate the code paths associated with having Outlook Express connect to an arbitrary NNTP server. Although this is certainly effective in reducing the analysis space, we can do better. Recall from a previous statement that every interaction with our target in turn results in instruction execution. In the current situation, this means that when we access a malicious NNTP server through the 'news://' URI handler in Internet Explorer, for example, our code coverage tool will unnecessarily record the code responsible for starting Outlook Express, the code responsible for painting on-screen items such as windows and dialog boxes, and the code responsible for processing user-driven GUI events such as clicking buttons. For example, when connecting to an NNTP server for the first time, the dialog box shown in Figure 23.4 is presented.

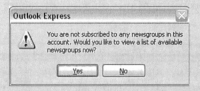

**Figure 23.4**  The Unfortunate Severity Decreasing Pre-Exploit dialog box

---

[6]  http://www.openrce.org/downloads/details/171/Process_Stalker

[7]  https://www.openrce.org/articles/full_view/12

The creation, handling, and tearing down of this dialog box are far from interesting for our purposes. To further narrow our analysis scope, we can use Process Stalker to record only the code responsible for handling various GUI tasks. We do this by attaching to and interacting with Outlook Express without actually connecting to an NNTP server. Next, we remove the overlapping coverage between our GUI-only and server-connect recordings to pinpoint specifically the code responsible for parsing the NNTP server request. When all is said and done, we are able to reduce our field of view to 91 functions. Of the 1,337 (we swear this number was not made up) basic blocks across those 91 functions, only 747 were actually visited in the server-connect recording. Compared with the 58,000 that we began with, this is a significant and helpful reduction!

Applying a simple script to locate the basic blocks responsible for moving server-supplied data around further reduces the number to a meager 26 basic blocks, the second of which reveals the exact specifics of the vulnerability: An arbitrary amount of server-supplied data, delimited by spaces, is copied into a static 16-byte stack buffer. Wonderful, we can now whip up the exploit . . . er . . . vulnerability protection filter and get back home in time for the latest episode of *The Sopranos*.[8]

## DISSECTING A CODE COVERAGE TOOL

The PyDbg library, which we previously worked with, is in fact a subcomponent of a larger reverse engineering framework, named PaiMei. PaiMei is an actively developed, open source Python reverse engineering framework freely available for download.[9] PaiMei can essentially be thought of as a reverse engineer's Swiss army knife and can be of assistance in various advanced fuzzing tasks, such as intelligent exception detection and processing, a topic we cover in depth in Chapter 24, "Intelligent Fault Detection." There already exists a code coverage tool bundled with the framework named PAIMEIpstalker (also called Process Stalker or PStalker). Although the tool might not produce the exact reports you want out of the box, as the framework and bundled applications are open source they can be modified to meet whatever your specific needs are for a given project. The framework breaks down into the following core components:

- *PyDbg*. A pure Python win32 debugging abstraction class.

---

[8]  http://www.hbo.com/sopranos/

[9]  http://openrce.org/downloads/details/208/PaiMei

- *pGRAPH.* A graph abstraction layer with separate classes for nodes, edges, and clusters.
- *PIDA.* Built on top of pGRAPH, PIDA aims to provide an abstract and persistent interface over binaries (DLLs and EXEs) with separate classes for representing functions, basic blocks, and instructions. The end result is the creation of a portable file, that, when loaded, allows you to arbitrarily navigate throughout the entire original binary.

We are already familiar with the interface to PyDbg from earlier. Scripting on top of PIDA is even simpler. The PIDA interface allows us to navigate a binary as a graph of graphs, enumerating nodes as function or basic blocks and the edges between them. Consider the following example:

```
import pida

module = pida.load("target.exe.pida")

# step through each function in the module.
for func module.functions.values():
    print "%08x - %s" % (func.ea_start, func.name)

    # step through each basic block in the function.
    for bb in func.basic_blocks.values():
        print "\t%08x" % bb.ea_start

        # step through each instruction in the
        # basic block.
        for ins in bb.instructions.values():
            print "\t\t%08x %s" % (ins.ea, ins.disasm)
```

We begin in this snippet by loading a previously analyzed and saved PIDA file as a module in the script. Next we step through each function in the module, printing the starting address and symbolic name along the way. We next step through each basic block contained within the current function. For each basic block, we continue further by stepping through the contained instructions and printing the instruction address and disassembly along the way. Based on our previous outline, it might already be obvious to you how we can combine PyDbg and PIDA to easily prototype a basic block-level code coverage tool. A layer above the core components, you will find the remainder of the PaiMei framework broken into the following overarching components:

- *Utilities.* A set of utilities for accomplishing various repetitive tasks. There is a specific utility class we are interested in, `process_stalker.py`, which was written to provide an abstracted interface to code coverage functionality.

- *Console.* A pluggable WxPython application for quickly and efficiently creating custom GUI interfaces to newly created tools. This is how we interface with the pstalker code coverage module.

- *Scripts.* Individual scripts for accomplishing various tasks, one very important example of which is the pida_dump.py IDA Python script, which is run from IDA Pro to generate .PIDA files.

The pstalker code coverage tool is interfaced through the aforementioned WxPython GUI and as we will soon see, relies on a number of the components exposed by the PaiMei framework. After exploring the various subcomponents of this code coverage tool, we examine its usage by way of a case study.

## PSTALKER LAYOUT OVERVIEW

The PStalker module is one of many modules available for use under the PaiMei graphical console. In the PStalker initial screen displayed in Figure 23.5, you can see that the interface is broken into three distinct columns.

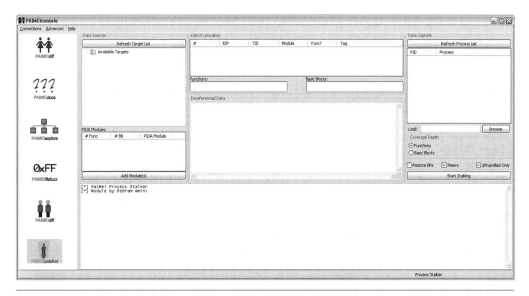

**Figure 23.5**   PaiMei PStalker module

The Data Sources column exposes the functionality necessary for creating and managing the targets to be stalked as well as loading the appropriate PIDA modules. The Data Exploration column is where the results of any individual code coverage run or stalk. Finally, the Data Capture column is where runtime configuration options and the target executable are specified. The general workflow associated with this tool is as follows (read on for specifics):

- Create a new target, tag, or both. Targets can contain multiple tags and each individual tag contains its own saved code coverage data.
- Select a tag for stalking.
- Load PIDA modules for every .DLL and the .EXE code for which coverage information is required.
- Launch the target process.
- Refresh the process list under the data capture panel and select the target process for attaching or browse to the target process for loading.
- Configure the code coverage options and attach to the selected target.
- Interact with the target while code coverage is being recorded.
- When appropriate, detach from the target and wait for PStalker to export captured items to the database.
- Load the recorded hits to begin exploring recorded data.

The online documentation[10] for PaiMei includes a full-length video demonstrating the use of the PStalker module. If you haven't ever seen it before, now is a good time to check it out prior to continuing.

## DATA SOURCES

Once consolewide MySQL connectivity is established through the Connections menu, select the Retrieve Target List button to propagate the data source explorer tree. This list will be empty the first time the application is run. New targets can be created from the context menu of the root node labeled Available Targets. Use the context menu for individual targets to delete the individual target, add a tag under the target, and load the hits from all tags under the target into the data exploration pane. The context menu for individual tags exposes a number of features:

---

[10] http://pedram.openrce.org/PaiMei/docs/PAIMEIpstalker_flash_demo/

- *Load hits.* Clear the data exploration pane and load the hits associated with the selected tag.

- *Append hits.* Append the hits associated with the selected tag after any existing data currently in the exploration pane.

- *Export to IDA.* Export the hits under the selected tag as an IDC script suitable for import in IDA to highlight the hit functions and blocks.

- *Sync with uDraw.* Synchronize the data exploration pane on the consolewide uDraw connection. Dual monitors are very helpful for this feature.

- *Use for stalking.* Store all recorded hits during data capture phase to the selected tag. A tag must be selected for stalking prior to attaching to a process.

- *Filter tag.* Do not record hits for any of the nodes or basic blocks under the selected tag in future stalks. More than one tag can be marked for filtering.

- *Clear tag.* Keep the tag but remove all the hits stored under the tag. PStalker cannot stalk into a tag with any preexisting data. To overwrite the contents of a tag it must be cleared first.

- *Expand tag.* For each hit function in the tag, generate and add an entry for every contained basic block, even if that basic block was not explicitly hit.

- *Target/tag properties.* Modify the tag name, view or edit tag notes, or modify the target name.

- *Delete tag.* Remove the tag and all the hits stored under the tag.

The PIDA modules list control displays the list of loaded PIDA modules as well their individual function and basic block counts. Prior to attaching to the target process, at least one PIDA module must be loaded. During the code coverage phase, the PIDA module is referenced for setting breakpoints on functions or basic blocks. A PIDA module can be removed from the list through a context menu.

## Data Exploration

The data exploration pane is broken into three sections. The first section is propagated when hits are loaded or appended from the Data Sources column. Each hit is displayed in a scrollable list box. Selecting one of the line items displays, if available, the context data associated with that hit in the Dereferenced Data text control. In between the list and text controls, there are two progress bars that represent the total code coverage based on the number of individually hit basic blocks and functions listed in the exploration pane against the number of total basic blocks and functions across all loaded PIDA modules.

## DATA CAPTURE

Once a tag has been selected for stalking, the selected filters have been applied, and the target PIDA modules have loaded, the next step is to actually attach to and stalk the target process.

Click the Retrieve List button to display an up-to-date process list, with newer processes listed at the bottom. Select the target process for attaching or browse to the target process for loading and select the desired coverage depth. Select Functions to monitor and track which functions are executed within the target process or select Basic Blocks to further scrutinize the individual basic blocks executed.

The Restore BPs check box controls whether or not to restore breakpoints after they have been hit. To determine what code was executed within the target, leave the option disabled. Alternatively, to determine both what was executed and the order in which it was executed, this option should be enabled.

The Heavy check box controls whether or not PStalker will save context data at each recorded hit. Disable this option for increased speed. Clear the Unhandled Only check box to receive notification of debug exception events even if the debuggee is capable of correctly handling them.

Finally, with all options set and the target process selected, click the Attach and Start Tracking button to begin code coverage. Watch the log window for runtime information.

## LIMITATIONS

There is one main limitation to this tool of which you should be aware. Specifically, the tool is reliant on the static analysis of the target binaries as provided by DataRescue's IDA Pro; therefore, the tool will fail when IDA Pro makes mistakes. For example, if data is misrepresented as code, bad things can happen when PStalker sets breakpoints on that data. This is the most common reason for failure. Disabling the Make final pass analysis kernel option in IDA Pro prior to the autoanalysis will disable the aggressive logic that makes these types of errors. However, the overall analysis will also suffer. Furthermore, packed or self-modifying code cannot currently be traced.

## DATA STORAGE

The typical user will not likely need to know how data is organized and stored behind the scenes of the PStalker code coverage tool. Such users can take advantage of the abstraction provided by the tool and utilize it as is. More detailed knowledge of the database schema will, however, be required in the event that the need to build custom extensions or reporting arises. As such, this section is dedicated to dissecting the behind-the-scenes data storage mechanism.

All of the target and code coverage data is stored in a MySQL database server. The information is stored across three tables: cc_hits, cc_tags, and cc_targets. As shown in the following SQL table structure, the cc_targets database contains a simple list of target names, an automatically generated unique numeric identifier, and a text field for storing any pertinent notes related to the target:

```
CREATE TABLE 'paimei'.'cc_targets' (
  'id' int(10) unsigned NOT NULL auto_increment,
  'target' varchar(255) NOT NULL default '',
  'notes' text NOT NULL,
  PRIMARY KEY ('id')
) ENGINE=MyISAM;
```

The next SQL table structure is of the cc_tags database, which contains an automatically generated unique numeric identifier, the identifier of the target the tag is associated with, the name of the tag, and once again a text field for storing any pertinent notes regarding the tag.

```
CREATE TABLE 'paimei'.'cc_tags' (
  'id' int(10) unsigned NOT NULL auto_increment,
  'target_id' int(10) unsigned NOT NULL default '0',
  'tag' varchar(255) NOT NULL default '',
  'notes' text NOT NULL,
  PRIMARY KEY ('id')
) ENGINE=MyISAM;
```

Finally, as shown in the following SQL table structure, the cc_hits database contains the bulk of the recorded runtime code coverage information:

```
CREATE TABLE 'paimei'.'cc_hits' (
  'target_id' int(10) unsigned NOT NULL default '0',
  'tag_id' int(10) unsigned NOT NULL default '0',
  'num' int(10) unsigned NOT NULL default '0',
  'timestamp' int(10) unsigned NOT NULL default '0',
  'eip' int(10) unsigned NOT NULL default '0',
  'tid' int(10) unsigned NOT NULL default '0',
  'eax' int(10) unsigned NOT NULL default '0',
  'ebx' int(10) unsigned NOT NULL default '0',
  'ecx' int(10) unsigned NOT NULL default '0',
  'edx' int(10) unsigned NOT NULL default '0',
  'edi' int(10) unsigned NOT NULL default '0',
  'esi' int(10) unsigned NOT NULL default '0',
```

```
'ebp' int(10) unsigned NOT NULL default '0',
'esp' int(10) unsigned NOT NULL default '0',
'esp_4' int(10) unsigned NOT NULL default '0',
'esp_8' int(10) unsigned NOT NULL default '0',
'esp_c' int(10) unsigned NOT NULL default '0',
'esp_10' int(10) unsigned NOT NULL default '0',
'eax_deref' text NOT NULL,
'ebx_deref' text NOT NULL,
'ecx_deref' text NOT NULL,
'edx_deref' text NOT NULL,
'edi_deref' text NOT NULL,
'esi_deref' text NOT NULL,
'ebp_deref' text NOT NULL,
'esp_deref' text NOT NULL,
'esp_4_deref' text NOT NULL,
'esp_8_deref' text NOT NULL,
'esp_c_deref' text NOT NULL,
'esp_10_deref' text NOT NULL,
'is_function' int(1) unsigned NOT NULL default '0',
'module' varchar(255) NOT NULL default '',
'base' int(10) unsigned NOT NULL default '0',
PRIMARY KEY  ('target_id','tag_id','num'),
KEY 'tag_id' ('tag_id'),
KEY 'target_id' ('target_id')
) ENGINE=MyISAM;
```

The fields from the cc_hits table break down as follows:

- *target_id & tag_id*. These two fields tie any individual row within this table to a specific target and tag combination.
- *num*. This field holds the numeric order in which the code block represented by the individual row was executed within the specified target–tag combination.
- *timestamp*. This stores the number of seconds since the UNIX Epoch (January 1 1970, 00:00:00 GMT), a format easily converted to other representations.
- *eip*. This field stores the *absolute* address of the executed code block that the individual row represents; this field is commonly formatted as a hexadecimal number.
- *tid*. This field stores the identifier of the thread responsible for executing the block of code at *eip*. The thread identifier is assigned by the Windows OS and is stored to differentiate between the code blocks executed by various threads in a multithreaded application.
- *eax, ebx, ecx, edx, edi, esi, ebp,* and *esp*. These fields contain the numeric values for each of the eight general-purpose registers at the time of execution. For each of the

general-purpose registers and stored stack offsets a *deref* field exists, containing the ASCII data behind the specific register as a pointer. At the end of the ASCII data string is a tag, which is one of *(stack)*, *(heap)* or *(global)*, representing where the dereferenced data was found. The moniker *N/A* is used in cases where dereferencing is not possible as the relevant register did not contain a dereferenceable address.

- *esp_4*, *esp_8*, *esp_c*, and *esp_10*: These fields contain the numeric values at their relevant stack offsets (esp_4 = [esp+4], esp_8 = [esp+8], etc.).
- *is_function*. This is a boolean field where a value of 1 denotes that the hit data block (at *eip*) is the start of a function.
- *module*. This field stores the name of the module in which the hit occurred.
- *base*. This field contains the numerical base address of the module specified in the previous field. This information can be used in conjunction with *eip* to calculate the offset within the module that the hit data block occurred at.

The open data storage provides advanced users with an outlet for generating custom and more advanced reports beyond what the PStalker tool provides by default. Let's put the tracker to the test with a full-fledged case study.

## CASE STUDY

For a practical case study, we will apply the PStalker code coverage tool to determine the relative completeness of a fuzz audit. Our target software is the Gizmo Project,[11] a VoIP, instant messaging (IM), and telephony communication suite. Figure 23.6 is a commented screen shot from the Gizmo Project Web site detailing the major features of the tool.

Gizmo implements an impressive number of features that are among the reasons for its soaring popularity. Seen by many as a possible Skype[12] "killer," Gizmo differentiates itself from the ubiquitous Skype by building on open VoIP standards such as the Session Initiation Protocol (SIP - RFC 3261), as opposed to implementing a closed proprietary system. This decision allows Gizmo to interoperate with other SIP compatible solutions. This decision also allows us to test Gizmo with standard VoIP security testing tools. Now that the crosshairs are set on the target software, we must next pick the target protocol and select an appropriate fuzzer.

---

[11] http://www.gizmoproject.com/

[12] http://www.skype.com/

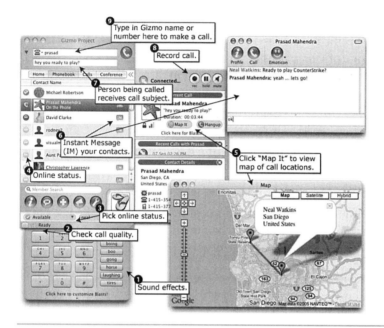

**Figure 23.6**    Gizmo Project feature list

## STRATEGY

We will be testing Gizmo's ability to handle malformed SIP packets. Although there are a few VoIP protocols we could target, SIP is a good choice as most VoIP telephony begins with a signaling negotiation through this protocol. There are also already a few free SIP fuzzers available. For our test, we will be using a freely available SIP fuzzer distributed by the University of Oulu Department of Electrical and Information Engineering named PROTOS Test-Suite: c07-sip.[13] The PROTOS test suite contains 4,527 individual test cases distributed in a single Java JAR file. Although the test suite is limited to testing only INVITE messages, it is perfectly suitable for our needs. A partial motivation for choosing this fuzzer is that the team responsible for its development has spun off a commercial version through the company Codenomicon.[14] The commercial version of the SIP test suite explores the SIP protocol in greater depth and bundles 31,971 individual test cases.

Our goal is as follows: Utilize PStalker while running through the complete set of PROTOS test cases to measure the exercised code coverage. This case study can be

---

[13] http://www.ee.oulu.fi/research/ouspg/protos/testing/c07/sip/

[14] http://www.codenomicon.com/

expanded on to accomplish practical tasks such as comparing fuzzing solutions or determining the confidence of a given audit. The individual benefits of utilizing code coverage as a metric are further discussed later in the chapter.

The PROTOS test suite runs from the command line and exposes nearly 20 options for tweaking its runtime behavior, shown here from the output of the help switch:

```
$ java -jar c07-sip-r2.jar -h

Usage java -jar <jarfile>.jar [ [OPTIONS] | -touri <SIP-URI> ]
  -touri  <addr>        Recipient of the request
                        Example: <addr> : you@there.com
  -fromuri <addr>       Initiator of the request
                        Default: user@pamini.unity.local
  -sendto <domain>      Send packets to <domain> instead of
                        domainname of -touri
  -callid <callid>      Call id to start test-case call ids from
                        Default: 0
  -dport <port>         Portnumber to send packets on host.
                        Default: 5060
  -lport <port>         Local portnumber to send packets from
                        Default: 5060
  -delay <ms>           Time to wait before sending new test-case
                        Defaults to 100 ms (milliseconds)
  -replywait <ms>       Maximum time to wait for host to reply
                        Defaults to 100 ms (milliseconds)
  -file <file>          Send file <file> instead of test-case(s)
  -help                 Display this help
  -jarfile <file>       Get data from an alternate bugcat
                        JAR-file <file>
  -showreply            Show received packets
  -showsent             Show sent packets
  -teardown             Send CANCEL/ACK
  -single <index>       Inject a single test-case <index>
  -start <index>        Inject test-cases starting from <index>
  -stop <index>         Stop test-case injection to <index>
  -maxpdusize <int>     Maximum PDU size
                        Default to 65507 bytes
  -validcase            Send valid case (case #0) after each
                        test-case and wait for a response. May
                        be used to check if the target is still
                        responding. Default: off
```

Your mileage might vary, but we found the following options to work best (where the touri option is the only mandatory one):

```
java -jar c07-sip-r2.jar -touri 17476624642@10.20.30.40 \
                        -teardown                       \
                        -sendto 10.20.30.40             \
                        -dport 64064                    \
                        -delay 2000                     \
                        -validcase
```

The delay option of two seconds gives Gizmo some time to free resources, update its GUI, and otherwise recover between test cases. The validcase parameter specifies that PROTOS should ensure that a valid communication is capable of transpiring after each test case, prior to continuing. This rudimentary technique allows the fuzzer to detect when something has gone awry with the target and cease testing. In our situation this is an important factor because Gizmo does actually crash! Fortunately for Gizmo, the vulnerability is triggered due to a null-pointer dereference and is therefore not exploitable. Nonetheless, the issue exists (Hint: It occurs within the first 250 test cases). Download the test suite and find out for yourself.

### Gizmo Context Dump at Time of Crash

```
[*] 0x004fd5d6 mov eax,[esi+0x38] from thread 196 caused access violation when
attempting to read from 0x00000038

CONTEXT DUMP
  EIP: 004fd5d6 mov eax,[esi+0x38]
  EAX: 0419fdfc (  68812284) -> <CCallMgr::IgnoreCall() (stack)
  EBX: 006ca788 (   7120776) -> e(ell111111111111111111111 (PGP1sp.dll.data)
  ECX: 00000000 (         0) -> N/A
  EDX: 00be0003 (  12451843) -> N/A
  EDI: 00000000 (         0) -> N/A
  ESI: 00000000 (         0) -> N/A
  EBP: 00000000 (         0) -> N/A
  ESP: 0419fdd8 (  68812248) -> NR (stack)
  +00: 861c524e (2250003022) -> N/A
  +04: 0065d7fa (   6674426) -> N/A
  +08: 00000001 (         1) -> N/A
  +0c: 0419fe4c (  68812364) -> xN (stack)
  +10: 0419ff9c (  68812700) -> raOo|hoho||@hoO@*@bOzp (stack)
  +14: 0061cb99 (   6409113) -> N/A

disasm around:
        0x004fd5c7 xor eax,esp
        0x004fd5c9 push eax
```

```
0x004fd5ca lea eax,[esp+0x24]
0x004fd5ce mov fs:[0x0],eax
0x004fd5d4 mov esi,ecx
0x004fd5d6 mov eax,[esi+0x38]
0x004fd5d9 push eax
0x004fd5da lea eax,[esp+0xc]
0x004fd5de push eax
0x004fd5df call 0x52cc60
0x004fd5e4 add esp,0x8
```

```
SEH unwind:
        0419ff9c -> 006171e8: mov edx,[esp+0x8]
        0419ffdc -> 006172d7: mov edx,[esp+0x8]
        ffffffff -> 7c839aa8: push ebp
```

The `touri` and `dport` parameters were gleaned through examination of packets traveling to or from port 5060 (the standard SIP port) during Gizmo startup. Figure 23.7 shows the relevant excerpt with the interesting values highlighted.

The number 17476624642 is the actual phone number assigned to our Gizmo account and the port 64064 appears to be the standard Gizmo client-side SIP port. Our strategy is in place. The target software, protocol, and fuzzer have been chosen and the options for the fuzzer have been decided on. Now, it's time to move to the tactical portion of the case study.

**Figure 23.7**   Gizmo startup SIP packet capture decoded

## TACTICS

We are fuzzing SIP and are therefore interested specifically in the SIP processing code. Luckily for us, the code is easily isolated, as the library name SIPPhoneAPI.dll immediately stands out as our target. First things first: Load the library into IDA Pro and run the pida_dump.py script to generate SIPPhoneAPI.pida. Because we are only interested in monitoring code coverage, specifying "basic blocks" as the analysis depth for the pida_dump.py script will result in a performance improvement. Next, let's fire up PaiMei and walk through the necessary prerequisites to get the code coverage operational. For more information regarding specific usage of PaiMei, refer to the online documentation.[15] The first step as depicted in Figure 23.8 is to create a target that we name "Gizmo" and add a tag named "Idle." We'll use the "Idle" tag to record the code coverage within Gizmo at "stand still." This is not a necessary step, but as you can specify multiple tags for recording and furthermore select individual tags for filtering, it never hurts to be as granular as possible. The "Idle" tag must then be selected for "Stalking" as shown in Figure 23.9 and the SIPPhoneAPI PIDA file must be loaded as shown in Figure 23.10.

Once the data sources are set up and a tag is selected, we next select the target process and capture options and begin recording code coverage. Figure 23.11 shows the configured options we will be using. The Refresh Process List button retrieves a list of currently running processes. For our example we choose to attach to a running instance of Gizmo as opposed to loading a new instance from startup.

**Figure 23.8**    PaiMei PStalker target and tag creation

---

[15] http://pedram.openrce.org/PaiMei/docs/

**Figure 23.9**  Selecting "Idle" tag for stalking

| # Func | # BB | PIDA Module |
|--------|--------|----------------|
| 22345 | 105174 | sipphoneapi.dll |

Add Module(s)

**Figure 23.10**  SIPPhoneAPI PIDA module loaded

Under Coverage Depth, we select Basic Blocks to get the most granular level of code coverage. As you saw previously from Figure 23.10, our target library has just under 25,000 functions and more than four times that many basic blocks. Therefore, if speed is a concern for us, we can sacrifice granularity for improved performance by alternatively selecting Functions for the coverage depth.

The Restore BPs check box flags whether or not basic blocks should be tracked beyond their first hit. We are only interested where execution has taken us so we can leave this disabled and improve performance.

Finally, we clear the Heavy check box. This check box flags whether or not the code coverage tool should perform runtime context inspection at each breakpoint and save the discovered contents. Again, as we are only interested in code coverage, the additional data is unnecessary so we avoid the performance hit of needlessly capturing it.

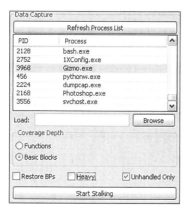

**Figure 23.11**    Code coverage capture options

Once we click "Start Stalking," the code coverage tool attaches to Gizmo and begins monitoring execution. If you are interested in the specific details of how the process ensues behind the scenes, refer to the PaiMei documentation. Once activated, log messages indicating the actions and progress of PStalker are written to the log pane. The following example excerpt demonstrates a successful start:

```
[*] Stalking module sipphoneapi.dll
[*] Loading 0x7c900000 \WINDOWS\system32\ntdll.dll
[*] Loading 0x7c800000 \WINDOWS\system32\kernel32.dll
[*] Loading 0x76b40000 \WINDOWS\system32\winmm.dll
[*] Loading 0x77d40000 \WINDOWS\system32\user32.dll
[*] Loading 0x77f10000 \WINDOWS\system32\gdi32.dll
[*] Loading 0x77dd0000 \WINDOWS\system32\advapi32.dll
[*] Loading 0x77e70000 \WINDOWS\system32\rpcrt4.dll
[*] Loading 0x76d60000 \WINDOWS\system32\iphlpapi.dll
[*] Loading 0x77c10000 \WINDOWS\system32\msvcrt.dll
[*] Loading 0x71ab0000 \WINDOWS\system32\ws2_32.dll
[*] Loading 0x71aa0000 \WINDOWS\system32\ws2help.dll
[*] Loading 0x10000000 \Internet\Gizmo Project\SipphoneAPI.dll
[*] Setting 105174 breakpoints on basic blocks in SipphoneAPI.dll
[*] Loading 0x16000000 \Internet\Gizmo Project\dnssd.dll
[*] Loading 0x006f0000 \Internet\Gizmo Project\libeay32.dll
[*] Loading 0x71ad0000 \WINDOWS\system32\wsock32.dll
[*] Loading 0x7c340000 \Internet\Gizmo Project\MSVCR71.DLL
[*] Loading 0x00340000 \Internet\Gizmo Project\ssleay32.dll
[*] Loading 0x774e0000 \WINDOWS\system32\ole32.dll
[*] Loading 0x77120000 \WINDOWS\system32\oleaut32.dll
[*] Loading 0x00370000 \Internet\Gizmo Project\IdleHook.dll
```

```
[*] Loading 0x61410000 \WINDOWS\system32\urlmon.dll
...
[*] debugger hit 10221d31 cc #1
[*] debugger hit 10221d4b cc #2
[*] debugger hit 10221d67 cc #3
[*] debugger hit 10221e20 cc #4
[*] debugger hit 10221e58 cc #5
[*] debugger hit 10221e5c cc #6
[*] debugger hit 10221e6a cc #7
[*] debugger hit 10221e6e cc #8
[*] debugger hit 10221e7e cc #9
[*] debugger hit 10221ea4 cc #10
[*] debugger hit 1028c2d0 cc #11
[*] debugger hit 1028c30d cc #12
[*] debugger hit 1028c369 cc #13
[*] debugger hit 1028c37b cc #14
...
```

We can now activate the fuzzer and track the code executed during idle time. To continue, we wait for the list of hit breakpoints to taper off indicating that the code within the SIP library that executes while Gizmo sits idly has been exhausted. Next we create a new tag and select it as the active tag through the right-click menu by choosing Use for Stalking. Finally, we right-click the previously created "Idle" tag and choose Filter Tag. This effectively ignores all basic blocks that were executed during the idle state. Now we can start the fuzzer and watch it run. Figure 23.12 shows the code coverage observed in response to all 4,527 PROTOS test cases.

In conclusion, the PROTOS test suite was able to reach only roughly 6 percent of the functions and 9 percent of the basic blocks within the SIPPhoneAPI library. That's not bad for a free test suite, but it illustrates why running a single test suite is not the equivalent of a comprehensive audit. After running the test suite we have failed to test the majority of the code and it's unlikely that we've comprehensively tested functionality within the code that we did hit. These coverage results can, however, be improved by

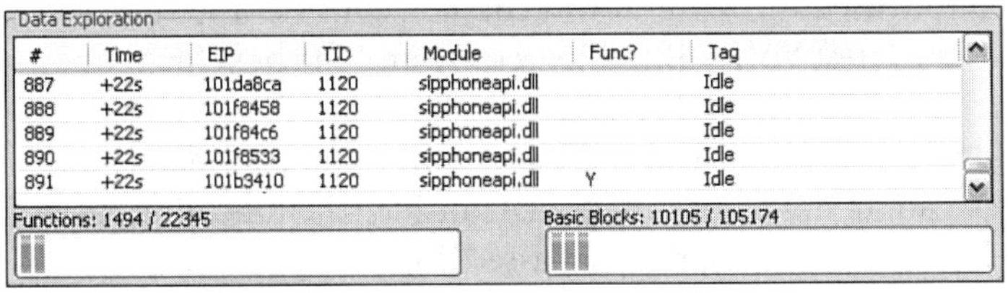

**Figure 23.12**  Code coverage results

adding a process restart mechanism in between short intervals of test cases. The reasoning behind this is that even though Gizmo successfully responds to the valid test cases, we instructed PROTOS to insert between malformed tests, Gizmo still ceases to operate correctly after some time and the code coverage suffers. Restarting the process resets internal state and restores full functionality, allowing us to more accurately and thoroughly examine the target.

Considering that PROTOS contains only 1/7 of the test cases of its commercial sister, can we expect seven times more code coverage from the commercial version? Probably not. Although increased code coverage is expected, there is no consistent or predictable ratio between the number of test cases and the resulting amount of code exercised. Only empirical results can be accurate.

So what do we gain from tracking fuzzers in this manner and how can we improve on the technique? The next section provides us with some answers to these questions.

## BENEFITS AND FUTURE IMPROVEMENTS

Traditionally, fuzzing has not been conducted in a very scientific manner. Frequently, security researchers and QA engineers hack together rudimentary scripts for generating malformed data, allow their creation to execute for an arbitrary period of time, and call it quits. With the recent rise in commercial fuzzing solutions, you will find shops that take fuzzing one step further toward scientific testing by utilizing an exhaustive list of the test cases developed by a commercial vendor such as Codenomicon. For security researchers simply looking for vulnerabilities to report or sell, there's often no need to take the process any further. Given the present state of software security, the current methodologies are sufficient for generating an endless laundry list of bugs and vulnerabilities. However, with increasing maturity and awareness of both secure development and testing, the need for a more scientific approach will be desired. Software developers and QA teams concerned with finding all vulnerabilities, not just the low-hanging fruit, will be more concerned with taking a more scientific approach to fuzzing. Fuzzer tracking is a necessary step in this direction.

Keeping with the same example used throughout this chapter, consider the various parties involved in developing the latest VoIP softphone release and the benefits they might realize from fuzzer tracking. For the product manager, knowing the specific areas of tested code allows him to determine more accurately and with more confidence the level of testing to which their product has been subjected. Consider the following statement, for example: "Our latest VoIP softphone release passed 45,000 malicious test cases." No proof is provided to validate this claim. Perhaps of the 45,000 malicious cases, only 5,000 of them covered features exposed by the target softphone. It is also possible that the entire test set exercised only 10 percent of the available features exposed by the target softphone. Who knows, maybe the test cases were written by really brilliant engineers and covered the entire code base. The latter case would be wonderful, but again, without code coverage analysis there is no way to determine the validity of the original claim. Coupling a fuzzer tracker with the same test set might lead to the following, more informative statement: "Our latest VoIP softphone release passed 45,000 malicious test cases, exhaustively testing over 90 percent of our code base."

For the QA engineer, determining which areas of the softphone were not tested allows him to create more intelligent test cases for the next round of fuzzing. For example, during fuzzer tracking against the softphone the engineer might have noticed that the test cases generated by the fuzzer consistently trigger a routine named parse_sip(). Drilling down into that routine he observes that although the function itself is executed multiple times, not all branches within the function are covered. The fuzzer is not exhausting the logical possibilities within the parsing routine. To improve testing the engineer should examine the uncovered branches to determine what changes can be made to the fuzzer data generation routines to exercise these missed branches.

For the developer, knowing the specific instruction set and path that was executed prior to any discovered fault allows him to quickly and confidently locate and fix the affected area of code. Currently, communications between QA engineers and developers might transpire at a higher level, resulting in both parties wasting time by conducting overlapping research. Instead of receiving a high-level report from QA listing a series of test cases that trigger various faults, developers can receive a report detailing the possible fault locations alongside the test cases.

Keep in mind that code coverage as a stand-alone metric does not imply thorough testing. Consider that a string copy operation within an executable is reached, but only tested with small string lengths. The code might be vulnerable to a buffer overflow that our testing tool did not uncover because an insufficiently long or improperly formatted string was passed through it. Determining what we've tested is half the battle; ideally we would also provide metrics for how well what was reached was tested.

## FUTURE IMPROVEMENTS

One convenient feature to consider is the addition of the ability for the code coverage tool to communicate with the fuzzer. Before and after transmitting each individual test case, the fuzzer can notify the code coverage tool of the transaction, thereby associating and recording the code coverage associated with each individual test case. An alternative approach to implementation would be through postprocessing, by aligning timestamps associated with data transmissions and timestamps associated with code coverage. This is generally less effective due to latency and imperfectly synchronized clocks, but also easier to implement. In either case, the end result allows an analyst to drill down into the specific blocks of code that were executed in response to an individual test case.

The current requirement to enumerate the locations of all basic blocks and functions within the target is a painstaking and error-prone process. One solution to this problem is to enumerate basic blocks at runtime. According to the Intel IA-32 architecture software developer's manual[16] volume 3B[17] section 18.5.2, the Pentium 4 and Xeon processors have hardware-level support for "single-step on branches":

### BTF (single-step on branches) flag (bit 1)

When set, the processor treats the TF flag in the EFLAGS register as a "single-step on branches" flag rather than a "single-step on instructions" flag. This mechanism allows single-stepping the processor on taken branches, interrupts, and exceptions. See Section 18.5.5, "Single-Stepping on Branches, Exception and Interrupts."

Taking advantage of this feature allows for the development of a tool that can trace a target process at the basic block level without any need for a priori analysis. Runtime speed benefits are also realized, as there is no longer a need for setting software breakpoints on each individual basic block at startup. Keep in mind, however, that static analysis and enumeration of basic blocks is still required to determine the full scope of the code base and to make claims on percent covered. Furthermore, although it might be faster to begin tracing using this approach, it will likely not be faster then the previously detailed method in the long run. This is due to the inability to stop monitoring blocks that have already been executed as well as the inability to trace only a specific model. Nonetheless, it is an interesting and powerful technique. Expanding on the PyDbg single stepper shown earlier in this chapter, see the blog entry titled "Branch Tracing with Intel MSR Registers"[18] on OpenRCE for a working branch-level stepper. The detailed investigation of this approach is left as an exercise for the reader.

On a final note for improvement, consider the difference between code coverage and path coverage (or process state coverage). What we have already discussed in this chapter is pertinent to code coverage; in other words, what individual instructions or blocks of code were actually executed. Path coverage further takes into the account the various possible paths that can be taken through a cluster of code blocks. Consider, for example, the cluster of code blocks shown in Figure 23.13.

---

[16] http://www.intel.com/products/processor/manuals/index.htm

[17] ftp://download.intel.com/design/Pentium4/manuals/25366919.pdf

[18] http://www.openrce.org/blog/view/535

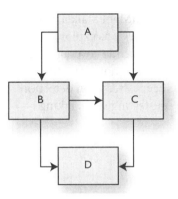

**Figure 23.13**   Example control-flow graph

Code coverage analysis might reveal that all four blocks A, B, C, and D were exercised by a series of test cases. Were all paths exercised? If so, what paths did each individual test case exercise? The answers to these questions require path coverage, a technique that can further conclude which of the following feasible path combinations were covered:

- A → B → D
- A → B → C → D
- A → C → D

If, for example, only the first and third paths in this list were exercised, code coverage analysis would reveal 100 percent coverage. Path coverage, on the other hand, would reveal that only 66 percent of the possible paths were covered. This additional information can allow an analyst to further tweak and improve the list of test cases.

## SUMMARY

In this chapter we introduced the concept of code coverage as it applies to fuzzing, beginning with a simplistic solution implemented in just a few lines of Python. By studying the building blocks of binary executable code, we demonstrated a more advanced and previously implemented approach. Although most of the public focus on fuzzing has previously been spent on data generation, that approach only solves half of the problem. We shouldn't just be asking "How do we start fuzzing?" We also need to ask "When do we stop fuzzing?" Without monitoring code coverage, we cannot intelligently determine when our efforts are sufficient.

A user-friendly and open source code coverage analysis tool, PaiMei PStalker, was introduced and shown. Application of this tool for fuzzing purposes was explored and areas for improvement were also discussed. The application of this code coverage tool and concept, or "fuzzer tracking," takes us one step further toward a more scientific approach to fuzz testing. In the next chapter, we discuss intelligent exception detection and processing techniques that can be further coupled into our testing suite, taking fuzzing to the next level.

# Intelligent Fault Detection

*"Never again in the halls of Washington, DC, do I want to have to make explanations that I can't explain."*

—George W. Bush, Portland, OR, October 31, 2000

We know how to choose a target. We know how to generate data. Thanks to the previous chapter, we know how to track where and how our data is processed. The next important concept to master is deciding when our fuzzer has successfully caused some trouble. This may not always be self evident as the result of a fault might not be easily detected external to the target system. Once again, this topic has not received great attention among today's currently available fuzzers. Unlike fuzzer tracking, however, we are starting to see strides in both the commercial and open source space.

We begin in this chapter by exploring the most primitive solutions toward fault detection, such as simple response parsing. We then move to the next advanced level by leveraging debugging tools and technologies. Finally, we briefly touch on the most advanced techniques of fault detection with an exploration of dynamic binary instrumentation (DBI). All in all, the tools, techniques, and concepts shown in this chapter will help us in determining when our fuzzer has done well by doing wrong.

## PRIMITIVE FAULT DETECTION

What do you get when you blindly fire off 50,000 malformed IMAP authentication requests, one of which causes the IMAP server to crash and never check on the status of the IMAP server until the last test case? Simple: You get nothing. Without at least having a general idea of which of the test cases actually caused the IMAP server to crash, you are left with as little information as you had prior to running the fuzzer in the first place. A fuzzer with no sense of the health of its target borders on being entirely useless.

There are a number of techniques a fuzzer can employ in determining whether or not an individual test case has discovered any abnormalities in the target, perhaps the simplest of which is to add a *connectivity* check in between test cases, as PROTOS did in the last chapter. Sticking to our example with IMAP, assume we are working with a fuzzer that generates the following first two test cases:

```
x001 LOGIN AAAAAAAAAAAAAAAAAAAAAAAAAAAA…AAAA
x001 LOGIN %s%s%s%s%s%s%s%s%s%s%s…%s%s%s%s%s
```

Between each generated test case, the fuzzer can attempt to establish a TCP connection on port 143 (the IMAP server port). In the event of failure, an assumption can be made that the last test case caused the server to crash. The commercial test suites produced by Codenomicon take this approach by including functionality to optionally send a legitimate or known good case after each test case. The resulting pseudocode to accomplish this task is very simple:

```
for case in test_cases:
    fuzzer.send(case)
    if not fuzzer.tcp_connect(143):
        fuzzer.log_fault(case)
```

We can improve this logic slightly by replacing the connectivity check with a known valid response test. For example, if we know that the username paimei and password whiteeyebrow are valid credentials on the IMAP server, then we can ensure the server is not simply available, but also behaving properly by attempting to successfully authenticate as the user paimei. In the event of a failure, an assumption can be made that the last test case caused the server to malfunction. Again, the resulting pseudocode to accomplish this task is very simple:

```
for case in test_cases:
    fuzzer.send(case)
    if not fuzzer.imap_login("paimei", "whiteeyebrow"):
        fuzzer.log_fault(case)
```

Earlier, we stated that the failure of either a connectivity or known valid response test allows us to make the assumption that the last test case caused a malfunction within the target. This is not entirely accurate. Consider, for example, that during an IMAP server fuzz session, after test case 500, we have a connectivity test failure. Great! We have discovered an input that can cause the server to crash. Before running down the hall to report our great find, however, we restart the IMAP server, rerun test case 500 individually, and to our dismay nothing happens. What's going on? The likely scenario is that one, or perhaps a combination of a dozens of our earlier test cases, placed the IMAP server into a state that allowed test case 500 to bring the server down. On its own, however, test case 500 appears to be properly handled. In such situations we can leverage another simple technique, which we call *fuzzer stepping*, to help narrow down the possibilities.

The generic problem is as follows: We know that somewhere in between test cases 1 and 499 the IMAP server was placed into a state that allowed test case 500 to crash the server, but we don't know what combination of test cases was responsible. There are a number of stepping algorithms we can use. Here is a simple one to start with:

```
# find the upper bound:
for i in xrange(1, 500):
    for j in xrange(1, i + 1):
        fuzzer.send(j)

    fuzzer.send(500)

    if not fuzzer.tcp_connect(143):
        upper_bound = i
        break

    fuzzer.restart_target()

# find the lower bound:
for i in xrange(upper_bound, 0, -1):
    for j in xrange(i, upper_bound + 1):
        fuzzer.send(j)

    fuzzer.send(500)

    if fuzzer.tcp_connect(143):
        lower_bound = i
        break

    fuzzer.restart_target()
```

The first half of the logic is responsible for locating the upper bound of the sequence responsible for generating the desired state. This is accomplished by incrementally testing from the 1st to the $n$th cases, followed by 500, where $n$ is continuously incremented by one. After each sequence is tested, the fuzz target is restarted to reset the internal state. Similar logic is then applied to locate the lower bound. Combined, our routine has isolated the sequence of test cases that when followed by 500 will cause the target to crash. Excitement resumes as we can run down the hallway again. This is, of course, a relatively simple algorithm and would not take into account the fact that it might actually be a couple of test cases in our identified range that put the server into a vulnerable state. For example, we might discover that test cases 15 to 20 followed by test case 500 causes a crash, when in reality a sequence of test cases 15, 20, and 500 in succession will actually cause the crash. The algorithm will nonetheless narrow down the possibilities

The simple solutions we just covered are the bare bones for malfunction monitoring. To get an even better understanding of what is happening within our fuzzer target, we can dig deeper and take a low-level view with a debugger. Before doing so, it is important for us to determine what exactly it is that we are looking for.

## WHAT ARE WE LOOKING FOR?

At the lowest level, the CPU informs the operating system when various faults, exceptions, or interrupts (hereby collectively referred to as events or exceptions) such as a memory access violation or divide by zero occur. Many of these events occur naturally. Consider, for example, what happens when a process attempts to access memory that is currently paged to disk. A page fault is generated and the operating system handles the event by loading the appropriate page into main memory from the disk cache. This transaction happens entirely transparent to the process that made the original memory access request. Events that are unhandled by the operating system are bubbled down to the process level. This is where our interest begins.

As our fuzzer trudges over a target process or device, there are a number of events it could trigger. Attaching a debugger to our fuzzer targets allows us to intercept these events as they occur. As soon as an event is captured, the target process is frozen pending an interactive instruction. When combined with the previously outlined simplistic approaches, once the debugger catches the event and pauses the fuzzer target, the subsequent connectivity or known valid input check will fail. This combined approach allows us to potentially uncover more issues in our example IMAP server. As the various exception events occur at the assembly level, it will be our responsibility to intelligently determine the higher level source of the event and, more important, determine if the event is significant from a security perspective. The following list enumerates the three underlying categories into which all software memory corruption vulnerabilities fall. We examine examples from each category as well as determine the types of exceptions that might be generated in response to each:

- Transferring control of execution to an address it should not
- Reading data from an address it should not
- Writing data to an address it should not

As an example of transferring control of execution to an address it should not, consider the classic stack overflow and the following C code excerpt from a function with a stack frame that resembles the one shown in Figure 24.1.

```
void taboo (int arg1, char *arg2)
{
    int x;
    char buf[16];
    int y;

    strcpy(buf, arg2);
}
```

This contrived function takes both an integer and a string argument, declares three local variables, and then copies the supplied string into the declared stack buffer with no regard for the size of the source string or destination buffer. When the function taboo() is called, its arguments will be pushed onto the stack in reverse order. The resulting assembly CALL instruction will implicitly push the current instruction pointer address (stored in register EIP) onto the stack. This is how the CPU knows where to transfer control back to once the called function has completed execution. Typically, the function prologue will next push the current frame pointer (stored in register EBP) onto the stack. Finally, space is set aside for the three declared local variables by subtracting the total variable size from the stack pointer (stored in register ESP). The resulting stack frame looks exactly like what you see in Figure 24.1.

As depicted in Figure 24.1, recall that the stack grows "down" from higher addresses to lower addresses. Data writes, however, occur in the opposite "up" direction. If the length of the string arg2 is longer than 16 bytes (declared size of buf) then the strcpy() will continue copying past the end of the allotted space for buf, overwriting the local integer variable x, then the saved frame pointer, then the saved return address, then the first argument, and so on. Assuming arg2 is a long string of A characters, then the saved EIP is overwritten with 0x41414141 (0x41 is the hex value for the ASCII character A).

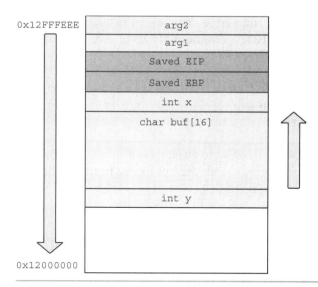

```
0x12FFFEEE                    arg2
                              arg1
                            Saved EIP
                            Saved EBP
                              int x
                           char buf[16]



                              int y


0x12000000
```

**Figure 24.1**   Example stack layout

When the function `taboo()` completes execution, the `RETN` assembly instruction will restore the overwritten saved EIP and transfer control to whatever instructions are found at address 0x41414141. Depending on the contents of the memory at address 0x41414141, a couple of different scenarios can take place. In most cases, no valid pages of memory will be mapped to this particular address and an ACCESS_VIOLATION exception will be generated when the CPU attempts to read the next instruction from the unreadable address 0x41414141. Note that in this specific example if `arg2` is longer than 16 bytes but less than or equal to 20 bytes, no exception will occur.

If there is valid data but not executable code at the address and the underlying processor has support for nonexecutable (NX[1]) page permissions, then again an ACCESS_VIOLATION exception will be generated when the CPU attempts to execute from the nonexecutable address 0x41414141. Most interestingly, if there is valid executable code at the address, then no exception is generated. This is a key point that is addressed later in the chapter. This example demonstrates one of the most straightforward forms of control-flow hijacking.

As an example of reading from addresses it shouldn't, consider the following C code excerpt from a function with a stack frame resembling that shown in Figure 24.1:

---

[1]   http://en.wikipedia.org/wiki/NX_bit

```
void taboo_two (int arg1, char *arg2)
{
    int *x;
    char buf[] = "quick brown dog.";
    int y = 10;

    x = &y;

    for (int i = 0; i < arg1; i++)
        printf("%02x\n", buf[i]);

    strcpy(buf, arg2);

    printf("%d\n", *x)
}
```

This function takes both an integer and a string argument, declares three local variables, and sets the integer variable x as a pointer to y. Next the function continues to print a variable number of hex bytes from buf specified by the integer argument arg1. As no sanity checking is done on the argument used as the loop terminator, a value longer than 16 will cause the printf() routine to access and display data it otherwise should not be doing.

Just as before the data is read up toward higher addresses, opposite to the direction of stack growth. Therefore the loop will expose the values for the local integer variable x, then the saved frame pointer, then the saved return address, then the first argument, and so on. Depending on the size of arg1, an ACCESS_VIOLATION on read might not ever occur, as short enough values simply cause the loop to access data that although the programmer might not logically want exposed, is happily shared by the CPU and operating system as they are unaware of its sensitivity.

Next, an unbounded string copy is made just as it was in the previous example. Assuming, however, that arg2 contains only 20 A characters (four bytes more than the size of buf), then only the local pointer variable x is overwritten. In this situation, the stack overflow would not lead to an invalid transfer of execution as before. However, during the call to printf() when the overwritten variable is dereferenced as a pointer, an ACCESS_VIOLATION will likely occur when attempting to read from the address 0x41414141.

For a more real-world example of reading from a place it should not, consider the following code snippet, which illustrates an exposure of the classic format string vulnerability:

```
void syslog_wrapper (char *message)
{
    syslog(message);
}
```

According to the `syslog()` API prototype, a format string followed by a variable number of format string arguments is expected. By directly passing the user-supplied string contained within the argument `message` to `syslog()`, any format string tokens contained within the argument will be parsed and the relevant format string argument will be dereferenced. As no such format string arguments exist, whatever values currently exist on the function stack will be utilized. For example, if the argument contains `%s%s%s%s%s`, then five addresses are read from the stack and dereferenced as a string pointer until a null-byte is seen. Supplying enough `%s` format string tokens typically causes an invalid pointer to be treated as a string, which leads to an ACCE_VIOLATION. In some cases, the pointer will be valid addressable memory, but the memory content will not be NULL terminated, leading to the function reading off the end of a page while searching for a NULL byte. Note that depending on the environment and the number of format string tokens supplied, no violation might occur. Again, this key concept is covered later in the chapter.

As an example of writing to an address it should not, consider the following C code excerpt from a function with a stack frame resembling that shown in Figure 24.1:

```
void taboo_three (int arg1, char *arg2)
{
    int x;
    char buf[] = "quick brown dog.";
    int y;

    buf[arg1] = '\0';
}
```

This function takes both an integer and a string argument, declares three local variables, and then truncates the string stored in `buf` at the index specified by the argument `arg1`. As no sanity checking is done on the supplied index, a value larger than 16 will cause an erroneous null-byte to be written to an address that should otherwise not be written to. Just as seen in a previous example, depending on where this address lies, an actual exception might or might not be generated. Even though no exception might be generated, when fuzzing we'd like to know when this occurs.

For a more real-world example of writing to a place it should not, consider the following code snippet and simplified example, which demonstrates an exposure of a typical heap overflow vulnerability:[2]

---

[2] http://doc.bughunter.net/buffer-overflow/free.html

```
char *A = malloc(8);
char *B = malloc(16);
char *C = malloc(24);

strcpy(A, "PPPPPPPPPPPPPPPPPPPPPPPPPPPPPPPPPPPP");
free(B);
```

In this code excerpt, three character pointers are declared and initialized to point to dynamically allocated memory, which is said to come from the heap. Among other stored inline information, each heap chunk contains both a forward and backward link to create the doubly linked list depicted in Figure 24.2.

**Figure 24.2**   Heap chunk doubly linked list

When the call to `strcpy()` is reached, the allocated buffer referenced by A will be over-run as it cannot store the long string of supplied P characters. As the overrun buffer is not stored on the stack, there is no opportunity to clobber a saved return address. So where is the problem? In the next line of code, the call to `free(B)` must unlink B from the chain and connect A and C to one another. This is accomplished via the following basic logic:

```
B->backward->forward = B->forward
B->forward->backward = B->backward
```

As the forward and backward pointers are stored at the start of each heap chunk, the overflow that resulted from the call to `strcpy()` will overwrite those pointer values in the B chunk with 0x50505050 (0x50 is the hex value for the ASCII character P). At the assembly level, this can translate to both invalid write and read attempts.

**A SAD ATTEMPT AT A SECURITY SOLUTION**

Although not directly related to the topic at hand, we cannot help but take this opportunity to point out a humorous effort at creating a precompile security solution. Some time ago a research paper surfaced from the Drexel University Computer Science department titled "Using Program Transformation to Secure C Programs Against Buffer Overflows."[3]

The paper stipulates the capability of eliminating all exploitable buffer overflows by simply replacing the usage of all stack buffers with buffers allocated from the heap.

The 10-page paper covers the dynamics of the transformation, discusses transformation efficiency, cites numerous references, and even demonstrates an example of how their groundbreaking transformation can convert a contrived code-execution exploitable vulnerability into a simple DoS. Unfortunately for the authors, at no point during their research did they come across the fact that heap overflows are also exploitable.

## A NOTE ON CHOOSING FUZZ VALUES

Now that we finished illustrating how a number of high-level snippets and software vulnerability concepts can translate into a generated low-level event, let's address a key issue involving the selection of fuzz values. You might have already noted that depending on various conditions, fuzz values that result as being referenced as a memory address might not actually result in an access violation and therefore the generation of an exception. This notion must be kept in mind when choosing values to utilize in fuzzed requests. Poorly chosen values can result in false negatives, situations where our fuzzer successfully traversed vulnerable code but was unable to identify it as such.

Consider, for example, the various situations in which four bytes of fuzzer-supplied data are utilized in a memory dereference. The classic string of A characters results in dereferencing the memory address 0x41414141. Although in most cases no valid pages of memory are mapped at this particular address, therefore resulting in the ACCESS_VIO-LATION we expect, there will be cases where the address is indeed valid and therefore no exception event is generated. Although in all likelihood our fuzzer has done enough

---

[3]  http://www.cs.drexel.edu/~spiros/research/papers/WCRE03a.pdf

damage at this point to trigger an exception even later down the line, we would like to know when things go awry as soon as possible. Given the opportunity to choose the four bytes used as an invalid memory address, what would you choose? Choosing an address in the kernel address space (typically 0x80000000–0xFFFFFFFF) works well, as kernel space is never accessible from user mode.

Taking a look at another example, consider the case of the format string vulnerability. We saw that if enough %s tokens were not supplied, then the subsequent stack pointer dereferences might not trigger any invalid memory references. On first inclination, you might be tempted to address the issue by simply increasing the number of %s tokens used in your various fuzz requests. Further analysis would, however, reveal that other factors, such as imposed string length limitations, could render this solution useless. How can we sidestep this issue more elegantly? Recall that the key to exploiting format string vulnerabilities is the capability to *write* to the stack utilizing the format string token %n and its derivatives. The %n format string token writes the number of characters that should have been output by the format string to the relevant stack pointer. By supplying a number of %n tokens instead of %s tokens, we might be more likely to trigger a fault given the limitation of a shorter input string. A combination of interspersed %n%s tokens is probably the wisest choice to account for situations where the %n token can be filtered or disabled (see Chapter 6, "Automation and Data Generation," for more information).

In short, being mindful of where your chosen fuzz data can end up and how it can be used can pay off in great magnitude. Refer to Chapter 6 for more information on choosing appropriate fuzz values.

## AUTOMATED DEBUGGER MONITORING

The downfall of debugger-assisted target monitoring is that as most debuggers are designed for interactive use, automatically extracting useful information from and controlling the actual debugger programmatically is out of the question. The last thing we want to do is manually check in on our fuzzer and restart the process whenever the debugger identifies an exception. Fortunately, we can once again leverage the help of the previously introduced PaiMei[4] reverse engineering framework. Utilizing the framework, we can architect a two-part fuzzing and monitoring system as illustrated in Figure 24.3. It should be noted that this reverse engineering framework is currently designed solely for use on the Windows platform and that similar to the rest of the book, our focus in this section is on the Intel IA-32 architecture.

---

[4]  https://www.openrce.org/downloads/details/208/PaiMei

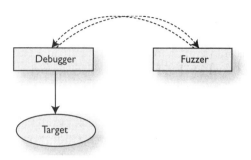

**Figure 24.3**    Fuzzer/monitor architecture

## A BASIC DEBUGGER MONITOR

Sticking with the designated example of the chapter, imagine our target is an IMAP server. The target can either be attached to or loaded directly under the control of the debugger we will be creating shortly. The debugger has a two-way communication back channel with our fuzzer. The back channel can be implemented in a number of ways. The most convenient choice would likely be sockets, as that allows us to not only write our fuzzer and debugger in different languages, but potentially run them on separate systems and even different platforms. Diving right in, consider the following Python code for the debugger component:

```
from pydbg import *
from pydbg.defines import *

import utils

def av_handler (dbg):
    crash_bin = utils.crash_binning.crash_binning()
    crash_bin.record_crash(dbg)

    # signal the fuzzer.

    print crash_bin.crash_synopsis()
    dbg.terminate_process()

while 1:
    dbg = pydbg()
    dbg.set_callback(EXCEPTION_ACCESS_VIOLATON, av_handler)
```

```
dbg.load(target_program, arguments)

# signal the fuzzer.

dbg.run()
```

It might not look like much, but true to the PaiMei framework mantra of "short and sweet," this Python snippet actually accomplishes a lot. You might recognize the first two lines from previous chapters, importing the necessary functionality and definitions from the PyDbg[5] Windows debugger library. The next library import, however, we have yet to see. The PaiMei.utils[6] module contains various reverse engineering support libraries. In this case, we will be using the crash_binning module, which is explained later. Skipping down a bit, you will find an infinite `while` loop. The loop begins by creating an instance of the PyDbg class and registering the function `av_handler()` as the callback handler for processing ACCESS_VIOLATION exception events. Whenever an invalid memory reference occurs, such as any of the previously mentioned examples, this registered function will be called. Next, the debugger loads the target program with any optional arguments.

At this point it is necessary to signal our fuzzer over the back channel, letting it know that our target is ready to receive a fuzz request. In the final line of the loop, the debugger allows the debuggee to execute through the `run()` member routine (and alias of `debug_event_loop()`).

In the remaining lines of our program is the definition of the `av_handler()` routine. As with any registered event callback, our function takes a single argument, the current instance of the PyDbg debugger object. The function begins by creating an instance of the PaiMei crash_binning utility mentioned earlier. This utility exists to simplify the collection process of various helpful attributes regarding the state of the current thread, which in this case triggered the ACCESS_VIOLATION exception we are handling. The following information is transparently recorded in the next line, during the call to `record_crash()`:

- *Exception address.* The address at which the exception occurred, in this case, the address of the instruction that caused the ACCESS_VIOLATION.
- *Write violation.* A flag that when raised specifies that the exception occurred during an attempt to write to a memory location. Otherwise, the exception occurred during an attempt to read from a memory location.

---

5  http://pedram.redhive.com/PaiMei/docs/PyDbg/

6  http://pedram.redhive.com/PaiMei/docs/Utilities/

*Violation address.* The address at which a read or write was attempted that resulted in the exception being generated.

- *Violation thread ID.* The numeric identifier of the thread in which the exception occurred. The first four attributes combined allow us to make statements such as "within thread 1234, the assembly instruction at 0xDEADBEEF was unable to read from the address 0xC0CAC01A and caused the application to terminate."

- *Context.* The saved CPU register values at the time the exception occurred.

- *Disassembly.* Disassembly of the instruction that caused the exception.

- *Disassembly around.* Disassembly of the five instructions both before and after the instruction that caused the exception at the specified exception address. Examination of the surrounding instructions in combination with the context information allows analysts to get a better feel for why the exception occurred.

- *Stack unwind.* The call stack of the offending thread at the time the exception occurred. Although this information is not always available on 32-bit Windows platforms, when it is available it shows analysts how the program got to where it is. An alternative to examining stack unwinding is to proactively record the actions of the target, as discussed in Chapter 23, "Fuzzer Tracking."

- *SEH unwind.* The Structured Exception Handler (SEH) chain at the time the exception occurred. Depending on whether or not we are processing first-chance exceptions (more on this later), an analyst can examine this chain to see which functions were registered from within the target itself for handling exceptions.

At this point, the debugger should once again signal the fuzzer, letting it know that the last test case caused an exception that requires further examination. The fuzzer can record this fact, then wait for the next signal from the debugger stating that the target has been reloaded and is ready to continue receiving the next fuzz requests. Once the debugger has signaled the fuzzer, it prints a human-readable synopsis of all the metadata captured in the call to `record_crash()` and terminates the debuggee. The `while` loop will take care of reloading the target. For more specifics on the underlying functionality of PyDbg, refer to Chapter 20, "In-Memory Fuzzing: Automation."

## STACK UNWINDING ON 64-BIT VERSIONS OF WINDOWS

An unfortunate reality when debugging on the various 32-bit Windows platforms is that in many cases, stack unwinding information is lost. The generic approach to unwinding the stack is simple. The current frame starts at stack offset EBP. The address of the next frame is read from the pointer at EBP. The return address of any given frame is stored at EBP+4. The stack range can be retrieved from the thread environment block (TEB), referenced by the FS register:[7] FS[4] for the address of the top of the stack and FS[8] for the address of the bottom of the stack. This process breaks down whenever a function exists within the call chain that does not use EBP-based stack framing.

Omitting the use of a frame pointer is a common optimization used by compilers because it frees the EBP register to be used as a general-purpose register. However, functions with EBP-based framing can reference local variables as offsets of the static EBP register:

```
MOV EAX, [EBP-0xC]          ; EBP-based framing
MOV EAX, [ESP+0x44-0xC]     ; frame pointer omitted
```

In the event that this optimization is used anywhere within the call chain being unwound, information about the true chain is lost. Microsoft has alleviated this pain in the newer 64-bit platforms by replacing the various calling conventions with a single call convention, the full details of which are available on MSDN.[8] Furthermore, every nonleaf function (a leaf function does not call any other functions) now has static unwind information stored within the Portable Executable (PE) file[9] that allows for full and accurate stack unwinds at any point in time.

There you have it. Adding this PyDbg script to your repertoire will place you at the forefront of the fuzzer monitoring software bundled with commercial fuzzers today. However, we can do even better. When fuzzing software, particularly software that isn't very well written, you will be faced with the daunting task of cataloging and sorting

---

[7] http://openrce.org/reference_library/files/reference/Windows%20Memory%20Layout,%20User-Kernel%20Address%20Spaces.pdf

[8] http://msdn2.microsoft.com/en-us/library/7kcdt6fy.aspx

[9] http://www.uninformed.org/?v=4&a=1&t=sumry

through potentially thousands of test cases that triggered an exception. On further analysis, you will likely reveal that many of the cases expose the same underlying issues. Another way of stating this is that the fuzzer discovered multiple vectors to the same vulnerability.

## A More Advanced Debugger Monitor

Going back to the IMAP example of this chapter, let's reexamine this issue in real-world terms. Here is the scenario: We have a custom fuzzer capable of generating 50,000 unique test cases. We run the fuzzer in conjunction with our recently created debugger script and discover that 1,000 of the test cases caused an exception. It's now our job as a researcher to manually scrutinize each of these cases and determine what went wrong. Let's take a look at the first couple of troublemakers:

```
Test case 00005: x01 LOGIN %s%s%s%s%s%s%s%s%s%s%s%s…%s%s%s
                 EAX=11223300 ECX=FFFF7248…
                 EIP=0x00112233: REP SCASB

Test case 00017: x01 AUTHENTICATE %s%s%s%s%s%s%s%s%s%s%s%s…%s%s%s
                 EAX=00000000 ECX=FFFFFF70…
                 EIP=0x00112233: REP SCASB

Test case 00023: x02 SELECT %s%s%s%s%s%s%s%s%s%s%s%s…%s%s%s
                 EAX=47392700 ECX=FFFEEF44…
                 EIP=0x00112233: REP SCASB
```

For the sake of brevity, only a partial context dump was included in the preceding excerpt. In each of the displayed cases an exception occurred due to an attempt to read from an invalid memory address (not shown). An educated guess based solely on the fuzz inputs leads us to believe that the underlying issue is either due to an improper ability to parse long strings, or it is due to a format string vulnerability. Noticing that the violation occurred at the same address while executing the instruction REP SCASB, we suspect that this pattern might exist across many of the 1,000 cases. After a couple of cursory checks we confirm our suspicion. Let's take a closer look. The SCASB IA-32 assembly instruction will scan a string in search of the byte stored in the first AL register (first byte of EAX). In each of the displayed cases AL=0. The REP instruction prefix loops the prefixed instruction and decrements the ECX register while ECX is not equal to 0. ECX has a high value in each of the displayed cases. This is typical of the assembly pattern used in determining string lengths. It appears that many of our crashes are occurring while scanning a string for its terminating null byte.

How frustrating. We have 1,000 test cases that we know result in a problem, but a large bulk of them appears to occur at or near the same place. Manually culling through the list is no task for a human (although perhaps suitable for an intern). Is there a better way? Sure there is, otherwise, we wouldn't have lead you down this path in the first place.

As the name might suggest, the PaiMei crash binning utility does more then simply display details regarding the current context. The utility was mainly designed for use as a persistent container for storing relevant contextual information across many, many crashes. Calls to the record_crash() member routine create a new entry in an internally maintained and organized list. Each created entry contains its own unique relevant contextual metadata. This method of organization allows us to transform our previous statement of "1,000 out of 50,000 test cases results in an exception" to the more useful "out of 50,000 test cases, 650 resulted in an exception at 0x00112233, 300 resulted in an exception at 0x11335577, 20 resulted in an exception at 0x22446688," and so on. The modifications to our original script are simple, as shown here outlined in bold:

```
from pydbg import *
from pydbg.defines import *

import utils
crash_bin = utils.crash_binning.crash_binning()

def av_handler (dbg):
    global crash_bin
    crash_bin.record_crash(dbg)

    # signal the fuzzer.

    for ea in crash_bin.bins.keys():
        print "%d recorded crashes at %08x" % \
            (len(crash_bin.bins[ea]), ea)

    print crash_bin.crash_synopsis()
    dbg.terminate_process()

while 1:
    dbg = pydbg()
    dbg.set_callback(EXCEPTION_ACCESS_VIOLATON, av_handler)

    dbg.load(target_program, arguments)

    # signal the fuzzer.

    dbg.run()
```

To achieve persistence, the crash bin declaration was moved into the global name-space. Logic was also added such that every time a new exception is recorded, the known faulting addresses are iterated and the number of monitored exceptions at each address is displayed. This is not the most useful method for displaying this information, but it is shown here as an example. As an exercise, try making the necessary modifications to the script such that a directory is created for every offending address. Within each of these directories, text files containing the human-readable output from crash_synopsis() should be created for each recorded crash.

For further improved automation and cataloging, we can extend the crash binning utility to reference the stack unwind information available from each recorded crash. In this sense, we can extend our storage data structure from a list of lists into a list of trees. This allows us to capture and group individual test cases by path as well as exception address. Consider Figure 24.4.

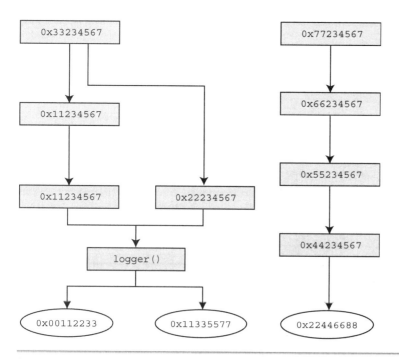

**Figure 24.4**    Crash binning stack unwind cataloging concept

The round data points in Figure 24.4 represent the previous exception address categories. The boxed data points represent addresses from the stack unwind. By adding the stack unwind data points into our view, we can start to see the paths that lead to our various faulty addresses. In essence, we are able to improve our last statement of "out of 50,000 test cases, 650 resulted in an exception at 0x00112233, 300 resulted in an exception at 0x11335577," and so on, to "out of 50,000 test cases, 650 resulted in an exception at 0x00112233 of which 400 took the path x, y, z and 250 took the path a, b, z." More important, analysis from such a view might allow us to determine the underlying source of repetitive faults. In our current situation, the bulk of our captured exceptions occurred at addresses 0x00112233 and 0x11335577. There are hundreds of paths to both of these points, but for the sake of brevity, only a few are shown. All of the paths in this branch of the graph go through the `logger()` routine. Could this be the source of the bulk of our problems? Perhaps a format string vulnerability exists within this routine. As this routine is called from numerous locations within our IMAP server, it makes sense that the passing of a format string to multiple IMAP verbs could result in the same problem. Although only deeper analysis can tell, we can immediately see the benefits of pre-human analysis automation. Again, the modifications required to achieve this added functionality are left as an exercise for the reader.

## FIRST-CHANCE VERSUS LAST-CHANCE EXCEPTIONS

An important concept we have yet to cover regarding exception handling is the notion of first-chance versus last-chance exceptions. When an exception occurs within the target process loaded under our debugger, the Microsoft Windows operating system presents our debugger with what is known as *first-chance notification.*[10] It is up to the debugger to choose whether or not to pass the exception on to the debuggee. In the event that the debuggee is passed the exception, one of two things can happen. If the debuggee is capable of handling the exception, then it will do so and execution will continue as normal. If the debuggee is unable to handle the exception, then the operating system once again presents the exception to the debugger, this time as the *last-chance notification.*. Whether or not the delivered exception is first or last chance is reflected by a value in the EXCEPTION_DEBUG_INFO[11] structure. When working with PyDbg, we can check this value from within a callback handler in the following manner:

---

[10] http://msdn.microsoft.com/msdnmag/issues/01/09/hood/

[11] http://msdn.microsoft.com/library/default.asp?url=/library/en-us/wcecoreos5/html/wce50lrfexceptiondebuginfo.asp

```
def access_violation_handler (dbg):
    if dbg.dbg.u.Exception.dwFirstChance:
        # first chance
    else:
        # last chance
```

A nonzero value for dwFirstChance means that this is the first time the debugger has encountered the exception and the debuggee has not yet had a chance to see and process it.

What does all this mean for our purposes? It means that we have a decision to make, on whether or not we will be ignoring first-chance exceptions. For example, assume that we are once again auditing our example IMAP server and that the following code excerpt is responsible for the format string vulnerability exposed in the logger() routine:

```
void logger (char *message)
{
    ...
    try
    {
        // format string vulnerability.
        fprintf(log_file, message);
    }
    except
    {
        fprintf(log_file, "Log entry failed!\n");
    }
    ...
}
```

The try/except clause around the vulnerable call to fprintf() creates an exception handler. In the event that the first fprintf() fails, the second fprintf() will be called. If, in this case, we were to choose to ignore first-chance exceptions, then we would not be able to detect the format string vulnerability as the IMAP server gracefully handles its own error. This is not to say that the vulnerability does not exist or is not exploitable! Simply put, we have a false negative. On the other hand, we will also find ourselves in situations where the majority of the exceptions we uncover are both gracefully handled and do not expose any security concerns. If we choose to process first-chance exceptions, we would have a number of false positives to deal with. As an independent security researcher, there is no blanket correct decision that you can make. Once aware of the matter, empirical testing can be applied for any given target to determine which side of the false positive versus false negative fence you would like to fall on. As a software developer or QA engineer testing to secure your own product, the safe decision would be to monitor first-chance exceptions and take the time to study the source of the exception in each case.

## DYNAMIC BINARY INSTRUMENTATION

Debugger-assisted monitoring can go a long way. However, as mentioned in Chapter 5, "Requirements for Effective Fuzzing," the panacea of error detection lies in DBI. Discussing this subject matter at the depth required to develop prototype tools is outside the scope of this book. However, the information provided in this section will assist you in gaining a clearer understanding of how some currently available advanced debugging tools function under the hood. DBI engines are able to instrument a target executable at the smallest logical fragment, the basic block.

Recall from Chapter 23 that a basic block is defined as a sequence of instructions where each instruction within the block is guaranteed to be run, in order, once the first instruction of the basic block is reached. DBI systems allow you to instrument individual instructions within each basic block by adding on, modifying, or otherwise altering the instruction logic. This is generally made possible by shifting execution control flow from the original instruction set into a modified code cache. With some systems, instruction-level instrumentation can be accomplished on a higher level RISC-like pseudo-assembly language. This allows developers to more easily develop DBI tools as well attempt to make the tools work across architectures. The exposed API from a DBI system allows for a wide variety of uses from profiling and optimization to machine translation and security monitoring.

A number of DBI systems exist today, examples of which include DynamoRIO,[12] DynInst,[13] and Pin.[14] The DynamoRIO system, for example, was developed as a joint project between the Massachusetts Institute of Technology and Hewlett-Packard. DynamoRIO is implemented on the IA-32 architecture, supporting both Microsoft Windows and Linux. DynamoRIO is both stable and high performance, as is evident by its usage in commercial software solutions such as Determina's[15] Memory Firewall.[16]

---

[12] http://www.cag.lcs.mit.edu/dynamorio/

[13] http://www.dyninst.org/

[14] http://rogue.colorado.edu/pin/

[15] http://www.determina.com

[16] http://www.determina.com/products/memory_firewall.asp

More information about Determina's usage of DynamiRIO can be found in the MIT research paper titled "Secure Execution Via Program Shepherding."[17] The Pin DBI is interesting because unlike most DBI systems it allows for development of tools that can attach to a target process as opposed to being limited to loading the target process under DBI control.

The utilization of DBI allows one to develop monitoring tools to further improve our fault-detection capabilities from detecting the occurrence of a fault to potentially detecting the source of the fault. Circling back to the previously used heap overflow example:

```
char *A = malloc(8);
char *B = malloc(16);
char *C = malloc(24);

strcpy(A, "PPPPPPPPPPPPPPPPPPPPPPPPPPPPPPPPPPPP");
free(B);
```

With debugger-based monitoring, we were unable to detect the actual overflow as it happened during the call to strcpy(). The same holds true for the stack overflows demonstrated earlier. In the case of the stack overflow, an exception might be generated and detected when the affected function returns. In the case of this and other heap overflows, an exception will not be generated until subsequent heap manipulation, such as the call to free() shown in the previous code segment. Building on DBI, it is possible to track and fence all memory allocations as they occur at runtime. The term *fence* refers to the ability to mark or otherwise remember the start and end of each heap chunk. Through instrumentation of all memory write instructions, a check can be added to ensure that the bounds of any individual heap chunk are not being exceeded. As soon as even a single byte is overrun past the end of an allocated chunk, notification can be made. Successful implementation of such a technology can save you hours of time, analysis, and ultimately money.

The learning curve associated with custom DBI tool development is not trivial. Fortunately, others before you have gone through the trouble of creating tools that can be expanded on for fuzzer integration. In the commercial space you will find products such as IBM Rational Purify,[18] Compuware DevPartner BoundsChecker,[19] OC Systems RootCause,[20] and Parasoft Insure++.[21] Purify, for example, is actually built on Static

---

[17] http://www.determina.com/products/memory_firewall.asp

[18] http://www-306.ibm.com/software/awdtools/purify/

[19] http://www.compuware.com/products/devpartner/visualc.htm

[20] http://www.ocsystems.com/prod_rootcause.html

[21] http://www.parasoft.com/jsp/products/home.jsp?product=Insure

Binary Instrumentation (SBI) and BoundsChecker is built on a combination of SBI and DBI. In either case, these products can deliver the error detection and performance analysis feature set one would expect. In the open source world, the most notable solution you might come across is Valgrind[22] (pronounced "val" as in "value" and "grind" as in "grinned"). Valgrind provides you with both a DBI system and a number of predeveloped tools such as Memcheck, which can be used to locate memory leaks and heap overrun vulnerabilities. A number of third-party add-ons are also available for Valgrind. For our specific purposes, the bounds checker version, Annelid,[23] is of most significance.

For most, the usage of debugger-assisted automation will already be a step up from their current fuzzing methodology. We encourage you, however, to explore some of these more advanced error detection paths.

## Summary

In this chapter, we covered fuzzer target monitoring from the most basic high-level techniques to more advanced debugger-assisted techniques. We also touched on the notion of DBI, introducing various DBI systems as well as some out-of-the-box solutions that you can explore for more advanced target monitoring.

With the knowledge gleaned from this chapter, you should be able to combine the powers of a custom debugger monitoring tool with a high-level fuzzer stepper. This combination can be used generically to accurately determine which individual test cases or perhaps groups of test cases caused your target to stray off track. With the added automation benefits, you will be able to transfer the labors of your interns from post-fuzzer analysis back to their traditional task of brewing you fresh coffee.

[22] http://valgrind.org/

[23] http://valgrind.org/downloads/variants.html?njn

# PART IV
## LOOKING FORWARD

# Lessons Learned

## 25

"*Rarely is the question asked: Is our children learning?*"

—George W. Bush, Florence, SC, January 11, 2000

We hope that at this point we have been able to paint a clear picture of what fuzzing is, why it is effective, and how it can be implemented to unveil hidden faults in program code. Up front, we mentioned that this book is geared toward three distinct target audiences that can benefit from the power of fuzzing: developers, QA team members, and security researchers. In this chapter we break down the software development lifecycle (SDLC) to determine where each of these groups can apply fuzzing to build secure software.

## SOFTWARE DEVELOPMENT LIFECYCLE

Fuzzing was once a technique used almost exclusively by security researchers after a product went "gold" and cycled through production, but software developers are now wisely learning to apply fuzzing to uncover vulnerabilities earlier in the SDLC. Microsoft has adopted fuzzing as a key component of their Trustworthy Computing Security Development Lifecycle.[1] That methodology openly encourages developers to "apply security-testing tools including fuzzing tools" during the implementation phase of what

---

[1]  http://msdn.microsoft.com/library/default.asp?url=/library/en-us/dnsecure/html/sdl.asp

they call the Security Development Lifecycle (SDL). Microsoft has developed the concept of an SDL, which mirrors the phases of their own SDLC, both of which can be seen in Figure 25.1.

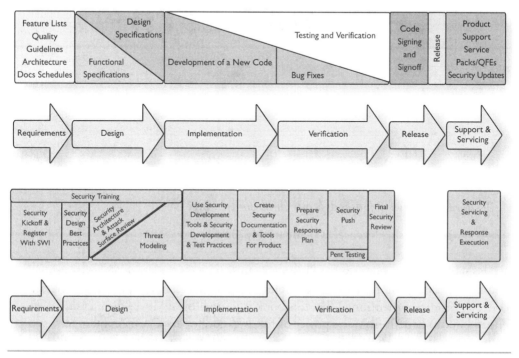

**Figure 25.1**    Microsoft's SDLC and Microsoft's SDL

You can see in these parallel processes that Microsoft has gone to the extent of identifying appropriate security involvement during each phase of their SDLC. This is an important acknowledgment of the integral role that security must play throughout the SDLC. What must also be implemented but cannot be reflected in these diagrams is the necessity for security to be woven into the fabric of the SDLC, not just as a parallel process. Developers, QA teams, and security researchers must work in unison and coordinate their efforts to work toward the common goal of secure code.

## MICROSOFT FOCUS ON SECURITY

It comes as no surprise that Microsoft is tightly weaving security into its SDLC. Having a dominant market share, Microsoft technologies are heavily targeted by security researchers. Although many argue that Microsoft has a long way to go on the security front, there is no denying that Microsoft has already made major strides in enhancing the security of its software.

As an example, consider Microsoft Internet Information Services (IIS),[2] the Microsoft Web server. There are currently 14 publicly disclosed vulnerabilities affecting the 5.x branch of IIS.[3] The 6.x branch, which was unveiled in early 2003, is only affected by three known faults,[4] none of which are rated as critical.

The improvements in security can be partially attributed to low-level security enhancements such as the /GS buffer security check,[5] Data Execution Prevention (DEP), and Safe Structured Exception Handling (SafeSEH)[6] and one of Windows Vista's most widely anticipated security enhancements, Address Space Layout Randomization (ASLR).[7] In addition to these security enhancements, Microsoft has dedicated human resources to security through programs such as the Secure Windows Initiative.[8] Fuzzing is one of many techniques utilized by the employees of this division to enhance the security of the software you see deployed today.

There are no shortage of SDLC methodologies but for our purposes, we'll use Winston Royce's original waterfall model[9] due to its simplicity and widespread adoption. The waterfall model uses a sequential approach to software development with development proceeding through five distinct phases throughout its lifecycle. Figure 25.2 illustrates the approach.

---

[2] http://www.microsoft.com/WindowsServer2003/iis/default.mspx

[3] http://secunia.com/product/39/?task=advisories

[4] http://secunia.com/product/1438/?task=advisories

[5] http://msdn2.microsoft.com/en-US/library/8dbf701c.aspx

[6] http://en.wikipedia.org/wiki/Data_Execution_Prevention

[7] http://www.symantec.com/avcenter/reference/Address_Space_Layout_Randomization.pdf

[8] http://www.microsoft.com/technet/Security/bestprac/secwinin.mspx

[9] http://en.wikipedia.org/wiki/Waterfall_process

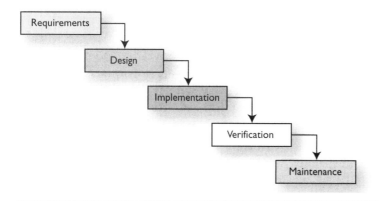

**Figure 25.2**   Royce's original waterfall model

Next, we consider how fuzzing can be implemented in each of these phases.

## ANALYSIS

The analysis phase involves all of the information gathering necessary prior to beginning a project. This phase includes working with end users to determine exactly what they're looking for. Although fuzzing would not play a direct role in this phase of the SDLC, it is important that developers, QA teams, and security professionals start thinking about whether or not fuzzing would be an appropriate testing tool for later phases.

## DESIGN

Designing an application involves producing an abstract representation of the project. This can involve various modeling techniques depending on the portion of the overall solution that is being modeled, such as the hardware, software, or database components. It is at this stage that decisions are made as to the programming languages and software libraries that will be used during the coding phase.

As design decisions are made, the feasibility of and possible approaches for fuzzing begin to come into focus. It is during this phase that two important details are defined that will affect the overall approach. First, decisions are made about the software and hardware platforms to be implemented. This will affect the fuzzing tools that can be used and the fuzzing classes that will apply. For example, if the project is a console application designed for use on the Linux operating system, then environment variable fuzzing is appropriate. If the project is designed for use on the Windows operating system, will it have ActiveX controls marked as "safe for scripting" that will expose functions to external Web sites? If that's the case, COM object fuzzing should be applied.

The network protocols for interprocess communications will likely be chosen during this phase of the SDLC. If, for example, the requirements for the specific project call for a built-in instant messaging solution perhaps the Extensible Messaging and Presence Protocol (XMPP) might be selected. This protocol is an open XML communications technology developed in 1999 by the open source community behind the Jabber[10] project. This is a good phase within the SDLC to pass the protocol specification along to the fuzzing team. This is also a good time to assign some resources to search for and enumerate currently available XMPP testing tools and previously discovered XMPP parsing vulnerabilities.

Another important decision made during the design phase relates to the input vectors that will be developed in the application. Remember that fuzzing is simply a technique for providing malformed input to an application and watching to see what happens. It is therefore key to identify all such input vectors and determine how best to fuzz them. It is also important to be creative when determining what exactly constitutes and input vector. Just because something is happening in the background and not directly exposed to an end user doesn't mean that an attacker couldn't create custom code to access the interface. The more complete the list of input vectors, the better the total code coverage that can be achieved with fuzzing.

## CODING

During the coding phase, development teams work to build the necessary components of the overall project and slowly pull them together into a unified application. The important point to remember here is that fuzzing can and should be used during development by developers. The burden of fault testing should not be solely carried by the QA teams and security professionals.

As sections of code are compiled and tested for appropriate functionality, they should also be tested for adequate security controls. Fuzzing can be applied to any of the possible input vectors identified during the design phase. If an exposed ActiveX control is ready, start fuzzing it. If a network service is complete, start fuzzing it. As we saw earlier in Chapter 19, "In-Memory Fuzzing," and Chapter 20, "In-Memory Fuzzing: Automation," in-memory fuzzing can also be applied at the function level. If a given function is designed to extract an e-mail address from a user-supplied string, try calling that function thousands of times with a number of random and cleverly chosen string values.

Poor input validation is often the weakness that leads to security vulnerabilities and fuzzing will help developers to better understand why input validation is so critical.

---

[10] http://www.jabber.org/

Fuzzing is designed to identify input that the developer did not account for and that the application is not capable of handling. When developers see this in action, they will be in the best possible position to build appropriate input validation controls and ensure that the same mistakes are not made in subsequent code. More important, the earlier in the SDLC that vulnerabilities are discovered, the lower the overall cost to correct them. When a developer finds his own mistakes, it's much easier to fix them.

## TESTING

As software moves into the testing phase, QA teams move in. Security teams should also participate in the testing phase before the project reaches production. Overall costs will always be lower if defects are uncovered before the software is released. Additionally, you can save the company damage to its corporate reputation by ensuring that vulnerabilities are discovered internally, rather than first appearing on a public mailing list.

It is important that QA teams and security researchers determine how best to work together during the testing phase to leverage one another's resources. Involving security specialists in the SDLC might be a new approach for some software vendors, but the growth of publicly disclosed vulnerabilities has demonstrated just how essential their involvement is.

Both QA teams and security researchers need to be aware of commercial and open source fuzzing tools that can be applied during testing. This is an area where peer training sessions can be implemented. Security researchers are more likely to have current knowledge of the latest and greatest fuzzing tools available and they can be leveraged to train QA teams and developers on appropriate tools that can be used to improve security. As an ancillary to this training, developers are made aware of common programming mistakes they can avoid and can gain a stronger understanding of secure programming practices.

## MAINTENANCE

Despite the best efforts of developers, QA teams, and security researchers, faults that result in both simple nuisances and critical security vulnerabilities will find their way into production code. Major software vendors have poured billions of dollars into security and although the situation is improving, vulnerable code is a reality that we will always have to deal with. It is therefore important to remain proactive in researching security vulnerabilities even when code moves to production. New fuzzing tools, knowledgeable researchers, and improved fuzzing techniques might provide fresh insight into previously tested code and uncover new vulnerabilities. Moreover, vulnerabilities might be implementation dependent and can therefore emerge after code is released to production due to a configuration change. As an example, some issues might not surface on a 32-bit platform but will on a 64-bit system.

Beyond internal efforts to proactively identify vulnerable code, it is important to have processes in place to respond to and work with independent researchers. Independent researchers are responsible for discovering the majority of public security vulnerabilities found in software. Although researchers have differing motives for uncovering vulnerabilities, their efforts are nonetheless important in further securing production code. Software vendors should be sure to have processes in place to allow independent researchers to report their findings to teams responsible for acting as a liaison between the researchers and the developers that will ultimately correct the bugs.

## IMPLEMENTING FUZZING IN THE SDLC

We recognize that the waterfall model provides an overly simplistic overview of the processes involved in all but the most simplistic development efforts. Most projects involve multiple teams working in combination and SDLC phases that occur in repetitive cycles as opposed to the neat sequential phases of the waterfall model. Regardless, any development model incorporates these same basic phases in some combination. Try not to focus on the model itself. Instead, use what has been discussed in this chapter to implement fuzzing into your own SDLC to better secure your code before it reaches production.

## DEVELOPERS

Developers are the first line of defense when it comes to implementing security in new projects and should be empowered with the ability to fuzz newly developed functions, classes and libraries as they develop them. By providing developers with the skills to recognize basic security problems, many costly security fixes can be addressed immediately and never reach the QA or security teams, much less the general public.

Developers typically conduct the majority of their programming within a particular integrated development environment (IDE) with which they are comfortable. Microsoft Visual Studio, for example, is the standard IDE for C# and Visual Basic coding on the Windows platform, whereas Eclipse is a popular choice for development in Java and various other languages. One recommended approach for encouraging developers to incorporate fuzzing into their development practices is to develop IDE plug-ins as opposed to requiring your developers to learn an entirely new suite of tools for security testing.

Although not specifically a fuzzing tool, SPI Dynamics' DevInspect[11] tool provides an example of this approach. DevInpect is a tool that extends Visual Studio and Eclipse functionality to provide developers with source code analysis and black box testing of ASP.Net and Java Web applications.

## QA RESEARCHERS

QA has historically focused on functionality testing as opposed to security. Fortunately, this is changing as end users become increasingly aware of the dangers posed by insecure software and demand more from their software vendors. Although QA teams should not be expected to become security experts, they should be expected to have a basic understanding of security and more important, know when to bring in a security expert. Fuzzing is a testing process that is ideally suited to QA teams as it can be highly automated. Reverse engineering would not, for example, be an appropriate skill to demand of QA researchers given that it is a highly specialized skill that requires substantial training. Running fuzzing tools, on the other hand, is a very realistic expectation of QA teams. Although it might require coordination with the security team to determine if a particular exception leads to an exploitable condition, during the testing phase, a crash of any kind is worthy of review and should likely be addressed by developers. At that point, the distinction between security and functionality isn't as critical. What is critical is fixing the problem at hand.

## SECURITY RESEARCHERS

Fuzzing is not new to security researchers. Fuzzing is a widely used approach to discovering security vulnerabilities due to its relative simplicity and high rate of return. In the recent past, security researchers were not involved in the SDLC at all. In many organizations that still remains the case. If your SDLC does not employ security specialists, it's time to revisit your software development processes. Microsoft, for example, hosts the BlueHat Security Briefings[12] in an effort to transfer knowledge from well-known security researchers to their staff.

The challenge for security researchers is to shift their focus to uncovering vulnerabilities earlier in the SDLC. There is always value in patching a hole, no matter when it is

---

[11] http://www.spidynamics.com/products/devinspect/

[12] http://www.microsoft.com/technet/security/bluehat/sessions/default.mspx

found, but the cost of implementing patches increases as the development project proceeds as noted in Figure 25.3. Security teams have specialized skills that can be leveraged to adapt the testing process to continually improve the fuzzing tools and techniques that are used. Although QA teams should be responsible for running standard fuzzing tools and scripts, it is up to security researchers to build custom tools or identify new technologies and continually educate QA teams and developers on their use.

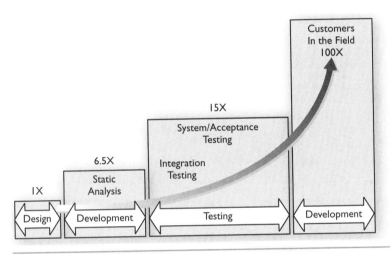

**Figure 25.3**   Cost of fixing software defects throughout the SDLC

## Summary

Gone are the days when anyone involved in software development can say "Security's not my problem; we have a team that takes care of that." Security is everyone's responsibility, including developers, the QA team, and security researchers. As a product manager, it does not suffice to simply ignore vulnerabilities and hope that they will magically vanish. Your people must also be empowered with the processes and tools to embed security into the SDLC, and fuzzing represents an automatable process that can be leveraged by all three groups. Fuzzing is not a magic bullet, but it is a methodology that lends itself to developing user-friendly security tools capable of uncovering a wide range of vulnerabilities.

# Looking Forward

*"But all in all, it's been a fabulous year for Laura and me."*

—George W. Bush, summing up his first year in office, three months after the 9/11 attacks, Washington, DC, December 20, 2001

Where does fuzzing go from here? The field has already begun migrating from the academic and underground worlds and is being embedded in enterprise test beds and throughout the SDLC. Given the increasing acceptance of fuzzing among software developers, it's not surprising to see commercial tools being developed to take advantage of this powerful methodology. In this chapter we look at where fuzzing is today and peer into the crystal ball to see if we can determine where it will be in the near future.

## COMMERCIAL TOOLS

An arguably strong indicator of a maturing industry is the entrance of commercial players into that space. This is the trend we are currently witnessing with fuzzing technologies. As large software developers such as Microsoft have adopted fuzzing as a means of identifying security vulnerabilities earlier in the SDLC, the doors have been opened for new products and companies to emerge to fill the need for robust, user-friendly fuzzers. In this section we take a look at some of the commercial entities that have emerged, listed in alphabetical order.

## BEYOND SECURITY beSTORM[1]

beSTORM is a black box testing tool that leverages fuzzing to identify vulnerabilities in various network-based protocols. The founders of Beyond Security were initially involved with the creation of the SecuriTeam[2] public Web portal that disseminates security news and resources. Protocols covered by beSTORM include the following:

- HTTP - Hypertext Transfer Protocol
- FrontPage extensions
- DNS – Domain Name System
- FTP- File Transfer Protocol
- TFTP- Trivial File Transfer Protocol
- POP3 – Post Office Protocol v3
- SIP - Session Initiation Protocol
- SMB – Server Message Block
- SMTP – Simple Mail Transfer Protocol
- SSLv3 – Secure Sockets Layer v3
- STUN - (Simple Traversal of User Datagram Protocol (UDP) Through Network Address Translators (NATs))
- DHCP – Dynamics Host Configuration Protocol

beSTORM runs on Windows, UNIX, and Linux platforms and has separate testing and monitoring components.[3] The inclusion of a target monitoring component is a feature we should expect to see more often in the next generation of commercial fuzzing technologies. In the case of beSTORM, the monitoring component is built as a custom debugger and currently limited to the UNIX and Linux platforms. A screen shot of beSTORM is shown in Figure 26.1.

---

[1]  http://www.beyondsecurity.com/

[2]  http://www.securiteam.com/

[3]  http://www.beyondsecurity.com/beSTORM_FAQ.pdf

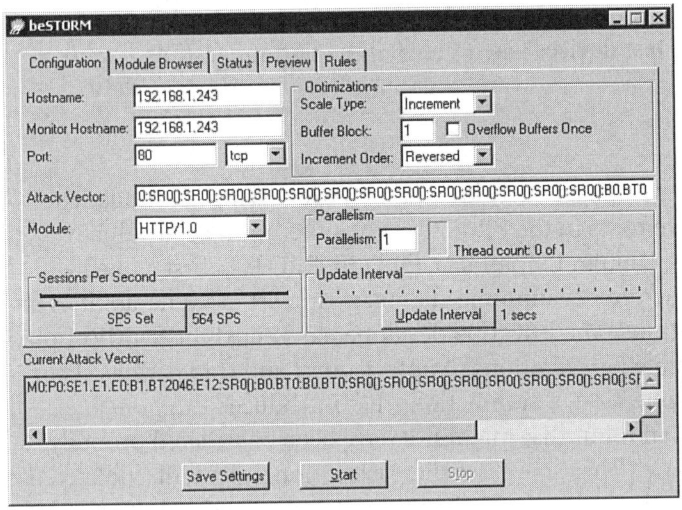

Figure 26.1   Beyond Security beSTORM

## BREAKINGPOINT SYSTEMS **BPS-1000**[4]

As the newest player on the block, BreakingPoint established a position in the market with a clear dominance in pure traffic generation horsepower. The BPS-1000 is a custom hardware solution capable of generating more than 5 million TCP sessions at 500,000 TCP sessions per second. Although not a fuzzer in the traditional sense, the BPS-1000 is capable of mutating generated traffic toward the purposes of fault induction and detection evasion.

Figure 26.2   BreakingPoint Systems BPS-1000

---

4   http://www.breakingpointsystems.com/

One of the more interesting features of the BPS-1000 is the front-side AC adapter, designed to power cycle target test devices when they fail to continue testing.

## CODENOMICON[5]

Codenomicon offers arguably the most widely known software fuzzing solutions. The founders of Codenomicon have roots in the PROTOS[6] test suite, a project originally sponsored by the University of Oulu in Linnanmaa, Finland. PROTOS first gained wide publicity back in 2002 when the project announced a staggering list of vulnerabilities in various SNMPv1 implementations. The PROTOS developers dissected the SNMPv1 protocol and enumerated all possible permutations of both request and trap packets. They then developed a substantial collection of transactions that introduced *exceptional elements,* a term they defined as "an input that might not have been considered properly when implementing the software."[7] In some cases these exceptional elements violated the protocol standard, whereas in other cases they adhered to the specification but included contents designed to break poorly written parsers. The results of the PROTOS SNMPv1 test suite garnered significant attention as they identified numerous vulnerabilities resulting in patch releases from dozens of affected hardware and software vendors.[8] The PROTOS project has since evolved and today consists of test suites for a variety of network protocols and file formats, including the following:

- WAP – Wireless Application Protocol
- HTTP – Hypertext Transfer Protocol
- LDAPv3 – Lightweight Directory Access Protocol v3
- SNMPv1 – Simple Network Management Protocol v1
- SIP – Session Initiation Protocol
- H.323 – A collection of protocols commonly used in videoconferencing
- ISAKMP – Internet Security Association and Key Management Protocol
- DNS – Domain Name System

The testing methodology behind the commercial product has not deviated greatly from its inception with PROTOS. Most notably the commercial test suites cover a larger

---

[5]  http://www.codenomicon.com/

[6]  http://www.ee.oulu.fi/research/ouspg/protos/

[7]  http://www.ee.oulu.fi/research/ouspg/protos/testing/c06/snmpv1/index.html#h-ref2

[8]  http://www.cert.org/advisories/CA-2002-03.html

number of network protocols and file formats and furthermore offer a friendly GUI as shown in Figure 26.3.

Codenomicon offers a separate product for each individual protocol at a premium price. The quoted retail price as of the time of writing was approximately $30,000 (U.S.) per protocol. This pricing model suggests that the company is targeting software developers that would require just a few protocol suites for the type of products that they produce versus a pure security research shop that would be interested in testing a wider variety of products and protocols. The biggest limitation of the product is the lack of target monitoring capabilities. Codenomicon utilizes known good test cases to poll the health of the target during testing. As discussed previously in Chapter 24, "Intelligent Fault Detection," this is among the most rudimentary monitoring techniques.

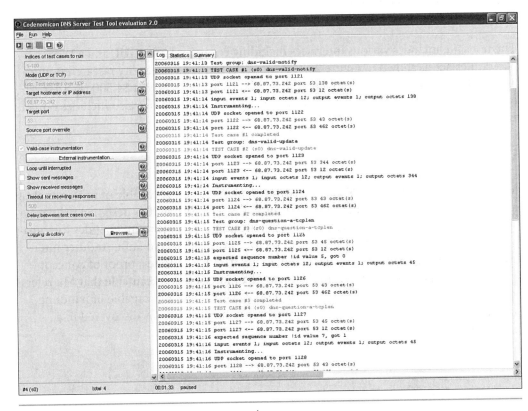

**Figure 26.3**   Codenomicon DNS server test tool

## GLEG PROTOVER PROFESSIONAL[9]

GLEG is a Russian company that was founded with the offering of VulnDisco,[10] a service comprised of monthly releases of newly discovered vulnerabilities in the form of exploit modules for Immunity Inc.'s CANVAS[11] exploitation framework. GLEG later expanded its offering to include the homegrown fuzzer it was using to uncover many of the vulnerabilities offered through the VulnDisco product. The resulting product is called ProtoVer Professional and is developed in the Python programming language. As of the time of writing, the following protocols are supported by this fuzzer:

- IMAP – Internet Message Access Protocol
- LDAP – Lightweight Directory Access Protocol
- SSL - Secure Sockets Layer
- NFS – Network File System

The test suite includes various interfaces including command line, GUI, and a Web-based interface as shown in Figure 26.4. ProtoVer is written by security researchers and appears to be targeted at that same market, with pricing currently at $4,500 (U.S.) to obtain an annual license for all supported protocols. The license fee also includes e-mail support.

## MU SECURITY MU-4000[12]

Mu Security offers the Mu-4000 as a hardware appliance that is capable of both mutating network traffic and monitoring the target for faults. The Mu-4000 is designed primarily for testing other network devices and, like the BreakingPoint solution, includes the capability of power cycling the target device to recover from a detected fault. Another interesting feature of the Mu-4000 is that it can automatically generate a proof of concept exploit when a fault is uncovered in the form of a Linux-based executable that Mu refers to as an external vulnerability trigger. Mu claims that its device is capable of handling any IP-based protocol. An example of a report detailing exceptions discovered in a DHCP implementation is shown in Figure 26.5.

---

[9]   http://www.gleg.net/protover_pro.shtml

[10]  http://www.gleg.net/products.shtml

[11]  http://www.immunitysec.com/products-canvas.shtml

[12]  http://www.musecurity.com/products/mu-4000.html

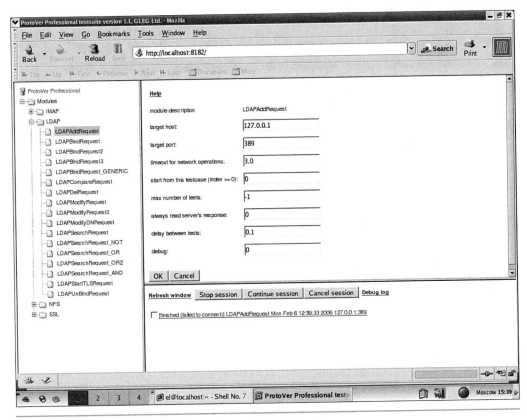

**Figure 26.4** GLEG ProtoVer Professional test suite Web interface

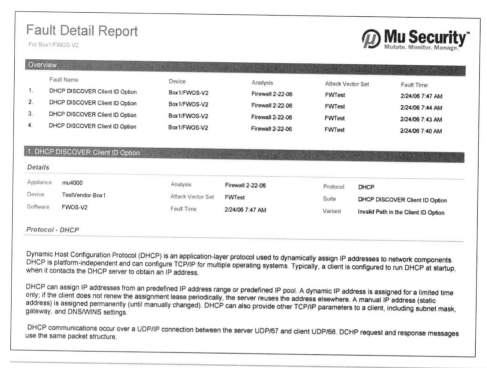

**Figure 26.5**   Mu Security–Mu-4000 report

## SECURITY INNOVATION HOLODECK[13]

Security Innovation's Holodeck is a unique software solution that allows developers to emulate unexpected failures to explore the robustness of implemented security and error handlers in software developed for the Microsoft Windows platform. The product exposes typical fuzzing behaviors, such as the ability to mutate both files and network streams. Among its more unique features, Holodeck is capable of triggering the following faults:

- Resource faults when attempting to access certain files, registry keys and values, and COM objects.

- System faults that might occur in environments with limited disk space, memory, and network bandwidth.

---

[13] http://www.securityinnovation.com/holodeck/

Holodeck carries a reasonable price tag of $1,495 (U.S.) for a single user license and exposes an open API, allowing power users to create automation tools and extensions around the product. A screen shot from the main view of Holodeck is shown in Figure 26.6.

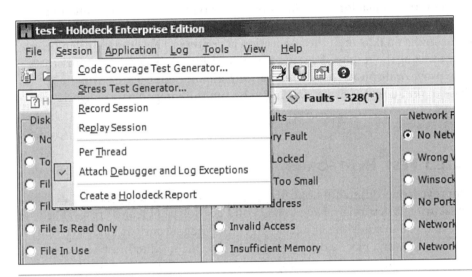

**Figure 26.6**   Security Innovation's Holodeck

This list of companies and products is by no means a complete list of all available commercial fuzzing solutions. It does, however, provide an indication of where the industry is presently. The majority of the listed solutions are relatively new "version 1" technologies. The industry for fuzzing technologies, although emerging, is still relatively immature.

## HYBRID APPROACHES TO VULNERABILITY DISCOVERY

The commercial fuzzers discussed largely represent niche products focused on a specific method of vulnerability discovery. If vulnerability research has taught us one thing, it has demonstrated that no single approach is a silver bullet. All approaches have benefits and limitations.

Knowing this, we expect security tools to move toward a form of hybrid analysis, combining multiple approaches. The goal here is to produce a solution where the sum of the parts is greater than the whole. Take, for example, combining source code analysis with fuzzing. A challenge with fuzzing is ensuring sufficient code coverage. In a pure black box testing scenario, how can you be sure that you have fuzzed all possible inputs? In Chapter 23, "Fuzzer Tracking," we discussed the usage of code coverage as a measurement for how complete fuzzing efforts have been. Consider for a moment an alternate approach, using hybrid analysis. The analysis would begin with an automated source code review. This traditional form of white box testing typically uncovers numerous "potential" vulnerabilities, but suffers from false positives, as it is incapable of confirming the results in the final form of the application at runtime. This limitation can be addressed by utilizing the results of a static scan to assist in the generation of fuzz cases that can help prove or disprove those potential vulnerabilities during the dynamic fuzzing phase of the audit. We expect fuzzing to become an integral part of hybrid security technologies.

## INTEGRATED TEST PLATFORMS

New and improved, one-off, stand-alone fuzzers will always continue to be invented and adopted by security professionals. However, QA and development teams are less likely to find the time and will to study the intricacies of cutting-edge security tools, given that security testing will always place a distant second behind the need to meet development requirements and deadlines. To gain widespread adoption in the QA and development communities, fuzzing technologies must find their way into the existing platforms with which these groups are already familiar and using on a daily basis. Expect to see fuzzing functionality integrated into development environments such as Microsoft Visual Studio and Eclipse. Likewise, popular QA platforms offered by vendors such as IBM and Mercury could benefit from fuzzing capabilities. These capabilities could be offered either by the vendors or maintainers of these applications, but initially are more likely to be developed by third parties and offered as application plug-ins. SPI Dynamics' DevInspect and QAInpect products, although not exclusively fuzzers, would be early examples of such an approach.

## SUMMARY

Where is the industry heading from here? Early indicators hint that more widespread adoption of fuzzing technologies is on the horizon. We encourage this trend and view fuzzing as a unique methodology within the security community for a number of reasons. Most important, alternative techniques such as binary reverse engineering and in-depth source code analysis require specialized skill sets that are not realistic for development and QA teams. Fuzzing, on the other hand, can be implemented as an automated process and is therefore accessible to both groups.

Although independent security researchers will continue to push the envelope and develop interesting fuzzing techniques, it will likely take the efforts of a commercial vendor to create the first easy-to-use fuzzing environment that will smoothly integrate into development environments. Among the most critical requirements is the advancement of error detection, as discussed in Chapter 24. The use of debugging techniques is rarely bundled with fuzzers available today. Even when debuggers are bundled with fuzzers, they tend to be far from optimal. More advanced techniques must be applied to accurately pinpoint and automatically categorize discovered faults. Fault-detection vendors such as those mentioned in Chapter 24, including IBM, Compuware, Parasoft, and OC Systems, are in a unique position to augment their capabilities and complete the package.

Examining the history of similar, yet more mature technologies, we can expect to see a few key events. First, larger, more established companies will move into the space to compete with early pioneers. Vendors could develop their own solutions from scratch but in many cases will acquire some of the pioneering commercial technologies. What entities are likely to move into this space? It's difficult to state with certainty butlook for established software vendors in the security and QA spaces to pick up on the opportunity to differentiate themselves from competitors by adopting fuzzing technologies.

# Index

PyDbg class, 332, 334, 332
  in-memory fuzzer implementation, 340-345
  single stepper tracking tool
    implementation, 445-446
PythonWin COM browser, 288
PythonWin type library browser, 288

**Q**

QA Researchers, 504

**R**

race condition vulnerabilities, 178
Raff, Aviv, 24, 42
random fuzzing, 367
random primitives, 389-390
random testing, 34
randomize() routine, 378
Rational Purify, 492
RATS (Rough Auditing Tool for Security), 7-8
RCE (reverse code engineering), binary auditing
  automated, 17-18
  manual, 14-16
reading
  addresses, 476-478
  process memory, 318
ReadProcessMemory() function, 318
RealPlayer
  RealPix format string vulnerability, 193-195
  shell script workaround, 192
RealServer ../ DESCRIBE vulnerability, 226
ReceivePacket() function, 259
recordings (tracking), filtering, 446
record_crash() routine, 483, 487
RECT struct, 378
Reduced Instruction Set Computer (RISC)
    architecture, 438
registering callbacks, 401-402
remote access services vulnerability, 226
remote code injection, 134
remote fuzzers, 39
  network protocol, 40
  web application, 41
  web browser, 41-42
repeaters as block helpers, 396
reporting exceptions, 183-184
reproducibility, 62
  black box testing, 13
  value of automation, 74
reproduction, in-memory fuzzing, 43
request-URI input (web applications), 126-128
requests
  HTTP, 144
  PTRACE_TRACEME, 187
  Sulley, 410-411
  timeouts, 147
  Web application fuzzing, 140-141
  WebFuzz, 153-155

Requests for Comment (RFCs), 54
researches
  QA, 504
  security, 504-505
resource constraints, 69
responses
  error messages, 146-147
  user input, 147
  Web application fuzzing, 143
  WebFuzz, 155-156
restores
  points
    fuzz_server.exe, 335
    OllyDbg, 338
  processes
    handling, 327-331
    memory block contents, saving, 329-330
    thread context, saving, 328-329
return codes, 179
reusability, 43, 62-64
reverse code engineering (RCE), 14
reverse engineering frameworks (PaiMei), 449-450.
    *See also* PStalker
RFCs (Requests for Comment), 54
RGB struct, 378
RISC (Reduced Instruction Set Computer)
    architecture, 438
Rough Auditing Tool for Security (RATS), 8
routines. *See also* functions; methods
  ap.getPayload(), 356
  av_handler(), 483
  bp_set(), 333
  ContinueDebugEvent(), 323
  DebugActiveProcess(), 321
  DebugSetProcessKillOnExit(), 321
  flatten(), 378
  func_resolve(), 333
  GetFuncDesc(), 296
  GetNames(), 295
  GetThreadContext(), 327
  GetTypeInfoCount(), 294
  handler_bp(), 333
  LoadTypeLib(), 294
  MMalloc(), 81
  parse(), 306
  process_restore(), 345
  process_snapshot(), 343
  randomize(), 378
  record_crash(), 483, 487
  s_checksum(), 396
  self.push(), 398
  setMaxSize(), 356
  setMode(), 356
  SetThreadContext(), 327
  set_callback(), 333
  smart(), 378

## THIS BOOK IS SAFARI ENABLED

### INCLUDES FREE 45-DAY ACCESS TO THE ONLINE EDITION

The Safari® Enabled icon on the cover of your favorite technology book means the book is available through Safari Bookshelf. When you buy this book, you get free access to the online edition for 45 days.

Safari Bookshelf is an electronic reference library that lets you easily search thousands of technical books, find code samples, download chapters, and access technical information whenever and wherever you need it.

**TO GAIN 45-DAY SAFARI ENABLED ACCESS TO THIS BOOK:**

- Go to **http://www.awprofessional.com/safarienabled**
- Complete the brief registration form
- Enter the coupon code found in the front of this book on the "Copyright" page

Addison
Wesley